Higher Education Finance Research

Policy, Politics, and Practice

A Volume in
Conducting Research in Education Finance:
Methods, Measurement, and Policy Perspectives

David C. Thompson, *Kansas State University*
Faith E. Crampton, *Crampton & Associates*

Conducting Research in Education Finance: Methods, Measurement, and Policy Perspectives

David C. Thompson and Faith E. Crampton, Series Editors

Higher Education Finance Research: Policy, Politics, and Practice (2014)
by Mary P. McKeown-Moak and Christopher M. Mullin

The purpose of this series is to offer researchers, practitioners, and policymakers indepth works on "best practices" in education finance research, inclusive of pre-K through higher education. The rationale for the series is the current lack of resources for those specifically interested in conducting education finance research. The volumes in this series are of particular interest to higher education faculty who work with graduate students doing research projects, theses, or dissertations

Higher Education Finance Research

Policy, Politics, and Practice

by

Mary P. McKeown-Moak
Moak, Casey & Associates

and

Christopher M. Mullin
Board of Governors of
the State University System of Florida

Information Age Publishing, Inc.
Charlotte, North Carolina • www.infoagepub.com

Library of Congress Cataloging-in-Publication Data

McKeown-Moak, Mary P., and Mullin, Chrisopher M.
Higher education finance research : policy, politics, and practice / by
Mary P. McKeown-Moak and Christopher M. Mullin.
pages cm. -- (Conducting research in education finance : methods,
measurement, and policy perspectives)
ISBN 978-1-62396-493-1 (paperback) -- ISBN 978-1-62396-494-8 (hardcover) --
ISBN 978-1-62396-495-5 (ebook) 1. Education, Higher--Finance--United
States--History. 2. Education, Higher--United States--Research--Methdology.
3. Education and state--United States--History. I. Title.
LB2342.M374 2013
378.1'06--dc23

2013037695

Printed in the United States of America

CONTENTS

SECTION II: REVENUES AND EXPENDITURES

SECTION III: ACCOUNTABILITY AND
RETURN ON INVESTMENT

SECTION IV: PRESENTING RESEARCH

List of Figures

List of Tables

ABOUT THE SERIES

David C. Thompson and Faith E. Crampton

Education in the U.S. is a multibillion dollar enterprise that encompasses preschool, elementary, secondary, and postsecondary institutions. Tax revenues from the local, state, and federal levels combine to support education across tens of thousands of communities nationwide. In particular, public elementary and secondary schools are charged with educating all children regardless of the challenges and additional costs incurred to ensure equality of educational opportunity. At the same time, many higher education institutions struggle to provide access to families and students of modest economic means by controlling tuition increases without compromising the quality of education students receive. However, tax revenues are limited and must be divided among a host of other public services we value as a society. The role of research in education finance is one that systematically analyzes the equity, adequacy, efficiency, accountability, and stability of education funding so that legislators, policymakers, educators, parents, communities, and other stakeholders can make informed decisions on how best to allocate and deploy fiscal resources to achieve multiple and sometimes competing educational goals. This series is designed to address the challenging issues raised above. The first volume in this series, *Higher Education Finance Research: Policy, Politics, and Practice*, bridges the constructs of efficiency and accountability. These are research topics of great importance, and the authors bring their considerable expertise to readers in order to empower them in the conduct and presentation of research in these domains.

Higher Education Finance Research: Policy, Politics, and Practice, pp. xv–xv
Copyright © 2014 by Information Age Publishing

FOREWORD

Three separate organizational structures, three levels of institution types, various financing partners (including various levels of government, individuals, families, and industry), all within 50 unique states plus additional territories and foreign operations, different philosophical assumptions, economic theories, and a nuanced vocabulary—all of these factors contribute to the complexity of financing postsecondary education in the United States. It is easy to see why, over the last hundred years, a number of books, papers, and position statements have been written about postsecondary finance.

When we began this book, the hardest part was trying to find a way to structure the text. We had a few ideas based upon the work that came before us but decided that what we needed first was a framework and guiding vision as to why we were writing. We came to the same idea from two different perspectives.

Mary McKeown-Moak is an experienced higher education finance researcher. A few accomplishments include being president of the American Education Finance Association (now the Association for Education Finance and Policy), serving as the chief financial officer of the Arizona Board of Regents, and penning an innumerable number of monographs and reports as a researcher and consultant with MGT of America. She has worked in almost every state in the country on both higher education and K–12 finance issues, enabling her to talk in two worlds. For her this book is about sharing what she has learned during her tenure.

On the other hand, the bulk of Christopher M. Mullin's experience and work in his role at the American Association of Community Colleges has focused on community college finance in particular with a focus on

Higher Education Finance Research: Policy, Politics, and Practice, pp. xvii–xix
Copyright © 2014 by Information Age Publishing
xvii

federal student aid and the policy and politics of the federal role in funding education. Previously he conducted state level research for Illinois as a member of the state's P-20 research arm, the Illinois Education Research Council. He has taught at three universities and regularly gives talks to national, state, and institutional leaders. His hope for the book is to provide the foundational knowledge requisite to engage in postsecondary finance discourse, as policies are decisions informed by financial considerations. More information on Mary and Chris is included in the section about the authors.

Together, we have developed this book to empower the reader. We do not hide what we know, we do not attempt to push a perspective, and we attempt to let the reader know when they may be being misled.

The book is structured in four parts. The first section provides a brief history and description of the general organization of American higher education, the sources and uses of funds over the last 100 years, and who is served in what types of institutions. Definitions of terms that are unique to higher education are provided, and some basic rules for conducting research on the economics and finance of higher education will be established. Although in some ways conducting research in higher education funding is similar to that for elementary/secondary education, there are some important distinctions that also will be provided.

The second section introduces guiding philosophies, sources of data, data elements/vocabulary, metrics, and analytics related to institutional revenues and expenditures. Chapters in this section focus on student-oriented revenues, institutionally-oriented revenues, and funding formulas.

The third section introduces accountability-related concepts by first comparing the accountability movement in higher education to that in K–12. We then examine performance-based approaches applied in budgeting and funding, methods to determine public and private returns on investment in postsecondary education, and we close with an examination of finance from the perspective of the primary consumer: students.

The fourth and last section of the book focuses on presenting postsecondary finance research to policy audiences. It is our attempt to assist in connecting academic research and policymaking. Chapters focus on accounting for time considerations in analysis, the placing of data in a context to make the data and findings relevant, and ways to effectively communicate your findings.

In putting this book together, we learned from each other, pushed ourselves, built upon the wisdom and knowledge of decades of friendships and scholarship, and diverted time away from our families.

Mary would like to thank her husband, Lynn Moak, for his support and tireless dedication to the field of education finance. Mary also would like to acknowledge the role of the many people from whom she learned about education finance and who served her well as mentors and friends, including Ron Brady, Fred Bradshaw, Bill McLure, Kent Caruthers, Kern Alexander, Forbis Jordan, and Lucie Lapovsky. She treasures her many friends in education finance, including state legislators, from whom she has learned many lessons about the translation of research into policy.

Chris would like to acknowledge the critical role David S. Honeyman, his doctoral advisor, played in his development as a scholar and person. His parents, Robert T. (who passed away during the writing of this book) and Jolie A. Mullin, introduced him early to the concepts of equity and opportunity that serve as beacons during his journey. It is Chris' hope that he made his father proud. Finally, he would like to thank his wife, Candide, and two children, Mila Jolie and Luke Hudson, for their understanding and support of this work. There were many missed dinners and absent nights. He hopes they understand his rationale and reason for all he does, is, and has always been to and for them.

SECTION I

Introduction to
Higher Education Finance Research

Postsecondary education in the United States is a complex enterprise, with almost 5,000 accredited degree- or certificate-granting institutions providing services to over 18 million undergraduate students and three million graduate students. These institutions expended over $490 billion in academic year 2011–2012 to increase the nation's human capital, conduct research expanding knowledge, and provide services to the general public. Revenues for the institutions came from the federal, state, and local governments; tuition and fees; private gifts and grants; and other sources. These revenues differ among institutional types and in each state.

Because of the complexity of the enterprise, research on the economics and finance of higher education also is complex and requires an understanding of how and why higher education is funded, by whom, at what cost, and who benefits.

This section of the book will provide a brief history of and describe the general organization of American higher education, the sources and uses of funds over the last 100 years, and who is served in what types of institutions. Definitions of terms that are unique to higher education will be given, and some basic rules for conducting research on the economics and finance of higher education will be established. Although in some ways, conducting research in higher education funding is similar to that for elementary/ secondary education, there are some important distinctions that also will be provided.

Higher Education Finance Research: Policy, Politics, and Practice, pp. 1–1
Copyright © 2014 by Information Age Publishing

CHAPTER 1

ORGANIZATION OF HIGHER EDUCATION

During 2011–2012, 4,599 postsecondary institutions enrolled 21.5 million students (Snyder & Dillow, 2012), representing nearly 8.5% of all Americans aged 15 or older (U.S. Census Bureau, 2012). In fall 2011, degree-granting institutions enrolled 18.6 million undergraduate and 2.9 million graduate students. Of the 18.6 million undergraduates, 57% were enrolled in 4-year institutions, 41% in 3-year institutions, and 2% in less-than-2-year institutions (Knapp, Kelly-Reid, & Ginder, 2012).

As an industry, a total of 3.8 million staff, including 1.5 million faculty members, 240,000 administrators, and 1.7 million other staff, in addition to countless other interested parties, engaged in the process of providing educational opportunity at the collegiate level. Together, the postsecondary education industry spent $497 billion in the 2009–2010 year (Snyder & Dillow, 2012). Institutions conferred a total of 4.3 million degrees, including 850,000 associate's, 1.65 million baccalaureates, 693,000 master's, and 159,000 doctoral degrees.

Yet, only a century earlier, the extent and cost of participation in higher education was substantially less. In 1909–1910, just 2.8% of the U.S. population aged 18 to 24 was enrolled in higher education, as compared to 41.7% in 2009–2010 (Snyder, 1993; Snyder & Dillow, 2012). In 1910, approximately 951 public and private non-profit

Higher Education Finance Research: Policy, Politics, and Practice, pp. 3–23
Copyright © 2014 by Information Age Publishing

colleges enrolled 355,000 students and received $76.9 million in revenue (McCarthy & Hines, 1986).

Why has postsecondary education participation grown at such a rapid rate? The answers to this question are as varied as the people and communities engaged in the enterprise. This chapter provides an overview of the diversity of institutions and funding partners created to enhance the nation's human capital, as well as information on the funding of higher education at the industry level. Numerous actors involved in the funding and provision of postsecondary education opportunities complicate an already complex enterprise.

The expanding role of community colleges and for-profit institutions over the last 50 years, the non-traditional students these institutions serve, the rise of the sub-baccalaureate credential as a valued postsecondary outcome, growing interest by policymaking bodies in regulating higher education (i.e., gainful employment regulations of the U.S. Department of Education), and the evolution of the 4-year university to use more selective enrollment practices all necessitate a reframing of postsecondary finance.

This book reexamines traditional concepts and calculations in higher education finance research, in some cases expanding them to illustrate the diversity of funders and institutions. As background, this chapter provides an overview of the who, what, where, when, and why of postsecondary finance. It is intended for the novice, while also reframing research perspectives for the experienced researcher or practitioner.

POSTSECONDARY EDUCATION SECTORS

Opportunities for postsecondary learning may occur in numerous settings including businesses, professionally-affiliated conferences, workshops, seminars, and community-based organizations. What makes postsecondary education institutions different is their accreditation and statutory recognition. For example, for an institution to be eligible to participate in federal student financial aid programs of the U.S. Department of Education, it must meet certain eligibility criteria found in the Code of Federal Regulations.

Diverse institutions offer educational opportunity in higher education and were founded to meet the demand for, and supply of, human capital. The intent of this section is to provide a foundational understanding of the defining characteristics of postsecondary institutions.

Postsecondary education includes academic, career, technical, and continuing professional education programs after high school. Institutions that provide these programs are divided into sectors based on control or governance: *public, private non-profit,* and *private for-profit institutions.* The sectors are *not* determined by the primary source of the institution's revenues; many public institutions no longer receive the majority of their support from public sources, and all accredited institutions (i.e., those that report to the U.S. Department of Education) receive governmental revenues in the form of federal student financial aid and in many cases may receive state and/or local funds either for student financial aid or for institutional operations. Not all institutions providing some form of postsecondary education are accredited, and non-accredited institutions are not included in the statistics in this volume.

For this book, a *public institution* is defined as "an educational institution whose *programs* and activities are operated by publicly elected or appointed school officials and which is supported primarily by public funds." Public institutions in general are governed by boards that are elected by the citizens of a state or appointed by governors or legislatures. Community colleges, in particular, may be governed by elected boards or by boards appointed by a governmental body.

Private institutions are not controlled, primarily supported, or operated by public governments. Their private status allows them to operate independently with fewer checks and balances than publicly controlled institutions (Carnegie Commission on Higher Education, 1973). They may be non-profit or for-profit in nature. A *private institution* is defined as: "An educational institution controlled by a private individual(s) or by a nongovernmental agency, usually supported primarily by other than public funds and operated by other than publicly elected or appointed officials." A *private non-profit institution* is: "A *private institution* in which the individual(s) or agency in control receives no compensation, other than wages, rent, or other expenses, for the assumption of risk. These include both independent not-for-profit schools and those affiliated with a religious organization." A *for-profit institution* is: "A *private institution* in which the individual(s) or agency in control receives compensation other than wages, rent, or other *expenses* for the assumption of risk."

Private non-profit institutions generally are governed by boards of lay people, or by representatives of the religious organization with which the college is affiliated. For- profit institutions also may have a lay governing board but may be controlled by a founder and/or the founder's successors.

Table 1.1 displays the number of institutions, the enrollments, and the revenues for institutions of higher education from 1850 to 2010. In 1910, there were no community colleges, and statistics were not kept on the number of private for-profit institutions providing postsecondary education, so the data are somewhat limited for the early years.

While it may be argued that each of the sectors was present in some form prior to the founding of the nation, we briefly trace the history of legal recognition of institutional control for purposes of distinction

Table 1.1.   Institutions, Students, and Revenues of Higher Education, 1850 to 2010

Year	Number of Colleges/ Universities	Number of Students	Total Income (in thousands)	Revenues per Student
1850	234	27,158	$1,916	$71
1860	467	56,120	$3,176	$57
1870	563	62,839	$21,464	$342
1880	811	115,850	$35,084	$303
1890	998	156,756	$76,883	$490
1900	977	237,592	$199,922	$841
1910	951	355,430	$554,511	$1,560
1920	1,041	597,880	$715,211	$1,196
1930	1,409	1,100,737	$2,374,645	$2,157
1940	1,708	1,494,203	$5,785,537	$3,872
1950	1,851	2,444,900	$21,515,242	$8,800
1960	2,004	3,639,847	$58,519,981	$16,078
1970	2,525	8,004,660	$117,340,109	$14,659
1980	3,152	11,569,899	$128,501,638	$11,107
1990	3,535	13,538,560	$139,635,477	$10,314
2000	4,056	15,312,289	$282,261,455	$18,434
2010	4,599	21,016,026	$496,703,609	$23,635

Source: Snyder and Dillow (2012).

among types of institutions, rather than a treatise on their evolution. A designation as "private" does not mean that the institution does not receive public funds (local, state, or federal monies). As indicated above, all institutions recognized as having students eligible for federal student financial aid receive federal funds.

Private Non-profit Institutions

Prior to 1800, almost all the colleges in the nation were affiliated with religious organizations. The first college in the "New World" (Harvard College, now Harvard University) was founded in 1636 to prepare ministers, and many of the small private colleges that exist today were founded to prepare ministers to serve local communities (Snyder, 1993). Even though these institutions were founded as private institutions, some of these institutions received public funds. For example, 400 British pounds for the establishment of Harvard and the president of the college's salary came from the Massachusetts General Court in 1636 and was thereafter supplemented by bank taxes and tolls paid to cross the Charles River (Cohen, 1998; Lucas, 1994; Roche, 1986). In another case, tracts of land, taxes on tobacco, export duties on furs and skins, and a tax on peddlers were directed toward the establishment and maintenance of William and Mary College in 1693 (Cohen, 1998; Lucas, 1994; Roche, 1986). Harvard's revenues were predominately from private sources, but the college also received public revenues. Other colleges of a private nature also were supported in part by public funds; for example, the first publicly funded university in Maryland was Washington College, which received colonial/state funds for its operations although it is a private non-profit college. In 1850, the 234 colleges that existed received about 90% of their revenues from private sources (McCarthy & Hines, 1986).

The tension between public fiscal support and public influence over institutional policymaking, in combination with rising tensions over the separation of church and state (given the predominant denominational affiliation of many private colleges), led to litigation to determine if these colleges were indeed private or public (Cohn & Leslie, 1980; Lucas, 1994). The United States Supreme Court in the case of Dartmouth College and the State of New Hampshire determined that Dartmouth was indeed a private college not controlled by the state. At question in the case was whether the state could abolish the corporation that ran Dartmouth because the institution received public funds. This case established the precedent that private colleges could receive public funds, provided that those funds were not used for sectarian purposes.

Public Institutions

Public institutions existed in the years prior to the distinction made in the Dartmouth case. In fact, four of the 37 colleges that existed prior to 1800 were public: the University of Georgia, University of North Carolina, University of Virginia, and the University of Maryland. The Northwest Ordinance of 1787 is seen by some as stimulating the growth of public colleges, although many of them struggled to remain solvent. Unlike private colleges, these institutions did not have endowments or related groups such as churches that provided funding. By 1860 there were 21 public colleges in 20 states, funded in part by public monies (Snyder, 1993), but there was no "national" or "federal" college.

Benjamin Franklin and Thomas Jefferson, as well as the other first presidents, were early proponents of a federally funded national university, not state universities. Although a national university has never been established in the manner that the founding fathers suggested, the service academies (the Military Academy at West Point, the Naval Academy, and the Air Force Academy) exist today as completely federally funded institutions as opposed to state or locally funded public institutions.

Lucas (1994) suggests that what saved the fledgling public college was the Morrill Act of 1862, which provided land grants for the creation and maintenance of agricultural and mechanical colleges. The 1890 Morrill Act provided annual federal appropriations lacking from previous efforts to establish institutions of higher education. The Morrill Acts were to function as an endowment of an educational system that eliminated the need for continued federal funding (McCarthy & Hines, 1986). Spurred on by a growing populist concern for agricultural advancements, Justin Morrill introduced a bill in Congress to support the establishment of agricultural and mechanical colleges with federal aid to the states (Roche, 1986). Up to and during this time, public financial support was sporadic at best for postsecondary education, which relied heavily on student fees, private gifts, and grants (Chambers, 1968; Cohen, 1998; Lucas, 1994; Roche, 1986).

Within a context of sectional differences along economic and social lines, Abraham Lincoln signed the Morrill Act of 1862 providing the means for states to begin operating their own postsecondary education institutions (Anderson, 1976; McDowell, 2001). The purpose of these new institutions was specified in the fourth section of the act, which stated "each State which may take and claim the benefit of this act, to the endowment, support, and maintenance of at least one college ... in order to promote the liberal and practical education of the industrial classes in the several professions and pursuits of life" (PL 37-108). The act was an effort to extend the opportunity for education to individuals via institutions that would reflect the unique local context and desires of each state (Eddy, 1957). In approximately twenty states, the land-grant college was an addition to an already present state college (Brubacher & Rudy, 1997). For example, Michigan had already established the University of Michigan in 1817 when Michigan State University was chartered as a land-grant institution in 1863 (Anderson, 1976).

The Servicemen's Readjustment Act of 1947 (PL 346- 268, GI Bill) significantly expanded enrollments at postsecondary education institutions, along with the belief that everyone could go to college (Cohen, 1998). For public higher education, the number of institutions expanded to include 66 land-grant colleges, 259 other undergraduate institutions, and 330 community colleges by 1950 (Mullin & Honeyman, 2008).

To assist in meeting the increased demand for participation in postsecondary education, states took innovative action with the expansion of the

2-year public community college in postsecondary education structures to provide educational opportunity (Longanecker, 2007). Termed "democracy's colleges," these institutions were believed to have brought educational opportunity to the masses through their open-door philosophy, proximity to a state's citizens, and low cost to the student (Carnegie Commission on Higher Education, 1970b). Medsker and Tillery (1971) attributed their growth to three other factors: (a) training programs of various duration and focus were needed to meet the growing job market, (b) the influx of participants taking advantage of the GI Bill, and (c) the perspective of adults after World War II that there was a broader world to which they belonged and should learn about.

While the ideal of increased educational opportunity via open-access institutions occurred at the end of the Second World War (Palmer, 1996), universal access to postsecondary education via the creation of localized institutions was not achieved until the decade spanning the years 1960 to 1969 (Lingenfelter, 2004; Longanecker, 2007); between 1960 and 1970 the number of community colleges grew from 412 to 909, an increase of 497 institutions or 121% (American Association of Community Colleges, n.d.) while the number of other public postsecondary education institutions remained constant.

The increased number of community colleges allowed undergraduate public institutions to expand in areas commensurate with increased status, such as graduate education, research, and research funding. As a result, these undergraduate institutions could redirect less-qualified students to community colleges by increasing their own admission standards (Cohen, 1998). Community colleges accepted their role as providers of postsecondary opportunity to those who were of lesser income, geographically bound, or older (Carnegie Commission on Higher Education, 1970a).

A salient theme in the evolution of the public American postsecondary enterprise was the notion of access via the material realization of institutions built to meet diverse needs, whether those needs were secular, demographic, or geographic. Many of the first state colleges were normal schools, established to train teachers for the rapidly expanding elementary and secondary school population. These normal schools began as 2 year institutions and could be considered the precursors to community colleges.

For-profit Institutions

The development of for-profit institutions is less well documented than their public and private non-profit counterparts. Claims of education as a profit-oriented business may be traced to antiquity, but like the origins of public institutions, the date of demarcation for the establishment of for-profit institutions relates to their recognition in policy as a defined institution of higher education. In fact, there continue to be a large number of profit-minded businesses offering education and training opportunities, yet these entities are not considered institutions of higher education. The training programs provided by large accounting firms or by Walmart are examples of the postsecondary programs that are not included in the statistics collected by the Institute for Education Sciences (IES) of the U.S. Department of Education.

Prior to the 1970s, for-profit or proprietary institutions like Strayer University were excluded from eligibility for federal student aid. During congressional hearings leading to reauthorization of the Higher Education Act of 1965 (HEA), for-profit institutions sought accreditation to obtain access to public subsidies and to legitimize their role in higher education (Scanlon & McComis, 2010). In the years immediately following passage of the HEA, accrediting agencies began to recognize for-profit institutions, and the number of for-profit institutions recognized by the U.S. Department of Education increased from 55 in 1976–1977 to 1,104 in 2008–2009 (Snyder & Dillow, 2010; Harcelrod, 1989). The large increases in enrollments shown in Table 1.1 in the last 20 years are attributable in large part to increases in the number of for-profit or proprietary institutions.

LEVELS AND CLASSIFICATION OF POSTSECONDARY EDUCATION INSTITUTIONS

Control type of an institution (public, private non-profit, or for-profit) is just one of two important distinctions, the other being the *level* of the institution. *Level* refers to the length of an institution's program of greatest duration. In the federally maintained Integrated Postsecondary Education Data System (IPEDS), an institution is classified into one of three levels: 4-year and higher, 2 to 4 years, and less than 2 years.

When control type and levels are combined, nine sectors result (see Figure 1.1). The qualities that place institutions into one of nine sectors are unique to both the programs they offer and the way they are governed. These differences, in turn, influence how the institutions are financed. For example, the University of Florida (public 4-year) is substantially different than Chippewa Valley Technical College (public 2-year), just as Columbia University (private non-profit 4-year) is much different than Franklin Academy (private non-profit < 2-year), University of Phoenix (for-profit 4-year), Heald College (for-profit 2-year) and ABC Beauty College, Inc. (for-profit < 2-year).

		Control		
		Public	Private nonprofit	For-profit
Level	<2-year	Public, <2-year	Private nonprofit, <2-year	For-profit,<2-year
	2-year	Public, 2-year	Private nonprofit, 2-year	For-profit, 2-year
	4-year	Public, 4-year	Private nonprofit, 4-year	For-profit, 4-year

Figure 1.1.   Sectors of postsecondary education.

Despite the differences, in policy discussions—which are primarily focused on issues directly or indirectly related to finances—sectors of higher education generally are grouped into one of four types: public 4-year, public 2-year or community colleges, private non-profit, and private for-profit. There are several reasons for the use in policy discussions of four sectors as opposed to nine.

For-profit institutions constituted a small percentage of the higher education universe for an extended period of time. Only recently have they been identified as a separate classification of institutions in widely distributed and referenced publications such as the College Board's annual *Trends in College Pricing* or the National Center for Education Statistics' annual *Digest of Education Statistics*.

A second distinction is the relatively small attendance at institutions whose programs are less than 2 years in duration; these institutions are excluded from many analyses or combined with other sectors with a similar governance or control type.

For research purposes, different distinctions or classifications may be used. Colleges and universities also are classified into Carnegie groups depending on their research activities and scope of program. In 1973, the Carnegie Commission on Higher Education developed and published a classification of colleges and universities that was derived from empirical data on colleges and universities. Classifications were updated in 1976, 1987, 1994, 2000, 2005, and 2010 to reflect changes among colleges and universities. This framework has been widely used in the study of higher education, both as a way to represent and control for institutional differences, and also in the design of research studies to ensure adequate representation of sampled institutions, students, or faculty (Carnegie Foundation for the Advancement of Teaching, 2012).

The 2010 Carnegie classes of institutions are shown in Table 1.2. The five basic types are described below and are further delineated into subgroups. The associate's colleges category is the only classification where control is a major determination of sub-group or sub-classification.

- *Associate's Colleges:* institutions where all degrees are at the associate's level, or where bachelor's degrees account for fewer than 10% of all undergraduate degrees.
- *Baccalaureate Colleges:* institutions where baccalaureate degrees represent at least 10% of all undergraduate degrees and where fewer than 50 master's degrees or 20 doctoral degrees were awarded.
- *Master's Colleges and Universities:* institutions that awarded at least 50 master's degrees and fewer than 20 doctoral degrees.
- *Doctorate-granting Universities:* institutions that awarded at least 20 research doctoral degrees (excluding doctoral-level degrees that qualify recipients for entry into professional practice, such as the JD, MD, PharmD, DPT, etc.).
- *Special Focus Institutions:* institutions awarding baccalaureate or higher-level degrees where a high concentration of degrees (above 75%) is in a single field or set of related fields, such as engineering schools.

Table 1.2.   Carnegie Classifications of Institutions

Category	*Sub-category*
Associate's Colleges	Assoc/Pub-R-S: Associate's—Public Rural-serving Small
	Assoc/Pub-R-M: Associate's—Public Rural-serving Medium
	Assoc/Pub-R-L: Associate's—Public Rural-serving Large
	Assoc/Pub-S-SC: Associate's—Public Suburban-serving Single Campus
	Assoc/Pub-S-MC: Associate's—Public Suburban-serving Multi-campus
	Assoc/Pub-U-SC: Associate's—Public Urban-serving Single Campus
	Assoc/Pub-U-MC: Associate's—Public Urban-serving Multi-campus
	Assoc/Pub-Spec: Associate's—Public Special Use
	Assoc/PrivNFP: Associate's—Private Not-for-profit
	Assoc/PrivFP: Associate's—Private For-profit
	Assoc/Pub2in4: Associate's—Public 2-year Colleges under Universities
	Assoc/Pub4: Associate's—Public 4-year, Primarily Associate's
	Assoc/PrivNFP4: Associate's—Private Not-for-profit 4-year, Primarily Associate's
	Assoc/PrivFP4: Associate's—Private For-profit 4-year, Primarily Associate's
Baccalaureate Colleges	Bac/A&S: Baccalaureate Colleges – Arts & Sciences

(Table continues on next page)

Table 1.2. Continued

Category	*Sub-category*
	Bac/Diverse: Baccalaureate Colleges—Diverse Fields
	Bac/Assoc: Baccalaureate/Associate's Colleges
Master's Colleges and Universities.	Master's/L: Master's Colleges and Universities (larger programs)
	Master's/M: Master's Colleges and Universities (medium programs)
	Master's/S: Master's Colleges and Universities (smaller programs)
Doctorate-granting Universities	RU/VH: Research Universities (very high research activity)
	RU/H: Research Universities (high research activity)
	DRU: Doctoral/Research Universities
Special Focus Institutions	Spec/Faith: Theological seminaries, Bible colleges, and other faith-related institutions
	Spec/Medical: Medical schools and medical centers
	Spec/Health: Other health profession schools
	Spec/Eng: Schools of engineering
	Spec/Tech: Other technology-related schools
	Spec/Bus: Schools of business and management
	Spec/Arts: Schools of art, music, and design
	Spec/Law: Schools of law
	Spec/Other: Other special-focus institutions
Tribal Colleges	Tribal: Tribal Colleges

Source: Carnegie Foundation for the Advancement of Teaching

INSTITUTIONAL CHARACTERISTICS

The vast majority of postsecondary institutions have fewer than 5,000 undergraduate students enrolled; 58% of institutions have fewer than 1,000 undergraduate students. Each sector varies greatly in the number of institutions and the size of undergraduate enrollments, with a greater percentage of public institutions having large enrollments; 55% of public institutions, 89% of private non-profit, and 95% of for-profit institutions enrolled fewer than 5,000 students in fall 2009 (see Table 1.3).

Institutions are not distributed equally by geographic region; 23% of institutions are located in the Southeast, and 4% in the Rocky Mountain area. Almost half (47%) of all institutions are located in a city, 26% are located in the suburbs, with the remaining 26 percent split equally

Table 1.3.   Institutional Characteristics of Postsecondary Institutions, by Control of Institution and Level: Fall 2009

	Public			Private			For-profit		
	4-year	*2-year*	*Less-than-2-year*	*4-year*	*2-year*	*Less-than-2-year*	*4-year*	*2-year*	*Less-than-2-year*
Geographic Location (number of institutions)[a]									
Rural	81	350	102	164	17	7	55	86	84
Town	168	242	63	237	21	8	7	72	125
Suburban	126	196	58	410	41	31	171	321	588
City	318	329	40	841	112	57	345	516	800
Total[b]	693	1,120	263	1,652	191	103	578	995	1,597
Region (number of institutions)									
Far West	73	167	10	190	12	22	92	158	214
Great Lakes	80	91	45	190	18	8	47	157	137
Middle Atlantic	121	92	62	334	76	17	38	141	225
New England	44	44	6	150	16	4	13	18	115
Plains	59	115	21	174	21	4	82	74	74
Rocky Mountains	31	46	5	24	3	1	47	67	30
Southeast	179	358	39	329	17	18	160	237	321
Southwest	74	133	32	81	5	3	64	91	217
Outlying Areas and US Service Schools	24	11	0	39	6	11	7	11	54
Total[b]	693	1,120	263	1,652	191	103	578	995	1,597
Size of Undergraduate Student Body (number of institutions)									
Under 1,000	40	173	231	728	177	91	374	865	1,458
1,001–4,999	225	456	8	722	10	3	164	121	41
5,000–9,999	156	259	0	109	0	0	18	0	1
10,000–19,999	141	155	1	54	0	0	7	0	1
20,000 or more	130	69	0	17	0	0	11	0	0
Total[b]	693	1,120	263	1,652	191	103	578	995	1,597
Title IV Student Aid									
% of institutions that participate in Title IV	100	100	99	98	97	91	99	98	93
Degree-granting									
% of institutions that are degree-granting	100	91	0	99	50	0	100	66	0
Institutional Housing									
% of institutions that provide on-campus housing	78	21	1	76	21	3	11	4	1

Source: U.S. Department of Education, National Center for Education Statistics, Integrated Postsecondary Education Data System (IPEDS).

Note: (a) Institutions may offer a substantial number of courses online. (b) Total does not include 84 administrative units and 40 institutions whose sectors were unknown.

between towns and rural locations. These data are informative but must be interpreted with caution, as many for-profit institutions operate primarily in online environments, which makes geographic analyses difficult. When for-profit institutions are removed, there is a 5% and 6% decrease in city and suburban-located institutions, respectively, and a 5% increase in the number of institutions in both towns and rural locations. (Regional location does not change more than 2% for any region.)

The majority of institutions participate in federal Title IV student aid programs. All 4-year institutions are degree-granting, but only 50% of private non-profit 2-year institutions are degree-granting, as compared to 91% and 66% of public and private for-profit institutions respectively. On-campus housing is a phenomenon most prevalent on 4-year campuses at public and private non-profit institutions.

Admissions Practices

Institutions make decisions to establish admission thresholds that set the minimum qualification needed to pursue the opportunities postsecondary education provides. Colleges that permit students with all academic backgrounds the opportunity to advance their level of educational attainment are termed "open access."

Open access institutions are found in every sector of higher education. In 2009–2010, 17.2% of public 4-year, 96.3% of public 2-year, 13.2% of private non-profit 4-year, 45.8% of private non-profit 2-year, 47.9% of for-profit 4-year, and 62.1% of for-profit 2-year institutions classified themselves as open admission (Snyder & Dillow, 2011, T. 338). (See Table 1.4).

Some of the remaining institutions are highly selective in their admission practices. Institutions are called "highly selective" if they admit fewer than 10% of applicants. In 2010, 0.2% of public 4-year, 0.6% of private non-profit 4-year, and 0.0% of for-profit 4-year institutions admitted fewer than 10% of those who applied (Snyder & Dillow, 2011, T. 339).

The distinction between open access and highly selective institutions is an important one in higher education finance because open access institutions must provide a fuller range of services to students who come to college less well-prepared. These services require additional resources, especially if the institution provides remedial education or other "success" services.

Table 1.4.   Academic Characteristics of Postsecondary Institutions, by Control of Institution and Level: Fall 2009

	Public			Private			For-Profit		
	4-year	*2-year*	*Less-than-2-year*	*4-year*	*2-year*	*Less-than-2-year*	*4-year*	*2-year*	*Less-than-2-year*
Remediation									
% of institutions offering remedial services	76	99	84	60	55	64	80	36	16
Admission Practices									
% of institutions that are open admission	16	95	61	11	31	72	45	67	76
% of institutions requiring SAT/ACT test scores	69	2	0	51	12	1	2	0	0
% of institutions charging an application fee	88	39	61	71	87	58	57	65	69
Prior Learning									
% of institutions accepting dual credit	87	93	16	63	38	6	46	15	3
% of institutions accepting credit for life experiences	33	56	5	36	14	4	43	14	5
% of institutions accepting Advanced Placement (AP) credits	93	88	20	72	39	5	72	22	3
Distance Learning									
% of institutions offering distance learning opportunities	88	92	17	50	22	4	78	19	2
Library									
% of institutions owning a library	98	89	50	95	89	64	98	92	85
Instructional Staff[a] (Not Including Medical Schools)									
Total	437,858	369,363		337,742	3,708		93,707	23,139	
Full time	281,610	112,473		168,240	1,427		13,724	10,295	
Part time	156,248	256,890		169,502	2,281		79,983	12,844	
Faculty Status (Full time staff involved in instruction, research, and/or public service)[b]									
Total	365,618	112,800		224,618	1,353		13,666	10,070	
With Tenure	168,420	45,669		83,039	101		107	124	
On Tenure Track	74,042	15,864		45,162	54		124	4	
Not on Tenure Track	109,357	9,833		59,706	145		93	1	

(Table continues on next page)

Table 1.4. Continued

	Public			Private			For-profit		
	4-year	*2-year*	*Less-than-2-year*	*4-year*	*2-year*	*Less-than-2-year*	*4-year*	*2-year*	*Less-than-2-year*
Faculty Status (Full time staff involved in instruction, research, and/or public service)[b]									
No Tenure System	2,546	40,514		20,226	1,045		13,117	9,858	
No Faculty Status	11,253	920		16,485	8		225	83	
Academic Rank (Full time instructional staff)[c]									
Total	280,092	111,658		167,485	1,353		13,462	9,949	
Professor	84,847	14,427		50,975	95		1,104	201	
Associate Professor	71,911	10,327		43,697	203		811	67	
Assistant Professor	74,494	11,556		46,117	263		669	65	
Instructor	21,392	45,432		10,913	603		7,597	9,174	
Lecturer	19,784	697		7,481	10		5	0	
No Academic Rank	7,664	29,219		8,302	179		3,276	442	
Adjusted 9-month Average Salaries[d]									
Professor	$104,903	$71,285		$109,695	$53,028		$57,408	$44,584	
Associate Professor	$75,825	$60,081		$74,641	$47,757		$53,741	$39,582	
Assistant Professor	$63,741	$53,743		$61,919	$45,789		$55,262	$34,288	
Instructor	$46,365	$63,896		$47,141	$41,868		$41,904	$36,579	
Lecturer	$53,679	$52,568		$56,884	$30,214		$22,166	n/a	

Source: NCES (2012a)
Note: Adapted from data presented in NCES Winter 2009 Compendium Tables (a) Table 5, (b) Table 18, (c) Table 28, (d) Table 34 [data adjusted for 11/12 month contract to equate to 9-month contract]

Remedial Education

As aspect of open admission practices is the acknowledgement that students arrive at college, either after high school of later in life, with some academic deficiencies. The extent to which remedial services are available to students varies somewhat by institution type and year (see Table 1.4). In the 2009–2010 academic year, nearly all public 2-year institutions (99.6%) offered students the opportunity to participate in remedial education, compared to roughly half (49.4%) of all for-profit 2-year institutions.

These deficiencies impact the likelihood of students meeting traditional measures of attainment, such as completion of a degree or certificate, and is a point of considerable conversation at the time this book was written because completion rates relate to performance funding mechanisms and incenting student success. This issue will be discussed in Chapter 7.

STUDENT CHARACTERISTICS

In the early years of American higher education, as indicated earlier, students were those interested in becoming ministers and those who could afford a liberal education. In 1850, only 27,000 students were enrolled in postsecondary institutions. Access to higher education for all is attributed to the Morrill Act of 1862 and was further expanded by the extension of educational benefits to veterans returning from World War II and by the passage of the National Defense Education Act. Following passage of the 1862 Morrill Act, enrollment more than doubled but still was limited to almost all males.

In the 21st century, a postsecondary education is seen as the best route to increased earnings, so significantly more individuals, and a significantly greater proportion of the over 18-year-old population, were enrolled in postsecondary education. Each sector varied greatly in the number of institutions and the size of enrollments. Table 1.5 displays information not only on the headcount enrollment but also the "full-time equivalent enrollment" (FTE). The full-time equivalent enrollment is calculated by the U.S. Department of Education using a formula that varies by institutional type. Up until 1998, the conversion from headcount to FTE was the same for all institutions and was calculated as the number of headcount full-time students plus one-third of the number of part-time students. The concerns this difference raises in conducting research in higher education finance will be discussed in the next chapter.

Table 1.5.   Headcount and FTE Enrollments by Sector, Fall 1970 to Fall 2010

Number of Institutions	Fall 1970	Fall 1980	Fall 1990	Fall 2000	Fall 2009	Fall 2010
Total	2,556	3,226	3,501	4,056	4,474	4,589
Public	1,089	1,493	1,548	1,676	1,671	1,652
Private non-profit**	1,467	795	709	729	734	736
Private for-profit**		164	322	724	1,181	1,310
Enrollment						
Total Headcount	8,580,887	12,096,895	13,818,637	15,312,289	20,427,711	21,016,126
Public	6,261,502	9,457,394	10,844,717	11,752,786	14,810,642	15,142,809
Private non-profit	2,134,420	2,527,787	2,760,227	3,109,419	3,765,083	3,854,920
Private for-profit	18,333	111,714	213,693	450,084	1,851,986	2,018,397

(Table continues on next page)

Table 1.5.   Continued

Number of Institutions	*Fall 1970*	*Fall 1980*	*Fall 1990*	*Fall 2000*	*Fall 2009*	*Fall 2010*
Full-time Equivalent Enrollment						
Total FTE	6,737,819	8,819,013	9,983,436	11,267,025	15,495,892	15,943,343
Public	4,953,144	6,642,294	7,557,982	8,266,932	10,750,132	11,020,752
Private non-profit**	1,676,853	2,176,719	2,250,453	2,601,179	3,177,702	3,262,699
Private for-profit**			175,001	398,914	1,568,058	1,659,892
Average Headcount Enrollment by Type of Institution						
Total	3,357	3,750	3,947	3,775	4,566	4,580
Public	5,750	6,334	7,006	7,012	8,863	9,166
Private non-profit*	1,467	3,180	3,893	4,265	5,130	5,238
Private for-profit		681	664	622	1,568	1,541
Average FTE Enrollment by Type of Institution						
Total	2,636	2,734	2,852	2,778	3,464	3,474
Public	4,548	4,449	4,882	4,933	6,433	6,671
Private non-profit*	1,143	2,270	3,174	3,568	4,329	4,433
Private for-profit			543	551	1,328	1,267

** Data not available to separate private institutions into non-profit and for-profit.
Source: Snyder and Dillow (2012), Tables 206 and 227; Snyder 1993, Table 25.

The number of public and private non-profit institutions has remained relatively constant since 2000, but the number of private for-profit institutions has quadrupled since 1990, in part due to the expansion of eligibility for federal student financial aid programs. Total enrollment at for-profit institutions also has increased dramatically since 1990.

Average enrollment also varied by sector, with public institutions being the largest, with average enrollment increasing from 5,750 in Fall 1970 to 9,166 in Fall 2010, about twice the size of the average private non-profit institution. At private non-profit institutions, average enrollment increased from 3,180 in Fall 1980 to 5,238 in Fall 2010. Private for-profit institutions increased in size from an average of 681 students in Fall 1980 to 1,541 in Fall 2010.

REVENUES AND EXPENDITURES

Higher education is an immense industry supported by a balance of revenue sources that differs by state and by institutional type. Funding comes from four primary sources: students and their families, who pay tuition and fees; state and local governments, through direct institutional appropriations, financial aid, and contracts and grants; the federal government, through direct institutional appropriations, financial aid, and contracts and grants; and through gifts and endowments. Revenues also are received from investment income and sales and services. Those revenues are used for instruction, research, public service, academic support, student services, institutional support, student financial aid, operation and maintenance of the physical plant, auxiliary services, and at some institutions, hospital operations. The first eight of these expenditure categories are grouped together into "educational and general expenditures" (E&G). All institutions eligible for federal Title IV programs must annually report their revenues and expenditures to the U.S. Department of Education through the IPEDS finance survey.

In 1850, the 234 operating colleges and universities had a total of $1.9 million in revenue, of which only $200,000 came from public sources. By 2010, revenues had increased to $496 billion, of which 25% came from government or public sources. Revenues doubled between every decade after 1960, and state government support also increased dramatically. Tuition and fees as a percent of total revenues have remained at between 20 and 28% throughout the time period, except for 1950, when veterans returning from World War II paid little tuition and fees (see Table 1.6). Up until 1940, the federal government provided less than 10% of total revenues. The category of "other" support has always been the major source of income for institutions and includes revenues from endowments, contributions, and auxiliary services.

Table 1.6.   Revenues of Postsecondary Institutions, 1850 to 2010 (dollars in thousands)

	Total Revenue	Tuition & Fees	Federal	State	Local	Other
1849–50	1,916			200a		1,716
1859–60	3,177			160a		3,017
1889–90	21,464					
1899–1900	35,084					
1909–10	76,883	18,463	4,607	2,093		51,720
1919–20	199,922	42,255	12,783	61,690		83,194
1929–30	554,511	144,126	20,658	150,847		238,880
1939–40	715,211	200,897	38,860	151,222	24,392	299,840
1949–50	2,374,645	394,610	524,319	491,636	61,700	902,380
1959–60	5,785,537	1,157,482	1,036,990	1,374,476	151,715	2,064,874
1969–70	21,515,242	4,419,845	4,130,066	5,873,626	778,162	6,313,543
1979–80	58,519,982	11,930,340	8,902,844	18,378,299	1,587,552	17,720,947

(Table continues on next page)

Table 1.6. Continued

	Total Revenue	Tuition & Fees	Federal	State	Local	Other
1989–90	139,635,477	33,926,060	17,254,874	38,349,239	3,639,902	46,465,402
1999–2000	282,261,456	62,498,447	29,342,866	57,559,210	6,511,404	126,349,530
2009–10	496,703,609	134,660,394	28,397,667	74,319,548	20,277,167	239,048,833
Percent of total revenues						
1849–50				10%		90%
1859–60				5%		95%
1889–90						
1899–1900						
1909–10		24%	6%	3%	0%	67%
1919–20		21%	6%	31%	0%	42%
1929–30		26%	4%	27%	0%	43%
1939–40		28%	5%	21%	3%	42%
1949–50		17%	22%	21%	3%	38%
1959–60		20%	18%	24%	3%	36%
1969–70		21%	19%	27%	4%	29%
1979–80		20%	15%	31%	3%	30%
1989–90		24%	12%	27%	3%	33%
1999–2000		22%	10%	20%	2%	45%
2009–10		27%	6%	15%	4%	48%

Source: McCarthy and Hines (1986) for 1850 and 1860; Snyder 1993 for 1890–1990; and Snyder and Dillow (2012) for 2000 and 2010.

As shown in Table 1.7, tuition and fees comprised 18% of total revenues for public institutions, 33% of private non-profit revenues, but 91% of private for-profit revenues. State appropriations, grants, and contracts comprised 24% of public institutional revenues, but only around 1% of private institutional revenues. On the other hand, investment return provided 17% of private non-profit revenues, but only 3% of public institutional revenues.

Table 1.7. Revenues by Sector, 2010

Revenue Source	Total $	Total %	Public $	Public %	Private non-profit $	Private non-profit %	Private for-profit $	Private for-profit %
Total	496,703,609	100%	303,329,538	100%	168,689,242	100%	24,684,829	100%
Net Student tuition and fees	134,660,394	27%	55,930,482	18%	56,355,862	33%	22,374,050	91%
Federal appropriations, grants, and contracts	76,154,992	15%	51,289,997	17%	22,913,792	14%	1,951,202	8%

(Table continues on next page)

Table 1.7.   Continued

Revenue Source	Total $	%	Public $	%	Private non-profit $	%	Private for-profit $	%
State appropriations, grants, and contracts	74,319,548	15%	72,483,814	24%	1,721,659	1%	114,075	0%
Local appropriations, grants, and contracts	20,277,167	4%	19,805,742	7%	471,425	0%	0	0%
Private gifts grants, and contracts	27,712,020	6%	5,876,450	2%	18,017,260	11%	38,299	0%
Investment return	38,512,306	8%	10,046,610	3%	28,425,581	17%	40,115	0%
Educational activities	20,071,688	4%	14,814,344	5%	4,821,825	3%	435,519	2%
Auxiliary enterprises	36,739,245	7%	22,173,700	7%	14,080,329	8%	485,216	2%
Hospitals	45,778,392	9%	29,236,931	10%	16,541,461	10%	0	0%
Other	22,477,857	5%	21,671,469	7%	5,340,047	3%	−753,647	−3%

Source: Snyder and Dillow (2012), Tables 366, 370, and 372.

Expenditures also increased commensurate with revenues but varied significantly by sector. Table 1.8 displays the total expenditures by type from 1930 to 2010. Education and general expenditures varied from 75 to 84% between 1930 and 2010, while student aid was 25% of total expenditures in 1930 but had declined to 4% in 2010.

Table 1.8.   Expenditures From 1930 to 2010 (dollars in thousands)

Year	Total $	E & G $	%	Auxiliary $	%	Student Aid $	%
1930	$507,142	$377,903	75%	$3,127	1%	$126,112	25%
1940	674,688	521,990	77%	124,184	18%	121,514	18%
1950	2,245,661	1,706,444	76%	476,401	21%	453,121	20%
1960	5,601,376	4,685,258	84%	916,117	16%	172,050	3%
1970	21,043,113	16,845,212	80%	2,769,276	13%	984,594	5%
1980	56,913,588	44,542,843	78%	6,485,608	11%	2,200,468	4%
1990	134,655,571	105,585,076	78%	13,203,984	10%	6,655,544	5%
2000	236,784,231	184,573,397	78%	22,892,749	10%	7,992,583	3%
2010	446,483,758	345,744,328	77%	34,810,190	8%	16,387,785	4%

Source: Snyder and Dillow (2012), Tables 377, 389, and 391.

When expenditures by control are examined, there are differences. Table 1.9 displays expenditures by functional area for public, private, and for-profit institutions in 2010. Private non-profit institutions spent a larger proportion of their budgets on instruction than did public institutions or for-profit institutions. Private for-profit institutions spent the majority of their budgets on student services, academic, and institutional support. Unfortunately, no further delineation of those expenditures was available to determine in which of the three categories for-profit institutions spent the most. The next chapter will provide information on how to use data such as these in research.

Table 1.9. Expenditures by Sector, 2010 (dollars in thousands)

	Public		Private Non-Profit		Private For-Profit	
Expenditure Category	$	%	$	%	$	%
Total	281,368,314	100%	145,141,785	100%	19,973,659	100%
Instruction	76,292,102	27%	47,486,299	33%	4,750,829	24%
Research and public service	39,584,345	14%	18,245,219	13%	13,257	0%
Student services, academic and institutional support	54,702,049	19%	43,788,779	30%	13,086,981	66%
Auxiliary enterprises	20,457,106	7%	13,887,042	10%	466,042	2%
Net grant aid to students	15,435,492	5%	832,078	1%	120,215	1%
Other	74,897,220	27%	20,902,369	14%	1,536,334	8%

Source: Snyder and Dillow (2012), Tables 379, 377, and 381.

CHAPTER 2

FOUNDATIONS OF FISCAL ANALYSES

The previous chapter traced the evolution of the three distinct institution types under different types of control: public, private non-profit, and private for-profit. While an understanding of control type helps to understand an institution's motives as they relate to mission and governance, control type also is important for appropriate fiscal analyses.

The purpose of this chapter is to provide further background knowledge on the various types of finance data in postsecondary education, highlighting the characteristics and considerations necessary to note where comparative research may be problematic. To illustrate that point, in Chapter 1, data were presented on the numbers of institutions and students, revenues, and expenditures as if the data were comparable over some time period. However, counts of the number of institutions and students have been defined differently during the time shown in the tables, and definitions of revenues and expenditures also have changed. In conducting finance research, it is important to note these changes and make the data comparable before analyzing the information.

Higher Education Finance Research: Policy, Politics, and Practice, pp. 25–58
Copyright © 2014 by Information Age Publishing

FUNDING MAGNITUDE

Comparing fiscal data from 1 year to another can provide valuable information when funds are allocated irrespective of the number of students impacted by the funds, for example, capital revenues for the construction of a new building or for equipment. However, in postsecondary education, financial data are by and large tied to students, either through direct grants or through capitation, in other words, based upon the number of students enrolling or completing some level of academic success. As such, fiscal data often need to be adjusted to understand their magnitude; one cannot rely solely on volume. This is often done by dividing an amount of revenues or expenditures by the number of students that enroll in postsecondary education or in a particular program to arrive at a "per student" value.

While per student values are commonly reported, it is important to understand how the number of students is calculated. Student data usually are reported either as headcount, or count, of actual persons or as full-time equivalent students (FTES), a value derived a number of different ways depending on the purpose of the count. In elementary and secondary education, there also are multiple ways to count students, including membership or attendance.

HEADCOUNT

Headcounts reflect the actual number of people served during a period of time, usually an academic year. An unduplicated headcount, when a student is counted only once during the time period being studied (the fall, spring, or summer semester during an academic year; or only once even if enrolled at more than one institution), is one type. Since these data are reported by institutions to IPEDS, in the national reporting data, students who are enrolled at two or more institutions, about 11% of students, may be counted at least twice. (A 2012 push for a national count of student-level data, currently prohibited by federal law, would limit this problem.)

Unduplicated counts are most frequently used to represent enrollment in the fall semester. Historically, students enrolled in college as full-time students and did not change during the academic year, so this count made sense. Headcount also is a workload measure for student services programs, where a counselor or admissions officer works with one individual at a time, irrespective of the number of courses or credit hours the student is taking,

Another type of headcount is the duplicated headcount. A student is counted every time enrolled for the fall, spring *and* summer semester during an academic year, or counted at each of the institutions in which the student is enrolled. Rarely are duplicated counts published or shared. However, unless the data being used expressly define the type of student count, a duplicated count cannot be eliminated. Whether headcounts are reported for federal purposes, by state agencies, or by institutions, researchers must determine if the number is an unduplicated or a duplicated headcount.

DERIVED STUDENT COUNTS

In addition to headcount, there are a number of student counts that are derived for specific purposes. Among these are credit hours, contact hours, FTES, and weighted credit hours or FTES.

Credit and Contact Hours

How did one account for the varying graduation requirements from high school (i.e., number of math courses) and the non-compulsory nature of postsecondary education as high school graduation rates rose at the turn of the 20th century? Wellman and Ehrlich (2003) suggest that the credit hour was developed to represent a standardized measure of education, which allowed for educational institutions to maintain their autonomy through the provision of elective courses. An added benefit was that packing courses as credit hours allowed specialized knowledge to be portable between institutions.

The credit hour, as determined by the National Center for Education Statistics (NCES) for IPEDS purposes, is defined as a fifty-minute class session offered for 16 weeks. Similar to the credit hour is the contact hour, which, as defined by NCES for IPEDS, equals a sixty-minute class session. The number of credit or contact hours is multiplied by the number of students in the course and then summed across all courses in an academic year to arrive at an instructional activity value (from the 12-month enrollment survey) for the institution.

It is important to note that there are other calculations to determine credit and contact hours. The lack of a standardized definition of the credit hour in federal legislation led to a discussion of the topic in the program integrity negotiated public rulemaking process of 2010–2011 (http://www2.ed.gov/policy/highered/reg/hearulemaking/2009 credit.html). The debate centered on the realization that in awarding over $150 billion in federal student financial aid, a common definition for the credit hour did not exist, even though credit hours measure degree completion (U.S. Department of Education, 2010). On October 29, 2010, in the final federal regulations, a credit hour for federal purposes was defined as "an institutionally established equivalency that reasonably approximates some minimum amount of student work reflective of the amount of work expected in a Carnegie unit" (Ochoa, 2011, p. 1).

Full-time Equivalent (FTE) Students

According to NCES (2010a), "The full-time equivalent (FTE) of students is a single value providing a meaningful combination of full-time and part-time students." Implicit in this definition is the assumption that all institutions define a "full-time" student in the same way. Federal reports define a full-time student as one taking 12 or more credit hours in a term or semester. Definitions of "full-time" vary from state to state and from institution to institution. For example, some institutions define a full-time student as one taking 10 or more credit hours in a term. Not all recent reports or studies use the NCES conversion factors for FTE, and consequently, researchers must be very clear on which conversion factors were used.

In 2013, for federal reporting purposes, there are two calculations utilized to determine the number of FTE students at an institution. One calculation consists of full-time students plus an adjusted number of part-time students. Prior to the 1990s, NCES defined an FTE student as the headcount of full time students plus one-third the headcount of part-time students. In 2013, weights for the adjustment of part-time students vary by sector from 0.403543 for public 4-year institutions to a low of 0.335737 for students at public 2-year and less-than-2-year institutions (Snyder & Dillow, 2011). These values were set in the mid-1990s and have remained unchanged to allow for comparable data over the years. This version of the FTE was used in tables 226, 227, 228, 245, 255, 257, 258, 362, 366, 367, 368, 369, 373, 375, 376, 377, and 378 (personal communication, Tom Snyder, 2011) in the 2010 and 2011 editions of the *Digest of Education Statistics* (Snyder & Dillow, 2011), but not in other tables. The 2012 version of the FTE count is not the same as that used prior to 1990, and even in federal documents, care must be taken to ensure comparability of data.

The other NCES calculation of FTE for IPEDS is based upon an institution's 12-month instructional activity—total credit and contact hours—and calendar system. If an institution has a quarter calendar system, the total number of credit hours over a 12-month period for undergraduate students is divided by 45 to arrive at the total number of FTEs. If the institution reports contact hours, the divisor is 900; for graduate students in credit hour programs the divisor is 36. If an institution has a semester/trimester or 4-1-4 calendar system, the total number of credit hours over a 12-month period for undergraduate students is divided by 30 to arrive at the total number of FTEs. If the institution reports contact hours, the divisor is 900, and for graduate students in credit hour programs, the divisor is 24. For institutions with continuous enrollment programs, FTE is determined by dividing the number of contact hours attempted by 900.

It should be noted that this is the NCES or federal methodology, and that a definition of "full-time equivalent students" can vary by state and institution. Some states measure FTE in the fall term only; other states define a full-time undergraduate student as one taking 15 or more credit hours per term or 30 per academic year; a full-time master's student as one taking 12 or more credit hours per term or 24 hours in an academic year; a full-time doctoral student as one taking 10 or more credit hours per term or taking 20 credit hours in an academic year; and a full-time professional student (law, medicine, dentistry, veterinary medicine) as a headcount student. Others define a full-time undergraduate student as one taking 12 or more credit hours per term, a master's student as one taking 10 hours per term, and a doctoral student as one taking 8 or more credit hours per term.

A difference in credits used in the denominator could make a substantial difference in FTE calculations. For example, if an institution provided 60,000 undergraduate credit hours in a given year, using a 30 credit hour policy for full-time status to determine an FTE (the denominator) would result in an undergraduate FTE of 2,000. Alternatively, if a 24 credit hour policy were implemented to determine an FTE at the same institution, the result would be 2,500 FTEs.

To illustrate the differences for financial analysis, assume that each institution received $10,000 per FTE. A 30 credit hour policy would result in $20 million, but a 24 credit hour policy would result in $25 million, a $5 million difference for an institution simply by changing the calculation of an FTE.

In all cases, an FTE is a derived variable used to estimate the number of full-time students attending a campus. FTE is calculated from credit/contact hours or weighted headcounts. It is important to remember that the FTE used in federal counts is not the same as the FTE used by states to distribute state aid, or by institutions to determine the tuition and fees of a full-time student.

USING STUDENT COUNTS IN RESEARCH AND ANALYSIS

The student count is a critical component of postsecondary finance research and analysis. When using or analyzing fiscal data, it is imperative to know what definition of student count is being used so that the researcher can determine if this particular definition is appropriate for this study. Additionally, there are instances where enrollments experience sharp increases or declines, such as happened to institutions in the state of Louisiana after Hurricane Katrina. Colleges in the affected area experienced sharp declines, while others taking those displaced students experienced sharp, but temporary, increases. Stochastic analysis must account for these types of variations.

Weighting Student Counts

In comparative analysis, student counts are weighted because the distribution of institutional enrollments that comprise a sector influences averages. For example, the College Board, in its annual *Trends in College Pricing* reports, weights enrollments to control for the size of the enrollment and different tuition and fee price structures. This calculation adjusts for structural differences such as the low tuition and fees in the California community colleges, which enroll a large number of students. The correct calculation of the average tuition and fees paid by a "typical" student is illustrated in Table 2.1.

Table 2.1. Weighted Enrollments and Tuition and Fee Revenue at Three Colleges

College	Enrollment	Tuition and Fee (T&F) Price	Total T&F Revenue	Weighted T & F Price
A	100	$2,000	$200,000	
B	100	$3,000	$300,000	
C	1,000	$900	$900,000	
Total	1,200		$1,400,000	$1,166.67

Three colleges (A, B, and C) have enrollments of 100, 100, and 1,000 respectively. Each college charges a different tuition and fee amount ($2,000, $3,000 and $900, respectively), and College C, which has the highest enrollment, has the lowest tuition and fees. Without weighting, the average tuition and fees for students at the three colleges would be $1,966.67, or ($2,000 + $3,000 + $900)/3. This calculation, resulting in the simple mean average or the average of the averages, does not result in the average tuition and fees paid by the 1,200 students enrolled at the three institutions.

In this example, the majority of enrollments were in low-cost institutions, and the simple mean average is determined by the higher tuition and fee prices at institutions with lower enrollments. To adjust for this imbalance, the data must be enrollment weighted. To weight, multiply the enrollment by the tuition and fee price, and then add the totals together. Then divide the resulting amount by the total number of enrollments. In this correct calculation, average tuition and fees paid by students at these three institutions is $1,167.

In many cases, the total tuition and fees received by the institution and the total number of students are known, but not the average. In this case, to calculate average tuition and fees per student, across institutions, add the total tuition and fee revenues and divide the sum by the total student count.

Credit hours also may be weighted. In funding formulas (discussed in Chapter 5), credit hours often are weighted by a factor that represents their cost. Through a cost study, a state may determine that a lower division (freshman or sophomore) credit hour in business costs $100, while a doctoral credit hour in physics costs $650. To equate those credit hours in a formula, the business credit hour would be given a weight of "1" while the doctoral physics credit hour would have a weight of "6.5."

As will be discussed in other chapters, FTEs, credit hours, and headcounts are incorporated into higher education finance allocations, analysis, and research in a number of ways.

Which Count to Use

Different student counts may be used in analysis, having a dramatic impact on the results. As shown in Table 2.2, fall and 12-month unduplicated headcounts can vary significantly. If used as a denominator in a "cost" per student calculation, the resulting data likely will be skewed. Aligning the proper student count with fund total is difficult. As a consumer and producer of fiscal research and analysis, it is imperative that the type of student count being used is expressed clearly in the text or noted as a footnote or endnote.

Aligning Student Counts and Revenues or Expenditures

Fiscal research, in its most basic form, will take the total sum of either revenues or expenditures and divide that by the number of full-time equivalent students to derive revenues or expenditures per FTE. The resulting value will be used independently in discussing a trend, as in the State Higher Education Executive Officers' (SHEEO) State Higher Education Finance (SHEF) survey, or as a dependent or independent variable

Table 2.2. Undergraduate Enrollment, by Student Count and Sector: 2007–2008

	Type of Student Count			
Sector	*12-month unduplicated headcount*	*12-month full-time-equivalent enrollment*	*Fall 2007*	*Full-time, first-time undergraduates*
Public				
< 2-year	96,907	67,856	54,598	28,677
2-year	9,972,804	4,287,110	6,374,245	702,478
4-year	6,911,037	5,215,234	5,813,773	972,855
Private				
< 2-year	17,466	13,958	12,349	9,068
2-year	61,024	44,180	44,843	12,413
4-year	2,909,759	2,331,026	2,436,958	483,959
For-profit				
< 2-year	427,320	406,933	232,934	260,948
2-year	567,726	505,648	321,221	230,238
4-year	1,334,889	774,551	735,536	209,978

in quantitative analysis. The appeal in using this calculation is that the cost per FTE is easy to understand.

Cost per FTE also has drawbacks in analysis. As mentioned earlier and perhaps most importantly, FTE as determined by the U.S. Department of Education's Institute of Education Sciences (IES) or NCES is not the same as state or institutional determinations of FTE. In distributing resources to public or private institutions, states have their own definitions of FTE. In some cases, the definition is in statute. In addition, state appropriations may include contract and grants that may be based upon student headcounts or equalization funds, which may be components of funding formulas detailed in Chapter 5. Also, some states (e.g., North Carolina and California) may fund non-credit courses with state appropriations, but not count the non-credit students in enrollment or FTE.

While difficult to apply in practice, in theory it is most appropriate to determine cost per student or revenues per student based upon whether the revenue or expenditure was allocated using a student headcount or credit hour or some other measure. As discussed in the chapter on funding formulas, the mathematical derivation of a formula used to allocate resources may be based on a regression model that is using a particular student count or other factor that explains a significant percentage of the variation in expenditure.

We propose, for standardizing fiscal data for analysis across institutions, a method that appropriately reflects the nature of the services being offered. The calculations listed in Table 2.3 provide a simple guide for unitizing fiscal data. It is important, however, to ensure that comparisons across institutions done in anything other than macro-analysis are comparisons among peer institutions. Methodologies for selecting peers are discussed in Chapter 11. It also should be noted that comparable data may not be available for one or more of the preferred methodologies. This is especially true for weighted student credit hours or FTE comparisons where the definitions of FTE and the weights vary from state to state. This proposed method of standardizing fiscal data, and alternative methods, will be discussed in greater detail in Chapter 4.

In this section, the denominator of a "cost" per FTE equation has been discussed. Before delving into more sophisticated concepts and calculations, it is prudent to examine the numerator of the equation.

THE IMPACT OF ACCOUNTING PRACTICES ON FINANCE DATA

All degree-granting institutions, as a condition of remaining eligible to participate in Title IV federal student financial aid programs, report data to the Integrated Postsecondary Education Data System (IPEDS) of the National Center for Education Statistics (NCES) in nine different surveys throughout the year. One of the surveys is finance. These data have been used for cross-sector comparisons, and prior to 1997, this was appropriate because all institutions reported the data in specific categories as defined by NCES. However, in 1997, the Financial Accounting Standards Board (FASB) and the Governmental Accounting Standards Board (GASB) altered their accounting standards so that private and some public institutions (those that have taxing authority) report under FASB standards and most public institutions report under GASB standards. As a result, data that are reported to IPEDS differ substantially by sector and generally are not appropriate for cross-sector analyses. This section explains in further detail why this is the case and offers alternative data sources for analysis.

FASB and GASB

Fiscal data for colleges and universities are reported to IPEDS in a standardized format and under standard definitions. Prior to the mid-1990s, public and private non-profit institutions produced comparable financial statements under the auspices of the American Institute of Certified Public Accountants' Guide *Audits of Colleges and Universities*. While

Table 2.3. Preferred Measures for Standardizing Data for Comparisons

Revenue or Expenditure Category	Preferred Measure(s)								
	FTE	Credit Hours	Weighed Credit Hours	Headcount	Unduplicated Headcount	Number of Faculty Members	Number of Staff	Number of Administrators	Building Square Footage
State Appropriations	X	X	X						
Local Appropriations	X	X	X						
Contracts and Grants						X			
Sales and Services of Auxiliaries				X					
Instruction	X	X	X						
Public Service				X		X	X	X	
Academic Support				X	X				
Student Services				X	X				
Institutional Support				X	X	X	X	X	
Physical Plant Operation & Maintenance					X	X	X	X	X

comparable, these data did not present a complete measure of operating costs because certain items were omitted from the reporting (Goldstein, 2005). The two accounting standards utilized by postsecondary institutions now differ depending on whether the institution reports under FASB or GASB, and whether the institution is for-profit or not-for-profit. The standards differ in many ways, and each has adjustments that are beyond the scope of this discussion (Goldstein, 2002; Goldstein & Menditto, 2005), but the result is misalignment of revenue and expenditure categories (see Table 2.4). GASB and FASB each publish manuals and provide workshops to understand the adjustments needed under their differing formats. Definitions of revenue and expenditure categories, and how these items are reported to IPEDS, are discussed later in this chapter.

Table 2.4. Revenues and Expenditures Collected on FASB Forms for Private For-profit Institutions, FASB Forms for Private Non-profit Institutions and Some Public Institutions, and GASB Forms for Public Institutions

Revenue Categories	*FASB Forms for for-profit institutions*	*FASB Forms for non-profit institutions and some public*	*GASB forms for public institutions*
	Report only total amounts for revenue categories	Report total amounts; unrestricted; temporarily restricted; and permanently restricted amounts for revenue categories	Report total amounts, with revenues split into operating, non-operating, and other revenues and additions
Federal government appropriations, grants, contracts	Combined on one line	Appropriations; grants & contracts	Federal appropriations; federal operating grants and contracts; federal non-operating grants and contracts
State and local appropriations, grants, contracts	Combined on one line	State appropriations; local appropriations; state grants and contracts; local grants and contracts	State operating grants; local operating grants; state appropriations; local appropriations; state non-operating grants; local non-operating grants

(Table continues on next page)

Table 2.4.   Continued

Revenue Categories	FASB Forms for-profit institutions	FASB Forms for non-profit institutions and some public	GASB forms for public institutions
Private gifts, grants, contributions from affiliated entities	Not reported	Private gifts; private contracts; contributions from affiliated entities	Private operating grants and contracts; non-operating gifts including affiliated entities; capital grants and gifts
Investment income and gains	Only the amount included in net income	Investment return	Non-operating investment income; Additions to permanent endowments
Sales and services of educational activities	Sales and services of educational activities	Sales and services of educational activities	Sales and services of educational activities
Sales and services of auxiliary enterprises	Sales and services of auxiliary enterprises	Sales and services of auxiliary enterprises	Sales and services of auxiliary enterprises
Hospital operations	Not applicable	Hospital	Hospital
Independent operations	Not applicable	Independent operations	Independent operations
Net assets released from restriction	Not reported	Reported	Not reported
Capital appropriations	Not reported separately	Included with government appropriations, as applicable	Capital appropriations
Capital grants and gifts	Not reported separately	Included in other categories	Capital grants and gifts
Additions to permanent endowments	Not applicable	Not split out	Additions to permanent endowments

Source: Developed from NCES IPEDS Survey Instructions, U.S. Department of Education (NCES, 2012) http://nces.ed.gov/ipeds/surveys/2011.asp

There are four formats that have been used at the national level to collect data from public and private institutions: Old Form (pre-1997), FASB for non-profit, FASB for for-profit, and New GASB. The Old Form was used by all institutions until 1997; some public institutions continued to use this version through fiscal year 2003. Private non-profit institutions and some public institutions have used FASB since 1997, as have for-profit institutions with slightly different standards. Public institutions phased in use of the New GASB over a 3-year period from 2002 to 2004. The major areas affected by the changes in accounting standards over time are revenues, expenses or expenditures, and scholarships and fellowships.

The most notable difference for purposes of comparisons is that state and local appropriations are not counted as operating revenues under GASB standards, but are operating revenues under FASB standards. In addition, prior to the change in the mid-1990s, public institutions did not report depreciation expenses; the new standards require institutions to show depreciation as an expense. Because of these two major changes, operating revenues and expenditures for public institutions before 1997 are not comparable to those after 1997 unless adjustments are made. Later in this chapter we will discuss methods for making the data comparable to pre-1997 reporting and among the various formats of post-change reporting.

Knowing this, a reasonable person may suggest it is still possible to compare certain categories that have similar titles. However, the difference is not only in how the GASB or FASB standards categorize similar revenue or expenditures, but how they are classified. Specifically, the U.S. Department of Education has noted,

> Different institutions may classify certain funds differently as a scholarship or fellowship or as a pass-through. One common area of differences is Pell Grants. Private institutions (and a few public institutions) operate under accounting standards adopted by the Financial Accounting Standards Board (FASB). The vast majority of public institutions use accounting standards adopted by the Governmental Accounting Standards Board (GASB). Public institutions using current GASB accounting standards are required to treat Pell Grants as scholarships, using the logic that the institution is involved in the administration of the program (as evidenced by the administrative allowance paid to the institution). *FASB standards give private institutions the option to treat Pell Grants as scholarships or as pass-through transactions, using the logic that the federal government determines who is eligible for the grant, not the institution.* Because of this difference in requirements, public institutions will report Pell Grants as federal revenues and as allowances (reducing tuition revenues), whereas FASB institutions may do this as well or (as seems to be the majority) treat Pell Grants as pass-through transactions. *The result is that in the case where a FASB institution and GASB institution each receive the same amount of Pell Grants on behalf of their students, the GASB institution will appear to have less tuition and more federal revenues, whereas the FASB institution treating Pell as pass-through will appear to have more tuition and less federal revenues.* (NCES, 2010b, n.p., emphasis added)

These points of differentiation are critical to understanding postsecondary finance. In essence, these differences restrict analysis to within sector, although even within sector analysis should be done with caution, as some public institutions utilize FASB accounting standards. Chapter 1 presented comparisons of expenditures across sectors and pointed out that private institutions receive a greater share of revenues from tuition and fees than do public institutions. This difference (at least since 2000) in percentage shares is due in part to the differences in FASB and GASB reporting standards. Data across time also were presented, and again these data must be viewed with caution, as the change in accounting standards resulted in a lack of fully comparable data before and after the standards changed.

DATA SOURCES

To this point, this chapter has discussed a data set that is inappropriate for comparative analysis of finance data across sectors. There are, however, other public sources of information that allow for comparative calculations (see Table 2.5).

Table 2.5. Sources of Data

	Level of Data			Frequency		
	Institutional	State	Inst. Control	Quarterly	Year-to-Date	Annually
U.S. Department of Education						
National Center for Education Statistics (NCES):						
Integrated Postsecondary Education Data System (IPEDS)—www.nces.ed.gov/ipeds						
Institutional Characteristics	X	X	X			X
Completions	X	X	X			X
12-month Enrollment	X	X	X			X
Student Financial Aid	X	X	X			X
Fall Enrollment	X	X	X			X
Graduation Rates	X	X	X			X
200% Graduation Rates	X	X	X			X
Finance	X	X	X			X
Human Resources	X	X	X			x
Sample Surveys—http://nces.ed.gov/surveys/SurveyGroups.asp?group=2						
Baccalaureate and Beyond (B&B)	X		X			
Beginning Postsecondary Students Study (BPS)	X		X			
National Postsecondary Student Aid Study (NPSAS)	X		X			
Office of Postsecondary Education (OPE):						
Application Volume Reports—http://federalstudentaid.ed.gov/datacenter/application.html						
Number of FAFSA Applications processed	X	X		X	X	
Title IV Program Volume Reports—http://federalstudentaid.ed.gov/datacenter/programmatic.html						
Direct Loan Program	X	X	X	X	X	
Federal Family Education Loan Program	X	X	X	X	X	

(Table continues on next page)

Table 2.5. Continued

	Level of Data			Frequency		
	Institutional	*State*	*Inst. Control*	*Quarterly*	*Year-to-Date*	*Annually*
Grant Volume (Pell, ACG, SMART, TEACH)	X	X	X	X	X	
Campus-based Volume (FWS, Perkins, FSEOG)	X	X	X			X
Default Rates—http://federalstudentaid.ed.gov/datacenter/cohort.html						
Official cohort default rates	X		X			X
Budget lifetime default rate			X			X
Cumulative lifetime default rate			X			X
Federal Perkins Loan Program	X	X				X
Foreign Gifts -						
Foreign gifts	X	X	X			
Proprietary School 90/10 Revenue Percentages from Financial Statements—http://federalstudentaid.ed.gov/datacenter/proprietary.html						
Proprietary School 90/10 Revenue Percentages	X	X				X
Financial Responsibility Composite Scores—http://federalstudentaid.ed.gov/datacenter/compositescores.html						
Financial Responsibility Composite Scores	X	X	X			X
Discretionary and Formula Grant Database—http://wdcrobcolp01.ed.gov/CFAPPS/grantaward/start.cfm						
Federal Grants	X	X	X			X
Equity in Athletics Disclosure Act—http://ope.ed.gov/athletics/						
Equity in Athletics Disclosure Act Data	X	X	X			X
National Science Foundation						
www.webCASPAR.nsf. gov research expenditures	X					
Census Bureau: American Community Survey						
NACUBO www.nacubo.org						
Endowment Study						
Tuition Discounting Study						
Benchmarking studies for various departments						
State Data:						
Grapevine—http://ilstu.grapevine.edu						
Annual Survey		X	X			X
State agency websites—state fact books and other data	X	X	X	X	X	X
Data/Fact books- either institutional or state level	X	X	X			X
Delta Cost Project— www.deltacostproject.org Cost information	X					X

(Table continues on next page)

Table 2.5.   Continued

	Level of Data			Frequency		
	Institutional	State	Inst. Control	Quarterly	Year-to-Date	Annually
Council for Aid to Education—www.cae.org Survey of giving, endowments	X					X
Moody's Financial—www.moodys.com Financial and operating ratios	X					X
Society of College and University Planning—www.scup.org Facilities Survey		X				X
College and University Professional Association for Human Resources (CUPA-HR)—www.cupahr.org Salaries of administrative and faculty	X	X				X
Delaware Study of Costs and Productivity—http://kudsu.ipr.sc.edu/delaware/ Faculty Salary Costs	X					X
American Association of University Professors (AAUP)—www.aaup.org Faculty salary survey	X	X				X
Association of Physical Plant Administrators—www.appa.org Facilities Core Data Study	X					X
National Association of State Student Grant and Aid Programs (NASSGAP)—www.nassgap.org						
Annual Survey		X	X			X
State Higher Education Executive Officers (SHEEO)—www.sheeo.org						
State Higher Education Finance (SHEF)		X				X

Federal Sources: Department of Education

The federal government invests heavily in students and research. These data are hosted in a variety of databases within various departments, agencies, and other organizations. While some of the data sources are listed on a new website www.data.ed.gov, many are not. The following is a brief description of the databases; the user is encouraged to revisit the particulars of any data set, as the categories may change overtime. Additionally, website links were checked before publishing but also may have changed.

The U.S. Department of Education (ED) has numerous databases. There are two primary offices that provide data accessible to the public. The first is an institutionally-based data collection and reporting system (IPEDS), which is run by the NCES of the Institute of Education Sciences at ED. In addition to IPEDS, NCES maintains several sample surveys of students. The second office is the Office of Postsecondary Education (OPE), which houses data related primarily to the funding of postsecondary programs run by ED such as the Pell Grant or Title III-A Strengthening Institutions grant programs.

The IPEDS data system is a source for postsecondary data collected at the institutional level. Postsecondary institutions are required to submit data to IPEDS as a condition of being eligible to participate in federal student aid programs. Institutions submit data to IPEDS three times a year—fall, winter and spring—with each collection period comprising of multiple survey submissions. For example, the 2012–2013 collection cycle included the following:

- Fall: institutional characteristics, completions, and 12-month enrollment data;
- Winter: student financial aid data; and
- Spring: fall enrollment, graduation rates, 200% graduation rate, finance, and human resources.

Each survey component provides data that may be informative to fiscal analysis and research. Each survey is briefly described in this section. (Note, the surveys may change slightly from year-to-year, and some of the human resources information is collected every other year.)

- *The Institutional Characteristics Survey.* Data submitted as part of the institutional characteristics survey provide descriptive detail about institutions. Most often, as discussed in Chapter 1, institutions are divided into control, level, or sector for analysis. In addition, there is information about the city and state of location, tuition and fees and room and board charges, types of programs and credentials awarded, and an OPEID that is required to crosswalk data from IPEDS to other databases from the U.S. Department of Education such as grant and loan data.
- *The Completions Survey.* The completions survey provides information about credentials earned at institutions. These data can be disaggregated by program type (education, nursing, engineering, etc.) and credential level (certificate, bachelor's degree, etc.). These data are helpful for productivity analyses. It is important to remember, however, that these data reflect the number of credentials awarded, not the number of students earning credentials. In some instances a student may earn more than one credential in a given award year. Starting in the 2012–2013 year, the number of students completing will also be reported by institutions.

- *The 12-month Enrollment Survey.* Enrollment in postsecondary education has traditionally been and continues to primarily be discussed in terms of fall enrollments. It is the case, however, that institutions enroll students at times other than just the fall semester. For this reason, IPEDS collects 12-month enrollments from institutions. A comparison (Mullin, 2012b) of fall 2008 headcount enrollments to 12-month unduplicated headcount enrollments in 2008–2009 found that the student body increased between 18 and 102%, depending on sector. In addition to 12-month unduplicated headcounts, the survey collects instructional activity—total credit and contact hours—during the academic year to allow for the derivation of full-time equivalent students.

- *The Student Financial Aid Survey.* Institutions report various data concerning student financial aid for undergraduate students. Elements in this data collection include, but are not limited to, the percent of first-time, full time students receiving various types of student financial aid; the average dollar amount of aid awarded by the institution; and the net price at the institution for specific types of students.

- *The Fall Enrollment Survey.* Enrollment during the fall semester is the traditional way postsecondary enrollment has been measured. Institutions submit fall headcount enrollment disaggregated in a number of ways including, but not limited to, gender, race/ethnicity, level of study, and enrollment status (full or part-time).

- *Graduation Rates Surveys.* The purpose of the survey is to track the completion status of first-time, full-time cohort of students at 100 and 150% of "normal" time to earn a degree. Institutions report both graduation and transfer-out counts for the cohort, which may be revised due to allowable exceptions such as death or military service. In 2012, the Committee on Measures of Student Success (2011) concluded that these rates, while comparable across institutional sectors, understated the success of students at 2-year institutions. At the time of writing, NCES was in the process of providing alterations to the graduation rate survey. The related 200% graduation rates survey collects similar data for 200% of normal time.

- *The Finance Survey.* As described earlier in this chapter, the finance survey of IPEDS collects basic financial information for institutions according to either FASB or GASB accounting standards. These data are not consistent across institution types. Because of the importance of the Finance Survey in conducting research, more detail on the survey will be provided later in this chapter.

- *The Human Resources Surveys.* The human resources survey was restructured for the 2012–2013 year in a number of ways. For example, non-instructional staff occupations will be aligned with the 2010 Standard Occupational Categories (SOC) codes of the U.S. Department of Labor (DoL); a question will determine if an institution has graduate assistants; the primary instruction category will differentiate between credit and non-credit teaching; and the salaries section will change the way data are collected (https://surveys.nces.ed.gov/ipeds ViewContent.aspx?contentId=22). These substantial changes will provide greater detail but will limit the ability to examine trend data over time. In addition, parts of the human resources survey have been collected only every other year.

In addition to institutional data collected in IPEDS, NCES administers a number of sample surveys to better understand students' experiences in postsecondary education. These data may be used for analysis through web-based analytic tools on the NCES DataLab website (http://nces.ed.gov/datalab/) such as QuickStats and PowerStats or the Data Analysis System (http://nces.ed.gov/das/), each with increasing levels of sophistication. While some analytical functions are available with these web tools, restricted-use data files are available for researchers who agree to a set of terms regarding use of the data.

The three primary data sets used in postsecondary research are the Baccalaureate and Beyond Longitudinal Study, the Beginning Postsecondary Student Longitudinal Study, and the National Postsecondary Student Aid Study.

The Baccalaureate and Beyond Longitudinal Study (B&B) follows students who completed a bachelor's degree to understand employment experiences, educational expectations, and undergraduate experiences. Of special interest are students who enter the teaching profession.

The purpose of the Beginning Postsecondary Students Longitudinal Study (BPS) is to follow cohorts of first-time students for 6 years, interviewing them in the first, third and sixth year. Data pertaining to students' demographic information, school and work experiences, academic progress and attainment, and family are collected.

The primary focus of the National Postsecondary Student Aid Study (NPSAS) is to better understand how students finance their education. The detail provided in this study allows for analysts and researchers to answer very specific questions related to student financing of postsecondary education nationally. NPSAS serves as the base-year sample for both the BPS and B&B studies.

The datacenter of the Office of Federal Student Aid hosts an extensive amount of institutional level data. These data are primarily, but not exclusively, related to legislation and regulations pertaining to federal student aid.

- *Application Volume Reports.* The Free Application for Federal Student Aid (FAFSA) is a form students are required to complete when applying for federal student aid. Data for the number of applications are available at the institution, state, and high school level over an 18 month period of time as applicants can start submitting the FAFSA in January of 1 year through the end of June of the following year (e.g., January 1, 2012 through June 30, 2013). When using data in the Application Volume Reports, be careful to understand if the data provided are for applications or applicants, as applicants (students) can submit applications to multiple institutions.

- *Title IV Program Reports.* Title IV student aid programs include grants and loans. Data for some grant and loan programs are available on a quarterly basis, typically within a month after the fiscal quarter ends. Campus-based aid data are available on an annual basis. In addition to these quarterly data, there are annual reports for grant and loan programs. For the Pell Grant, the End-of-Year report provides more detailed information and is available a year after the program year ends at (http://www2.ed.gov/finaid/prof/ resources/data/pell-data.html). Annual data books for campus-based aid also provide greater detail and are available online (http:/ /www2.ed.gov/finaid/prof/resources/data/cb-data.html).

- *Default Rates.* Title IV federal student aid in the form of loans must be repaid. Defaulting, according to regulations, is a failure to repay the loans within a set period of time. All student loans must be repaid, as they are not dischargeable. If an institution has too high of a cohort default rate over a set period of time, then the institution can risk losing eligibility to offer Title IV aid; for current details of the program see 34 Code of Federal Regulations 668. Cohort default rate (CDR) data are available by institution, lender, state, and institution type. Historical CDR data are available in press releases and take some searching to locate.

- *Foreign Gifts.* Data on foreign gifts to institutions are available from OPE. The data include the institution name, state, control, the date the gift was received, the amount, the type, country of origin, and name of grantor.

- *Proprietary 90/10 Revenue Percentages.* Proprietary (for-profit) institutions are not allowed to have greater than 90% of their revenue come from Title IV federal student aid. Each year, according to section 487(d)(4) of the Higher Education Act, a report as to the Title

IV and non-Title IV revenue sources of for-profit institutions is to be submitted to U.S. House and Senate authorizing committees. These data are available by institution.

- *Financial Responsibility Composite Scores.* Private institutions, non-profit and for-profit, must demonstrate that they are maintaining a standard of fiscal responsibility to continue participation in Title IV federal student aid programs as prescribed by the Higher Education Act. A composite score is derived from three ratios—a primary reserve ratio, equity ratio, and net income ratio—as determined from an institution's audited financial statement. Composite scores by institution are provided in the database.

- *Grant Database.* The Office of Postsecondary Education manages a number of grant programs. Data for the various grant programs are provided via a data display tool that allows the user to "cut" the data in many ways and then export the data as an Excel spreadsheet. Programs include but are not limited to Title III-A Strengthening Institutions, Minority Science Initiative, Fund for the Improvement of Postsecondary Education (FIPSE), and Gaining Early Awareness and Readiness for Undergraduate Programs (GEAR-UP).

- *Equity in Athletics Disclosure Act.* A data tool also is available for statistics pertaining to participation in and financing athletics in postsecondary education. Data files also may be downloaded and are provided by institution and sport.

Other Federal Data Sources

The U.S. Census Bureau maintains a large data repository of information that pertains to postsecondary education that may be accessed at www.census.gov. Some of the Census Bureau data is reported by institutions on the IPEDS finance survey. Of particular interest for postsecondary research are the statistical abstracts, which give complete data by state resulting from the 2010 or earlier census, and the American Community Survey, which provides information on many population demographics (including education) by state, region, and standard metropolitan statistical area. These data are used most often in studies and research of the economic impact of higher education.

The National Science Foundation provides information on research grants and contracts awarded to institutions and matches these data with information from IPEDS. Information may be accessed at www.webCASPAR.nsf.gov.

Non-Governmental Databases

There are any number of national associations related to postsecondary education that collect data on an annual or regular basis. Six associations are members of the Washington Higher Education Secretariat (http://www.whes.org/). These institutions represent public land-grant colleges and universities (Association of Public and Land-grant Universities [APLU]), public 4-year colleges and universities (American Association of State Colleges and Universities [AASCU]), research universities of public and private non-profit affiliation (Association of American Universities [AAU]), community colleges (American Association of Community Colleges [AACC]), and private non-profit universities and colleges (National Association of Independent Colleges and Universities [NAICU]). The American Council on Education (ACE) serves as a coordinating body and has members from all institution types. Not included in "the six," but of note is the Association of Private Colleges and Universities (APSCU), which represents for-profit colleges.

Each of these organizations maintains significant data files on their membership. For example, the National Association of College and University Business Officers (http://www.nacubo.org/), in partnership with the Commonfund, annually publishes a national endowment study and with its members publishes comparative data on the costs of particular programs or offices. In another example, the Council for the Advancement and Support of Education (CASE) has a compensation database for those in the advancement disciplines (http://www.case.org/). Another example is the faculty salary survey of the American Association of University Professors (www.aaup.org).

In addition to educational organizations, trade publications such as *The Chronicle of Higher Education* (www.chronicle.com) and *Inside Higher Education* (www.insidehighered.com) collect compensation data for college presidents and administrative positions, respectively. The College Board has developed both a survey of tuition and fees and a survey of student financial aid that have proven to be very valuable in policy discussions due to the ability to provide college pricing data in October for the current academic year (www.trends.collegeboard.com).

Besides the various data sources mentioned thus far, there are groups that aggregate data from numerous sources such as the U.S. Census Bureau or the U.S. Department of Labor. Examples include the National Center for Higher Education Management Systems (NCHEMS; www.higheredinfo.org), Complete College America (www.completecollege.org), the Delta Cost Project (www.deltacostproject.org), and the Federal Education Budget Project of the New America Foundation (http://febp.newamerica.net/).

State and Institutional Sources

For public institutions, institutional and state level data may be available via a state data or fact book. These reports are not uniform across states and may include data for private institutions. Data books or fact books are very rich in terms of understanding a particular state. Of particular note are the websites of the Illinois, Florida, Texas and Ohio governing and/or coordinating boards. These sites have a wealth of data, collected over long periods of time, and may be accessed at the following:

- www.flbog.edu
- www.ibhe.org
- www.ohiohighered.org
- www.thecb.state.tx.us

The data on the costs per credit hour or costs of instruction are particularly informative for those doing research in higher education finance. Each of these state agencies has been collecting finance data for over 30 years, and each has longitudinal data bases with comparable data across institutions and, in some cases, across sectors.

In addition to the data provided by the state agencies overseeing higher education, each institution may have its own data or fact book, available through the institution's website. Public and private institutions must provide a certain amount of information to the public, and that information must be easily accessible. Some institutions provide a significant amount of data, including a dashboard that provides performance measures.

Institutions also must prepare audited financial statements that are prepared under generally accepted accounting principles, either under the GASB or FASB standards. Institutional financial statements, called Consolidated Annual Finance Reports or CAFRs, contain a wealth of data presented in consistent formats. The CAFRs also may be found on institutional websites.

National, standardized, state level data for public institutions are provided by the State Higher Education Executive Officers in their annual State Higher Education Finance Survey (SHEF), typically released in February. These reports are an extension of reports initially created by Kent Halstead, who worked for the ED before his retirement. In 2009, SHEF merged with the *Grapevine* survey of state and local tax appropriations for higher education of Illinois State University initiated in 1960 by M. M. Chambers. Since 1960, *Grapevine* has published annual compilations of data on state tax support for higher education, including general fund appropriations for universities, colleges, community colleges, and state higher education agencies. Each year's *Grapevine* survey has asked states for tax appropriations data for the new fiscal year and for revisions (if any) to data reported in previous years. *Grapevine* may be accessed at www.grapevine.illinoisstate.edu.

Information on state budgets may be obtained from the National Association of State Budget Officers (NASBO), which publishes information detailing state budget revenues and expenditures for current, past, and projected budget years. The NASBO documents may be accessed at www.nasbo.org.

Data pertaining specifically to state student grant and aid programs is available in an annual report from the National Association of State Student and Grant Aid Programs (NASSGAP). Data are available by sector and cover over 40 years.

IPEDS FINANCE SURVEY AND INSTITUTIONAL FINANCIAL STATEMENTS

Colleges and universities report a significant amount of data on the IPEDS Finance Survey, including information in a special format for the Census Bureau. These data are consistent with the institution's Consolidated Annual Financial Report (CAFR). Information includes the Statement of Financial Position, changes in net assets, student financial aid, revenues, expenditures, and value of the institution's endowments. For research purposes, the revenues and expenditures sections of the survey receive the most attention. The discussion that follows will explain what the categories of revenue and expenditure are under the post-1997 standards, compared to Old Form categories, so that researchers may make comparisons of revenues over time.

Reporting under the Old Form (as compared to FASB and New GASB) included only current funds, which were classified as "unrestricted," "restricted," and "auxiliary funds." Unrestricted funds are revenues or assets that may be used for the benefit of the institution without restriction or limitation by the donor or other external agency. Restricted funds are revenues whose use is limited by the donor or other external agencies; grants to carry out research projects were considered restricted funds. Auxiliary funds are those related to units that are fee-driven or self-supporting, such as residence halls, food service, and bookstores (McKeown-Moak, 2000a).

The Old Form did not include plant funds, loan funds, or endowment funds. Plant funds are resources for renewal and replacement of institutional properties, debt service, and the cost of long-lived assets such as furniture. Plant funds include the value of land and buildings. Loan funds are resources provided by various sources that may be lent to students, faculty, or staff and are not part of current funds. Endowment, and similar, funds are those donated funds from which the earned income may be spent, but not the corpus of the donated funds.

FASB and New GASB include all funds, but new GASB does not differentiate by restricted or unrestricted. Many financial studies done using Old Form examined only unrestricted funds, and unrestricted funds still are included on the FASB standards for non-profit institutions. Institutional finance data reported under the Old Form does not include revenues such as contributions to endowments, interest from student loans, and capital appropriations for the construction or renovation of facilities; both FASB and New GASB include these data. Many institutions collect student fees to pay bonded indebtedness; under accounting standards prior to 1997, these student fees would be included in plant funds and reported only in the institution's Consolidated Annual Financial Reports (CAFR), not in the Old Form. These funds are included in reporting under FASB and New GASB standards (NCES, 2012). Thus, it is not possible to take total revenues under the Old Form and compare them to total revenues under the new GASB or FASB. Some equating across categories can be done, as indicated below.

In the Old Form, tuition and fees and auxiliary enterprise revenues were reported as a gross amount; all student charges, no matter how they were paid, were included in the revenue amount. Under FASB and New GASB, tuition and fees as well as auxiliary enterprises are reported net of scholarships and fellowships used to pay these fees, or as net of allowances; and the amount of allowances is reported in the scholarship section. Adding the allowance amount back to the revenues reported in tuition and fees and in auxiliary enterprises should result in a gross amount somewhat comparable to the amount reported in the Old Form. The allowance amount is called "discounts and allowances" on the New GASB form and "allowances (scholarships)" on both FASB forms (NCES, 2012).

Revenues under the New GASB format are categorized as "Operating," "Non-operating," and "Other Revenues." FASB does not make the distinction between operating and non-operating revenues. For several categories, such as grants and contracts, addition of the amounts from each section (e.g., state operating grants and contracts and state non-operating grants) should give a value comparable to the category (state grants and contracts) that was collected in the Old Form or in FASB. For appropriations, however, simple addition of items that look comparable will not work. First, capital appropriations were not included in the Old Form, and FASB does include capital appropriations in the appropriations revenue amount without differentiation, whereas GASB separates out capital (NCES, 2012).

The Old Form included a schedule requesting hospital revenue by source. This schedule is not included in either New GASB or FASB. Investment income was not reported separately in the Old Form, but is a separate revenue item in FASB and New GASB. Additions to permanent endowments appear as a revenue source in the New GASB form but do not appear separately in the FASB, where endowments are included in private gifts, grants and contracts or contributions from affiliated entities, depending on the source. These amounts do not appear anywhere on the Old Form since they were considered endowment fund activity and were not within the scope of the Old Form used to report nationally (NCES, 2012). These data, however, were included in the institution's CAFR.

Revenue Categories

Total revenues include all operating revenues, non-operating revenues, and other additions for the reporting period, including unrestricted and restricted revenues and additions, whether expendable or non-expendable. Excluded from revenue (and expenses) are inter-fund or intra-organizational charges and credits. Inter-fund and intra-organizational charges and credits include interdepartmental charges, indirect costs, and reclassifications from temporarily restricted net assets (NCES, 2012).

In the New GASB, *operating revenues* result from providing services and producing and delivering goods, while *non-operating revenues* are those generated from "non-exchange" transactions, such as appropriations, gifts, and investment earnings. These funds often are used to support the operations of the institution. The term "non-operating" does not preclude use for operating expenses (NCES, 2012). "Non-exchange" in the case of appropriations means that, for roll-up purposes for one state-wide CAFR, appropriations came from the state's general or other fund and were expended out of the fund.

This is the most controversial of the categorizations the new GASB made. Classifying appropriations as non-operating revenues placed almost every public institution (except those that had taxing authority and could report under FASB) in an operating deficit position; that is, operating revenues less operating expenses almost always were negative for public institutions, meaning that the institution was operating at a "loss." In truth this was not the case but was merely an accounting change. However, in congressional and legislative hearings, many presidents or chancellors had to explain that, unlike private institutions for which appropriations were considered an operating revenue, their institutions really were not in a negative position and were not abusing the public trust for the effective stewardship of public funds.

In some cases an institution may report certain revenues in an operating or non-operating category different from that shown on the IPEDS forms. The IPEDS component is not intended to dictate how an institution reports such revenues in its own financial statements or CAFR. However, for consistency of reporting on federal forms, information is reported according to the rules set forth in the IPEDS survey instructions.

Both new GASB and FASB use the same definitions for certain categories of revenue, although GASB will report certain revenues as "operating" or "non-operating," while FASB makes no distinction between operating and non-operating.

Tuition and fees. All tuition and fee revenues are included in this category, after deducting for discounts and allowances for institutional scholarships and waivers. Student activity fees assessed against students, such as Internet fees, are reported in this category. Also included in this category are those tuition and fees that are remitted to the state as an offset to state appropriations. Charges for room, board, and other services rendered by auxiliary enterprises are not reported here (NCES, 2012). To equate this category with the Old Form tuition and fees, add back the discounts and allowances to get a gross tuition and fee amount, which was the amount reported on the Old Form.

Federal operating grants and contracts, federal appropriations, and federal non-operating grants and contracts. Included in these categories are revenues from federal governmental agencies as direct appropriations and revenues that are for specific research projects or other types of programs and under GASB are classified as either operating or non-operating revenues. Examples are research projects and similar activities for which amounts are received or expenditures are reimbursable under the terms of a grant or contract. Federal land grant appropriations are included on this line on the GASB form, but Pell Grants or other federal student aid is not included in this category. For-profit institutions do not differentiate between federal grants and contracts and federal appropriations.

It is very difficult to equate these categories to the Old Form federal grants and contracts because of the inclusion of federal appropriations for land grant activities, which were reported as federal appropriations on the Old Form and in FASB. For institutions under New GASB, adding federal operating grants and contracts, federal non-operating grants and contracts, and federal appropriations will approximate the old "federal appropriations" plus the old "federal grants and contracts" category. For non-profit institutions under FASB, this category should match the Old Form because federal land grant appropriations are reported under federal appropriations.

State operating grants and contracts, state non-operating grants and contracts, and state appropriations. Revenues from state governmental agencies that are for specific research projects or other types of programs are included in the grants and contracts categories. Examples are research projects and similar activities for which amounts are received or expenditures are reimbursable under the terms of a grant or contract. Under GASB, these revenues are classified either as operating or non-operating, but no distinction exists under FASB. GASB includes state appropriations separately as a non-operating revenue. For-profit institutions report state and local appropriations, grants, and contracts on one combined line.

To equate to the Old Form for non-profit institutions, adding state operating grants and contracts and state non-operating grants should be a good approximation, and this can be compared to FASB state grants and contracts. Capital appropriations were not included on the Old Form, so this component of New GASB should not be included in comparisons. To equate with for-profit institutional reports, it would be necessary to add state and local operating and non-operating grants and contracts and state and local appropriations, but not capital appropriations.

Local government operating grants and contracts, local government non-operating grants and contracts, and local appropriations. Revenues from local governmental agencies that are for specific research projects or other types of programs are included in the grants categories. Examples are research projects and similar activities for which amounts are received or expenditures are reimbursable under the terms of a local grant or contract. Under GASB, these revenues are classified either as operating or non-operating revenues, but no distinction exists under FASB. To equate GASB reporting to the Old Form and FASB, add operating and non-operating local grants and contracts. To equate with for-profit institutional reports, it would be necessary to add state and local operating and non-operating grants and contracts and state and local appropriations.

Private operating grants and contracts (GASB), gifts (GASB), private gifts (FASB) and private grants and contracts (FASB). Revenues from nongovernmental agencies and organizations that are for specific research projects or other types of programs are reported as private operating grants and contracts under GASB and as private grants and contracts under FASB (NCES, 2011). Examples are research projects and similar activities for which amounts are received or expenditures are reimbursable under the terms of a grant or contract. Gifts (GASB) include contributions from affiliated entities, while that is a separate category under FASB. Under New GASB, these categories cannot be fully compared to the Old Form by adding private operating grants and contracts and gifts, because contributions from affiliated entities were not included on the Old Form. For institutions under FASB, the operating and gifts total can be compared to the sum of private gifts, and private grants and contracts. Contributions from affiliated entities is a separate category in FASB reports for non-profit organizations. The similar item on for-profit reports is private grants and contracts.

Sales and services of auxiliary enterprises. Revenues (net of discounts and allowances) generated by auxiliary enterprises that exist to furnish a service to students, faculty, or staff, and that charge a fee that is directly related to the cost of the service are included in this category. Examples are residence halls, food services, student health services, intercollegiate athletics, college unions, college stores, and movie theaters. However, intercollegiate athletics may be reported in several other categories, at the discretion of the institution. To equate to the Old Form, add back the discounts and allowances.

Sales and services of hospitals. This category includes the operating revenues (net of patient contractual allowances) for a hospital operated by the institution and for clinics associated with training, but clinics that are part of the student health services program should be reported as student services or as auxiliary services, as appropriate. This category should equate to the Old Form and is not a factor for most institutions because only a small percentage of colleges and universities operate an affiliated hospital.

Sales and services of educational activities. All operating revenues derived from the sales of goods or services that are incidental to the conduct of instruction, research, or public service activities, and revenues of activities that exist to provide instructional and laboratory experience for students and that incidentally create goods and services that may be sold to the public are included in this category. Examples include scientific and literary publications, testing services, university presses, dairies, and patient care clinics that are not part of a hospital (NCES, 2012). This category equates across forms.

Independent operations. This category includes all operating revenues associated with operations independent of the primary missions of the institution. This category generally includes only those revenues associated with major federally funded research and development centers. Very few institutions have revenues in this category, which equates across report formats. If an institution that is not a major research university reports revenue in the independent operations category, it is likely that these revenues are misreported.

Other sources. This is a calculated amount that includes all operating revenues not included in the previous categories, but not capital appropriations, capital gifts and contracts, and additions to permanent endowments. These categories were not included in the Old Form and should not be included in total revenues in comparisons to the Old Form or across sectors.

Expenditure Categories

The expenditure categories on the Old Form by and large are the same categories on the New GASB and FASB for non-profit organizations. Some functional categories are combined in for-profit reporting. What has changed, however, for non-profit institutions, is that the functional category expenditures are delineated into salaries and wages, fringe benefits, operations and maintenance of physical plant, depreciation, interest, and other. Depreciation and interest are expenditures that were not included on the Old Form, and therefore, across all categories, the expenditures for depreciation and interest must be subtracted in comparisons. However, the non-profit FASB and GASB formats are equivalent, with certain exceptions explained below. For-profit institutions do not separate expenditures into the expenses (salaries, etc.), reporting only a total expenditure; for-profit institutions also report certain functional areas on one line. Definitions of the functional categories are the same for all institutions.

Included in the expenditure categories are all operating and non-operating expenses and deductions, integrating the costs incurred for salaries and wages, goods, and other services used in the conduct of the institution's operations, but not the acquisition cost of capital assets, such as equipment and library books, which are capitalized under the institution's capitalization policy (NCES, 2012).

Instruction. This function includes all expenses of the colleges, schools, departments, and other instructional divisions of the institution for both credit and non-credit activities and expenses for departmental research and public service that are not separately budgeted. Not included are expenses for academic administration where the primary function is administration (e.g., academic deans); dean's offices are included in the academic support category. The instruction category includes academic instruction, occupational and vocational instruction, community education, preparatory and adult basic education, and remedial and tutorial instruction conducted by the teaching faculty for the institution's students (NCES, 2012). This category is equivalent across non-profit and for-profit institutions; however to equate to the Old Form instruction expenditures, subtract out depreciation and operation and maintenance of plant.

Research. This functional category includes all expenses for activities specifically organized to produce research outcomes and commissioned by an agency either external to the institution or separately budgeted by an organizational unit within the institution. Training activities, even if separately funded by a grant or contract, should not be included here.

For-profit institutions report research and public service expenditures on one line, and thus, to compare expenditures at for-profit institutions to those of non-profit, research and public service must be added together, after subtracting out depreciation and operation and maintenance of plant. To equate to the Old Form research expenditures, subtract out depreciation and operation and maintenance of plant.

Public Service. This category includes expenses for all activities budgeted specifically for public service and for activities established primarily to provide non-instructional services beneficial to groups or individuals external to the institution. Examples are seminars and projects provided to particular sectors of the community. Expenditures for community services and cooperative extension services at land grant institutions are included (NCES, 2012).

For-profit institutions report research and public service expenditures on one line, and thus, to compare expenditures at for-profit institutions to those of non-profit, research and public service must be added together, after subtracting out depreciation and operation and maintenance of plant. To equate to the Old Form public service expenditures, subtract out depreciation and operation and maintenance of plant.

Academic Support. This category includes expenses for the support services that are an integral part of the institution's primary missions of instruction, research, and public service. Included are expenses for museums, libraries, galleries, audio/visual services, ancillary support, academic administration (dean's offices), personnel development, and course and curriculum development. Expenses for veterinary and dental clinics are included if their primary purpose is to support the institutional program (NCES, 2012).

For-profit institutions report academic support, student services, and institutional support expenditures on one line, and thus, to compare expenditures at for-profit institutions to those of non-profit, these three functional areas must be added together, after subtracting out depreciation and operation and maintenance of plant. To equate to the Old Form academic support expenditures, subtract out depreciation and operation and maintenance of plant.

Student Services. This category includes expenses for admissions, registrar activities, and activities whose primary purpose is to contribute to students' emotional and physical wellbeing and to their intellectual, cultural, and social development outside the context of the formal instructional program. Examples are career guidance, counseling, and financial aid administration. This category also includes intercollegiate athletics and student health services, except when operated as self-supporting auxiliary enterprises (NCES, 2012). Most NCAA Division I athletic programs are included in the auxiliary enterprises category.

For-profit institutions report academic support, student services, and institutional support expenditures on one line, and thus, to compare expenditures at for-profit institutions to those of non-profit, these three functional areas must be added together, after subtracting out depreciation and operation and maintenance of plant. To equate to the Old Form student services expenditures, subtract out depreciation and operation and maintenance of plant.

Institutional Support. This category includes expenses for the day-to-day operational support of the institution. Incorporated are expenses for general administrative services, executive direction and planning, legal and fiscal operations, and public relations/development (NCES, 2012).

For-profit institutions report academic support, student services, and institutional support expenditures on one line, and thus, to compare expenditures at for-profit institutions to those of non-profit, these three functional areas must be added together, after subtracting out depreciation and operation and maintenance of plant. To equate to the Old Form institutional support expenditures, subtract out depreciation and operation and maintenance of plant.

Operation and Maintenance of Physical Plant. Plant expenses are allocated to the other functional areas, but it is possible to add the totals across the functional areas to get a total plant expenditure. This category includes all expenses for operations established to provide service and maintenance related to grounds and facilities used for educational and general purposes as well as expenses for utilities, fire protection, property insurance, and similar items (NCES, 2012).

For-profit institutions do not report a separate operation and maintenance of plant category. To equate to the Old Form operation and maintenance of physical plant, add together all of the plant expenditures allocated to the other functional areas.

Scholarships and Fellowships. All institutions report scholarships and fellowship expenses as net of discounts and allowances. This category includes outright grants to students selected and awarded by the institution and is the amount that exceeds fees and charges assessed to students by the institution and that would not have been recorded as discounts and allowances. This classification will include the excess of awards over fees and charges from Pell Grants and other resources, including funds originally restricted for student assistance. Loans to students or amounts where the institution is given custody of the funds but is not allowed to select the recipients are not included; these are transactions recorded in balance sheet accounts and not revenues and expenses (NCES, 2012).

To equate to the Old Form, add back the discounts and allowances reported in the financial aid part of the IPEDS form.

Auxiliary Enterprises. This category includes expenses of essentially self-supporting operations of the institution that exist to furnish a service to students, faculty, or staff, and that charge a fee that is directly related to, although not necessarily equal to, the cost of the service. Examples are residence halls, food services, student health services, intercollegiate athletics, college unions, college stores, and barber shops when the activities are operated as auxiliary enterprises (NCES, 2012).

This expenditure category is consistently reported across all types of institutions but to equate to auxiliary enterprises under the Old Form, any discounts or allowances must be added back, and depreciation and operation and maintenance of plant must be subtracted out.

Hospital Services. Very few institutions have this expenditure category, which includes all expenses associated with the operation of a hospital, including nursing expenses, other professional services, general services, administrative services, fiscal services, and charges for physical plant operations (NCES, 2012). This category equates to the Old Form after subtracting out depreciation and operation and maintenance of plant.

Independent Operations. This category includes all expenses for operations that are independent of or unrelated to the primary missions of the institution (i.e., instruction, research, public service), although they may contribute indirectly to the enhancement of these programs. This category is generally limited to expenses of major federally funded research and development centers, and consequently, very few institutions have this category of expenditure. Not included are the expenses of operations owned and managed as investments of the institution's endowment funds (NCES, 2012). This category equates to the Old Form, after subtracting out depreciation and operation and maintenance of plant, and is the same for all types of institutions.

Table 2.6. Revenue and Expenditure Categories Used in the Old Form

Old Form Categories	*Restricted Funds*	*Unrestricted Funds*
Revenues:		
Tuition and Fees	X	X
Federal Appropriations	X	X
State Appropriations	X	X
Local Appropriations	X	X
Federal Grants and Contracts	X	X
State Grants and Contracts	X	X
Local Grants and Contracts	X	X
Private Gifts, Grants, and Contracts	X	X
Sales of Educational Activities	X	X
Sales of Auxiliary Services	X	X
Hospitals	X	X

(Table continues on next page)

Table 2.6.   Continued

Old Form Categories	Restricted Funds	Unrestricted Funds
Revenues:		
Investment Income	X	X
Independent Operations	X	X
Other Income	X	X
Expenditures:		
Instruction		
Research		
Public Service		
Academic Support		
Institutional Support		
Operation and Maintenance of Plant		
Scholarships and Fellowships		
Auxiliary Enterprises		
Hospitals		
Independent Operations		
Other		

CONCLUSION

This chapter has provided examples of what to consider when comparing fiscal data, conducting fiscal analysis, and consuming financial data. In addition, the IPEDS Finance Survey was discussed in detail, with definitions of revenue and expenditure categories, program areas, and differences between reporting under FASB and GASB standards. With the foundation set, the following chapters provide more advanced concepts and calculations to consider when discussing postsecondary finance.

SECTION II

Revenues and Expenditures

This section introduces guiding philosophies, sources of data, data elements/vocabulary, metrics, and analytics related to *institutional* revenues and expenditures. Chapter 3 examines these concepts as they relate to *student-oriented* revenues, including tuition and fees and student financial aid, as well as student-oriented expenses. Chapter 4 examines these aspects as they relate to *institutionally-oriented* revenues, including state appropriations and restricted revenue in the form of contracts and grants for activities such as research, and institutionally-oriented expenditures such as education and general (E&G) expenses. Chapter 5 examines the use of funding formulas, the derivation of formulas, and formulas used by the states from the perspectives both of researchers and of institutional managers such as budget or chief financial officers.

The three largest sources of funding for higher education are tuition and fees, state and local appropriations, and federal contracts and grants. Students pay tuition and fees, and generally state and local appropriations are related to a student count of some sort. A large portion of federal contracts and grants come to the institutions as student financial aid. Thus, the three largest sources of funding are connected to students.

Students bring "resources" to the institution, and have "costs" associated with college attendance. Most of the student expenditures or "costs" in turn become revenues to the institution, which then expends those revenues to provide services to students. Table II.1 provides a typography of revenues and expenses from the student's and from the institution's perspectives. As can be seen, students have "costs" in the form of foregone income and lost investment income that are not included in the price of a

Higher Education Finance Research: Policy, Politics, and Practice, pp. 59–61
Copyright © 2014 by Information Age Publishing

college education. When students use family's or their own savings to cover their "costs" or expenses, those monies become revenues to the institution, which in turn converts those revenues to expenditures to provide services. In Chapter 2, we discussed that how institutions report revenues was revised in 1995 so that the revenues that students bring in the form of tuition and fees and room and board were no longer "double counted" because of the booking of grants, scholarships, and loan funds, at least at most institutions. Prior to revision of GAAP, revenues and expenditure both were double counted. We will discuss these concepts in detail in the following chapters.

Table II.1.   Typography of Revenues and Expenses

Student Revenues	Student Expenses/Costs	Institutional Revenues	Institutional Expenses
	Foregone investment return or income Foregone compensation Foregone earnings		
	Room and board	Room and board charges i.e. Sales and services of auxiliary enterprises	Auxiliary enterprises expenditures
Institutional student aid (loans) State and local student aid (loans) Federal student aid (loans) Third-party student aid (loans)	Childcare and other conditional expenses Transportation Healthcare costs Books and supplies	State contracts and grants Local contracts and grants Private contracts and grants Federal contracts and grants	Institutional student aid (loans)
Institutional student aid (grants)			Institutional student aid (grants)
Federal student aid (grants)			
Third-party student aid (grants)			
State and local student aid (grants) Family's income/savings Student's savings/income	Tuition and fees	Tuition and fees	

(Table continues on next page)

Table II.1. Continued			
Student Revenues	*Student Expenses/Costs*	*Institutional Revenues*	*Institutional Expenses*
		Federal appropriations	Instruction Research Public service Academic support Institutional support Operation of physical plant Capital expenditures Hospital operations Independent operations
		State appropriations	
		Local appropriations	
		Gifts	
		Sales and services of hospitals	
		Sales and services of educational activities	
		Independent operations	
		Other operating revenues	
		Federal non-operating grants	
		State non-operating grants-	
		Local non-operating grants	
		Investment income	
		Other non-operating revenues	
		Capital appropriations	
		Capital grants and gifts	
		Addition to permanent endowments	
		Other	

CHAPTER 3

STUDENT-ORIENTED REVENUES AND EXPENDITURES

This chapter examines concepts and calculations related to institutional revenues originating from students over the three phases of postsecondary education. The reasons students pursue postsecondary education in the first place are not included in this discussion but may be found in Chapter 8. A discussion of the student perspective on college "price" may be found in Chapter 9.

The first phase of postsecondary revenues and expenditures related to students actually occurs prior to entering college for the first time. In a general model, this time is thought to be while the student is in high school, but this time period is quite different for non-traditional students, that is, for students who may have been out of high school for some time and have been working. For these students, the first phase is the period between completion of high school or the GED and first enrollment in college and includes work or other life activities. The second phase begins with the first time a student is enrolled in college. In a traditional model, students are enrolled full-time, but the majority of college enrollments in 2013 are not traditional. The third and final phase depicts the time period after leaving the college upon earning a credential, likely a degree.

Higher Education Finance Research: Policy, Politics, and Practice, pp. 63–90
Copyright © 2014 by Information Age Publishing

PRIOR TO ENROLLMENT

In the first phase of postsecondary education, a student/prospective student will have a number of "costs" or expenditures even before enrollment on a campus. Some of these costs are out-of-pocket or cash expenditures, and others are prospective opportunity costs such as foregone income.

Among the out-of-pocket costs are testing fees for exams such as the PSAT, SAT, or ACT. In some states, the state waives all these potential fees or covers the charges for the students. Taking the PSAT is the entry point for becoming eligible for National Merit Scholarships. In the 1980s and 1990s, colleges and universities competed to attract the most national merit scholars. Having the most nationally, or even the most in a state, was a mark of the quality of the institution and was used by states such as Maryland, Georgia, and South Carolina as one of the institutional performance indicators, along with the average SAT or ACT score of the entering class. Higher, of course, was better.

However, attracting National Merit scholars came at a cost for some institutions. Schools like Michigan State University expended resources to attract bright students; that is, MSU "bought" students by giving them a merit scholarship that was counted as a National Merit Scholarship. Revenues to support the scholarships came from donations as well as from other institutional revenues, including tuition and fees of other students.

Application fees are another of the costs of postsecondary education that occur before actual enrollment. Before the 1980s most colleges and universities did not charge an application fee, or if there was a fee, it was only nominal, less than $25. As college budgets became more constricted, administrators looked for ways to increase fees, and larger application fees became the norm. A fee of $100 is common, and some institutions charge a $500 application fee. For students who apply to five or more colleges, the application fees can add up quickly.

There are other costs that prospective students incur before actual enrollment at an institution—a visit to the institution where the student stays in a residence hall is one example of this type of cost. If the student is not charged a fee, then this "expenditure" of time could be perceived as an opportunity cost for the university. If the student is charged a fee, then this, as well as the opportunity cost of time invested, is an additional cost to the student prior to enrolling.

From the institution's perspective, campus visits can be either an expenditure or, if the prospective student pays something to stay (like high school students who attend summer camps on campus), the fees are a revenue and expenditure in the auxiliary enterprises category. Institutions run summer camps to attract prospective students to the campus, and there is a belief that this is positive public relations expenditure for the institution. However, there is no scientific research that indicates that these types of public relations or "advertising" expenditures actually result in enrollment of students that the institution would not have enrolled anyway.

WHILE ENROLLED

In phase two of the cost continuum (during enrollment), students have a variety of costs, as were listed in the introduction to this section. There are tuition charges, mandatory fees that all undergraduate and/or graduate students pay, special class fees that apply to only those students taking certain classes such as language labs, usage fees for copying and duplication or for computer use, room and board charges, books and supplies, transportation, child care expenses (for students with children), health-care costs, and some miscellaneous costs. There also are the opportunity costs of foregone income, or lost investment income. These costs to the student become revenues to the institution or, in some cases, flow through revenues and expenditures that become student revenues that are expended for the "costs" of higher education, as depicted in Table II.1 (in the introduction to Section II) and also shown in Figure 3.1.

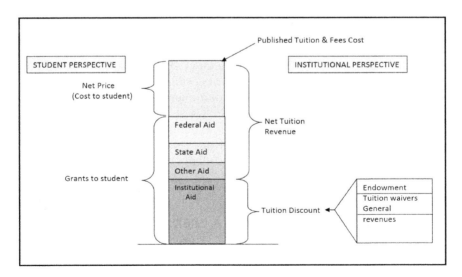

Figure 3.1. Revenues and expenditures from the student and institutional perspectives.

The differentiation between what constitutes a "tuition" and revenues that constitute a "fee" has been defined since the 1930s. Specifically, the term tuition refers to a fee associated with the cost of instruction. All other costs incurred in the education of the individual at a postsecondary institution are termed fees. Some systems of higher education have a "registration fee" that is charged to all students, and in addition, on top of the registration fee, a tuition charge that may be charged only to out-of-state students. A few institutions do the reverse—have a tuition charge that is differentially administered to all students, and then a registration fee that is charged to only certain students. Institutions have a variety of other fees including lab fees, computer fees, student union fees, facilities fees, student activities fees, and so on that are charged to all students and are called "mandatory fees." The mandatory fees may be assessed as a lump sum for the semester or term, or the fees may be on a per credit hour/unit basis. To ensure comparability among institutions, all institutions that report to IPEDS report the total of tuition and mandatory fees for the typical, full-time undergraduate student because not all institutions have tuition. For example, the University of California institutions are prohibited from charging tuition but not from charging fees, which cover everything outside of instruction, including such things as academic counseling, facilities, labs, computer rental, and so on. Some institutions charge relatively low tuition but have relatively high fees and vice versa. Including both tuition and mandatory fees equates what institutions charge for attendance.

Some institutions differentiate tuition and fees among classes of students. Different tuition and fees may be charged to in-state and to out-of-state students, or to undergraduate and graduate students, or to freshmen and sophomores versus juniors and seniors. There also may be differential tuition charges for classes offered at certain times, or for specific programs. How and why institutions set tuition and fee rates will be discussed later in this chapter.

Students have "revenues" that they expend to cover these "costs" just as the institution receives revenues from the students, and from other sources, which may flow back to the students in the form of financial aid, and expends those revenues to provide services.

AFTER EARNING A CREDENTIAL

The third phase of college costs begins after the student has graduated or left the institution, even without earning a credential. There are costs for copies of the student's transcript, graduation fees, alumni association fees, and others. Included in the after-commencement costs for students are loan repayment charges for all those students who financed their education by taking out a loan. In 2012, the College Board estimated that over 57% of undergraduate students who graduated from public institutions in 2010–2011 graduated with an average debt of $23,800 at graduation, while about 66% of students who earned bachelor's degrees in 2010–2011 from the private non-profit 4-year colleges at which they began their studies graduated with debt of $29,900; and among students earning bachelor's degrees in 2010–2011 from either the public or private non-profit 4-year colleges at which they began their studies, the 60% who borrowed graduated with an average debt of $25,300. For all of these bachelor's degree recipients, including those with no debt, the average amount borrowed was $15,100 (College Board, 2012b). The College Board also reported that students who earn their bachelor's degrees at for-profit institutions are more likely to borrow than those who attend public and private non-profit colleges, and borrowers at for-profit colleges tend to accumulate higher average levels of debt than borrowers at other types of institutions.

However, the additional income that a graduate can expect to earn after completion of college is thought to justify the debt burden associated with getting the degree. There has been some research into this area, mostly descriptive statistics of the debt burdens of graduates, especially for graduates of for-profit institutions, a fact that led to congressional action. The College Board includes loan information in its report *Trends in Student Aid* (2012b) describing average debt burden by type of institution, and by undergraduate and graduate students, and average default and loan interest rates.

TUITION AND FEE PHILOSOPHIES

Why do U.S. students pay tuition and fees to attend postsecondary institutions? Some European and Asian countries do not charge tuition for those students who are selected to attend their institutions, likely because the benefits of higher education are expected to accrue to the country and improve its economy.

When Harvard was founded in the 1600s, wealthy benefactors such as Lady Anne Mowlson provided endowment funding to help needy students who could not afford the cost of college. Institutions like New York University were founded on the principle of low tuition to provide educational opportunity to many citizens (Brademas, 1983). There was no distinction between the public good and private higher education, so that individuals, organizations, and governments made available assistance to keep tuition and fees affordable to even impoverished students (Rudolph,

1962). In the 1800s, only about 10% of what is thought of as the "college age group" attended institutions of higher education, and nearly all of these students were young men of considerable family means.

It was not until the Morrill Land Grant Act of 1862 that a college education became more widely sought after and more affordable. Section 4 of the Morrill Land Grant Act set forth the intent of expanding free educational opportunities to more citizens. It was the intention of the Morrill Act to provide free or almost free education to students through federal appropriations for higher education. The impact on annual appropriations for institutions slated to receive Morrill land grant funds would not come until the Morrill Act of 1890, which provided a more stable source of revenue to the institutions. Morrill expected that the land grant funds would constitute many of the funds that institutions needed to operate and that needy students would have to pay low or no charges for instruction. Later, in the 1940s, the Truman Commission recommended that community colleges with low or no tuition be established to reduce the cost of college attendance (Fenske, 1983).

There have been various policies enacted by the states that reflect several philosophies on tuition and student aid (Cunningham & Merisotis, 2002). From the theoretical perspective, the "cost" to the student and to society should be reflective of the benefits; in other words, who gets the benefits should pay. Because students and their families received part of the benefits, they should pay part of the cost, with the rest borne by society, at least theoretically.

Low Tuition

One philosophy that certainly was the rule rather than the exception after the Morrill Act was that institutions should have as little student cost for instruction as possible, because the benefits of higher education accrued mostly to society, rather than to the student. The other costs associated with participating in higher education, inclusive of forgone earnings discussed in Chapter 8, however, were costs to the student. Some states such as Arizona have a constitutional provision (arising from the Morrill Acts) that education "should be as nearly free as possible," which applies to all levels of education, and established a low tuition rule for Arizona's public colleges and universities.

With the advent of community colleges and with the recommendations of the Truman Commission, low tuition and fees were thought to be ideal because community college students were learning work skills that would improve the quality of life in the community. Thus, community college tuition was kept low, and in some states, the local community and the state provided sufficient funding for the community college so that students were not charged tuition and fees.

It was not only the community college sector itself (and the Truman Commission) that believed in low tuition and fees for students. The Carnegie Commission on Higher Education in 1977 suggested that community colleges operate at no cost to the student because of the benefits to society in general. Texas and California kept tuition low for many years following the suggestion of the Carnegie Commission.

High Cost, High Aid

The low to no tuition movement did not last long, however. The perspective of many was that a low to no tuition policy does not take a student's ability to pay into account. In effect, it would be inefficient to not maximize the amount of money a student may be able to pay for postsecondary education. Tuition and fees should, therefore, be in some way contingent on the student's ability to pay. In 1972 the Illinois State Scholarship Commission (ISSC) suggested that Illinois higher education institutions should charge tuition that was based on the student's and student's family's ability to pay (McKeown, 1974). This would be in effect a high cost, high aid policy that would have charged as much tuition and fees as the legislature (which determined total tuition revenues at the time) would permit, but that sticker price would be charged only to those students with the ability to pay. All others would receive financial aid to offset the high tuition. The ISSC policy recommendation was never enacted.

However, other states had a high cost, high aid policy until recently when the economy led to reductions in student aid. Maryland and Pennsylvania charged students relatively high tuition and mandatory fees at the public 4-year institutions but had relatively large aid programs to offset the price for those students with less ability to pay.

Percent of the Cost of Education

Another philosophy of tuition was that students and their families should provide the percentage share of the costs of education that was equivalent to the student's benefit from the education. So, if the perception was that the student received 25% or 33% of the benefit, then the student should pay 25 or 33% of the cost of that education. Determining what the "cost" was required research on college campuses and in state governing or coordinating boards.

For many years, until the mid-1980s when budgets and state appropriations for higher education became more constrained, Virginia set tuition at Virginia's community colleges at 25% of the cost of education; at the state colleges at 30% of cost; and at the research universities at 33 to 35% of cost. "Cost" was defined by a formula that included expenditures for instruction, academic support, student services, institutional support, and operation and maintenance of physical plant. Virginia eliminated this formula when state revenues were reduced, and institutions were forced to increase tuition charges to maintain quality programs.

McMahon (2009) argued that the social benefits of higher education are not recognized by most states, resulting in an underinvestment in higher education by the state. Under McMahon's calculations, the state and/or local community should support more than 60% of the cost of higher education because the state and local community receives more than 60% of the benefits. McMahon's research is robust, although policymakers likely would disagree with the implications of his findings.

TUITION AND FEES AS INSTITUTIONAL REVENUES

The *revenues* in the category "tuition and fees" are a primary revenue source for both public and private higher education institutions. At the same time, tuition and fees, institutional revenue, is a student cost, as noted above. Table 1.6 showed that total tuition and fees for all higher education institutions increased from $18.5 million in 1910 to $134.7 billion in 2010, and it increased from 24% of total revenues in 1910 to 27% in 2010 (Snyder & Dillow, 2012). Even though these percentages appear to be relatively equivalent, it is important to note that the 2010 figure is net tuition and fee revenues while the 1910 number is gross revenues. It also is important to remember that those are figures averaged across all institutions and that tuition revenues make up a larger share of the budgets of private institutions than of public institutions, especially large research universities.

Scholarship and fellowship expenditures, which were discussed in the prior chapter, were reported on the Old Form as a gross amount of awards granted. FASB presents net grant aid to students (total scholarships and fellowships minus the amount used to pay tuition and fees and other institutional charges). The same amounts that affect tuition and fees and auxiliary enterprises also affect this expense category. New GASB reports the net amount in a category called "scholarships and fellowships expenses," excluding discounts and allowances. Again the gross amount can be found on the scholarships and fellowships section of the form (Part C for FASB and Part E for New GASB).

Part E of the Old Form displayed student scholarships and fellowships by source. These data are essentially the same on the FASB and New GASB forms, with more detail added. Institutional scholarships are further broken down as funded and unfunded on the FASB form (Part C). The amount of the scholarships applied to tuition and fees is reported, as well as scholarships applied to auxiliary enterprise revenues (such as room and board or bookstore charges). These amounts may be different among FASB schools due to the variance in accounting method for Pell Grants. When the new FASB accounting standards were adopted, institutions could choose to treat Pell Grants as pass-through funds (the institution is simply a conduit for the funds) or as federal grant revenue and expense (or allowance). New GASB reporters use Part E to report scholarships and fellowships. Discounts and allowances applied to tuition and fees and discounts and allowances applied to sales and services of auxiliary enterprises are also reported on this part. All New GASB reporters treat Pell Grants as federal revenue and include them as discounts and allowances (if used to pay for tuition and fees or other institutional charges) or as net grant aid to students (if paid to the student to offset other expenses).

A direct crosswalk cannot be made from the Old Form to either the FASB or New GASB forms. There also is not a direct crosswalk between FASB and New GASB, although comparisons are somewhat easier between FASB and New GASB. The changes in scope and data collected cause some major and some minor obstacles to comparing data before and after the accounting changes for private and public institutions. The changes described above should help to bridge some of the gaps between the types of data collected and aid the reader in understanding where direct comparisons cannot be made.

IPEDS defines scholarships and fellowships as outright grants-in-aid, trainee stipends, tuition and fee waivers, and prizes awarded to students by the institution, including Pell Grants. Regardless of the source of funds, it is considered a scholarship or fellowship if the institution awards it. Financial aid may be need-based or merit-based and still fall into this category. Awards to undergraduate students are most commonly referred to as "scholarships" and those to graduate students as "fellowships." These awards do not require the performance of services by the recipient (such as teaching) while a student is receiving them or subsequently. The term does not include loans to students (subject to repayment), College Work-Study Program (CWS), or awards granted because of faculty or staff status. Also not included are awards to students where the selection of the student recipient is not made by the institution. Examples of this would include Lions Club scholarships where the club selects the recipient and Walmart scholarships where the company names the recipient.

A common misconception regarding scholarships and fellowships is to include work-study as scholarships in reporting in IPEDS. Because work-study requires the student to work to earn these wages, it cannot be considered an outright grant or scholarship. Expenses related to work-study are wages to be classified within the function that benefits from the student's work. For example, if the student works in the library, the wages should be classified as academic support. If the student works in the student aid office, their wages should be classified as student services.

Credits applied to students' accounts may come from many sources. Some originate within the institution, referred to as institutional scholarships. Some come from the federal government in the form of Pell Grants or SEOG grants. Others are from outside private sources such as local clubs and organizations. State scholarships may come to the institution in the form of tuition exemptions. Still others are payments from the students or their parents and other family members on the students' behalf. The accounting treatment of the credit determines whether it is a scholarship (or fellowship) or a pass-through transaction.

One characteristic that often affects how the credit is handled from an accounting standpoint is what role the institution plays in determining the recipient of the payment. In the case of payments from students or their families, the person paying determines who the recipient is. In the case of some state scholarship programs, the state determines that the student is eligible at any institution the student attends. Similarly, private clubs and organizations may send the payment with the student specifically named. In these cases, the institution has no input as to the recipient. The payment is simply applied to the student's account, and no revenue or expense is recorded. This is considered a pass-through transaction. The payment simply passes through the institution for the specific student's benefit. When the institution names the recipient, as in institutional scholarships, SEOG, and privately donated scholarships, it is a scholarship from the institution's perspective, generating an expense (or allowance). When the institution receives the private donation or federal funds, it is treated as revenue.

Different institutions may classify certain funds differently as a scholarship or fellowship or as a pass-through. One common area of differences is Pell Grants. Private institutions (and a few public institutions) operate under accounting standards adopted by the Financial Accounting Standards Board (FASB). The vast majority of public institutions use accounting standards adopted by the Governmental Accounting Standards Board (GASB). Public institutions using current GASB accounting standards are required to treat Pell Grants as scholarships, using the logic that the institution is involved in the administration of the program (as evidenced by the administrative allowance paid to the institution). FASB standards give private institutions the option to treat Pell Grants as scholarships or as pass-through transactions, using the logic that the federal government determines who is eligible for the grant, not the institution. Because of this difference in requirements, public institutions will report Pell Grants as federal revenues and as allowances (reducing tuition revenues), whereas FASB institutions may do this as well or (as seems to be the majority) treat Pell Grants as pass-through transactions. The result is that in the case where a FASB institution and GASB institution each receive the same amount of Pell Grants on behalf of their students, the GASB institution will appear to have less tuition and more federal revenues, whereas the FASB institution treating Pell as pass-through will appear to have more tuition and less federal revenues. This is the reason why FASB institutions are asked to answer the General Information question about how the institution treats Pell Grants. The answer to this question will make selection of peers easier for private institutions.

Scholarships and fellowships may be used to pay tuition and fees and other institutional charges such as room and board or bookstore charges. Under GASB and FASB accounting standards, the amounts used to pay tuition and other institutional charges are considered discounts or allowances, reducing the amount the student actually pays to attend the institution. The amount of any aid left over, usually refunded to the student, would be considered an expense. The following example may help to understand this concept:

Suppose a student is charged $3,000 for tuition and fees, and $1,500 in room and board charges. The student receives an institutional room and board scholarship of $1,500 and a Pell grant for $2,000. Below is a summary of how this situation would be represented.

Student Charges

Tuition	$3,000
Room and Board	$1,500

Scholarships and Payments

Institutional scholarship	$1,500
Pell grant (not treated as pass-through)	$2,000
Cash	$1,000

The institution would report in its accounting records:

Tuition Revenues	$1,000
Auxiliary revenues	$0
Federal revenues	$2,000

If the institution treated Pell grants as pass through, tuition revenues would be $3,000 and there would be no federal revenue.

Discounts and allowances have been netted against the amounts reported in the above representation of the accounting treatment. Institutions maintain records of the amounts of these allowances for each revenue source against which they are applied (tuition and fees or auxiliary enterprises). When reporting on IPEDS, scholarships appear in two different areas of the survey. One is on a part where the institution is required to report amounts of each type of scholarship, categorized by source, such as Pell Grants, other federal grants, state, local, and institutional grants and should be reported at the full amount of the grant or scholarship. This is Part E for GASB institutions and Part C for all others. Institutions also are required to report the amount of discounts and allowances applied to tuition and fees and to auxiliary enterprises, such as room and board charges. The other component is on the expenses part of the survey. The amount reported in this section is the part of aid that was not considered pass-through and not applied to tuition and fees or auxiliary enterprises. Generally this is the amount refunded to the student.

It is critical for researchers comparing student financial aid revenues and expenditures to understand under which rules the institution was reporting and to equate revenues and/or expenditures across the institutions included in the comparison. Otherwise, false conclusions could be reached.

TUITION AND FEE AMOUNTS

Table 3.1 displays average tuition and fees for public and private institutions from 1969–1970 to 2011–2012, as reported in the *Digest of Education Statistics* (Snyder & Dillow, 2012). Also included are the same data as reported by the College Board (2006), although College Board data prior to 2000 were not available, and the College Board stopped reporting data for private 2-year institutions after 2003. Of interest to researchers is the difference between the average tuition and fees reported by the College Board and those reported in the *Digest of Education Statistics*. As noted in Chapter 2, the averages are different because of different weights applied. College Board data are weighted by the number of students, while *Digest* data are not. Both data sources are considered excellent, but the researcher must know which data source used which type of data to reach relevant conclusions from the data. The College Board information is more current than the ED data, moreover, providing 2012–2013 information, while the ED data are preliminary even for 2011–2012.

Between 1999–2000 and 2011–2012, tuition and mandatory fees doubled at public 2-year institutions, increasing form $1,348 to $2,647, a $1,299 or 96% increase, using the *Digest* data. At public 4-year institutions, tuition and fees increased 130%, a $4,352 increase from $3,349 in

Table 3.1. Average Tuition and Mandatory Fees by Type of Institution

	Public 2-year	Public 4-year	Private 2-year	Private 4-year
As reported in the Digest of Education Statistics:				
1969–1970	178	358	1,034	1,561
1979–1980	355	738	2,062	3,225
1989–1990	756	1,780	4,817	8,396
1999–2000	1,348	3,349	8,225	14,616
2009–2010	2,285	6,695	14,876	21,908
2010–2011	2,439	7,136	14,467	22,771
2011–2012	2,647	7,701	13,879	23,479
As reported by the College Board:				
1999–2000	1,649	3,362	6,968	15,518
2009–2010	2,558	7,050		26,129
2010–2011	2,713	7,605		27,293
2011–2012	2,959	8,256		27,883
2012–2013	3,131	8,655		29,056

Sources: Snyder and Dillow, Table 349 (2012); College Board (2012a).

1999–2000 to $7,701 in 2011–2012. At private institutions, the increase was larger in dollars, but smaller in percentage: at 2-year, the increase of $5,654 from $8,225 to $13,879 or 69%, and from $14,616 to $23,479 at 4-year private institutions, an increase of $8,863 or 61%.

If the College Board data are used, then the percentage increases change; for 2-year, there was a 79% increase, or $1,310; for public 4-year, the increase was $4,894, or 146%; and for private institutions, the increase was $12,365, or 80%. With the College Board data, change through 2012–2013 can be calculated.

How these data are presented vary, depending on who is doing the reporting. Both data sources are respected and have excellent information. If the researcher or reporter is an advocate for public institutions, that person likely would report that the increase was fewer dollars than the increase at private institutions. If the researcher or reporter is an advocate for private institutions, then likely that person would report the percentage increase as being less than that of public institutions.

The data reported by both the NCES and College Board are for undergraduate, full-time students who are state residents at the public institutions. There are many other categories of students—part-time students, for example, who pay a charge per credit hour or per course. Graduate students also pay different tuition and fee amounts at most institutions, and professional students such as those enrolled in medicine, dentistry, or law are charged yet a different amount. As mentioned earlier, there may be differential charges for courses offered at off-peak times, for special programs such as an Executive Master's of Business Administration, or for programs that are sponsored by businesses. Determining how much to charge is a difficult process, as explained below.

TUITION SETTING

How do institutions determine how much tuition and fees to charge? Tuition setting is one of the most difficult decisions administrators have to make because this is an emotional issue for many students, their parents, college administrators, and board members. Tuition and fees often are used as the balancer in determining the institution's budget and so must be accurately projected if the institution is to have sufficient resources to operate (Division of Performance Audit, 2006). Staff agonizes over any tuition increase and how it will be perceived by the public, students, and their families. Research on the tuition setting process itself is limited and mostly descriptive, with the exception of the issue of tuition discounting, which will be discussed later in this section.

In some states, like Louisiana, for public institutions the legislature determines how much tuition will be, based on recommendations from legislative staff as well as the institutions and the statewide coordinating board. In states such as Arizona, the governing board sets tuition and fees for the public universities, while the governing boards for each community college set their tuition levels. However, tuition is constrained by the constitutional provision that "education be as nearly free as possible." The Arizona Board of Regents has interpreted that to mean that tuition should be in the bottom third of tuition and fee rates of the major research universities in the other states. In states such as Virginia, tuition levels for the public institutions were set as a specified percentage of the "cost of education." In South Carolina, institutions are required to set out-of-state tuition at a price at least equal to the "cost of education," which is calculated by the state coordinating board. Institutions have the flexibility to modify tuition levels to meet the required level, but an amount equal to the number of out-of-state students multiplied by the cost of education is subtracted from the formula-generated "resource requirement" for that institution.

In most cases, public institutions and/or systems and private institutions complete a significant amount of analysis and research in the tuition setting process. First, institutions will look at what they have charged over the past several years and also gather information on the tuition and fees charged by "peer" institutions or systems, or by all the institutions in the surrounding states. For example, the Washington Student Achievement Council (formerly the Washington Higher Education Coordinating Board) each year collects tuition and fee information from colleges and universities in all 50 states. Their excellent database provides comparison information for each Washington institution to the charges at "peer" institutions across the nation. Information can be accessed at www.wsac.wa.gov/planningandresearch/systemfunding/tuitionandfees.

Once an institution or board has comparison information, they may decide to change tuition levels to reposition themselves relative to peers, although this is unusual. Generally tables will be prepared that simulate changes in revenues generated by increases at various levels across student groups. For example, 1, 5, and 10% increases in in-state or resident tuition would be applied to the student body projected to attend the institution. Similar increases in out-of-state or non-resident tuition would be simulated. In addition, there would be calculation of the elasticity of demand, based on assumptions on the impact a particular dollar increase would have on enrollment. Some institutions have complicated elasticity calculations, while others rely on research done by outside consultants or by other institutions/systems. In addition, many institutions and systems also calculate past years', current, and projected tuition and fees as a percentage of average family income. This is a measure of affordability and access for public institutions. Because average family incomes were lower in inflation-adjusted dollars in 2011 than a decade earlier (College Board, 2012a), for most institutions, tuition and fees were a higher percentage of average family income, putting pressure on the provision of student financial aid.

All of the above work can be completed without regard to the institution's financial aid policies, which generally are considered in the "tuition discounting" process. The institution's enrollment management office likely will have significant impact on the information presented, including the impact of an increase on the makeup of the student body. Enrollment management is defined as the enrollment planning, recruitment, enrollment, and retention of students to achieve a student body that meets the goals of the college or university (Lapovsky & Hubbell, 2003). Through enrollment management, institutions seek to enroll a class of a specific size, with certain characteristics, while providing access to students and maximizing net revenue. Enrollment management is a complex strategic process.

Information gathered on peer tuition levels, increases in revenues, and impact on the student body would be made available to the decision makers and also to students and their families. Likely, a hearing would be held to get input from students, parents, college/university staff, and others on the impact of the various increases. In California and Missouri, and in other states, the increase in tuition and fees is subject to an agreement with the governor or legislature that state appropriations will either increase or not decrease if the institutions maintain current tuition levels, or reduce any increase to below the change in the consumer price index (CPI). In some states, a specified percentage of the increase may be earmarked for student financial aid, either by the institution's policy or by legislative mandate, in what is called "tuition discounting."

TUITION DISCOUNTING

During the 1800s, private colleges discovered that they did not need scholarship funds or endowments to provide aid to needy students. The colleges could reduce costs for needy students by waiving some or all of the tuition and fees, and calling the reduction a "scholarship." Tuition was set higher than needed to fund operating expenditures, and students who paid full tuition in effect paid the tuition for needy students (Fenske, 1983). This type of tuition policy is a form of the ability to pay practice of charging high tuition offset by financial aid. The practice of giving this type of scholarship actually continues today under the guise of "tuition remissions" or "tuition discounting."

Tuition discounting is defined as the art and science of establishing the net price of attendance for students at amounts that will maximize tuition revenue while achieving certain enrollment goals (Davis, 2003) or price discrimination by charging different students different prices for the same educational opportunities (Baum & Lapovsky, 2003). Private institutions have long used discounting, and it has become a standard practice at public institutions during the last 20 years as state and federal expenditures for student aid have not kept pace with rising tuition costs and enrollment levels. The most important reason that colleges engage in discounting is to generate or enhance net tuition revenue (Lasher & Sullivan, 2005).

Tuition discounting has been widely studied, and some claim that this technique can be used to build enrollments, increase institutional net revenue, and shape an incoming class to fit the institution's strategic objectives (AASCU, 2007; Lapovsky & Hubbell, 2004). Discounting generally was intended to permit an institution to balance ability to pay with willingness to pay while achieving other institutional objectives, such as improving the school's academic profile, serving more minority students, or other goals (Davis, 2003). Others claim that tuition discounting has unintended consequences and may result in the institution realizing less revenue or reducing access.

The National Association of College and University Business Officers (NACUBO) has monitored tuition discounting practices for over 20 years through an annual tuition discounting survey and published analyses in *Business Officer*. NACUBO has defined discounting as both need-based institutional grant aid and also reductions to published tuition and fee rates given to increase the probability of particular students choosing to enroll. The discount rate is defined as (Lapovsky & Hubbell, 2003):

$$\text{Tuition discount rate} = \frac{\text{Total Institutional grant aid}}{\text{Total gross tuition and required fee revenue}}$$

or

$$\text{Tuition discount rate} = \frac{\text{Average institutional aid per student}}{\text{Published tuition and required fee rate}}$$

The NACUBO publications, as well as other articles by Lapovsky and Hubbell (2003), Baum and Lapovsky (2006), Baum, Lapovsky and Ma (2010), and Hillman (2010a), describe the complicated process for designing a system of discounting to reach institutional goals. They also describe the unanticipated results of discounting, and the reader is encouraged to review these studies for methodology.

Hillman (2010a) used NCES data to identify the characteristics of students who benefit from tuition discounting at public 4-year colleges and universities. Using a binary logistic regression, he found that low-income students, minorities, freshmen, and non-resident students were more likely to receive discounts than other students, although the discount rate for low-income students is less than or just equal to that of upper-income students receiving discounts.

In another study on public 4-year colleges between 2002 and 2008, Hillman (2010b) found that tuition discounting can be a tool for enhancing net tuition revenue, but only to a limited extent. He found that colleges whose discount rate was greater than 13% yielded less net tuition revenues. Similarly, the Association of Governing Boards (AGB) determined that tuition discounting was not a viable long-term strategy and may threaten an institution's ability to offer educational opportunities (AGB, 2012).

Baum, Lapovsky and Ma (2010) reported that the overall tuition discount rate for private 4-year institutions had increased from 28.6% in 2000–2001 to 33.1% in 2008–2009, and NACUBO reported that the rate had increased to 36.4% in 2010–2011 and was projected to increase to 42.8% in 2011–2012 (Biemiller, 2012). The discount rate for freshmen at 4-year private institutions increased to 45.0% in 2011–2012 (Kiley, 2013).

For public 4-year institutions, the average discount rate had declined from 20.5% in 2000–2001 to 18.3% in 2008–2009, well in excess of the 13% rate Hillman found as a critical point. For public 2 year institutions, the rate had decreased from 12.0% in 2000–2001 to 10.6% in 2007–2008, although the rate had declined to a low of 7.8% in 2005–2006 (Baum & Lapovsky, 2010).

HOW STUDENTS PAY FOR COLLEGE

Students receive revenues to cover college expenses from a variety of sources, as was shown in the introduction to this section: from their families' and their own savings, from family income, from grant aid (which may be given by the federal, state, or local governments; from the institution itself; or from outside sources such as foundations and local civic organizations), from loans (which may be from federal, state, or local governments; from the institution itself; or from outside sources), or from income working during enrollment. In 2012 approximately $150 billion of federal student financial aid was available, and over $94 billion of aid from other sources was granted to students (College Board, 2012b). See Figure 3.2.

Despite this seemingly large amount of aid, equivalent to almost 50% of total college and university expenditures, on average, parental income and savings paid for approximately 28% of college costs, with grants and scholarships covering approximately the same percentage, and student borrowing, parental borrowing, student savings and income, and relatives and friends providing the rest (Glaser, 2013), as shown in Figure 3.3.

Each year, the College Board (www.collegeboard.org) provides information on the costs of college across the nation through a report called *Trends in College Pricing* and on student financial aid through *Trends in Financial Aid*. These series of reports contain the best, and some think the most accessible, information on college and university prices and financial aid and have been published since 1983. Data going back to 1963 are available from the College Board to established researchers.

Trends in College Pricing relies on data from the College Board's Annual Survey of Colleges (ASC) to provide information on changes in undergraduate tuition and fees, room and board, and other estimated expenses related to attending colleges and universities. Although data for *Trends in Student Aid 2012* go through only the 2011–2012 academic year, *Trends in College Pricing 2012* includes information on published prices for the 2012–2013 academic year. The *Trends* website makes data easily available for reference and downloading. *Trends in Financial Aid* is described by the College Board as

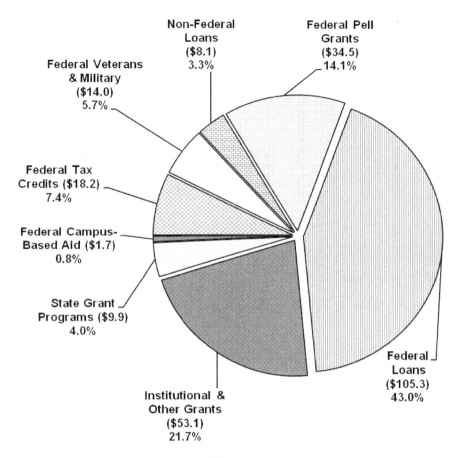

Non-Federal
Loans
($8.1)
3.3%

Federal Pell
Grants
($34.5)
14.1%

Federal Veterans
& Military
($14.0)
5.7%

Federal Tax
Credits ($18.2)
7.4%

Federal Campus-
Based Aid ($1.7)
0.8%

State Grant
Programs ($9.9)
4.0%

Institutional &
Other Grants
($53.1)
21.7%

Federal
Loans
($105.3)
43.0%

Source: Calculated from College Board (2012b).

Figure 3.2.   Estimated student aid by source, FY2012. Total aid awarded: $244.8 billion, including $8.1 billion of non-federal loans.

a compendium of detailed, up-to-date information on the funding that is available to help students pay for college. This report documents grant aid from federal and state governments, colleges and universities, employers, and other private sources, as well as loans, tax benefits, and Federal Work-Study assistance. It examines changes in funding levels over time, reports on the distribution of aid across students with different incomes and attending different types of institutions, and tracks the debt students incur as they pursue the educational opportunities that can increase their earnings, open doors to new experiences, and improve their ability to adapt to an ever-changing society. (College Board, 2012b)

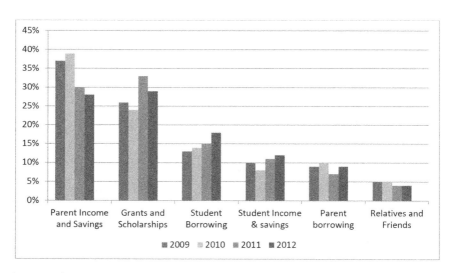

Source: Glaser (2013).

Figure 3.3.   How the typical family pays for college.

Because of this long history and the excellent research methodology employed by the College Board staff, these documents are invaluable to researchers in higher education finance. For examples, see a series of reports on the status of higher education funding published by the State Higher Education Executive Officers (SHEEO) (McKeown-Moak, 1999, 2000b, 2001a, 2002, 2003, 2004, 2005). The documents also are used extensively by colleges and universities and their governing or coordinating boards in setting tuition and fees and demonstrating the value of a college education. Researchers are encouraged to review the College Board website not only for the *Trends* reports but for other valuable information on how students and their families pay for college and for how colleges and universities set tuition and fees.

The *Digest of Education Statistics* also provides data on student financial aid and on tuition and fee prices, and those data were used earlier. The biggest drawback to the federal data is that it is not reported in a timely manner—for example, only some preliminary data for 2011–2012 were made available in January 2013. Not all data are included in the preliminary release, and this delay makes timely analysis problematic. Researchers also need to understand what student counts were used in the NCES data because different tables use differing counts.

FEDERAL STUDENT FINANCIAL AID

The federal government provided over $150 billion of student financial aid in 2011–2012. The first step for a student to receive federal aid is to complete a special application form. All students who apply for student financial aid (and their parents) must fill out the "Free Application for Federal Student Aid," commonly called the FAFSA, whether they are applying for federal student financial aid or not. Most states and institutions, as well as many private providers of student aid, use the FAFSA to determine eligibility for need-based grants and aid. As mentioned above, not all financial aid is need-based, and institutions and private providers of student financial aid may also use the FAFSA to determine merit-based aid. Moreover, institutions still use the FAFSA, as it is a standardized methodology. The FAFSA may be found at www.studentaid.ed.gov/fafsa, and readers are encouraged to visit the site for a wealth of information on how the expected family contribution is calculated, how institutions use the FAFSA, how aid is calculated, and how the federal government interacts with institutions. The site also provides information to guide prospective students and their families through the financial aid application process.

The FAFSA asks for a significant amount of information about the family and its taxed and untaxed income and assets to determine how much the student's family can afford to pay for the student's college education (GAO, 2005). Various factors including the size of the family, equity in a home, savings, and so on are considered in determining how much a family can afford. As can be imagined, the FAFSA is a complicated form, and many prospective students and their families are intimidated by the form. This is especially true for first-generation college students and for low-income, non-English speaking, and minority families. More discussion of the FAFSA can be found in Chapter 9.

In 1965 Congress passed the landmark Higher Education Act (HEA). The Higher Education Act Title IV authorized the programs that comprise the foundation of federal financial aid today: the Stafford Guaranteed Student Loan (GSL), Educational Opportunity Grant (EOG now called Pell Grant), and College-Work-Study programs. The HEA of 1965 also reauthorized the National Defense Student Loan (NDSL) program, which began in 1958 and was the beginning of low-interest federal student loans for "students in need" (Chambers, 1968). Each of these aid programs distributed aid to institutions for distribution to needy students, primarily through loans. Entitlements were not a component of Title IV aid; rather, aid was delivered through institutions to the "needy." Nevertheless, each of the aid programs was intended to promote access to a higher education. Over the next 8 years, federal student aid grew by 900%.

Since that time, there has been continuing debate over the appropriate federal government role or roles in funding postsecondary education. In 1968, Clark Kerr summarized the debate into five broad options (see Table 3.2): direct aid to institutions, direct aid to states, direct aid to students (and their parents), direct aid for research, and aid in the form of tax benefits for students. Direct aid to students, in the form of student aid, was perceived as the best option at the time as it aided families on the lower end of the economic spectrum, thereby reducing economic barriers to enrollment, while also reinforcing a market-based approach to postsecondary education, maintaining institutional neutrality with respect to control and level and recognizing the private returns to non-compulsory education (Mullin, in press).

Table 3.2.   Typology of Options for a Federal Role in Financing Postsecondary Education

Options for a Federal Role	Financial Impact	Power Impact
Tax relief to families and donors	Aids high and median-income families Aids private colleges (through higher tuition) more than public institutions	Works against equality of financial opportunity
Loans and grants to students	Aid families at lower end of the income scale (if based on need)	Aids equality of opportunity (grants) and offers additional resources (loans)
		Reinforces market mechanism
		Neutral between institution types
		Recognizes individual returns to education
Grants to states	Aids state taxpayers at expense of federal taxpayers	Concentrates too much control in a single center of power
		Limits an important source of diversity in funding
Categorical grant programs	Have an uneven impact by nature	Are responsive to quality and supportive of diversity
Formula-based grants to institutions	Treats all institutions equally, but states with higher enrollments get most	Depends on the purpose of the grant
		May raise constitutional issues about aid to religiously controlled institutions

In 1972, Congress reauthorized the Higher Education Act, making minor adjustments to existing programs and adding the State Student Incentive Grant (SSIG) and the Basic Education Opportunity Grant (BEOG, now called Pell Grant) programs. The SSIG program provided federal funds on a one-to-one match with state dollars to create additional aid for needy students within that state. SSIG can be perceived to have been a continuation and expansion of the apparent federal policy of granting need-based aid to students that would be delivered through existing institutions or agencies. The creation of the Pell Grant program, on the other hand, signaled a major change in federal student financial aid policy.

BEOGs, or Pell Grants, were, at their conception, entitlements for needy students that replace, or at least were designed to mitigate, the need for loans. Pell Grants were intended to be the base for packaging aid to needy students, would not have to be repaid, and would follow the student to whichever institution the student chose. Because Pell Grants were an entitlement program, Congress appropriated each year funds sufficient to cover program costs determined by formula. Although now Pell Grants are perceived by some to be a program to provide access, Pell Grants were a program that focused on student choice, not access, since the aid was directed to the student and his/her choice of an institution. Thus, the 1972 Reauthorization of the Higher Education Act altered the federal role in student aid from a policy focus on access to focus on access and choice, with aid delivered through a combination of grants, loans, and work from institutions and directly to the student (McKeown, 1994). Federal appropriations for student financial aid increased over 50% during the 5 years following reauthorization. By 1980, 2.5 million students participated in the Pell program and received $2.5 billion in aid (Mullin, in press).

The 1978 Reauthorization of the Higher Education Act ushered in a new era of federal student financial aid. Congress passed the Middle Income Student Assistance Act of 1978, greatly expanding eligibility for Pell Grants and Guaranteed Student Loans (GSL) to students from middle and upper income families. Removal of the income cap from the GSL program, increases in college enrollments and costs, and inflation contributed to significant increases in federally funded student aid. Between 1978 and 1981, aid grew 114% from $1.6 billion to $4.8 billion. Aid, predominately in the form of loans delivered to students instead of through institutions, became focused on middle income and upper income students, moving away from low income or needy students. The huge cost of GSLs shifted funds away from the entitlement program (Pell Grants) that was to have been the federal government's primary student aid vehicle. By 1981–1982, only 24% of the combined Pell and GSL funding came through Pell Grants. During the 1980s, the federal government retreated from the policies that made nearly every student eligible for GSLs by placing restrictions on the program. The focus of aid continued to be loans directly to students; however, the concept of attendance at any college of choice was undermined for low income students, who were less likely to attend a university than a community college or proprietary school.

During the 1980s, several entitlement programs were eliminated or severely restricted. As the majority of Vietnam War veterans completed college, veterans' educational benefits were phased down. Social security survivors' benefits for college were eliminated entirely. Thus, the focus of federal student financial aid moved away from entitlement programs and grant programs for the needy to loans with expanded eligibility.

Enactment of the Taxpayer Relief Act of 1997 (TRA97) provided new federal "student aid" through the use of income tax credits, savings incentives, and limited deductibility for interest paid on student loans. These programs were projected to cost about as much as all other existing federal financial aid programs combined and represent a significant shift in how the federal government provides funding for higher education. These tax credits are not need-based, represent revenue foregone rather than expenditures, and benefited primarily middle and upper-middle income students and their families. Lower income students who owe no federal taxes do not benefit, and those students whose family tax bill is less than the credit receive partial benefits.

Federal tax expenditures (such as the Hope and Lifetime Learning Credits) that represent foregone income were estimated to total about double the amount of Pell Grants in FY2000, and that amount has gone up since. Some provisions of federal law related to tax treatment of some "financial aid" were amended in 1999 tax changes. Continued expansion of tax expenditures instead of increased traditional financial aid implied that the goal of access to higher education had changed.

In 2011–2012, $236.7 billion in financial aid was distributed to undergraduate and graduate students, available to students at public, private non-profit, and for-profit institutions in the form of grants from all sources: Federal Work-Study, federal loans, and federal tax credits and deductions. In addition, students borrowed about $8.1 billion from private, state, and institutional sources to help finance their education (College Board, 2012). Undergraduate students receiving aid received an average of $13,218 per year (Glaser, 2013), including $6,932 in grant aid from all sources, and $5,056 in federal loans (College Board, 2012b). Graduate students received an average of $25,152 per FTE in aid, including $7,417 in grant aid and $16,796 in federal loans.

Federal grant aid almost tripled in constant dollars between 2001–2002 and 2011–2012, increasing from 20% to 26% of the total $185.1 billion in undergraduate aid. An estimated 13.1 million tax filers benefited from federal education tax credits and deductions in 2010—more than the number of students benefiting from any other federal aid program in 2011–2012. About 9.4 million students received Pell Grants, and about 10.4 million took out Stafford Loans. There were 1.4 million recipients of the Federal Supplemental Educational Opportunity Grant (FSEOG), 684,000 Federal Work-Study participants, and 524,000 Perkins Loan recipients in 2011–2012 (College Board, 2012b).

The number of students receiving Pell Grants, the central federal grant program providing funding for low-and moderate-income students, increased from 2.7 million in 1981–1982 and 3.8 million in 1991–1992 to 4.3 million in 2001–2002 and to 9.4 million (37% of all undergraduates) in 2011–2012. Total Pell Grant expenditures increased from $12.7 billion (in 2011 dollars) in 2001–2002 to $37.0 billion in 2010-11 but declined to an estimated $34.5 billion in 2011–2012. Only undergraduate students who have an expected family contribution of zero and enroll full-time/full-year receive the maximum Pell Grant. In 2010–2011 (when some students could receive more than one grant in a 12-month period), 31% of Pell Grant recipients received at least $5,550 in Pell funding, the maximum for a single award. In 2008–2009, 25% of Pell Grant recipients were awarded the maximum Pell Grant of $4,731 (in current dollars). The average Pell Grant per recipient was $2,094 (in 2011 dollars) in 1981–1982, $2,538 in 1991–1992, $2,925 in 2001–2002, and $3,685 in 2011–2012.

The $5,550 maximum Pell Grant in 2011–2012 was about equal to the 1976–1977 maximum grant of $1,400 after adjusting for inflation. The number of recipients in 2011–2012 was five times as high as it was in 1976–1977 (College Board, 2012b). About half of all 2010–2011 Pell Grant recipients were age 24 or older. Sixty percent of Pell Grant recipients are independent students. These data are shown graphically in Figure 3.3.

The American Opportunity Tax Credit (AOTC), introduced in 2009, increased the total tax savings for college students and their parents claiming education credits and tuition deductions from $7.0 billion (in 2011 dollars) in 2008 to $15.4 billion in 2009 and to $18.8 billion in 2010 (College Board, 2012b). Veterans' benefits and military aid increased from 19% to 27% of total federal grants over the decade from 2001–2002 to 2011–2012.

In 2011–2012, 44% of all grant aid (and 49% of undergraduate grant aid) came from the federal government. Ten years earlier, only 32% of all grant aid (and 37% of undergraduate grant aid) was federal (College Board, 2012b). Although the majority of aid was from the federal government in the form of loans, a significant amount of funding was available from other sources, including the states. In 2011–2012, 37% of all grant aid came from colleges and universities, 9% came from state governments, and 10% came from employers and other private sources.

There is a significant body of research on federal financial aid and whether that aid is effective in meeting its purposes of access and educational opportunity. Some of this research is descriptive, like the information from the College Board cited above, or historical summaries of financial aid such as McKeown's 1994 article that traces the role of federal financial aid. Other financial aid research addresses the issue of whether financial aid is effective, such as Gillen's 2009 research, or the work of Cornwall, Mustard and Sridhar (2006) and Mustard (2005) in Georgia, which evaluates the failure of the Georgia Hope Scholarship. Some of this research is politically motivated and advances a particular political position about the role of financial aid. Others are descriptions of the state of affairs.

As the Congress gears up for reauthorization of the Higher Education Act, all of the federal financial aid programs are likely to be scrutinized in detail, and certain agendas will be highly publicized. Groups such as the Lumina Foundation, the Bill and Melinda Gates Foundation, and the Washington higher education associations all have entered into the discussion on how federal financial aid should be revised to not only improve access to higher education but also increase the number of college graduates. It is in the context of a restricted Pell Grant program, with award amounts reduced for most students, that Congress will redo federal student financial aid.

For example, the Bill and Melinda Gates Foundation made grants to a group of 14 organizations working on postsecondary financial aid solutions. The 14 organizations are: Alliance for Excellent Education (AEE), Association of Public & Land-Grant Universities (APLU), Center for Law & Social Policy (CLASP), Committee for Economic Development (CED), Excelencia in Education (EE), HCM Strategists (HCM), Institute for Higher Education Policy (IHEP), National Association of Student Financial Aid Administrators (NASFAA), National College Access Network (NCAN), New America Foundation (NAF), The Education Trust (ET), The Institute for College Access & Success (TICAS), U.S. Chamber of Commerce's Institute for a Competitive Workforce (CofC-ICW), and Young Invincibles (YI). These grants, part of a project, Reimagining Aid Design and Delivery (RADD), resulted in "research" papers published in January and February 2013 on how financial aid can be redesigned to help more students be successful in college, with the goal of sparking a robust discussion about how financial aid can be used as a lever to increase student success, especially for low-income and middle-income students (Gates Foundation, 2012).

Analysis of these research reports indicates that these are basically policy papers, some of which are based on research into the question of how to make federal student financial aid an effective policy lever to improve student success, and some of which are backed by research on what programs are most effective in the quest to make federal student financial aid more efficient. Others are policy statements of the group writing or guiding the paper. The majority of the reports can be classified into policy themes revolving around reform of the Pell Grant program to target aid to low-income students, reform of student loans restricting amounts, simplification of the aid application process, reducing debt burdens, and reforming tax credits in a coordinated approach.

Table 3.3 lists the papers and their authors. Readers are encouraged to read the papers because of their implications for the process as Congress reauthorizes higher education aid in an era of sequestration. In addition, readers may wish to note the differences in presentation among the papers, some of which are short while others exceed 70 pages.

Presentation of research to a policy audience will be covered in more detail in Section IV.

A recent study by Dynarski and Scott-Clayton (2013) reviewed 50 years of financial aid practice and research to determine how well student aid programs work. They concluded that money matters for college access, and discounts work, although program complexity undermines aid effectiveness. The authors concluded that evidence on the effect of loans is limited and that academic incentives appear to improve aid effectiveness. However there already has been criticism of this study by other higher education researchers, leading to the conclusion that the jury is still out on the issue.

In the final analysis, this is a fertile area for research into the impacts of financial aid and for improvements in the way in which students and their families pay for postsecondary education. Little "good" research is available to judge what works and what just appears to work.

Table 3.3. Gates Funded Papers on Federal Financial Aid

Organization	Authors	Research Paper Title
AEE	Mercer, C., Roc, M. & DeBraun, B.	Repairing a Broken System: Fixing Federal Student Aid
APLU	Tanner, R.M.	Federal Student Aid: Access and Completion
CLASP	Reimherr, P. Harmon, T. Strawn, J. & Choitz, V.	Reforming Student Aid: How to Simplify Tax Aid and Use Performance Metrics to Improve College Choices and Completion
CED	CED	Boosting Postsecondary Education Performance
EIE	Santiago, D.A.	Using a Latino Lens to Reimagine Aid Design and Delivery
HCM	HCM	Doing Better for More Students: Putting Student Outcomes at the Center of Financial Aid
IHEP	Huelsman, M. & Cunningham, A.F.	Making Sense of the System: Financial Aid Reform for the 21st Century Student
NASFAA	NASFAA	Reimagining Financial Aid to Improve Student Access and Outcomes
NCAN	NCAS	Increasing Return on Investment from Federal Student Aid
NAF	Burd, S., Carey, K., Delisle, J., Fishman, l., Holt, A., Latinen, A. & McCann, C.	Rebalancing Resources and Incentives in Federal Student Aid
ET	Dannenberg, M. & Voight, M.	Doing Away with Debt: Using Existing Resources to Ensure College Affordability for Low and Middle-Income Families
TICAS	Abernathy, P., Asher, L., Cheng, D. Cochrane, D. Mais, J. & Thompson, J.	Aligning the Means and Ends: How to Improve Federal Student Aid and Increase College Access and Success
CofC-ICW	ICW	Redesigning Federal Financial Aid
YI	Mishory, J. & O'Sullivan, R.	The Student Perspective on Federal Financial Aid Reform

CHAPTER 4

INSTITUTIONAL REVENUES AND EXPENDITURES

Chapter 3 discussed institutional revenues that are student expenditures or costs, as well as institutional expenditures in the form of scholarships, fellowships, and loans that become revenues for students, as was documented in the introduction to this section. This chapter focuses on other institutional revenues and expenditures and includes information on how colleges and universities develop their revenue and expenditure budgets, restricted revenue in the form of contracts and grants for activities such as research, and how state allocations to institutions are determined. The funding formulas or models that allocate state appropriations in many states (both to public and private institutions) are discussed in Chapter 5.

Before we begin the discussion on those institutional revenues and expenditures that were not discussed in Chapter 3, let us quickly review some of the data issues that make research in college and university revenues and expenditures difficult. As was discussed in Chapter 2, prior to 1995, all colleges and universities classified and reported their revenues and expenditures according to generally accepted accounting principles (GAAP) for colleges and universities. There was no difference between the financial reports of public and private institutions. After 1995, there are differences in financial reports for institutions that report under GASB (most public institutions) and under FASB (private institutions and some public).

Higher Education Finance Research: Policy, Politics, and Practice, pp. 91–118
Copyright © 2014 by Information Age Publishing

Revenue categories under GASB were changed so that state, local, and federal appropriations are not considered an operating revenue but continue to be operating revenues for institutions reporting under FASB. Care must be exercised when comparing institutional revenues to ensure that the proverbial "apples" are being compared to "apples." Specifically, it is not correct to compare total operating revenues for institutions reporting under GASB to operating revenues of those operating under FASB, without first ensuring that all the revenue sources are included for both groups with the exception of capital revenues, which should be excluded for both FASB and GASB institutions. We discussed the changes to the reporting of tuition and fee revenues and auxiliary enterprises in Chapter 3, and these changes should be carefully adjusted in longitudinal studies. Also, in longitudinal studies, revenues from years prior to the change to New GASB must be equated to the New GASB, or vice versa.

On the expenditure side, the basic functional expenditure categories reported on the forms have not changed, with the exceptions of depreciation and operation and maintenance of plant. FASB does not consider operation and maintenance of plant as a separate function but rather allocates these expenses to the other functions such as instruction, research, public service, and academic support. Operation and maintenance (O&M) of plant is a distinct functional category on the Old Form and on the New GASB, although O&M is distributed across the other functional categories. This difference causes an otherwise comparable FASB institution to have higher expenses in functions such as instruction than a New GASB or an Old Form reporter. However, these differences can be accommodated by careful researchers. These are important caveats when conducting research on college and university revenues and expenditures.

Depreciation is a new concept for public higher education institutions after the FASB change. It is included in the FASB form and the New GASB form. Depreciation (a system of allocating the cost of long-lived assets over the time they are expected to be used) is calculated and expensed for items such as equipment, vehicles, and furnishings, as well as buildings. Essentially no expenses related to building purchases or construction appear in the Old Form because they were outside the scope of the form (plant fund). Equipment, vehicle, and furniture purchases appear as expenditures in the year they occurred in the Old Form. This change makes it extremely difficult to crosswalk from the Old Form to either FASB or New GASB.

Conducting research on the revenues and expenditures of colleges and universities is fraught with many perils because of the differences in reporting among institutions, states, and systems of higher education. In the sections that follow, we will examine revenues and expenditures, provide data sources, and note places where care must be taken to ensure quality research results.

REVENUES

As discussed earlier, the four main sources of revenues for colleges and universities are students and their families who pay tuition and fees; state and local governments through appropriations and other grants; the federal government through appropriations, financial aid, and other grants; and gifts and endowments. We discussed revenues from tuition and fees and federal, state, and other grants as student financial aid in the preceding chapter, and so this chapter focuses on the other sources of revenue.

Table 4.1 displays all revenues for higher education by sector in 2009–2010, along with the percent share of total revenues. Net tuition and fees provided 27% of the revenues for all institutions of higher education in 2009–2010, but the percentages varied widely by sector. Tuition and fee revenues made up 18% of public institutional revenues, 33% of private, non-profit revenues, but 91% of private, for-profit revenues. State and local appropriations, grants, and contracts comprised 19% of all institutional revenues, but 31% of public institutional revenues, 1% of private, non-profit revenues, and less than 1% of for-profit institutional revenues. Federal appropriations, grants, and contracts comprised 15% of total revenues, 17% of public revenues, 14% of private, non-profit revenues, and 8% of private, for-profit. Private gifts, grants, and contracts and investment return together comprised 5% of public institutions' revenues but 8% of private, non-profit revenues (Snyder & Dillow, 2012).

Federal Revenues: Federal Appropriations and Contracts and Grants

For almost 150 years, the federal government has been one of the major sources of funding for both public and private colleges and universities not only through student financial aid, but also through direct appropriations for both operations and capital projects, and through federal grants and contracts for research. Table 1.6 showed that federal support increased from $4.6 million, or 6% of total revenues, in 1910 to $28.4 billion, or 6%, 100 years later. In terms of share of revenues, 1945 marked the high point when federal revenues were 30% of all higher education revenues (Snyder, 1993). The numbers are not totally comparable though, given the change in the way that Pell Grants are included

Table 4.1. Total Revenues for Higher Education Institutions by Sector, 2009–2010

Revenue Source	Total $	Total %	Public $	Public %	Private Non-profit $	Private Non-profit %	Private for-Profit $	Private for-Profit %
Total	496,703,609	100%	303,329,538	100%	168,689,242	100%	24,684,829	100%
Net Student tuition and fees	134,660,394	27%	55,930,482	18%	56,355,862	33%	22,374,050	91%
Federal appropriations, grants, and contracts	76,154,992	15%	51,289,997	17%	22,913,792	14%	1,951,202	8%
State appropriations, grants, and contracts	74,319,548	15%	72,483,814	24%	1,721,659	1%	114,075	0%
Local appropriations, grants, and contracts	20,277,167	4%	19,805,742	7%	471,425	0%	0	0%
Private gifts grants, and contracts	27,712,020	6%	5,876,450	2%	18,017,260	11%	38,299	0%
Investment return	38,512,306	8%	10,046,610	3%	28,425,581	17%	40,115	0%
Educational activities	20,071,688	4%	14,814,344	5%	4,821,825	3%	435,519	2%
Auxiliary enterprises	36,739,245	7%	22,173,700	7%	14,080,329	8%	485,216	2%
Hospitals	45,778,392	9%	29,236,931	10%	16,541,461	10%	0	0%
Other	22,477,857	5%	21,671,469	7%	5,340,047	3%	-753,647	-3%

Source: Snyder and Dillow (2012).

in university reporting. Nevertheless, the federal government has been an important source of funding for the last 100 years.

With the passage of the Morrill Act of 1862, the federal government believed that it had endowed an educational system that eliminated the need for continued federal funding (McCarthy & Hines, 1986). As we now know, that was not the outcome. Between 1910 and 1940, the federal government provided between 4 and 7% of funding, mostly to the land grant colleges started by the two Morrill Acts (Snyder, 1993). During World War II federal funding reached a high of 30% of higher education funding, some earmarked for research, and some for training programs specifically contracted by the federal government. After the war, the proportion of revenues coming from the federal government began to decline, dipping to 14% in 1955–1956. After some rises during the early 1960s, the proportion of revenues from the federal government began a long, slow slide to 10% in 1989–1990, and to 6% in 2010. Federal support did average about 12% of college and university budgets between 1920 and 1982 (McCarthy & Hines, 1986).

The majority of federal funding since the 1950s has been for student financial aid, beginning with the G.I. Bill and continuing through the National Defense Act of 1958 and the Higher Education Act of 1972 and its reauthorizations. The federal government also funds a number of workforce programs through the Perkins, WIA, and TAA programs, most of which are formula-funded, with states receiving a percentage share in some cases based on their population. However, the federal government does provide a significant amount of funding for land grant programs and for research. Land grant funds are distributed based on a formula that considers the population of the state. Most of other federal funding is provided to large public and private research universities and is distributed through competitive grants.

In addition to competitive grant funding, the federal government provides earmarked funding to campuses for special programs or for buildings. Earmarks are often referred to as "pork" and are inserted into appropriations bills by a member of Congress for use generally in his or her home district or home state. *The Chronicle of Higher Education* maintains a database on earmark funding for colleges and universities, and these data may be accessed for a particular college to determine if the college received earmark funding. In 2008, 2,300 earmarks were granted to 920 institutions, totaling about $2.25 billion (Chronicle of Higher Education, 2008). In 1998, federal spending on earmarks totaled $528 million (Brainard & Hermes, 2008). Earmarks are not regulated, and there is little study of their impact on higher education institutions. Delaney (2011) studied the relationship between earmark funding and state appropriations for higher education to determine if state funds are reduced, increased to augment the federal funds, or have no impact on state appropriations. She concluded that for every dollar increase in federal earmarks received, state appropriations increased from $1.98 to $4.75, depending on how appropriations were measured.

Data on federal funding of higher education can be obtained from a variety of sources that were listed in Table 2.6, including the Institute for Education Sciences, the National Science Foundation, the National Institutes of Health, the *Chronicle of Higher Education*, and the Department of Labor. Also state governing and coordinating boards, as well as each institution, provide information on the sources of funds in their budgets. Analyses of these data generally are descriptive in nature; for example, the National Science Foundation issues an annual report on the federal funding of institutions of higher education without much analysis. Institutions use these data to compare their research funding to that of their peers. The Carnegie Foundation also uses the data to place institutions into the Carnegie categories listed in Table 1.2.

State and Local Appropriations

State and local governments have supported higher education since the first days of Harvard College, when the college received the proceeds from the toll for crossing the Charles River (Rudolph, 1990). Four of the 37 first institutions founded before 1800, including the University of North Carolina, the University of Georgia, and the University of Virginia, were state-supported institutions. Public colleges also expanded in the first half of the 19th century, and by 1860, there were 21 state colleges in 20 different states whose funding was predominately from state and local sources (Rudolph, 1990).

With the advent of normal schools in the 1800s, state funding increased to around 30% of total funding between 1909–1910 and 1931–1932 and then fell significantly during the Great Depression of the 1930s (Snyder, 1993). Normal schools were designed to help prepare teachers for the expanding school systems. The first of the normal schools was founded in 1823. Later, in 1839, Horace Mann established the first public normal school in Massachusetts. These schools typically offered a 2-year program. The proportion of revenues from state sources increased in the 1950s, 1960s, and 1970s, and by 1980, state support alone accounted for 30% of all income for higher education, including private institutions. It should be remembered that states, especially on the east coast, provided funding for private institutions, many by a funding formula such as those used by New York and Maryland, to maintain a diverse system of higher education. Local government support for institutions of higher education has remained relatively constant as a percent of the total budget since 1920, averaging about 3% of total higher education revenues (McCarthy & Hines, 1986).

Table 4.2 displays state higher education appropriations from FY 1988 to FY 2013 and includes appropriations for public and private institutions as well as for student financial aid. Over this 25 year period, state appropriations increased from $34.3 billion in FY 1988 to $72.0 billion in FY 2013 (Grapevine, various years). However, state appropriations across all 50 states reached a peak of $80.7 billion in FY 2008 (SHEEO, 2012) and dropped precipitously to $73.7 billion 2 years later, reflecting the state of the national economy.

Note that these totals for state appropriations are not the same as those reported by NCES in the *Digest of Education Statistics, 2012*. NCES reported that state appropriations were $57.6 billion in FY 2000, compared to $56.7 billion reported by Grapevine. Similarly, NCES reported $74.3 billion in FY 2010 compared to $73.7 billion reported by Grapevine. The Census Bureau has numbers similar to the NCES numbers. These differences in data may be related to the point at which data are reported. Grapevine data are reported by the state coordinating or governing boards early in the fiscal year; that is, Grapevine data are reported by November of the fiscal year. NCES data are reported after the fiscal year is completed and include any mid-year changes to appropriations, including employee benefits that may not be known at the point at which Grapevine data are reported. The main benefit of the Grapevine data is its timeliness.

Table 4.3 displays the percentage change in state appropriations over 25 years, 5 years, 2 years, and 1 year. Over 25 years, the average state increase was 109% and varied from a low of 17% in Massachusetts to a high of 320% in Nevada. Over the last 5 years, the average state appropriations decreased 11%, varying from a decrease of 37% in Arizona to an increase of 35% in North Dakota. Over the last 2 years, the average change was 0.0%, varying from a decrease of 8% in Florida to an increase of 14% in Wyoming. Finally, between FY 2012 and FY 2013, state appropriations decreased 5% on average, varying from a decrease of 38% in New Hampshire to an increase of 7% in Montana (McKeown-Moak, 2013b).

Another way of examining state support for higher education is to examine appropriations per capita and appropriations per $1,000 of personal income as measures of effort. Effort is a statistic often used in court cases on the equity of funding or in desegregation court cases (McKeown-Moak, 2006b). Grapevine displays the per capita and per $1,000 of personal income numbers for FY 2012 and FY 2013 in its report for FY 2013. Table 4.4 displays state appropriations per capita and per $1,000 of personal income for FY 2008, 2012, and 2013. Effort has decreased since FY 2008; the national average funding per $1,000 of personal income

Table 4.2. State Appropriations for Higher Education, FY 1988 Through FY 2013 (dollars in thousands)

State	FY1988 State Approp.	FY1998 State Approp.	FY2000 State Approp.	FY2008 State Approp.	FY2010 State Approp.	FY2011 State Approp.	FY2012 State Approp.	FY2013 State Approp.
Alabama	669,992	974,992	1,094,839	1,961,808	1,423,842	1,424,917	1,494,583	1,405,064
Alaska	150,190	168,614	176,494	298,615	333,415	342,154	357,025	365,195
Arizona	490,301	787,659	865,828	1,325,906	1,088,562	1,087,837	823,654	840,321
Arkansas	270,530	516,971	605,439	879,882	882,692	901,799	894,531	906,501
California	5,111,825	6,379,332	7,683,934	11,620,239	9,993,730	11,004,708	9,379,003	8,843,276
Colorado	441,070	651,419	719,221	747,481	448,293	676,318	647,496	640,629
Connecticut	414,174	577,502	699,290	1,034,481	1,064,476	1,076,131	949,946	957,256
Delaware	101,339	155,128	175,621	243,130	226,646	212,456	213,194	216,493
Florida	1,367,174	2,248,424	2,785,631	4,448,930	3,665,469	3,766,832	3,631,070	3,341,629
Georgia	759,404	1,383,597	1,560,155	2,959,754	2,608,183	2,899,569	2,635,157	2,757,056
Hawaii	243,118	348,407	342,247	554,292	523,279	489,556	512,328	513,517
Idaho	139,136	248,249	279,390	410,596	352,039	343,297	333,670	360,071
Illinois	1,332,240	2,250,609	2,554,402	2,948,632	3,291,307	3,251,432	3,594,470	3,566,692
Indiana	705,577	1,091,733	1,226,677	1,525,217	1,561,530	1,564,731	1,549,460	1,555,283
Iowa	441,369	743,226	826,589	873,724	757,896	758,712	740,352	787,420
Kansas	361,178	562,484	622,198	825,698	753,701	754,759	739,612	759,216
Kentucky	494,949	717,175	924,048	1,320,540	1,214,580	1,230,451	1,237,726	1,178,977
Louisiana	494,506	725,989	885,055	1,707,668	1,303,920	1,292,584	1,237,070	1,175,660
Maine	141,411	185,929	213,454	271,117	259,467	266,112	269,153	264,065
Maryland	614,216	875,428	1,042,683	1,555,048	1,600,560	1,615,987	1,609,180	1,612,476

(Table continues on next page)

98

Table 4.2. Continued

State	FY1988 State Approp.	FY1998 State Approp.	FY2000 State Approp.	FY2008 State Approp.	FY2010 State Approp.	FY2011 State Approp.	FY2012 State Approp.	FY2013 State Approp.
Massachusetts	894,998	906,702	1,047,475	1,347,345	978,455	1,138,650	1,049,107	1,049,107
Michigan	1,303,202	1,827,908	2,073,579	2,033,709	1,837,466	1,869,659	1,547,833	1,596,325
Minnesota	815,663	1,180,519	1,280,627	1,560,644	1,425,439	1,381,065	1,283,690	1,285,247
Mississippi	360,036	727,918	917,087	1,045,937	1,006,477	932,495	954,184	924,953
Missouri	503,019	838,559	977,626	1,021,705	980,393	959,556	933,329	931,240
Montana	110,380	126,734	138,477	196,548	171,514	172,375	202,105	202,188
Nebraska	227,974	415,858	473,939	657,012	641,402	653,935	650,437	659,571
Nevada	112,551	291,721	305,983	620,033	396,485	550,169	473,148	472,368
New Hampshire	66,901	88,813	96,428	133,093	138,883	137,555	82,698	85,622
New Jersey	970,459	1,352,032	1,519,546	2,044,508	2,009,930	2,050,400	1,998,300	1,888,439
New Mexico	262,813	484,858	544,091	1,016,381	887,961	835,346	798,972	799,406
New York	2,874,893	2,851,604	3,126,582	4,853,313	4,760,680	4,750,906	4,718,901	4,989,658
North Carolina	1,284,076	2,007,092	2,293,097	3,837,233	3,768,537	3,947,442	3,914,552	4,092,304
North Dakota	115,723	171,690	187,459	253,901	311,677	311,678	343,964	343,806
Ohio	1,265,213	1,863,307	2,060,555	2,288,295	1,996,930	1,994,909	2,013,731	2,039,964
Oklahoma	386,265	666,024	739,520	1,098,881	1,077,228	1,046,030	997,857	981,069
Oregon	349,940	551,133	650,142	725,762	642,906	626,985	566,032	582,208
Pennsylvania	1,173,572	1,715,676	1,879,605	2,193,274	2,031,695	2,008,025	1,800,947	1,792,655
Rhode Island	117,921	138,813	150,790	191,330	159,761	157,434	160,767	164,147
South Carolina	521,016	744,238	812,709	1,211,068	924,157	814,866	859,409	942,770

(Table continues on next page)

Table 4.2. Continued

State	FY1988 State Approp.	FY1998 State Approp.	FY2000 State Approp.	FY2008 State Approp.	FY2010 State Approp.	FY2011 State Approp.	FY2012 State Approp.	FY2013 State Approp.
South Dakota	73,731	120,649	130,345	198,949	187,178	185,251	181,016	190,251
Tennessee	636,948	904,670	984,860	1,639,551	1,490,255	1,659,586	1,414,996	1,455,169
Texas	2,231,787	3,559,663	4,093,434	6,347,753	6,434,942	6,270,812	6,464,047	6,425,707
Utah	257,218	469,938	546,774	812,338	687,173	696,896	728,923	748,759
Vermont	49,990	56,991	63,378	90,801	93,255	93,732	90,026	87,996
Virginia	915,836	1,153,457	1,480,258	1,885,553	1,727,005	1,702,243	1,624,027	1,703,083
Washington	710,143	1,103,896	1,238,035	1,768,291	1,572,442	1,592,882	1,361,782	1,372,858
West Virginia	237,404	352,763	372,505	562,253	492,835	500,524	543,309	545,761
Wisconsin	705,430	1,001,525	1,075,238	1,242,537	1,247,697	1,330,088	1,153,559	1,182,780
Wyoming	114,560	135,034	139,711	290,508	307,864	344,287	337,989	384,199
National Total or Average	34,393,361	49,402,652	56,683,050	80,681,264	73,742,209	75,676,124	72,098,316	71,966,407

Sources: Grapevine, various years; SHEEO (2011).

decreased from $6.59 in FY 2008 to $5.60 in FY 2012 and $5.42 in FY 2013. Similarly, the national average of appropriations per capita decreased from $257.46 in FY 2008 to $231.85 in FY 2012 and to $229.72 in FY 2013. Part of the decline is due to an increase in the population in some states.

The State Higher Education Executive Officers (SHEEO) publishes an annual report, *State Higher Education Finance (SHEF)*. *SHEF* provides information on policy issues in state higher education finance and includes analyses of funding that consider state wealth, tax effort, and other indicators. These research reports are used by policymakers who want information on their state's relative position on higher education funding. *SHEF* may be accessed at www.sheeo.org Grapevine data are now collected jointly with SHEEO for the *SHEF* reports. Up until 2008 Grapevine also contained detailed data on the appropriations to each institution for most states, but since combining with *SHEF*, these detailed data are no longer collected.

SHEF is an important resource for those doing research on higher education funding. In addition to the data on appropriations, tax effort, and state wealth, *SHEF* includes tables on full-time equivalent (FTE) enrollment in public higher education, appropriations per FTE, the percent change in appropriations per FTE, net tuition revenues as a percentage of total public higher education revenues, total educational revenues per FTE, and the methods used to calculate these numbers. SHEEO staff members then analyze the data in an interesting scatterplot format that places each state's condition into an easy-to-understand presentation. The data on state wealth and tax effort also are displayed in a manner that makes the information accessible for policymakers. As we discuss in Section 4, presentation to a policy audience requires a different orientation than presentation to an academic audience. The *SHEF* reports provide a format that appeals to both audiences.

One of the measures that *SHEF* uses to gauge state funding for higher education is to examine the sum of the revenues available from state and local appropriations and from net tuition revenues. This is an important concept when comparing among states because states differ in their philosophies of funding higher education. As was mentioned in Chapter 3, some states have a philosophy of low tuition and low financial aid, while other states are high tuition, high financial aid. Some states therefore provide a greater share of institutional funding, while others provide relatively low appropriations to institutions, resulting in higher tuition. Goldin and Katz (1999) found that these relationships are closely related to when the state joined the Union and to a history of private higher education institutions in the state that did not receive the majority of their funding from the state.

Table 4.3. Percent Change in
State Appropriations for Higher Education

State	25 Yr. Change	5 Yr. Change 2008–2013	1 Yr. Change 2012–2013	2 Yr. Change 2011–2013
Alabama	110%	–28%	–6%	–1%
Alaska	143%	22%	2%	7%
Arizona	71%	–37%	2%	–23%
Arkansas	235%	3%	1%	1%
California	73%	–24%	–6%	–20%
Colorado	45%	–14%	–1%	–5%
Connecticut	131%	–7%	1%	–11%
Delaware	114%	–11%	2%	2%
Florida	144%	–25%	–8%	–11%
Georgia	263%	–7%	5%	–5%
Hawaii	111%	–7%	0%	5%
Idaho	159%	–12%	8%	5%
Illinois	168%	21%	–1%	10%
Indiana	120%	2%	0%	–1%
Iowa	78%	–10%	6%	4%
Kansas	110%	–8%	3%	1%
Kentucky	138%	–11%	–5%	–4%
Louisiana	138%	–31%	–5%	–9%
Maine	87%	–3%	–2%	–1%
Maryland	163%	4%	0%	0%
Massachusetts	17%	–22%	0%	–8%
Michigan	22%	–22%	3%	–15%
Minnesota	58%	–18%	0%	–7%
Mississippi	157%	–12%	–3%	–1%
Missouri	85%	– 9%	0%	–3%
Montana	83%	3%	0%	17%
Nebraska	189%	0%	1%	1%
Nevada	320%	–24%	0%	–14%
New Hampshire	28%	–36%	4%	–38%
New Jersey	95%	–8%	–5%	–8%
New Mexico	204%	–21%	0%	–4%
New York	74%	3%	6%	5%
North Carolina	219%	7%	5%	4%
North Dakota	197%	35%	0%	10%
Ohio	61%	–11%	1%	2%
Oklahoma	154%	–11%	–2%	–6%
Oregon	66%	–20%	3%	–7%

(Table continues on next page)

Table 4.3.   Continued

State	25 Yr. Change	5 Yr. Change 2008–2013	1 Yr. Change 2012–2013	2 Yr. Change 2011–2013
Pennsylvania	53%	−18%	0%	−11%
Rhode Island	39%	−14%	2%	4%
South Carolina	81%	−22%	10%	16%
South Dakota	158%	−4%	5%	3%
Tennessee	128%	−11%	3%	−12%
Texas	188%	1%	−1%	2%
Utah	191%	−8%	3%	7%
Vermont	76%	−3%	−2%	−6%
Virginia	86%	−10%	5%	0%
Washington	93%	−22%	1%	−14%
West Virginia	130%	−3%	0%	9%
Wisconsin	68%	−5%	3%	−11%
Wyoming	235%	32%	14%	12%
National Total or Average	109%	−11%	0%	−5%
Minimum	17%	−37%	−8%	−38%
Maximum	320%	35%	14%	17%

Source: Calculated from Grapevine data.

The National Science Foundation (NSF) also regularly tracks statistics related to government spending on universities, especially at research universities, and issued a report in October 2012 depicting cuts in per student state support at major research universities over the past decade as a threat to the country's long-term economic health (Baskin, 2012). NSF indicated that it was critical for policymakers in the states to understand that cuts to higher education funding endanger the U.S. economy.

In addition, the National Center for Higher Education Management Systems (NCHEMS) published several analyses of state funding for higher education. NCHEMS reports on funding specifically may be found at www.higheredinfo.org as well on the NCHEMS website, www.nchems.org. NCHEMS reports for each state an evaluation of whether institutions of higher education were using resources efficiently and other measures of effectiveness in an easy-to-use web format. The College Board's publication, *Trends in College Pricing 2012*, also includes an analysis of state funding for higher education, and the reader is encouraged to examine these studies for examples of well-designed research on state appropriations, tuition and fees, and resources for higher education.

Table 4.4.   State Appropriations Per $1,000 of Personal Income and Per Capita, 2008, 2012, 2013

States	2008 Per $1,000 in Personal Income	2008 Per Capita	2012 Per $1,000 in Personal Income	2012 Per Capita	2013 Per $1,000 in Personal Income	2013 Per Capita
Alabama	12.97	418.45	8.94	311.13	8.19	291.38
Alaska	10.68	460.55	10.87	493.22	10.77	499.28
Arizona	6.10	200.01	3.63	127.36	3.57	128.23
Arkansas	10.15	302.65	9.06	304.41	8.88	307.38
California	7.31	302.63	5.70	248.89	5.21	232.46
Colorado	3.71	151.75	2.87	126.56	2.74	123.49
Connecticut	5.24	282.51	4.56	264.85	4.54	266.62
Delaware	7.01	281.15	5.64	234.76	5.60	236.06
Florida	5.41	206.36	4.79	190.29	4.32	172.98
Georgia	7.63	252.57	7.47	268.55	7.59	277.93
Hawaii	11.11	431.90	8.71	371.76	8.39	368.82
Idaho	8.50	265.88	6.40	210.68	6.73	225.65
Illinois	5.64	227.16	6.37	279.51	6.18	277.02
Indiana	7.20	240.89	6.68	237.78	6.44	237.91
Iowa	8.42	294.85	5.89	241.62	6.06	256.14
Kansas	8.07	297.44	6.31	257.67	6.37	263.08
Kentucky	10.18	316.48	8.35	283.44	7.68	269.15
Louisiana	11.71	385.94	7.01	270.41	6.48	255.47
Maine	6.22	208.60	5.31	202.59	5.03	198.67
Maryland	6.10	280.04	5.46	275.56	5.31	274.02
Massachusetts	3.35	163.03	2.95	158.79	2.91	157.85
Michigan	5.83	202.88	4.35	156.71	4.33	161.52
Minnesota	7.43	303.43	5.38	240.06	5.22	238.93
Mississippi	12.69	357.42	10.03	320.47	9.41	309.87
Missouri	4.65	159.05	4.09	155.32	3.99	154.64
Montana	6.12	197.84	5.63	202.58	5.40	201.15
Nebraska	9.50	347.15	8.33	353.07	8.20	355.46
Nevada	6.23	250.04	4.69	173.95	4.60	171.21
New Hampshire	2.45	101.54	1.36	62.75	1.38	64.83
New Jersey	4.81	234.88	4.32	226.19	3.99	213.03
New Mexico	15.65	488.05	11.24	384.37	10.93	383.31

(Table continues on next page)

Table 4.4. Continued

	2008		2012		2013	
States	*Per $1,000 in Personal Income*	*Per Capita*	*Per $1,000 in Personal Income*	*Per Capita*	*Per $1,000 in Personal Income*	*Per Capita*
New York	5.70	266.17	4.74	241.97	4.93	254.96
North Carolina	12.35	413.38	11.25	405.61	11.44	419.63
North Dakota	11.51	401.49	10.78	502.33	9.87	491.41
Ohio	5.98	207.36	4.63	174.48	4.50	176.71
Oklahoma	8.29	280.64	7.02	263.69	6.64	257.17
Oregon	5.55	192.23	3.89	146.33	3.86	149.31
Pennsylvania	4.58	176.41	3.34	141.32	3.24	140.45
Rhode Island	4.35	170.33	3.47	153.02	3.49	156.29
South Carolina	7.21	221.18	5.49	183.90	5.86	199.58
South Dakota	6.94	235.73	4.98	219.79	5.12	228.30
Tennessee	6.68	221.22	6.04	221.10	6.00	225.39
Texas	6.85	253.44	6.29	252.19	6.01	246.58
Utah	9.68	301.76	7.74	259.00	7.62	262.24
Vermont	3.91	141.96	3.45	143.68	3.26	140.57
Virginia	5.90	242.56	4.36	200.39	4.45	208.05
Washington	6.93	276.28	4.56	199.58	4.40	199.05
West Virginia	8.38	245.68	8.76	292.90	8.51	294.15
Wisconsin	6.33	227.03	5.10	202.03	5.09	206.55
Wyoming	12.42	536.96	12.47	595.73	13.68	666.54
National Average	6.59	257.46	5.60	231.85	5.42	229.72
Minimum	2.45	101.54	1.36	62.75	1.38	64.83
Maximum	15.65	536.96	12.47	595.73	13.68	666.54

Source: Grapevine (2008 & 2013).

The Southern Regional Education Board (SREB) and the Western Interstate Commission on Higher Education (WICHE) both publish fact books on higher education that are compendia on higher education indicators, funding, and statistics. Both SREB and WICHE compare funding by institutional type for institutions within their region and are an excellent source of good data that are collected in a robust research effort. Significant effort is expended to ensure that the data are comparable across states.

Unfortunately, there is not a similar body of research and data on funding from local appropriations. Community and technical colleges receive almost all local appropriations, although there are a few 4-year institutions, such as Washburn University and Wichita State University, that receive local appropriations. Until 2008, Grapevine included data on local funding, but there was very little analysis included with the descriptive data, and local appropriations for 4-year institutions were not part of the data provided. *The Digest of Education Statistics* includes a detailing of local appropriations by state, and this is the best source for national data. Data on local appropriations by state generally can be obtained from the state community college coordinating board for those states where community colleges receive local funds, and the American Association of Community Colleges also maintains some data files available at www.aacc.nche.edu.

Community and technical colleges in 25 states do not receive local appropriations or local tax revenues for their operations. Table 1.6 showed that local appropriations for higher education increased from $24.4 million in FY 1940 to $6.5 billion in FY 2000 and to $20.3 billion in FY 2010. This may seem like a very large increase, but it is important to remember that the number of students at 2-year colleges also increased from less than 200,000 in 1940 to 2.1 million by 1970, 5.7 million in FY 2000, and to 7.7 million in FY 2010.

State and Local Methods of Funding Higher Education

How do states and local governments decide how to fund higher education institutions and how much that funding should be? State budgeting for higher education has been said to resemble a family's attic: everything is added, but nothing is thrown away (Burke, 2004). Burke and Serban (1998a) noted that state resource allocation has objectives that have varied over the decades, from adequacy in the 1950s, distributive growth in the 1960s, redistributive equity in the 1970s, quality in the 1980s, and to accountability/reform in the 1990s. Caruthers and Marks (1994), however, claimed that each decade's new objective to be served by the state funding process became an additional rather than a replacement objective.

The state and local funding process usually takes four basic forms: formula, incremental (or decremental), initiative, and performance funding. States use one or all of these forms for the budget stages of preparation, justification, and allocation. However, in the final analysis, available resources determine the final allocation to higher education.

Formula funding actually is a form of zero-based funding that considers complex ratios, such as enrollment by level and academic discipline; the number of faculty, staff, and students; and gross square feet of buildings by building type. Calculations in formula funding have become more complex in the pursuit of adequacy and equity, the chief purposes of formula budgeting and resource allocation (McKeown, 1996a). Chapter 5 will discuss formula funding in detail.

Incremental funding builds on base budgets of historical costs and adds (or subtracts) funds for enrollment growth or decline, inflation, and special initiatives, depending on the availability of state resources. Although formula funding and incremental funding appear to be different, in reality they both reach essentially the same conclusion (Burke, 2004). Many states used formulas to set a base budget and then consider changes in enrollments and inflation. In the past, the bottom line in state resource allocation is that the allocation reflects current costs, student enrollment, and inflation (Caruthers & Marks, 1994).

The third form of state and local funding for higher education is the funding for special initiatives. This form really is incremental funding for special projects and was used by Ohio and Virginia, among other states, to fund certain items that were of special interest to the states' economies. Initiative funding provided up-front money to encourage a campus activity based on future promises (such as more nurse graduates) rather than achieved results (Burke & Serban, 1998a). However, almost all initiative programs were eliminated by the budget problems of the states. Although campus leaders favored initiative funding, when faced with budget cuts, they opted to fund their first priority, the funding of base budgets. Special initiatives generally funded only some campuses, while base budgets benefited all colleges and universities, so funding the base budget received more support not only from campus leaders but also from legislators who had campuses in their districts.

Whichever the budget approach among the first three methods, enrollments really were the driving factor in state funding for public colleges and universities. During the years of enrollment growth in the 1970s, these approaches brought additional funding to campuses, at least in states with increasing state revenues. However, in the 1980s, enrollments at many campuses became stable or declined, and so additional funding was limited. Some colleges did have increasing enrollments, but limited state resources made fully funding enrollment growth not possible.

To mitigate the impact of decreasing, or increasing, enrollment, many states began to fund enrollments by using a 3-year rolling average. There are three ways to calculate a rolling average. One is to give each year equal weight by adding up the 3 years of data and dividing by three. A second way is to allow for the more recent years to account for a larger proportion of the enrollments by weighting the 3 years of data by differential amounts such as 20, 30 and 50% respectively. The third example is the reverse, where the most recent year has the least influence, resulting in weighting enrollment data by 50, 30, and 20% respectively. These weights, or alternatives (25/25/50, 20/20/60, etc.), have differing impacts that may be exacerbated by increasing or decreasing enrollment trends. Some state legislators prefer the third example, weighting actual enrollments more heavily than budgeted or predicted enrollments.

For example, during a period of enrollment increase, a college would benefit most from a 20/30/50 weighing approach, where greater weight is given to the most recent enrollments, as compared to an approach that treats each year equally (33/33/33) or where the most recent year influences the calculation the least (50/30/20). In times of decreasing enrollments, the outcome reverses, however, and the weighting approach where the most recent year influences the calculation least (50/30/20) results in the lowest weighed total.

The budget crisis of the early 1990s produced major shifts in state allocations and budgeting away from equity and adequacy toward goals or objectives of accountability and efficiency (McKeown, 1996a). This shift in the 1990s led to the popularity, at least in the late 1990s, for the fourth type of state budgeting: performance budgeting or performance funding.

As previously discussed, state budgets for higher education traditionally were based on input measures (i.e., enrollments) rather than outcomes or, alternately, resources rather than results. Although the traditional methods of funding used workload measures, such as the credit hours offered or the number of staff, the focus on inputs encouraged institutions to enroll students in courses and not be concerned with satisfactory completion of the courses or other outcomes. The performance funding movement sought to change this focus, by tying funding directly to the institutional outcomes measured.

Although performance funding peaked in the late 1990s, in the early 2010s, performance funding is back as a major way to allocate state resources to higher education. One of the main differences between performance-based funding in the 1990s and in 2013 is the change in the focus from meeting the needs of higher education to meeting the needs of students, the state, and its economy.

Performance funding prior to 2000 generally was linked to, and a component of, the funding formula for higher education institutions. In the first part of the 21st century, however, funding formulas for public higher education underwent a radical change. State after state shifted their funding formulas from the old methods to a new wave of formulas that examine the need for public resources for colleges and universities in a fundamentally different way.

As the national economy went into a period of recession in the last half of the first decade of the 21st century, state appropriations for higher education declined and, in some cases, declined more than 20%. Because higher education enrollments are counter-cyclical, enrollments increased while state appropriations decreased, putting significant pressures on institutional budgets. At the same time, there was a national focus on performance and on increasing the numbers of college "completers" as a means of improving the economy. Indeed, in 2013, developing and implementing state performance-based higher education funding systems has been identified as one of the top ten policy issues facing higher education (AASCU, 2013). These funding formulas dominate the current higher education policy landscape—33 states have expressed interest or are currently implementing performance-based funding systems, up from fewer than 10 states just 2 years ago.

Performance funding takes away the traditional bottom line of determining appropriations based on enrollments—performance funding bases funding on completions and other indicators of institutional performance. In general, not all state appropriations are based on performance indicators; rather, it is a small part of the budget allocation, usually 5 to 10%, that is performance funding. In recent years, when state appropriations have been decreasing, performance funding has been limited. Even in Tennessee, which purports to fund 100% on performance, there is a substantial base budget that is protected in the state appropriations process. Performance funding is discussed in detail in Chapter 7.

Local funding for higher education in general follows the same process as that of state funding, with allocations based on formulas, incremental funding, or special allocations. There have been no reports of local funding being based on performance yet. However, local funding may be limited by state law. For example, in Texas, the amount of the local levy for a community college is restricted by law and limited to certain percentage levies that vary based on voter approval of the levy. In Arizona, state laws related to the community colleges limit the ability of a district to spend tax funds. The limitation does not include funds from tuition and fees, federal funds, bond proceeds, debt service, and state capital funding. Expenditure limits are adjusted annually to reflect changes in student enrollments and in inflation. Limits are calculated using FY 1980 as the base and are calculated by taking the base expenditure limit and multiplying by the enrollment increase and inflation. Even if tax rates raised additional resources, if the amount was over the expenditure limit, the college could not spend those additional tax revenues.

There are a number of academic research studies that examine how states appropriate funds for higher education. Clotfelder (1976) found a positive effect on appropriations of per capita enrollment and a negative impact of out-migration. Other researchers found that the politics, inter-party competition, voter turnout, term limits, and partisanship impact state appropriations levels (McLendon, Hearn, & Mokher, 2009; Peterson, 1976). Not surprisingly, several research studies concluded that state appropriations were linked to enrollment (Betts & McFarland, 1995; Clotfelder, 1976; Leslie & Ramey, 1986).

Hovey (1999) theorized that higher education serves as a "balance wheel" for state budgets: in good economic times, higher education is funded well, and increases in appropriations are greater than for other categories; in bad economic times, the reverse is true. Higher education is often the first budget category cut. Delaney and Doyle (2011) tested this theory over time and found the balance wheel explanation to be correct. This is not a surprising finding to institutional or state agency staff, who typically track higher education appropriations as a percent of the total state budget. Since 1979 the National Association of State Budget Officers (NASBO) and the National Governor's Association (NGA) jointly have published an annual Fiscal Survey of the States, which contains information on state budgets and appropriations as well as on higher education's share of the state budget. This report may be accessed at www.nasbo.org. In the 1970s, higher education's share of state budgets exceeded 18% on average, but it dipped to less than 12% in the 1990s and stood at 9.9% in FY 2012 (NASBO, 2012). These percentages also are tracked in the *SHEF* publications mentioned above.

Endowments, Investment Income, and Gift Funding

The fourth major source of funding for institutions of higher education, particularly private institutions, is endowment funding, investment income, and private gifts, grants, and contracts. The first institutions in the U.S. were started with endowments or gifts from private individuals or from sponsoring churches and other organizations. Institutions like Harvard and Stanford today have large endowments that provide a substantial proportion of the institution's operating revenues. However, public institutions did not have large endowments to assist in their operations. It was not until the 20th century that public institutions began to raise private donations and endowments in substantial amounts.

In 1909–1910, endowments comprised 16% of all institutional revenues, but that percentage declined to 10% by 1939–1940 (Snyder, 1993). The decline as a share of revenues may be attributed in part to the rising number of public institutions that did not have the history of resources from private sources as the long-established private institutions. In addition, the stock market crash of 1929 reduced available funds for gifts and endowments. Between 1950 and 1999, the percentage share of revenues from endowments and from private gifts has shown only small fluctuations in total. However, that is not the case after the accounting change to GASB.

Under fund accounting prior to the change in accounting under GASB, endowments were kept in a separate fund group. Endowments were defined as monies for which donors or other external parties have stipulated that the principal of the fund may not be expended but is to be invested and the income generated expended or added to principal. There are true endowment funds, term endowment funds, and quasi-endowment funds. Term endowment funds function just like endowments, except that after a specified period of time, or at the occurrence of a particular event, all or part of the principal may be expended. Quasi-endowment funds are monies that the governing board, not an external party, has determined are to be retained and invested. Since an external donor has not required that the funds be retained and invested, the principal may be expended at the discretion of the governing board, subject to any donor restrictions on its use. Each endowment and similar fund was accounted for separately. Many endowment funds were held in separate foundations, and their revenues were not reported to NCES (McKeown, 1995).

Prior to the accounting change to the new GASB, all institutions reported these types of monies as endowments or gifts if the funds came directly to the institution, not to an affiliated foundation or other organization. After the change in accounting, all institutions were required to show the revenues of affiliated entities. In addition, the reporting was not parallel across GASB and FASB institutions. Private, non-profit institutions reported endowment funding as investment income, and gifts remain reported as gifts. Private for-profit institutions report private gifts and investment return. Public institutions reporting under GASB report gifts, investment income, capital grants and gifts, and additions to permanent endowments, all as non-operating revenues.

Table 4.5 displays funding from endowments, investment income, and private gifts from 1920 through 2009–2010. Prior to 2000, data are reported only for all institutions, and data for 1999–2000 and 2009–2010 are shown separately for public institutions, private non-profit institutions, and private for-profit. It must be emphasized that the information for the latter 2 years is not consistent with prior years' data and that the only general conclusion is that endowments increased substantially between the $26.4 million reported in 1919–1920 and the $3.1 billion reported in 1989–1990. Similarly, gifts increased from $7.6 million in 1919–1920 to $7.8 billion in 1989–1990. Private non-profit revenues from endowments declined by 25% between 1999–2000 and 2009–2010, reflecting the state of the economy and declining returns on investments held by the institutions.

For the last 38 years, NACUBO and the Common Fund have collected information on college and university endowments through an annual survey. The annual survey analyzes return data and a wide range of

Table 4.5. Endowment, Investment Income, and Gift Revenues (dollars in thousands)

Year	Endowment and Investment Income				Private Gifts			
	Total	Public	Private Non-profit	Private for-profit	Total	Public	Private Non-profit	Private for-profit
1919–1920	$26,482				,$7,584			
1929–1930	68,605				26,172			
1939–1940	71,304				40,453			
1949–1950	96,341				118,627			
1959–1960	206,619				382,569			
1969–1970	516,038				1,129,438			
1979–1980	1,176,627				2,808,075			
1989–1990	3,143,696				7,781,422			
1999–2000	38,952,218	1,170,163	37,763,518	18,537	23,979,916	7,488,781	16,488,984	2,151
2009–2010	39,382,256	10,916,560	28,425,581	40,115	27,712,021	9,656,462	18,017,260	38,299

Source: Snyder and Dillow (2012).

112

related information gathered from a broad cross section of U.S. colleges and universities, both public and private, as well as their supporting foundations. The size and scope of the survey make it the most comprehensive annual report on the investment management and governance practices and policies of U.S. institutions of higher education (NACUBO, 2013). Of the 831 institutions participating in the 2012 survey, 525 are private, and 306 are public. This year's survey for the fiscal year ended June 2012 showed that returns were essentially flat but volatile (Troop, 2013). College and university endowments have had an average gain of 6.2% over the last 10 years, outperforming the Standard and Poor's 500 Stock Index return of 5.3% (NACUBO, 2013).

The *Chronicle of Higher Education* maintains a searchable database on college and university endowments that is available to researchers at www.chronicle.com. Data available cover multiple years of information on over 800 colleges and universities. It must be remembered that these data are self-reported and are not subject to audit.

There has been limited research on college and university endowments other than descriptive data of the size of endowments and historical information. Some research has been done on the ideal size of endowments (Schneider, 2006), and the General Accounting Office (2010) produced a report (*College and University Endowments Have Shown Long-Term Growth, While Size, Restrictions, and Distributions Vary*) for Congress that describes differences among institutions in endowment assets. The Association of American Universities (AAU) also maintains data on university endowments and conducts some research into the area. Goetzman and Oster (2012) examined asset allocation in university endowments and found that there was evidence of changes in investments depending on university objectives and strategic goals.

In 2007, the issue of wealthy university endowments became front page news. Members of the Senate Finance Committee, most notably Sen. Charles Grassley (R-IA), questioned why some university endowments were amassing vast amounts of tax-subsidized wealth while those universities were simultaneously raising tuition on average families to greater and greater levels. Miller and Munson (2008) responded with a commentary. While not the foremost issue facing higher education today, the proper role of endowments remains a hotly contested debate. The possibility of Congressional action raised fundamental questions about the role of government in regulating non-profits, the importance of federalism, and the investment responsibilities of endowment money managers. At the same time, higher education's inability to contain costs in a meaningful way has led many to reasonably argue that universities should begin to spend some of their own resources before asking the taxpayers for even more government dollars. This debate continues.

INSTITUTIONAL EXPENDITURES

Institutions expend revenues to provide services to students, faculty, staff, other stakeholders, and the general public. Expenditures may be classified in a variety of ways such as by program, function, organizational unit, project, or class of expenditure (e.g., travel, supplies). Classification by program cuts across the other categories and enables the greatest comparability of data among institutions. IPEDS classifies expenditures into the functional categories that were listed in Chapter 2, and the reader is encouraged to review the definitions of what is included in each functional area and what is needed to ensure comparability of data over time.

NCES maintains historical information on college and university expenditures, as does the Census Bureau. For the period from 1930 to 1990, data were shown in three broad budget categories: educational and general expenditures, auxiliary enterprises, and student aid. Table 1.8 displayed institutional expenditures from 1930 to 2010 in these three categories. It is important for researchers to remember that the data for 1999–2000 and 2009–2010 are not comparable to prior years' data because of the change in accounting. Educational and general expenditures comprised 84% of total expenditures for all institutions in 1960, dropped to a low of 75% in 1930, and have remained at about 78% since 1980.

Table 1.9 displayed information for 2009–2010 by functional category (instruction, research, etc.) by sector. Because of the differences in reporting expenditures under GASB and under FASB for private non-profit and private for-profit institutions, several functional categories are combined, masking real differences in the distribution of expenditures among types of institutions. Research and public service categories have been combined to enable comparisons across sectors, as have student services, academic support, and institutional support. There are differences in the percentages of the budget spent by public and private institutions. Public institutions spent 27% of their budgets on instruction, while private non-profit spent 33%, and private for-profit institutions spent 24%. The biggest difference is that private for-profit institutions spent the majority of their revenues, 66%, in the categories of student services, academic support, and institutional support. Public and private non-profit institutions had a more even distribution of resources. This underscores the suggestion that comparisons among institutions across sectors require care to ensure that the comparison is appropriate.

Table 4.6 displays expenditures by functional area for public and private non-profit institutions for FY 2010. Even though the categories were made as close to one another as possible, there still are differences in reporting that require caution in interpretation. Because public institutions report depreciation and plant expenditures separately and private institutions do not, the most relevant comparison is total educational and general expenditures (E&G). In FY 2010, public and private institutions expended approximately the same percent of their total budgets on E&G, 75 and 76% respectively.

Table 4.6. Expenditures by Functional Category for Public and Private Non-Profit Institutions

| Category | *Institution Type* | | | |
| | *Public* | | *Private* | |
	Amount	*% of Total*	*Amount*	*% of Total*
Instruction	76,292,102	27%	47,486,299	33%
Research	28,077,991	10%	16,155,474	11%
Public Service	11,506,354	4%	2,089,745	1%
Academic Support	18,878,483	7%	12,939,489	9%
Student Services	13,137,932	5%	11,416,177	8%
Institutional Support	16,348,654	6%	19,433,113	13%
Operation of Plant	18,052,279	6%	NA	NA
Depreciation	14,306,697	5%	NA	NA
Net Grant Aid	15,435,492	5%	832,078	1%
Subtotal, Ed. & General	212,035,984	75%	110,352,374	76%
Auxiliary Enterprises	20,457,106	7%	13,887,042	10%
Hospitals	26,674,882	9%	13,174,405	9%
Independent Operations	1,236,092	0%	5,154,851	4%
Other	14,627,269	5%	2,573,113	2%
Total	281,368,314	100%	145,141,785	100%

Source: Snyder and Dillow (2012), Tables 377 and 379.

E&G are most directly related to instructional cost at any particular institution and are the most often researched, debated, and considered by policymakers. Because of this, the specific functional categories in education and general expense have been examined in great detail by a variety of researchers as well as policymakers. State coordinating and governing boards use expenditure information to develop funding formulas and to compare institutions on what is an appropriate or efficient expenditure of funds. NACUBO completes benchmarking research to determine if institutions are expending an appropriate amount in each functional category. The Delta Cost Project provides information on average costs for each functional category across types of institutions. Institutions provide information on their web sites comparing their expenditures by functional area to those of their peers. The Delaware Study of Instructional Costs and Productivity (available at www.udel.edu/IR/cost/

brochure.html) provides an analytical tool for benchmarking workloads, productivity, and instructional costs by academic discipline. With all this information available, it is possible to design and carry out any number of research projects. The important constraint for all researchers is the comparability of data, especially in longitudinal research.

Most of the research completed on an individual institution's state and local revenues is done by institutional or state agencies and is not published in well-known or easily available places. Institutions and their governing or coordinating boards maintain databases on funding that include information on tuition and fee revenues, state appropriations, local appropriations (if any), characteristics of the student body, enrollments, expenditures by functional category and by discipline, and other information that may be critical for that institution. These data may be published in a fact book or some other information format available to the public. Data also may be maintained on the funding of the institution's peers or comparison institutions. Readers are encouraged to inventory how much information is available for their own institution.

SETTING OF INSTITUTIONAL BUDGETS

All institutions of higher education go through an internal budgeting process within their own institution, one with their own boards, and some must also go through a statewide coordinating board process. Public institutions must go through the annual (or biennial) state budgeting process. Universities and community colleges who receive local tax funds also must go through the process for the local government, whether it is for their own board, or whether the college is dependent on county or regional government. In short, it sometimes seems like the budgeting process is continual; at a particular point in time, an institution may be reporting the results of last year's operations, monitoring this year's budget operations, and preparing next year's budget.

How do institutions develop their budgets? Just like the state or local budgeting process, most institutional budgeting is done incrementally. However, in best practice budgeting, the development of the budget is linked closely with the institution's strategic plan, for the budget is the short-term action plan for carrying out the activities needed to reach the goals and objectives of the strategic plan.

State budgeting agencies require public institutions to develop and submit budgets that follow special regulations. Most budget requests are incremental, although performance funding may change that. Most budget requests identify the institution's major functions and activities.

Universities' internal budget processes establish the needs and priorities for current and planned programs and activities and the funding requirements for their support, including state appropriations in the case of public institutions, and local appropriations for those institutions with local funding. Institutions identify program needs that support their missions and short and long-range goals. This process typically works up from the departmental level to the college level and then to the institutional level, with decisions made along the way on what will best serve the institution's goals and objectives.

Private institutions, and to a lesser degree, public institutions, determine how their enrollment management will enable them to meet their revenue goals and the goals for the make-up of the student body. The process provides the framework to describe and justify to their boards and other policymakers their needs and plans. The process should also provide decision makers with the tools to rationally and equitably allocate resources in support of university plans and programs.

State budgeting processes typically begin approximately eighteen months prior to the fiscal year of the budget request. Presidents issue to their vice presidents guidelines that establish general university goals and objectives for the budget year and identify priorities within their mission and scope. Colleges and departments develop their funding requests within the parameters of the president's guidelines and with any additional directions from the responsible vice president.

For public institutions, at the state level, or the system level, depending on the governance structure of the organization, about 15 months before the start of the fiscal year, budget guidelines may be issued by the state budgeting office and/or the system office. Most budget requests include two parts: a continuation or base budget that is adjusted by changes in enrollments, outcome measures, or inflation; and a request for special initiatives. About a year before the budget year begins, institutions submit their requests to the governing board and/or state budget office. By this point, the institution has been through its own internal review and analysis processes. In general, an institution's internal process includes vice presidential review of the requests submitted from within his or her own area of responsibility. The vice presidents then delete or submit amended or unchanged requests to a college/university budget office. The budget office will analyze the requests before forwarding them, with recommendations, to an institutional budget committee composed of administrators, faculty, staff, and others. This committee will make recommendations to the president on priorities for funding.

After the internal review, budget documents will be submitted to an institution's board and, in the case of public institutions, likely will go to an executive and/or legislative state agency for review and further recommendations. Budget analysts at these agencies will review the requested budget, visit the institutions, and work with institutional (and system) staff to identify issues, request additional information, and develop their own recommendations for presentation to the legislature or governor.

Public institutions then go through a legislative budget review during which both house and senate staff and committees will review the budget requests, hold hearings, and determine appropriation amounts. The average budget hearing generally takes from one to two hours but can extend to eight hours of testimony, questions, and deliberations. Outside the formal subcommittee and committee hearings, institutional and/or system staff will spend time informing appropriations committee members and other key legislators of institutional budget issues and details. Once a final budget is approved by the appropriations committee(s), a final appropriations bill will be introduced and go through a regular hearing process.

Readers are encouraged to familiarize themselves with their own institutions' budgeting processes.

CHAPTER 5

STATE FUNDING FORMULAS

Funding formulas used for higher education are among the best researched aspects of higher education funding, in the sense that funding formula development requires more research and more advanced statistical techniques than are used in describing or reporting revenues and expenditures or in setting tuition and fees. However, the majority of *published* research on funding formulas in higher education is either historical or descriptive in nature. The real research to develop or update funding formulas is conducted by legislative or executive staff, by state governing or coordinating boards, or by a combination of the two.

This chapter provides not only the history of funding formula use and descriptive information on the types of formulas used to allocate resources to colleges and universities but also information on how to develop funding formulas, examples of best practice formulas, and a list of data sources used in formula development.

FUNDING FORMULA USE

At the majority of public colleges and universities, and for a large number of private colleges and universities, the allocation of state appropriations as a component of budget planning is determined by funding formulas or guidelines. The terms "formulas" or "guidelines" are used interchange-

Higher Education Finance Research: Policy, Politics, and Practice, pp. 119–159
Copyright © 2014 by Information Age Publishing

ably in this discussion because some states use the first term and other states the second term to describe their methodologies for calculating the amount of revenues an institution needs.

State-level funding formulas or guidelines for higher education have been in use in the United States for over 60 years. Originally envisioned as a means to distribute public funds in a rational and equitable manner (Hale & Rawson, 1976), just like formulas for distributing resources to elementary and secondary schools, higher education funding formulas have continually evolved into often-complex methodologies for determining institutional funding needs, allocating public funds, or rewarding performance. (A discussion of performance funding may be found in Chapter 7.) During the past 60-plus years, and indeed from the conception of formula use, there has been ongoing controversy among participants in the state budgeting process surrounding the design and usage of these funding mechanisms. Some see the use of funding formulas as a means to bring equity and predictability into the budgeting process, while others may perceive formula use as intrusive, inequitable, and burdensome (McKeown-Moak, 1999a).

Participants in the process have alternately praised and damned formulas, depending upon the impact of the formula on a participant's institution (Van Wijk & Levine, 1969). The only point on which participants in the policy process are likely to agree is that there is no perfect formula. Formula budgeting in the abstract is neither good nor bad, but there are good formulas and bad formulas (Caruthers, 1989).

In fact, funding formulas have changed from their original purposes of identifying an adequate and predictable resource base and distributing those resources equitably. Although funding formulas provide some rationale and continuity in allocating state funds for higher education, formulas are designed and utilized for many purposes, including measurement of productivity. Even though the genesis of funding formulas may lie in rational public policy formulation, the outcome may not. Formulas are products of political processes, which implies that formulas result from compromise and that what is acceptable in one political subdivision may not be acceptable in another. What is acceptable to one institution will not be acceptable to another, and wise financial officers often can influence formula methods to benefit their campuses by compromising when appropriate (McKeown-Moak, 1999b).

Although the basic purpose of funding formulas remains the rational and equitable allocation of state funds for public higher education, guidelines are designed and utilized by different groups for many purposes, including the following:

- by the state higher education agency or governing board as a means of recommending resources for each institution to the legislature and governor;
- by the legislative and executive budget offices as a means of evaluating higher education budget requests;
- by the governing or coordinating board and/or legislature as a means of measuring and rewarding productivity;
- by the state higher education agency as a means to distribute the state's higher education budget allocation to each institution; and
- by the governing or coordinating board and/or legislature as a means to provide funding to private colleges and universities on a per capita basis (McKeown & Layzell, 1994).

In general, formulas used only for the request phase of activities are often less complex than those used to distribute a lump-sum appropriation within a system.

States use at least seven different methods to recommend or allocate funding or to articulate funding adequacy: funding formulas based on credit hours or enrollment relative to cost factors, benchmarks or peer institutions, performance funding or performance metrics, performance contracting, vouchers, a base plus or minus incremental changes to base appropriations, or a hybrid among the methods. States may use multiple methods to allocate funding or to articulate funding adequacy (McKeown, 1986). As mentioned in Chapter 4, in truth most states use an incremental (or decremental) approach, with a formula or performance metrics determining the amount of the increment or decrement.

Development of an optimal or best formula is complex because there are differences in institutional missions, even within the same system, and in the capacities of institutions to perform their missions. These differences do not negate the value of formulas but suggest that formulas can be used to provide a fiscal base to which (or from which) funding can be added (or subtracted), if justified. Formulas typically are considered enrollment driven because they are based on credit hours, students, degrees produced, or faculty members, which makes it relatively easy to evaluate change. If additional funds are justified, then formulas can provide the basis to target supplemental funding. Because formulas may be enrollment or production driven, when enrollments or degrees produced are steady or decline, funding may decrease (Caruthers, 1989). This aspect of formula use brought formulas under attack in several states when institutions experienced declines in enrollment.

When enrollments decline or remain constant, methods are sought to provide additional resources. Development of new programs and services to meet the varied needs of a changing clientele may require different configurations of resources in addition to different programs. The use of alternative instructional delivery methods, including Internet delivery of instruction, may require a shift in the paradigm on funding, as will large increases in enrollments at a time of declining state resources (McKeown, 1982). Virtual universities, like Thomas Edison State College or Strayer University, or those where delivery of courses is shared among several public and private universities require a shift in funding methods and formulas (McKeown-Moak, 2006a).

To accomplish the purpose of providing an equitable distribution of available resources, a majority of states and systems have used funding formulas or guidelines in budget development or in resource allocation to higher education institutions. Early researchers defined funding formulas in different ways. Robins (1973) defined a formula as a procedure designed to estimate the anticipated expenditures of an institution using predetermined ratios or cost parameters. Rourke and Brooks (1966) define a formula as "a set of program-cost relationships used to estimate future budget requirements for one or more institutions of higher education" (p. 73) Miller (1964, 1968) defined a funding formula as an objective procedure for estimating the future budgetary requirements of an institution through the manipulation of data about future programs and by using relationships between programs and costs. Gross (1973) noted that a funding formula is a set of statements that specify a procedure for manipulating pertinent variable data through pre-established fixed data to estimate the future funding requirements of one or more institutions. Hale and Rawson (1976) distinguish between a cost analysis procedure and a state funding formula, noting that cost analysis uses historical data to establish relationships between programs and costs, while a funding formula is used to estimate future financial requirements; in other words, a cost analysis uses past expenditures, while a formula estimates future financial needs.

For the purposes of this discussion, a *formula* is defined as a mathematical representation of the amount of resources needed, or expenditures for an institution as a whole or for a program at the institution. Programs in this context refer to the categories into which expenditures are placed, as defined by the National Association of College and University Business Officers (NACUBO). The programs, functional categories, or budget areas commonly used were listed in Chapter 2 and include instruction, institutional support, research, operation and maintenance of physical plant, public service, scholarships and fellowships, academic support, and student services. Many states or systems provide funding based on these functional or budget programs. These areas are included in educational and general (E&G) expenditures, which result from the three basic missions of colleges and universities: instruction, research, and public service. Funding for the remaining NACUBO categories may be based on formulas in the determination of the total resource allocation to the institution.

However, as noted above, in most states and systems total institutional needs are not determined by a formula mechanism. Additions are made to the amounts determined by formula to recognize special needs or special missions. Similarly, given political structures, competition for funds from other state agencies, and shortfalls in revenue projections, the amount determined by a formula calculation may be reduced to conform to total funds available.

The breadth and coverage of funding formula and guideline usage varies as well among the states. States may use formulas for all public higher education sectors (4- and 2-year) or just a particular segment. Further, states may use formulas or guidelines for specific program areas such as instruction and academic support, or they may be all-inclusive. A trend over time has been to have more "non-formula" components in the higher education budget, given the feeling that formulas are not adequate for meeting the funding needs of certain specialized activities (e.g., co-located instruction, public service activities, cooperative extension).

DEVELOPMENT OF FUNDING FORMULAS

Funding formulas have been considered the offspring of necessity (Gross, 1979). The development of an objective, systematic method of dealing with the funding of many diverse institutions prompted many states to begin using formulas (Miller, 1964). Prior to 1946, institutions of higher education served a limited and relatively homogenous clientele. After World War II, enrollments increased dramatically, and each state or system had a variety of liberal arts colleges, land-grant colleges, teacher training colleges, and technical schools to meet the needs of its citizens.

As the scope and mission of campuses increased and changed (i.e., introduction of community colleges, teachers' colleges becoming regional universities), so did the complexity of distributing resources equitably among competing campuses. Because state resources did not keep pace with increasing enrollments, the competition for funding became greater. And, because no two campuses are alike, methods were sought to allocate available funds in an objective manner, to provide sufficient justification to the legislature for additional resources, and to facilitate inter-institutional comparisons (McKeown, 1982).

The desire for equity was a prime factor in the development of funding formulas, but other factors served as catalysts: the desire to determine an "adequate" level of funding, institutional needs to gain stability and predictability in funding levels, and increased professionalism among college and university business officers (Moss & Gaither, 1976). The objective of equity in the distribution of state resources is to provide resources to each of the campuses according to its needs. To achieve an equitable distribution of funds required a distribution formula that recognized differences in size, clients, location, and the mission of the college (Millett, 1974).

The concept of "adequacy" is more difficult to operationalize in the distribution of resources. What might be considered to be adequate for the basic operation of one campus would be considered inadequate for a campus offering similar programs but having a different client base (McKeown-Moak, 1999a).

Texas was the first state to use funding formulas for higher education, although the formula concept was pioneered by Russell somewhat earlier (Russell, 1954). By 1950, California, Indiana, and Oklahoma also were using funding formulas or cost analysis procedures in the budgeting or resource allocation process (Gross, 1979). In 1964, 16 states were identified as using formulas; by 1973, the number had increased to 25 states, to 33 by 1992 (McKeown & Layzell, 1994); by 2006, the number had increased to 38, a high point of formula usage before the recession of that decade (McKeown-Moak, 2006a). In 2010, information from state governing or coordinating board websites indicated that 35 states were using some form of a formula in the resource allocation process (McKeown-Moak, 2010a). (See Table 5.1.)

Formulas evolved over a long period of time and contributed to a series of compromises among institutions, governing or coordinating boards, and state budget officials. For example, institutions sought autonomy while governing or coordinating boards and budget officials sought adequate information to have control over resources. The development of the Texas formulas is an example of the trade-offs between accountability and autonomy.

When sudden enrollment increases in the late 1940s caused confusion in the amounts to be appropriated to Texas public colleges, each institution lobbied the legislature for additional funds. Texas legislators felt that the institutional requests were excessive and that the division of resources among institutions was inequitable. Consequently, the legislature asked for some rational mechanism to distribute funds. In 1951 a teaching salary formula based on workload factors was developed; this formula did not recognize differences among the campuses in roles and missions. By 1957 a series of budget formulas developed by institutional representatives, citizens, and the new Commission on Higher Education was presented to the legislature. These formulas were developed only after completion of a major study of the role and scope of the institutions. The study included an inventory of program offerings and

**Table 5.1.   States/Systems Using Formulas in
1984, 1992, 1996, 2006, and 2010**

State	*Using Funding Formulas*				
	1984	*1992*	*1996*	*2006*	*2010*
Alabama	X	X	X	X	X
Alaska		X			
Arizona	X	X	X	X	X
Arkansas	X	X		X	X
California	X	X	X	X	X
Colorado	X	X	X		
Connecticut	X	X	X	X	X
Delaware					
Florida	X	X	X	X	X
Georgia	X	X	X	X	X
Hawaii				X	X
Idaho		X	X	X	X
Illinois	X	X	X	X	X
Indiana				X	X
Iowa					
Kansas	X	X	X	X	
Kentucky	X	X	X	X	X
Louisiana	X	X	X	X	X
Maine					
Maryland	X	X	X	X	X
Massachusetts	X			X	
Michigan	X			*	X
Minnesota	X	X	X	X	X
Mississippi	X	X	X	X	X
Missouri	X	X	X	X	X
Montana	X	X	X	X	X
Nebraska				X	
Nevada	X	X	X	X*	X
New Hampshire					
New Jersey	X				
New Mexico	X	X	X	X	X
New York	X			*	
North Carolina				X	X
North Dakota	X	X	X	X	X
Ohio	X	X	X	X	X
Oklahoma	X	X	X	X	X
Oregon	X	X	X	X	X

(Table continues on next page)

Table 5.1.   Continued

State	Using Funding Formulas				
	1984	*1992*	*1996*	*2006*	*2010*
Pennsylvania	X		X	X	X
Rhode Island					
South Carolina	X	X	X	X	X
South Dakota	X	X	X	X	X
Tennessee	X	X	X	X	X
Texas	X	X	X	X	X
Utah		X	X		
Vermont				X	X
Virginia	X	X		X	
Washington	X				X
West Virginia	X	X	X		
Wisconsin	X				
Wyoming				X	X
N	36	32	30	38	35

* State did not complete survey; information taken from websites.

attempted to measure costs by program. After 1958 a cost study committee was established that recommended adoption of five formulas for teaching salaries, general administration, library, building maintenance, and custodial services. In 1961 two formulas for organized research and departmental operating costs were added. By 1996 Texas used 13 separate formula calculations that were developed through complex cost studies of each of the program offerings on the campuses. Texas continued to use advisory committees to revise and improve its formulas to encompass two broad objectives: provide for an equitable distribution of funds among institutions and assist in determining the funding needed for a first-class system of higher education (Ashworth, 1994).

At each phase of Texas formula development, compromises were reached between the desire for additional data for increased accuracy and for differentiating among the institutions and the cost and burden of providing the data. This method of using advisory committees who studied the costs at the various institutions was used in the dramatic changes to the Texas funding models in 2010 (McKeown-Moak, 2010b).

The trend in formula development in many states parallels the experience of Texas: refinement of procedures, greater detail and reliability in collection and analysis of information, improvement in the differentiation between programs and activities, and eventual inclusion of performance or accountability factors.

States have used different methods over time to develop their formulas for both 4-year and 2-year institutions. Some states have developed their methods from the ground up. Many of these formulas have been based on the statistical analysis of institutional data (i.e., regression modeling) or the determination of an "average cost" among institutions in a state for providing a particular type of service. Others have been based on staffing ratios and external determinations of "standard costs" or workload factors based on national norms.

The key to the process seems to be the isolation or identification of variables or factors that are directly related to actual program costs. Isolation of variables that are detailed, reliable, not susceptible to manipulation by a campus, and sufficiently differentiated to recognize differences in institutional role and mission requires the collection of myriad amounts of data. Data must be collected and analyzed in a manner that does not raise questions of preferential treatment for any campus. It is not unusual to run more than 50 separate regression equations before finding one that explains a sufficient percentage of the variance to be acceptable for policy purposes. The resulting formula also must be easily explainable to policymakers, which is the biggest constraint on formulas that distribute hundreds of millions of dollars. (A discussion of how to identify the variables to develop a formula from the ground up is included later in this chapter.)

Other states have developed their formulas by borrowing existing formulas from other states. For example, Alabama adapted the formulas used by Texas to the particular circumstances of Alabama and continued to modify the formulas to reflect circumstances specific to Alabama and to incorporate judicial interventions (McKeown, 1996a). Adaptation rather than development of a new formula appears to be the preferred method because of the time and effort required to complete a sound cost study. Accounting procedures are not refined enough in some states or systems to permit the calculation of costs differentiated by academic discipline and level of student and to separate professorial time into the multiple work products generated by carrying out the three main missions of most institutions of higher education: teaching, research, and service. States continue to adapt formulas from other states because methods that work in one state may work equally well in another at considerable savings of time and resources.

States or systems use funding formulas for a variety of reasons, including the following:

- Formulas provide an objective method to determine institutional needs equitably;
- Formulas reduce political competition and lobbying by the institutions (Rawson, 1975);

- Formulas provide state officials with a reasonably simple and understandable basis for measuring expenditures and revenue needs of campuses and determining the adequacy of support;
- Formulas enable institutions to project needs on a timely basis;
- Formulas represent a reasonable compromise between public accountability and institutional autonomy (Glenny, 1959);
- Formulas ease comparisons between institutions; and
- Formulas permit policymakers to focus on basic policy questions (McKeown, 1982).

Funding formulas also can provide for equity among institutions, depending on how the formulas are constructed. Two types of equity are achieved through formula use: horizontal and vertical. *Horizontal equity* is defined as the equal treatment of equals, and *vertical equity* is defined as the unequal treatment of unequals. An example of a horizontal equity element is a formula that provides a fixed dollar amount for one credit hour of lower division English instruction, no matter where or how the class is taught. Texas and Alabama used this element in their instruction funding formulas. An example of a vertical equity element in a formula is the allowance of $2.80 per gross square foot (GSF) of space for maintenance of a brick building, but $3.20 per GSF for maintenance of a frame building

However, formulas do have shortcomings, and there have been many heated debates over whether the advantages of formulas outweigh the downside of use. Some disadvantages of funding formulas are the following.

- Formulas may be used to reduce all academic programs to a common level of mediocrity by funding each one the same because quantitative measures cannot assess the quality of a program (Gross, 1973).
- Formulas may reduce incentives for institutions to seek outside funding.
- Formulas may lead to allocation of funds that will generate maximum future revenues under the formula (Dressel & Faricy, 1972).
- Formulas may be inappropriately used for the internal allocation of institutional resources even though neither the procedure not the parameters were designed for that purpose (Miller, 1964).
- Formulas may perpetuate inequities in funding that existed before the advent of the formula (Cope, 1968).
- Enrollment-driven formulas may be inadequate to meet the needs of changing client bases or new program initiatives.
- Formulas cannot serve as substitutes for public policy decisions.

- Formulas are only as accurate as the data on which the formula is based.

- Formulas may not provide adequate differentiation among institutions.

- Formulas may incent institutions to behave in certain ways, such as enrolling increasing numbers of students without regard to student success (Wilson, 1971).

- Formulas are linear in nature and may not account for sudden shifts in enrollments and costs (McKeown, 1982).

In early research on funding formulas, two types were identified: base formulas and functional formulas (Boling, 1961). A base formula was defined as one that uses pre-defined percentage factors to estimate the future funding requirements of a specific functional area; for example, library acquisitions budget may be 3% of instructional salaries (Hale & Rawson, 1976). Functional formulas were defined as those using factors directly related to a specific budget area to estimate future funding requirements; for example, a specific cost per square foot might be multiplied by the total square footage in a building to determine maintenance costs. Examples of both of these types of formulas are used in 2013.

Miller (1964) noted that base formulas have the advantage of simplicity of preparation and presentation. However, their simplicity leads to several disadvantages, including the lack of a consistent relationship between workload factors and base factors (Hale & Rawson, 1976). In addition, there may not appear to be a logical relationship among budget areas. Wilson (1971) noted that base formulas were appropriate when historical data are well-analyzed and when the roles of a particular institution are relatively stable.

Miller also noted that functional formulas are more dependable for long-range projections because the workload factors are included in the calculation. But functional formulas require a large database and sophisticated methods for maintaining, updating, and manipulating those data sets (Hale & Rawson, 1976). Because of the lack of large and well-developed data sets, many states did not adopt functional formulas until staff expertise was developed (McKeown, 1996a). Boling (1961) found that functional formulas encouraged efficiency and economy within institutions and were sensitive to the diverse needs of institutions.

In any event, guidelines or formulas reflect one of two *computational approaches*: the all-inclusive approach, where the total allocation for a program area such as instruction or academic support is determined by one calculation; and the itemized approach, where more than one calculation or formula is used in each budget area. Most state funding formulas have used the itemized approach (McKeown, 1982). Three *computational methods* have been identified under which every formula calculation can be classified:

- Rate per base factor unit (RPBF),
- Percentage of base factor (PBF), and
- Base factor/position ratio with salary rates (BF-PR/SR) (Gross, 1979).

The RPBF method starts with an estimate of a given base, such as credit hours completed or number of full time equivalent students (FTES), and then multiplies the base by a specific unit rate. Unit rates generally have been determined by cost studies and can be differentiated by discipline, level, and type of institution.

The PBF method assumes there is a specific relationship between a certain base factor like faculty salaries and other areas like departmental support services. The PBF method can be differentiated by applying a varying percentage to levels of instruction or type of institution, but this is unusual. Reportedly, the PBF was developed because of the perception that all support services are related to the university's primary mission of instruction (Boling, 1961).

The BF-PR/SR method is based on a predetermined "optimal" ratio between a base factor and the number of personnel. For example, ratios such as students per faculty member or credit hours per faculty member are used. The resulting number of faculty positions determined at each salary level is then multiplied by the applicable salary rate for that level, and the amounts are summed to get a total budget requirement. The BF-PR/SR method also is used commonly in plant maintenance and is the most complex of the computational methods (McKeown, 1981).

The *base factors* used in most formulas can be classified into five categories:

- head count,
- number of positions,
- square footage or acreage,
- FTE students or staff, and
- credit hours.

Square footage or acreage is used most often in the operation and maintenance of plant, whereas credit hours, FTE students or staff, or number of positions are the most prevalent bases in the instruction, academic support, and institutional support areas. Head count is used as the base unit most often in student services and the scholarships and fellowships area. Table 2.3 listed where these factors are most often used in functional areas.

States have also found it necessary to introduce factors that *differentiate* among institutions in funding formulas because each institution, if examined closely enough, has a different mission and mix of program offerings. Differentiation is used to recognize that there are legitimate reasons for costs to vary; reasons include economies and diseconomies of scale, method of instruction, and class size. Differentiation became more prevalent and more complex as accounting and costing methods improved and reliable cost data became available (McKeown & Layzell, 1994).

Differentiation is especially commonplace in formulas used to calculate funding requirements for the instruction program area. All of the states using formulas for instruction attempt to differentiate by discipline, institutional type, or level of enrollment. Enrollment may be based on credit hours attempted or credit hours completed. Only a few formulas in other budget areas differentiate by these three types of factors.

Formulas may differentiate among academic disciplines (such as education, sciences, and architecture), levels of enrollment (freshman and sophomore, called lower division; junior and senior, called upper division; master's; and doctoral), and types of institutions (community colleges, baccalaureate institutions, and research universities). Some states (e.g., Alabama) also include differentiation for historically Black institutions as an institutional type.

ECONOMIES OF SCALE AND SCOPE

Formulas also may include factors that consider the size and complexity of the institution so that *economies and diseconomies of scale and scope* may be recognized. Some higher education institutions long have contended that their small size makes it impossible to take advantage of factors that would reduce unit costs or, conversely, that the institution's large size introduces diseconomies that make unit costs higher. Similarly, institutions have argued that narrowness of offerings, such as being a liberal arts college only, results in a reduction of unit costs (because of factors such as less departmental overhead since there are fewer academic departments), while diversity of program offerings, addition of master's and doctoral programs, and diversity of mission cause additional costs, or diseconomies of scope. The economics literature and research provide evidence that not only economies and diseconomies of scale but also economies and diseconomies of scope exist in higher education.

One of the basic principles of economics is that the size or scale of operation is likely to affect the cost of one unit of production. In higher education, an increase in the size of the institution may result in reductions in unit costs, or cost of a full-time equivalent student; this phenomenon is called an *economy of scale*. Similarly, if increases in institutional size result in increases in unit costs or the cost of a full-time equivalent student, the phenomenon is called a *diseconomy of scale*. Formulas may recognize these differences by providing a fixed cost factor such as a minimum guaranteed funding base to ensure that smaller institutions have the necessary resources to offer a basic level of services or by providing differential amounts for more complex institutions.

A typical relationship between size and cost is shown in Figure 5.1. As institutional size increases, factors that appear to decrease unit cost tend to predominate until a point is reached when factors raising unit costs tend to be predominant. The result is a u-shaped curve where the minimal point on the curve represents the lowest unit cost. In higher education, this lowest point may actually be a range over which the factors that keep costs down and those that drive costs up are in balance.

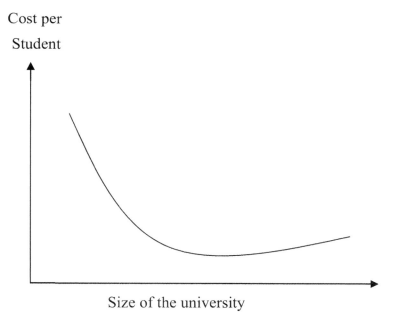

Figure 5.1.   Hypothetical cost curve between size of institution and cost per student.

Bowen (1980) noted that the primary factor that drives the costs of higher education down is what he calls the "lumpiness" of many of the resources used. For a college or university to operate at all, it must have some faculty, a few administrative officers, some buildings and grounds, books, and equipment whether the college enrolls five students or 5,000. These costs to operate an institution or program no matter how many students are involved are called "fixed costs." The cost per student for these initial overhead items or fixed costs decreases as the number of students increases, until a point is reached when the staff and facilities are fully employed and an additional student would require additional resources. The costs that are added for additional students or additional outputs are called "variable costs." "Marginal costs" are defined as those costs associated with the recent addition or deletion of students from a program; the terms "variable" and "marginal" costs are sometimes used interchangeably (McKeown, 1982).

As the institution expands further, more resources would be added in the lumpy fashion, with costs continuing to be spread over additional students, and unit costs again would fall. Large enrollments also increase average class size, resulting in further economies of scale because instructors' salaries remain the same but are spread over more students.

Bowen (1980) also noted that the "lumpiness" of resources gives rise to three different types of diseconomies of scale. One of these diseconomies is the rising cost of institutional coordination of larger and more academic units within the institution. While Bowen calls this a diseconomy of scale, other economists label this phenomenon a *"diseconomy of scope"* (Cohn, Rhine, & Santos, 1989, p. 285). Economies of scope are defined by Cohn et al. as "complementarity between outputs that results in lower per-unit costs when two more outputs are produced simultaneously." In other words, economies of scope occur when a college or university produces credit hours at multiple levels and it is cheaper to produce those credit hours at the undergraduate and graduate level together than to produce those credit hours in separate departments. Or, economies of scope occur when an institution produces multiple products with no increase in cost, as occurs when professors teach and also produce research and public service.

A second diseconomy of scale noted by Bowen (1980) is the possible deterioration in quality as the size of the institution increases. He calls deterioration in quality an increase in unit cost because the value of the service decreases.

The third diseconomy of scale occurs (Bowen, 1980) when increasing size results in additional recruitment expenditures and student financial aid, thus increasing unit costs.

Bowen was not the first economist to study economies and diseconomies of scale in higher education. Early studies were completed in the 1920s, but the first studies of note were completed in the 1960s, all showing that certain economies of scale did exist for colleges and universities (Hawley, Boland, & Boland, 1965; Hungate, Meeth, & O'Connell, 1964). In 1972, the Carnegie Commission on Higher Education determined that there was a definite relationship between size of an institution and cost per student. For public research institutions, cost reductions occurred at the breaking point between 5,000 and 5,500 students (Carnegie Commission on Higher Education, 1972). Earlier work by the Commission (1971) had resulted in these recommendations for optimal college/university size:

	Minimum	Maximum
Doctoral universities	5,000	20,000
Comprehensive universities	5,000	10,000
Liberal arts colleges	1,000	2,500
Community or junior colleges	1,000	5,000

In his seminal work on college or university costs, Bowen (1980) concluded the following:

- Large institutions spend a substantially smaller percentage of their educational expenditures for institutional support and student services than do small institutions.
- Most large institutions spend relatively less per student for plant operation and maintenance than do small institutions.
- Large institutions spend a greater percentage of their resources for teaching than do comparable small institutions.
- Size appears to have no consistent effect on the percentages spent for scholarships and fellowships and for academic support. However, large institutions spend relatively less on libraries than do small institutions (Bowen, 1980).

Bowen concluded that economies of scale appear to be most pronounced for institutional support, student services, and plant, resulting in large institutions being able to devote a larger share of their resources to instruction. As a result, larger institutions were able to pay higher average faculty salaries than smaller institutions could. Similarly, larger institutions had less building space per student than smaller institutions and also employed relatively more "other staff" than small institutions.

Paul Brinkman and Larry Leslie (1986) completed a meta-analysis on 60 years of research on economies of scale in higher education. The literature in the review included books, dissertations, reports, and journals dating from the 1920s. Their review of the studies found the following:

- Large economies of scale are found in expenditures for administration and operation and maintenance of plant.
- Total educational and general costs per student decrease as size increases.
- Substantive size-related economies of scale are most likely to occur at the low end of the enrollment range.
- Instructional expenditures have the least reductions in unit costs related to size.
- Evidence was inconclusive on whether large institutions experience diseconomies of scale.
- The extent to which a set of institutions (like a state system) experience economies or diseconomies of scale depends on the scope and variety of programs and services offered (i.e., economies and diseconomies of scope), salaries paid, and how resources are used on the campus.
- Institutions with between 1,000 and 2,000 FTE students can experience adverse economies of scale (Brinkman & Leslie, 1986).

In contrast to the meta-analytical results, using regression analysis Broomall, McMahon, McLaughlin, and Patton (1978) examined economies of scale for Virginia institutions and concluded that economies of scale are not a function of the type and size of a college or university. Moreover, no economies or diseconomies of scale or scope appeared as complexity or size of the institution increased (Broomall et al., 1978).

Koshal and Koshal (1999) examined economies of scale and scope in higher education and concluded the following:

- The marginal cost of graduate education is greater than that of undergraduate education.
- Ray economies of scale (the expansion of all outputs) exist for comprehensive universities. This means that increases in the size of graduate and undergraduate programs and in research and public service programs result in reduced marginal costs.
- Product specific economies of scale for undergraduate and graduate education do exist at all levels of output.
- Global economies of scope (due to complementarity among outputs like research and instruction) exist for all public institutions. For undergraduate and graduate instruction, both product-specific economies and diseconomies of scope exist.
- Comprehensive universities can reap benefits from both economies of scale and of scope. Large comprehensive universities are the more cost-efficient institutions (Koshal & Koshal, 1999).

Dundar and Lewis (1995) examined economies of scale and scope at public universities and concluded that average and marginal costs were highest for research outputs and lowest for undergraduate education. Social sciences have the lowest costs; contrary to conventional wisdom that costs of instruction increase by level, this was not found for all fields, and master's education in the social sciences is more costly than doctoral education. They concluded that the design of funding and tuition policies for universities should consider the joint costs of research and public service and the economies of scope possible with joint production. Most importantly, Dundar and Lewis (1995) concluded that economies of scale and scope exist at departmental levels and differ by discipline but not within the social sciences.

In what has been called "an important advance" (Hoenack & Collins, 1990) in the study of economies of scale and scope in higher education, Cohn, Rhine, and Santos (1989) examined three types of economies: ray economies (due to the expansion of all outputs), product-specific economies of scale, and economies of scope. They concluded that there were product-specific economies of scale for undergraduate and graduate enrollment and for sponsored research funding. For institutions engaging in only small amounts of research, they found ray economies of scale up to only 5,000 students while institutions with large amounts of research had ray scale economies up to 25,000 students. There also were significant economies of scope among all outputs, but especially for instruction and research. This means that the cost of producing research and instruction together is cheaper than the costs of producing them separately. Cohn et al. concluded that the most efficient institutions are major public research universities that have both large enrollments and substantial research enterprises (Cohn, Rhine, & Santos, 1989).

Lastly, Brinkman (1990) summarized the available information related to costs at comprehensive universities. Studies he reported concluded that total expenditures per student at institutions with 12,000 full-time equivalent students could be expected to be 22% lower than cost per student at an institution of 4,000 students. For master's-oriented institutions, economies of scale appear to be maximized at 3,000 to 4,000 students, and minimum average costs are reached at 5,000 students. Brinkman also reported that direct costs per credit hour for doctoral instruction were, on average, eight to nine times as much as lower division undergraduate costs per credit hour, master's level four to five times as much, and upper division 1.6 to 1.8 times as much. He concluded that factors associated with changes in marginal and average costs were size of institution, scope of services offered, level of instruction or student, and discipline.

Each of the studies noted above provides an example of "good" research into the economics of funding colleges and universities. However, seldom are those studies cited in development of funding formulas or in policies related to resource allocation. Nevertheless, in design of funding mechanisms, it is important to include factors that recognize economies and diseconomies of scale and scope.

GUIDING PRINCIPLES IN FORMULA/GUIDELINE USAGE

Over time, a number of researchers in the area of higher education finance have offered their concepts regarding desired characteristics in state higher education funding formulas. Frequently, what is offered as the "desired characteristic" is in direct response to a perceived shortcoming of a particular state's funding formula or guideline.

Fourteen characteristics, listed and summarized in Table 5.2 in no particular order of importance from A to N, often tend to be in opposition to one another. For instance, the desire to have a simple-to-understand funding formula may preclude features that might contribute to a greater degree of equity (e.g., more detailed sub-categories to reflect institutional differences). Similarly, a formula that is responsive to changes in enrollment levels may not be able at the same time to provide the desired level of stability. Use of the characteristics provides an objective framework for evaluating funding policy alternatives—both during the phase of review of the current formula and in subsequent years (McKeown & Layzell, 1994).

As shown in Table 5.1, in 2006, 38 states or systems reported that they were using funding formulas and guidelines in the budget or resource allocation process for public institutions, the most since 1980; the number of states using formulas declined to 35 in 2010. The number of states or systems employing formulas changes from year to year since states continually adopt, modify, and drop formulas and since what one person may consider a formula may be called by another name by another person. For example, Louisiana typically is identified as a formula state although the person responding to a 2006 survey used to collect the data indicated Louisiana was not using formulas. Table 5.3 provides information on the sectors to which formulas applied (McKeown-Moak, 2006a). However, when the recession of the late 2000s hit, the number of states actually using their funding formula to distribute revenues dropped, although the formulas continued to exist.

Although all of the southern states except North Carolina used funding formulas in the 1970s and 1980s and have been leaders in formula development and innovation, that picture changed during the last half of the 1990s. Delaware, Kentucky, Mississippi, and Virginia dropped the use of formulas in the resource allocation or budgeting process. Instead, these states focused budget requests and the allocation process on inflationary

Table 5.2. Sectors To Which Formulas Apply

State	All	All But Different	Research Universities	State Colleges/ Universities	Community Colleges	Voc/Tech College	Private Institution	Special Institution	Other
Alabama		X							
Arizona	X		X		X				
Arkansas			X	X	X				
California			X	X	X				
Connecticut			X	X					
Florida			X	X	X				
Georgia	X					X			
Hawaii	X								
Idaho			X	X	X	X			
Illinois					X				
Indiana	X								
Kansas					X	X			
Kentucky			X	X	X	X			
Louisiana	X								
Maryland		X					X		X
Massachusetts		X							
Minnesota				X	X	X			
Mississippi									X
Missouri			X	X	X				
Montana			X	X		X			
Nebraska					X				
New Mexico			X	X	X	X			
North Carolina			X	X	X		X		
North Dakota	X								

(Table continues on next page)

Table 5.2. Continued

State	All	All But Different	Research Universities	State Colleges/ Universities	Community Colleges	Voc/Tech College	Private Institution	Special Institution	Other
Ohio			X	X	X	X			
Oklahoma	X								
Oregon			X	X					
Pennsylvania				X					
South Carolina	X								
South Dakota				X					
Tennessee			X	X	X	X			
Texas			X	X	X	X		X	
Vermont			X	X	X	X			X
Virginia			X	X	X	X			X
Wyoming					X				
N	7	2	17	19	19	12	2	1	4

139

Table 5.3. Desired Characteristics of a Funding Formula or Funding Model

Characteristic	Summary Description
A. Equitable	The funding formula should provide both horizontal equity (equal treatment of equals) and vertical equity (unequal treatment of unequals) based on size, mission, and growth characteristics of the institutions.
B. Adequacy-Driven	The funding formula should determine the funding level needed by each institution to fulfill its approved mission.
C. Goal-Based	The funding formula should incorporate and reinforce the broad goals of the state for its system of colleges and universities as expressed through approved missions, quality expectations, and performance standards.
D. Mission-Sensitive	The funding formula should be based on the recognition that different institutional missions (including differences in degree levels, program offerings, student readiness for college success, and geographic location) require different rates of funding.
E. Size-Sensitive	The funding formula should reflect the impact that relative levels of student enrollment have on funding requirements, including economies of scale.
F. Responsive	The funding formula should reflect changes in institutional workloads and missions as well as changing external conditions in measuring the need for resources.
G. Adaptable to Economic Conditions	The funding formula should have the capacity to apply under a variety of economic situations, such as when the state appropriations for higher education are increasing, stable, or decreasing.
H. Concerned with Stability	The funding formula should not permit shifts in funding levels to occur more quickly than institutional managers can reasonably be expected to respond.
I. Simple to Understand	The funding formula should effectively communicate to key participants in the state budget process how changes in institutional characteristics and performance and modifications in budget policies will affect funding levels.
J. Adaptable to Special Situations	The funding formula should include provisions for supplemental state funding for unique activities that represent significant financial commitments and that are not common across the institutions.
K. Reliant on Valid & Reliable Data	The funding formula should rely on data that are appropriate for measuring differences in funding requirements and that can be verified by third parties when necessary.
L. Flexible	The funding formula should be used to estimate funding requirements in broad categories; it is not intended for use in creating budget control categories.
M. Incentive-Based	The funding formula should provide incentives for institutional effectiveness and efficiency and should not provide any inappropriate incentives for institutional behavior.
N. Balanced	The funding formula should achieve a reasonable balance among the sometimes competing requirements of each of the criteria listed above.

increases and special initiatives. Most of the other southern states modified their formulas since 1992, and the University of North Carolina system used formulas to determine increases or decreases in institutional funding requests based on changes in enrollment. Virginia developed a new funding formula that had performance components in the 1990s.

As indicated at the beginning of this section, there has been a constant evolution in both the design and usage of funding formulas and guidelines during the 60-plus years that they have been in use. Some of the major trends are listed below:

More Detailed Categories. One long-term trend has been the development of more detailed guideline categories. Within the instruction component, for example, there has been a tendency toward the use of more discipline categories, more levels of instruction, and separate add-on rates for non-personal services expenses. As discussed earlier, however, some states have found that adding more complexity in their formula has had adverse results (McKeown-Moak, 2006a).

Greater Use of Non-formula Categories. As a result of the increasing scale and complexity of state systems of higher education, there has been a greater use of non-formula categories as a supplement to formula/guideline calculations in recognition of the fact that the formula approach may not be adequate to meet the needs of some programs and activities (e.g., unique or specialized academic and administrative programs).

When state resources increased in the mid-2000s, states appeared to return to the use of funding formulas as a method to distribute available resources equitably or to calculate adequate resources. As state budgets became constricted again, college and university budgets again were restricted, causing tuition and fees to escalate.

In response to growing public concerns over accountability and quality, some states implemented funding mechanisms, either implicitly or explicitly, based on institutional performance. This change shifted the focus from equity and adequacy in funding to outcomes achieved with the funding received. As the national economy went into a period of recession in the last half of the first decade of the 21st century, state appropriations for higher education declined, and in some cases, declined more than 20%. Because higher education enrollments are counter-cyclical, enrollments increased at the same time that state appropriations decreased, putting significant pressures on institutional budgets.

At the same time, there was a national focus on performance and on increasing the numbers of college "completers" as a means of improving the economy. From the White House to state houses to foundations such as the Bill and Melinda Gates Foundation and the Lumina Foundation, the demand was made for increased graduation rates at lower costs for students and at a lower cost to taxpayers. The economic crisis of the states led to demands for graduation of more students, with higher quality educations, more efficiently, and more quickly (Albright, 2010).

This shift in focus away from the "needs" of the college or university to allocation methods that are student-centered, or based on measures of "success," is a sea change in college and university formula funding. Measures of success in this case relate to student success and institutional success in meeting the needs of the state or local community. In the time of financial crisis, there appeared to be a much greater recognition of the fact that higher education is a major driver of the economy and that the state and local community need higher education to provide educated citizens with their greater earning power and ability to pay more in taxes, as well as the other benefits of higher education, including the transfer of knowledge. Policymakers appeared to believe that higher education budgets are not aligned with state or local priorities and wanted institutions to produce graduates in high-demand fields like nursing or teaching.

Some of the new measures in the new wave of funding formulas may sound like the old measures: graduation rates, for example, used to mean the number of full-time first-time freshmen who complete within 150% of the traditional time to degree (i.e., 6 years for a 4-year institution, and 3 years for a community college). The new measure of graduation rate includes students who take longer because of their part-time status or adults who have other responsibilities and are neither first-time nor full-time. The new measure may be called "completions" and refers not only to graduations, but also to certificates, apprenticeships, and completion of the students' plans, which may be 12 hours of a computing programming strand, or qualifying for a teaching certificate, or some other credential.

The new funding models reflect the needs of the state and its citizens, not merely the needs of the institution. Instead of additional funding to educate more students and maintain quality, the economic crisis in states has led to reduced funding to educate more students and still maintain quality. This has been called the "upending of conventional ways" that are "out-of-touch with economic and demographic realities" (Albright, 2010, p. 1). Instead of funding based on the level of resources needed to maintain the "market basket" of courses, programs, and degrees, given the make-up of the student body, the new funding mechanisms shift to funding based on results as measured by course completions (not enrollments), degrees or other "completions" as mentioned above, and other measures of institutional success in meeting the state's and the students' needs. This new paradigm may be called "performance funding" with a twist. States adopting new models have taken their long-standing formulas and adapted those formulas to emphasize results (such as graduation or course completions) and cost-effectiveness. In Ohio, for example, the measure of "enrollment" has moved away from the number of credit hours in which students are enrolled at the beginning of the semester to the number of credit hours for which students successfully complete the course. The weighting of the credit hours remains the same to recognize differences in the costs of providing courses in different disciplines and at different enrollment levels (undergraduate, graduate). Texas has proposed to do the same—calculate credit hours at course completion rather than enrollment. Other calculations in the funding model in Ohio and Texas remain the same, with calculations for student services, academic support, physical plant, and so on.

Performance funding will be discussed in detail in Chapter 7.

FUNDING FORMULAS FOR 2-YEAR COLLEGES

In many states, 2-year colleges originally were governed under the auspices of state departments of education and/or local school boards. Because of this governance structure, early funding formulas for 2-year colleges were patterned from elementary and secondary education funding formulas. Funding generally was calculated at a dollar amount per student, with both the state and the local district contributing to total funding. The level of local funding was based on the district's ability to support the college, which generally was calculated based on an equalization formula using taxable property wealth per full-time equivalent student, just as is the case for elementary/secondary education. Use of ability to pay formulas is one method of distributing funds equitably across college districts within a state. Ability to pay is similar to the subtraction of different revenue amounts from the "needs" of 4-year institutions based on the amount of revenues that the institution can generate.

When governance for 2-year colleges was transferred from the local school district board (and the state board of education) to a board for the college (and either a statewide 2-year college board or other state higher education board), most funding formulas migrated away from the "ability to pay" formulas used for elementary and secondary education (Mullin & Honeyman, 2007). Many states (e.g., Georgia, North Dakota, Nevada, Montana, West Virginia) now incorporate funding for 2-year colleges within the funding formulas used for all higher education by differentiating by type of institution. Other states (e.g. Texas, Alabama, Arizona) have separate funding formulas for 2-year colleges, while some states (e.g., Wyoming) use funding formulas for 2-year colleges but not for the 4-year segment.

The Arizona, Indiana, Kansas, Missouri, Nebraska, and Illinois community college formulas continue to use the ability of the local community college district to support the college (as measured by local property wealth) as a formula component. Other states include equity factors in their formulas by recognizing variations in the cost of offering different types of educational programs and services (like South Carolina does) and by recognizing economies of scale (e.g., North Carolina) (McKeown-Moak, 2006a).

Several states determine the adequacy of their 2-year college funding formula by comparing funding to regional averages or to institutional peer groups. Alabama, Kentucky, and South Carolina compare funding for 2-year colleges to the Southern Regional Education Board (SREB) regional average funding for each type of college, as defined in the SREB Data Exchange. Oklahoma uses national peer group averages to determine the adequacy of institutional funding levels.

FORMULAS BY NACUBO CLASSIFICATION

Practices in formula use vary significantly among the states/systems. Formula usage and identification of "best practices" in each area are described below for each of the areas. In addition, how to calculate or develop a funding formula is described, and data sources are listed.

Instruction

This category includes all expenditures for credit courses; for academic, vocational, technical, and remedial (colleges only) instruction; and for regular, special, and extension sessions (most of these special and extension are self-supporting outside of state budget). Excluded are expenditures for academic administration when the primary assignment is administration (such as deans). Instruction is the most complex, and most expensive, component of an institution's expenditures, although research may have more revenues at a major research university.

To develop a funding formula for instruction, one must begin with the identification of appropriate cost factors. Identification of the cost factors or cost drivers is critical to the validity of the formula development process. Research has shown that the number of student credit hours by discipline and by level as well as both student/faculty ratios and faculty salaries and the distribution of faculty time across disciplines and functions are the major drivers of the cost of instruction (Brinkman, 1989; Hale & Rawson, 1976; Paulsen, 1989; Rutledge & Stafford, 1977). Minor drivers are supplies and expenses, travel, equipment, and other operating expenditures such as the costs of departmental offices. These expenditures vary significantly by discipline; for example, a chemistry lab will require chemicals, lab equipment, usually assistants to the instructor, and greater expenses for the space, which has to be vented properly. The number of students who may be in the lab at one time also is limited by the space available. On the other hand, an English literature course will not require the equipment and supplies and may be taught to over 100 students at a time. Likely, the salary of the English instructor is lower than that of the chemistry instructor (unless they are teaching assistants!).

When funding formulas were first developed, researchers completed regression analysis or another complex statistical technique or did a cost study to determine those cost drivers and develop a formula for instruction. In the 1970s and 1980s, it was not unusual to run more than 100 regressions to determine an appropriate formula for the instruction component, if a cost study was not completed. It usually took considerable time to find a regression that explained over 80% of the variance, was simple enough to be explainable to policymakers (such as governing board members or legislators and their staffs), was agreeable to the colleges and universities affected, *and* whose variables were not easily manipulated.

It is important to explain more than 80% of the variation in costs when millions of dollars will be distributed by the formula. Over 95% is better, of course. In using statistical analysis to determine a formula, it also is important to remember that statistical significance is irrelevant—the elements used are not a sample, but rather the whole population, making statistical significance moot.

In the regression equation, the constant is a proxy for the fixed costs of providing instruction, while the other factors in the equation are the variable costs. Data for the analysis generally comes from the institutions or the statewide governing or coordinating board. However, some data can come from the Delta Cost Project or the Delaware Cost Studies, as listed in Chapter 2. Most of the regression analysis is based on student/faculty ratios and faculty salaries by discipline and level or on costs that are unitized to costs per credit hour or per full-time equivalent student. Completing this type of study may be beyond the capacity of colleges and universities and their boards or legislative and/or gubernatorial staff because of the time commitments required and perhaps their statistical ability.

Institutional personnel, of course, want a formula that will provide a positive revenue flow for their institution. Regression equations may result in the average costs to provide instruction for a particular discipline and at certain levels. And it is possible to "skew" the results by loading costs into a discipline for which your institution has a monopoly, in other words, your institution is the only institution in the state offering that program. For example, if your institution had the only dental hygiene program, it would be possible to put into that program's costs all the salaries of higher-paid instructional staff as well as lab costs that could be shared by other programs, such as radiologic technology. Coupled with low student/faculty ratios, the higher salaries and higher operating costs would result in higher costs per credit hour.

State-level personnel involved in this kind of research, of course, want a result that is equitable to all the institutions. Institutional personnel want a result that recognizes the unique nature of their institution and which does not discriminate against their institution. Formulas can discriminate against an institution or institutional type by the use of different funding rates for different institutional categories. For example, a separate schedule of faculty salary rates for research universities, another for regional universities, and a third for community colleges is likely to provide additional resources for the research universities. If your institution is a research university, then you likely will favor this type of differentiation, but if you are with a community college, you likely will believe that the community college is the victim of discrimination.

Similarly, student/faculty ratios that are separate for research universities and for regional colleges or universities may appear to favor the research university. If the student/faculty ratios recognize economies of scale, then a large state college or university may perceive that it is being penalized for being "efficient." From the perspective of a small college, however, this type of differentiation may be favorable.

Since the largest component of the budget is instruction, an institution should be vigilant in determining if the factors in the instruction formula favor or discriminate against their type of institution. Most instruction formulas differentiate by level of instruction and by discipline. These formulas were designed to recognize the additional costs of graduate education and the additional costs of some disciplines such as the laboratory sciences. If the formulas recognize the true costs of providing these services, then the differentiation is legitimate. If, however, the differences are based on small class sizes in graduate classes when actual class sizes have changed (as they have for master's programs in business), the formula may warrant a revision. Alert institutional personnel watch for opportunities to shift credit hours to higher levels or more expensive disciplines (McKeown-Moak, 1999b). State level personnel likely would view this shifting as manipulation of the variables, as discussed above.

Because most funding formulas for instruction are based on regressions and average costs, large universities with many students can skew the state average cost of a particular discipline. Institutional personnel should examine the underlying data to ensure that the calculation of state average cost does not discriminate against their college or university. In the same vein, use of teaching assistants and adjunct faculty lowers the average cost of offering undergraduate courses. Colleges that do not enjoy the benefits of teaching assistants should be vigilant in the calculation of average costs for disciplines that make extensive use of teaching assistants and also be alert to unique disciplines offered by only one institution, which may have lowered the average costs of other disciplines (McKeown-Moak, 1999b). In any case, to determine whether a formula that differentiates by type is favorable to a particular institution, calculate the formulas for each of the institutional types with the data for the particular institution.

In the 21st century, it is unlikely that states and legislatures will complete regression studies to determine a funding formula for instruction. It is more likely that an instruction funding formula will build on the research completed by other states. As noted in Chapter 2, several states maintain databases on costs per credit hour, or weights for credit hours, or student/faculty ratios by discipline and level. These databases are valuable tools to use in constructing your own formula. Some states average the information from other states to use in their own instruction formulas. Table 5.4 provides some examples of average credit hour costs or weights used by states in 2012.

Other formulas were developed by completing a cost study, which examines the distribution of faculty time over courses, research, and the other activities in which faculty participate. A cost study is an expensive and time-consuming study, requiring a survey of the entire faculty and near 100% participation rates. As mentioned in Chapter 2, several states (notably Florida, Texas, and Illinois) complete cost studies periodically, and those cost studies may be used to approximate costs per credit hour by discipline and by level instead of doing a new cost study.

Since the instruction program is typically the major component of expenditures at institutions of higher education, formulas for this activity are often quite complex. Each of the states using formulas explicitly or implicitly utilizes at least one formula for instruction. States provide differential funding for activities within the instruction program to recognize differences in costs by level of instruction, among academic disciplines, and among institutional roles and missions. Over time, formulas for instruction have become more complex in part because improvements in cost accounting procedures have resulted in more accurate data.

States use both the all-inclusive approach and the itemized approach in the instruction area, but the majority uses the itemized approach. Explicitly, states have attempted to distribute in an equitable manner state funds for the instructional operations of public institutions within the state by recognizing the equality of class credit hours by discipline and level and the differences in institutional roles and missions. Since the formula allocations provide varying amounts based on enrollments by level and discipline, each institution in the state may receive differing amounts for

Table Table 5.4. Examples of Credit Hour Weights or Costs for Illinois, Ohio, and Texas

Program Type	Illinois				Ohio				Texas				Average			
	LD	UD	MS	DOC	LD	UD	MS	DOC	LD	UD	MS	DOC	LD	UD	MS	DOC
Agriculture	1.78	2.22	2.96	2.80	5.53	6.47	11.12	10.13	1.88	2.46	7.01	9.35	3.06	3.72	7.03	7.43
Natural Resources and Conservation	1.93	2.36	3.91	14.00	3.14	4.91	6.58	8.15	1.88	2.46	7.01	9.35	2.32	3.24	5.83	10.50
Architecture and Related	2.22	2.53	3.47	5.20	1.95	4.53	7.18	9.15	1.88	2.46	7.01	9.35	2.02	3.17	5.89	7.90
Area, Ethic, Cultural, and Gender Studies	2.00	3.42	5.09	7.84	2.41	3.31	8.19	9.32	1	1.7	4.1	9.26	1.80	2.81	5.79	8.81
Communications and Journalism	1.60	2.33	3.80	5.22	2.23	3.44	10.21	11.34	1	1.7	4.1	9.26	1.61	2.49	6.04	8.61
Computer and Information Sciences	2.11	3.24	4.62	5.07	3.07	4.5	7.63	8.95	1.44	2.4	3.85	4.8	2.21	3.38	5.37	6.27
Personal and Culinary Services	1.38	1.64	3.29	5.60	2.16	2.7	12.68	14.41	1.04	1.68	2.88	6.97	1.53	2.01	6.28	8.99
Education	1.49	1.89	2.82	3.24	3.18	3.28	5.11	8.65	1.41	1.73	2.34	7.58	2.03	2.30	3.42	6.49
Engineering	2.62	3.64	4.67	5.22	4.68	5.3	11.21	11.55	2.41	3.82	7.47	15.81	3.24	4.25	7.78	10.86
Engineering Technology	2.27	2.36	3.51	4.31	4.39	4.78	13.79	12.72	2.41	3.82	7.47	15.81	3.02	3.65	8.26	10.95
Foreign Languages	1.67	2.00	3.60	3.84	2.49	3.4	8.33	11.57	1	1.7	4.1	9.26	1.72	2.37	5.34	8.22
Family and Consumer Sciences					2.16	2.7	12.68	14.41	1.04	1.68	2.88	6.97	1.60	2.19	7.78	10.69
Legal Professions	2.29	1.58	3.07	7.53	2.58	3.01	7.66		1.74	2.95	3.1	3.92	2.20	2.51	4.61	5.73
English Language and Literature	1.76	2.20	4.44	3.89	2.42	3.36	8.23	8.82	1	1.7	4.1	9.26	1.73	2.42	5.59	7.32
Liberal Arts and Sciences	3.62	3.07	3.67	1.78	3.81	5.47	11.3	10.51	1	1.7	4.1	9.26	2.81	3.41	6.36	7.18
Library Science	4.00	5.24	3.07	6.69	1	10.72	4.77		1	1.7	4.1	9.26	2.00	5.89	3.98	7.97
Biological and Biomedical	1.40	2.29	4.51	4.84	3.04	4.25	10.63	9.78	1.74	2.95	8.07	20.3	2.06	3.16	7.74	11.64
Mathematics and Statistics	1.44	2.00	4.33	5.20	2.34	3.19	8.76	12.34	1	1.7	4.1	9.26	1.59	2.30	5.73	8.93
Multi/Interdisciplinary Studies	2.58	1.67	2.98	3.16	3.51	5.17	7.97	10.85	1	1.7	4.1	9.26	2.36	2.85	5.02	7.76
Nursing	1.33	2.62	5.87	11.22	3.46	3.96	10.77	11.15	1.96	2.35	4.45	9.94	2.25	2.98	7.03	10.77

(Table continues on next page)

Table 5.4. Continued

Program Type	Illinois				Ohio				Texas				Average			
	LD	UD	MS	DOC	LD	UD	MS	DOC	LD	UD	MS	DOC	LD	UD	MS	DOC
Parks, Recreation, and Leisure Studies	1.04	1.36	2.67	2.84	3.12	3.49	7.67	11.25	1	1.7	4.1	9.26	1.72	2.18	4.81	7.78
Basic Skills	1.24	7.76				3.36			1.35	1.2			1.67	4.11		
Philosophy and Religious Studies	1.38	2.00	3.73	6.24	2.39	3.19	9.57	11.52	1	1.7	4.1	9.26	1.59	2.30	5.80	9.01
Physical Sciences	1.27	2.44	4.91	4.78	3.28	4.78	12.98	11.25	1.74	2.95	8.07	20.3	2.10	3.39	8.65	12.11
Psychology	1.00	1.67	3.69	4.22	2.11	3.04	7.02	9.07	1	1.7	4.1	9.26	1.37	2.14	4.94	7.52
Security and Protective Services	1.27	1.56	4.71	6.44	2.12	2.68	4.49	6.36	1.9	2.03	2.93	14.4	1.76	2.09	4.04	9.07
Public Administration	1.33	1.69	2.96	4.78	2.75	3.32	4.24	6.61	1.9	2.03	2.93	14.4	1.99	2.35	3.38	8.60
Social Sciences	1.00	1.56	4.44	5.00	2.27	3.03	4.31	6.56	1.9	2.03	2.93	14.4	1.72	2.21	3.89	8.65
Construction and Other Trades	6.76	4.49	13.78	21.33	4.68	5.3	11.21	11.55	1.96	2.42	4.07	2.45	4.47	4.07	9.69	11.78
Visual and Performing Arts	2.22	3.67	4.33	3.89	2.72	4.58	10	9.26	1.4	2.31	5.44	7.07	2.11	3.52	6.59	6.74
Health Professions	1.13	1.73	2.49	6.67	3.46	3.96	10.77	11.15	1.23	1.89	3.23	9.14	1.94	2.53	5.50	8.99
Business, Management, and Related	1.53	2.11	3.80	9.82	2.56	3.43	5.85	21.15	1.09	1.7	3.26	24.41	1.73	2.41	4.30	18.46

Source: McKeown-Moak (2012)

149

instruction and different amounts per student from the formulas. Some of the states/systems, such as Pennsylvania, recognize economies of scale in the instruction formula by using fixed and variable costs.

Examples of two formulas for instruction follow. Student/faculty ratios by level by discipline vary in the first sample formula, while the rate varies by level in the second.

1. Eq. 5.1a: Instruction funding = the sum of (the number of faculty positions per discipline times the average faculty salary for that discipline), where the number of faculty positions is determined by student/faculty ratios, and the number of FTE students is determined by credit hours by level.

2. Eq. 5.1b: Instruction funding = Base amount plus the sum of [(a rate times the number of weighted credit hours in Discipline Group 1), (rate times the number of weighted credit hours in Discipline Group 2), and (rate times the number of weighted credit hours in Discipline Group 3)], where the number of weighted credit hours is the rolling 3-year average credit hours, and all academic disciplines are assigned to one of three discipline groupings based on cost factors. A discipline may be in Discipline Group 1 for undergraduate instruction and in Discipline Group 2 or 3 for master's or doctoral instruction.

Each state that uses a formula for instruction utilizes a unique methodology. In fact, no two states rely on the same parameters for determining funding needs for their institutions of higher education. A common problem faced by those states with large numbers of instructional cost categories in their funding formulas is the need to monitor the appropriateness of the classification of student credit hours by program or discipline. Formulas with too many program levels can create a temptation for institutions to assign their credit hour production to those program categories with the highest rate of reimbursement. The need to audit the correct reporting of student credit hour production exists in any enrollment-driven funding formula. However the problem grows exponentially with the level of differentiation.

In general, too much differentiation within the instructional component creates incentives for "gaming" the formula and leads to extra administrative expense in auditing enrollment reports and projecting future enrollment levels. For these and related reasons, some states (e.g., Florida) have refined their formulas in recent years to rely on a smaller number of cost categories in their instructional formulas. Other states also are evaluating the use of simpler formulas.

Research

This category includes expenditures for activities designed to produce research outcomes. Some states provide funding for the research mission of the system of higher education as a component of the basic funding formula, as performance funding, or as incentive funding. One of the most successful ways of funding research has been the research incentive funds of the Ohio Board of Regents. These funds were awarded to universities for increases in the amounts of externally funded research. The OBOR staff indicated that this incentive funding has resulted in hundreds of millions in increased research funding, much of which is directed to areas of special statewide need (Petrick, 2009).

Florida's formula is complex and involves computations related to the magnitude of research activities at each institution. The number of research positions is calculated based on a ratio by specific department and is then multiplied by a specified salary rate. Kentucky used a formula that calculated a level of support that recognizes differing roles and missions in research among institutions. None of these formulas were developed by a regression or other equation, but rather by compromise and agreements with the institutions.

Because different states have differing goals for the research component of an institution, there are no generic "best practice" research formulas. Two sample research formulas follow.

1. Eq. 5.2a: Research amount = 1% of outside funding for research.
2. Eq. 5.2b: Research amount = 2% of the sum of the formula amounts for instruction and academic support plus 5% of sponsored research.

Formulas that provide additional funding for research activities only to certain institutions (most likely, only those with a research mission) will be seen by other institutions as unfairly penalizing their institutions.

Public Service

This category includes funds expended for activities that primarily provide non-instructional services to individuals and groups external to the institution. Alabama, Kentucky, Maryland, Tennessee, and South Carolina were the only states who have reported using an explicit formula approach for the funding of public service activities. In Florida, public service positions were generated based on ratios specific to disciplines and then multiplied by a salary amount per position. South Carolina provided

25% of prior year sponsored and non-general fund public service expenditures; Alabama's funding formula was 2% of the combined allocations for instruction and academic support. Sample public service formulas are shown below. Just as with research formulas, public service funding generally was developed by compromises among the institutions. Land-grant universities, which typically are large research universities, include the activities of the cooperative extension service in the public service program area, and cooperative extension programs usually are funded incrementally.

1. Eq. 5.3a: Public service amount = 2% of the sum of instruction and academic support
2. Eq. 5.3b: Public service amount = $75,000 + 1% of instruction, or $150,750, whichever is greater

Academic Support

The category of academic support includes funds expended to provide support services for the institution's primary missions of instruction, research, and public service. The area includes expenditures for libraries, museums, and galleries; demonstration schools; media and technology, including computing support; academic administration, including deans; and separately budgeted course and curriculum development. However, costs associated with the office of the chief academic officer of the campus are included in the institutional support category.

To fund the library component of the academic support category, Alabama, Connecticut, Florida, Georgia, Kentucky, Maryland, Mississippi, Missouri, Nevada, Oregon, South Carolina, Tennessee, and Texas have had at least one formula. Texas allocated an amount per credit hour differentiated by level of instruction, a formula that was originally developed by a regression approach.

Standards on the size of library collections, number of support personnel, and other factors have been developed by the American Library Association (ALA) and the Association of College Research Libraries (ACRL). Formulas to apply these standards, like the Voight formula and the Clapp-Jordan formula, have been developed so that institutions may determine if their library holdings meet the minimum requirements established by professional librarians. Only four states used a library formula that would permit meeting the ACRL criteria.

However, library holdings calculated by formulas like the Clapp-Jordan are not sensitive to 21st century libraries or information storage and retrieval. No formula or standard currently in use accounts for the changes in resource requirements necessitated by increasing use of technology. In fact, the ALA and ACRL standards on size of collection do not consider the use of the "virtual library," where the text of some books may be accessed electronically via the Internet. These technological changes in media availability certainly have profound impacts on library resource needs. In fact, such changes could actually make the distinction between "libraries" and "academic computing" currently found on most campuses irrelevant in the future. As such, the practice of having separate formulas for libraries could become outdated. In 2010, the American Library Association issued new guidelines for funding of academic libraries. As of this point in time, those new standards have not been incorporated into any funding formula, although it is likely that states that have used the Clapp-Jordan or Voight formula may change in the near future.

Some states have developed the academic support formula by using a regression approach that identified variables that explained a significant portion of the variation in spending for academic support. Academic support, institutional support, and student services are areas where the student headcount is a much better predictor of expenditures. One student being advised on courses to take requires the same expenditure of staff time as another student who may be taking a different class load.

An example of a simple and a more complicated academic support formula is shown below.

1. Eq. 5.4a: Academic support funding = 5% of instruction formula calculation.
2. Eq. 5.4b: Academic support funding = $750,000 + 15% of instruction formula calculation + $10 per undergraduate credit hour over 50,000 credit hours + $20 per masters credit hour + $80 per doctoral credit hour + $5 per continuing education hour.

Florida, Kentucky, Missouri, South Carolina, and Texas each had at least one formula for other components of the academic support category. South Carolina calculated an amount based on the average expenditure per student by type of institution. Data from the most recent IPEDS surveys were updated using the Higher Education Price Index (HEPI) to arrive at the amount per student.

Student Services

This expenditure category includes funds expended to contribute to a student's emotional and physical wellbeing and intellectual, social, and cultural development outside of the formal instruction process. This category includes expenditures for student activities, student organizations, counseling, the registrar's and admissions offices, and student financial aid administration.

Several states developed their student services formulas using regression analysis. The student services formulas used by Alabama, Kentucky, and Texas provided a different amount per head count or FTE student. As the size of the institution increases, the rate per student decreases to recognize economies of scale. The formula implicitly does this by adding an amount per weighted credit hour to a base. Such a calculation inherently recognizes economies of scale. The formula was designed to allocate adequate resources to colleges or universities of any and every size (McKeown-Moak, 1999a).

South Carolina used a flat amount per student, determined as the average IPEDS expenditure by type of institution, updated by the HEPI. As was the case with instruction formulas, institutional personnel should run their data through each of the differentiated formulas for the various sectors to ensure that their institution is not being disadvantaged.

Two sample student services formulas follow, both including consideration of economy of scale.

1. Eq. 5.5a: Student services funding = $395 per student for the first 4,000 headcount + $295 per student for the next 4,000 headcount + $265 per student for all students over 8,000 headcount.
2. Eq. 5.5b: Student services funding = Base funding of $2,345,585 up to 4,000 headcount + $282 per student from 4,001 to 8,000 headcount + $255 per student over 8,000.

Institutional Support

This category includes expenditures for the central executive level management of a campus, fiscal operations, administrative data processing, employee personnel services, and support services. This formula can be simple or quite complex, as some states calculated regression formulas to generate the formula. Alabama, Mississippi, South Carolina, and Tennessee multiplied a specified percentage by all other E&G expenditures to calculate institutional support needs. Kentucky included some differentiation and a base amount to recognize economies of scale and complexity of operation, and Texas multiplied a specified rate by a measure of enrollment to determine institutional support amounts.

Most institutional support formulas recognized fixed and variable costs by including a base amount and a specified amount per student or percent of base. Examples of "best practices" institutional support formulas are shown below.

1. Eq. 5.6a: Institutional support = base amount + 15% of total E&G budget (excluding institutional support)
2. Eq. 5.6b: Institutional support = 11% of total E&G formula amount (excluding institutional support) for institutions with more than 8,000 headcount students or 15% of total E&G formula amount (excluding institutional support) for institutions with less than 8,000 headcount students.

Operation and Maintenance of Physical Plant

This category includes all expenditures for current operations and maintenance of the physical plant, including building maintenance, custodial services, utilities, landscape and grounds, and building repairs. Not included are expenditures made from plant fund accounts (for items such as building construction and major renovation, purchase of lands, etc.) or expenditures for operations and maintenance of the physical plant component of hospitals, auxiliary enterprises, or independent operations. Formulas calculate an amount separately for physical plant even though this "program area" is reported within each of the other areas in the IPEDS Finance Survey.

Because the physical facilities of colleges and universities are quite complex and each is unique, funding formulas for the operation and maintenance of the physical plant may be very complex. All of the states (except Montana) that reported using funding formulas provide state resources for plant operations through a formula. Connecticut, Oregon, South Carolina, and Texas use multiple formulas to calculate detailed plant needs. These complicated methods differentiate among types of building construction, usage of space, and size of institution and were originally developed by regression analysis that identified cost drivers. Differences among buildings on each campus are recognized, and the unequal costs of maintaining, cooling, heating, and lighting each building are built into the formulas.

On the other hand, some states provided a flat dollar amount per gross square foot of building space. A plant formula that uses this rate per base factor method has the advantage of being simple and easy to calculate. However, unless the dollar amount per square foot is differentiated by type of building construction (i.e., one rate for frame buildings, another for brick or masonry, and a third for steel), legitimate differences in maintenance costs are not recognized.

Examples of the more complex formulas for plant operations follow. Although this set of formulas is more detailed than a simple rate per gross square foot, it recognizes that there are important differences in a campus' physical facilities that impact on cost. Institutional personnel should be vigilant to ensure that their campus' physical facilities needs are included in the formula for plant operations and maintenance.

1. Eq. 5.7a: Plant funding = the sum of Building Maintenance + Custodial Services +Grounds Maintenance + Utilities.

    Where: Building Maintenance = a maintenance cost factor times the replacement cost of the building, and the maintenance cost factor varies by type of construction and whether or not the building is air-conditioned;

    Custodial services = square footage divided by the average square footage maintained by one person per year times a salary rate;

    Grounds maintenance = rate times the number of acres maintained; and

    Utilities = actual prior year expenditures, adjusted for inflation and other cost Increases.

2. Eq. 5.7b: Plant funding = $4.17 times the number of category I GSF space + $3.44 times the number of Category II GSF + $5.54 times the number of health care GSF + utilities + $2,267 per acre maintained + lease costs – 25% of indirect cost recovery funding.

One of the problematic issues in plant funding formulas is the decision of for which buildings and areas of campus the state should provide funding. Texas, for example, includes within the formula only the square footage and acreage of buildings and grounds that relate to instruction, research, and public service (or E&G buildings). When Arizona had a formula for plant renewal for the universities, that formula excluded research buildings constructed with private funds even though those buildings would be considered E&G buildings by other states. Some states include buildings and grounds used by intercollegiate athletics, while others exclude these facilities as "auxiliary."

Another issue related to plant funding is whether to include funding for building renewal within the operating budget formulas. Texas included an amount equal to a percentage of the replacement cost of the building, where the percentage varies by type of building. On the other hand, Arizona had a formula for the universities that allocates a percentage equal to the replacement cost of the building, but the funding was included in the capital budget appropriation, not the operating appropriation, and was placed in the plant fund portion of the universities' budgets (when this was funded). Arizona's community colleges also had a building renewal formula, which has been suspended for the last few years. From a different perspective, Maryland does not place any funding for building renovation in the college and university budgets but funds all building renovation and major maintenance from the budget of the state department of planning and construction.

Scholarships and Fellowships

This category encompasses all expenditures for scholarships and fellowships, including prizes, awards, federal grants, tuition and fee waivers, and other aid awarded to students for which services to the institution are not required.

Only Kentucky, Maryland, Mississippi, Montana, and Oklahoma calculated an allocation for scholarships and fellowships. One reason for the presence/absence of a formula here is whether the state has a robust statewide student financial aid program. In each case except Oklahoma, which calculated the amount as a dollar value times the number of FTE students, the formula amount was calculated as equal to a percentage of tuition revenues. These approaches all provide horizontal equity but fail to provide vertical equity in that neither the cost to the student or the institution nor the student's ability to pay are considered in the formula. Consequently, there really is no "best practices" example of a formula for this program area. Two examples of scholarships and fellowship formulas are given below.

1. Eq. 5.8a: Scholarships and fellowships amount = 10.5% of estimated income from undergraduate student tuition and fees.
2. Eq. 5.8b: Scholarships and fellowships amount = amount times the number of full-time equivalent students

Revenue Deduction Components

Many of the states that use funding formulas in the resource allocation process do not employ a revenue deduction component. In those states, the calculation of the formula funding amounts is intended to reflect only the state share of funding. Where a revenue deduction component is included in the formula, the most common calculation is to deduct a percentage or all of non-resident tuition and fees.

Alabama's revenue deduction was based on the weighted average credit hour charged to full-time students. Each institution charged a different tuition, so the average tuition charge per weighted average credit hour across all campuses was calculated and then multiplied by the number of credit hours. For historically Black institutions, the amount deducted was equal to 90% of the actual weighted credit hour charges.

Mississippi deducted a percentage of the total calculated by the formula, with the percentage varying by sector. Georgia deducted not only all unrestricted tuition and fee revenues but also certain other unrestricted revenues. Kentucky and Tennessee deducted an amount equal to a tuition rate times enrollment, plus a percentage of investment income. West Virginia deducted only tuition revenues generated by a higher percentage of non-resident students than average for each institution's peer group.

South Carolina deducted an amount equal to non-resident full-time student enrollment times the "cost of education," up to total non-resident tuition and fee revenues received, and resident tuition and fee revenues equivalent to 25% of the "cost of education." In this deduction step, a calculation was made to determine undergraduate and graduate cost of education, defined by a formula unique to South Carolina. South Carolina law requires that non-resident students pay at least the full cost of education, which results in the deduction on non-resident fees up to the cost of education. Institutions are permitted to retain any non-resident revenues above the calculated amount to encourage institutions to charge non-residents higher amounts to keep resident tuition and fees as low as possible. For resident students, the South Carolina Commission on Higher Education has interpreted the state policy of low tuition to mean that state residents pay 25% of the cost of education determined separately for undergraduate and graduate students. If total resident tuition revenues exceed 100% of the calculated "deduction" amount, then the institution may retain the first 10% of the excess, but all amounts over 110% of the calculated amount are deducted from the institution's allocation. In South Carolina, institutions charge different tuitions and have differing costs of education; consequently, the deduct amount must be calculated for each institution. Institutions have been critical of the deduction since the formula has not been fully funded for some time, and tuition has increased to supplant state revenues insufficient to meet the institutions' "needs" as calculated by the funding formula.

CONCLUSION

Formulas will never solve the resource allocation problems in higher education, and indeed, some of the new performance funding formulas are likely to exacerbate the resource allocation dilemmas. Formulas cannot recognize the full range of objective and subjective differences among institutions, nor can formulas anticipate changes in the missions of institutions such as those that have come about with the increased use of virtual technology to deliver courses.

On the other hand, formulas, when properly designed, may provide an objective allocation mechanism that can provide more equity in the distribution of resources than independent funding of each institution based on the power of the institution to lobby. Determining a method for funding higher education will continue to be part of a political process that involves the art of compromise (McKeown-Moak, 1999a).

SECTION III

Accountability and Return on Investment

The first two sections of this book have provided information on the revenues and expenditures for higher education, how these revenues and expenditures are reported, research related to college and university finance, and how budgets and funding are established. The third section of this book introduces accountability-related concepts. Chapter 6 examines the accountability movement as it relates to postsecondary education in contrast to K–12 education and presents various metrics used in the higher education community for accountability reporting. Chapter 7 examines performance-based approaches to maximize efficiency and productivity through funding or budgeting and discusses the current trend to state performance funding mechanisms. Chapter 8 presents methods for calculating both individual and public returns on investment in education and includes a basic discussion of human capital development. Chapter 9 focuses on methods to examine the cost of attendance to the student and discusses corresponding consumer protection metrics.

Higher Education Finance Research: Policy, Politics, and Practice, pp. 161–161
Copyright © 2014 by Information Age Publishing

CHAPTER 6

ACCOUNTABILITY IN HIGHER EDUCATION

The concept of accountability in higher education is not a new one, despite all of the recent popular press that treats higher education accountability as something that is a new idea. Higher education institutions reported on and were accountable for the effective stewardship of funds, whether to the board of the institution, the church with which the institution was affiliated, or the state which chartered the institution, or all of the above, from the first days of Harvard College. Despite this long history of "accountability," Burke (2004b) called "accountability" the most used and perhaps least analyzed and, therefore, the most misunderstood word in higher education. Although there is a great deal of interest in and discussion of accountability, there does not appear to be much agreement on what accountability in higher education means, who is accountable to whom, for what purposes, by what means of measuring, and with what, if any, consequences.

This chapter discusses the various meanings of "accountability," provides information on how accountability is measured, by whom, for what, and what calculations are appropriate. Information on how colleges, universities, and state systems have developed accountability or quality assurance programs and how accountability measures are reported also will be displayed, including how to provide information for the various stakeholders to whom higher education must be accountable. Chapter 7 will

Higher Education Finance Research: Policy, Politics, and Practice, pp. 163–219
Copyright © 2014 by Information Age Publishing

provide a more complete discussion of the latest round of the ultimate in financial "accountability," performance funding,

"Accountability" Concepts

Webster's New Encyclopedic Dictionary defines "accountability" as "being responsible for giving an account of one's acts or furnishing a justifiable explanation," and Roget's Thesaurus lists "answerability," "responsibility," and "liability" as synonyms. In higher education, accountability has come to have varied definitions or demonstrations that an institution is "accountable"—through financial and/or performance audits, through accreditation by regional or discipline-based accrediting agencies, by compliance with state and federal regulations, or through quality assurance programs. Institutions, their governing or coordinating boards, and institutional managers are accountable to many constituencies—agencies that provide funding, including federal, state, and local governments; students and their families; faculty; staff; governors; and the general public, among many interested parties.

Burke (2004b) identified six accountability demands on officials or their agents for government or public service organizations, including colleges and universities. First, they must demonstrate that they have used their powers properly. Second, they must show that they are working to achieve the mission or priorities set for their office or organization. Third, they must report on their performance. Fourth, they must demonstrate efficient and effective stewardship for the resources they use and the outcomes of the use of those resources. Fifth, they must ensure the quality of the programs and services produced. Sixth, they must show that they serve public needs. Most of these six accountability demands were perceived to be beyond the scope of those responsible for the financial operations of colleges and universities until the 1980s.

At the beginning of the 20th century, accountability typically referred to financial accountability, and college and university financial officers also were responsible for providing accountability for staff and the physical plant. Accountability for students and for student progress toward graduation or program completion was the purview of the faculty and staff in the student services areas. Financial accountability usually was provided through a financial audit by an accounting firm or, in the case of public institutions, by the state's auditor general. Some public institutions were required to have an outside audit as well as an audit by the state (Ruppert, 1994).

However, by the beginning of the 21st century, higher education accountability had moved beyond just financial accountability (Burke,

2003), with the institution's financial officers responsible in many cases for providing accountability for most of the six demands listed by Burke. Financial officers now may find themselves responsible for providing demonstrations not only of financial accountability but also academic accountability, the institution's productivity, and for maintaining the institution's quality assurance program. In most large colleges and universities, the financial officer will have the assistance of the institutional research and planning office to meet accountability requirements.

In 2013, the American Association of State Colleges and Universities (AASCU, 2013) identified accountability (defined as "improvement in the performance of states' public higher education systems and institutions, collectively aimed at boosting measures of college affordability, productivity and student success," p. 1) as the prevailing theme for state higher education policy. In this case, accountability was defined as identification and study of programmatic strategies to maximize public colleges' and universities' ability to achieve state goals, with continued strong emphasis on increasing college graduation rates and overall degree production.

Accountability is often thought of in terms of a triangle: *state priorities, academic concerns,* and *market forces* are the three facets of the triangle and often have competing interests in higher education (Burke, 1997). The accountability triangle assesses the responsiveness of accountability programs to the three interests and pressures that most affect higher education in this country: (1) *state priorities* reflect the public needs and desires for higher education programs and services, often as expressed by state officials but also by civic leaders outside government; (2) *academic concerns* involve the issues and interests of the academic community, particularly professors and administrators who are concerned with issues of autonomy; and (3) *market forces* relate to the customer needs and demands of students, parents, businesses, and other clients of colleges and universities. State priorities, academic concerns, and market forces also reflect, respectively, the civic, collegiate, and commercial cultures and interests. State priorities represent political accountability, academic concerns reflect professional accountability, and market forces are about market accountability (Burke, 2004b).

Each of the three corners of the accountability triangle reflects both broad needs and special interests. State priorities can constitute what the citizens of a state need most from higher education, such as better schoolteachers, more nurses, an educated workforce, and an informed citizenry but also can reflect the partisan interest of the party in power. Academic concerns can encourage free inquiry and discussion of ideas, beliefs, and institutions infused by openness, scholarship, and objectivity or can also reflect the resource-reputation model of higher education. This model is thought to view institutional quality as a matter of recruiting the brightest students, hiring the faculty stars, and raising the most resources through research grants or private donations. Market forces can mean meeting the real needs of citizens and society for programs and services or responding to the dominant economic interest in a state, commercial schemes, or consumer fads. However, the drive for prestige and reputation may be perceived as merging academic concerns, public priorities, and market forces and can result in production of more lawyers and physicians than society needs rather than the nurses and teachers that are needed (Burke, 2004a).

Accountability also may be described as upward, downward, inward, and outward accountability. *Upward accountability* represents the traditional relationship of a subordinate to a superior. It covers *procedural, bureaucratic, legal,* or *vertical accountability. Downward accountability* focuses on a manager being responsible to subordinates in participatory decision making or *collegial accountability* in higher education. *Inward accountability* centers on agents acting on professional or ethical standards and often appears in organizations dominated by professionals, such as in colleges and universities, where it becomes *professional accountability. Outward accountability* means responding to external clients, stakeholders, supporters, and to the public at large. It includes *market* and *political accountability* (Vidovich & Slee, 2001).

The purposes or goals of accountability in higher education have shifted over time from system *efficiency,* to educational *quality,* to organizational *productivity,* and to external *responsiveness* to public priorities or market demands. As is often the case in public policy, new purposes are always added, but earlier goals are seldom abandoned (Burke, 2004a). The new accountability in the 21st century is about managing, measuring, and rewarding results.

Despite all the rhetoric on accountability, one of the barriers is the metrics of analysis that do not translate well into program and performance measures (Delta Cost Project, 2009). For policymakers, the existing metrics do not provide assistance in decision making.

Productivity

Productivity is closely related to and often a component of an accountability system. Webster's New Encyclopedic Dictionary defines "productivity" as "the quality or state of being productive, as yielding or furnishing results, benefits, or profits." As with the term "accountability," "productivity" in higher education is a term that is used often and can mean many things, depending on who is measuring and what benefits or results are being measured.

Productivity often is measured by simple counts such as the number of associates, bachelor's, master's, and doctoral degrees awarded. In addition to simple counts, other calculations of productivity can be made. One such calculation is cost-per-completer (CPC). In this calculation, the total amount spent on education is divided by the total number of completers at institution (i) in year (t).

$$\text{Eq. 6.1} \quad CPC = \frac{\text{Total Cost}_{it}}{\text{Total Number of Completers}_{it}}$$

The benefit of this equation is that it is easily understood by the layperson and makes common sense to policymakers. This formula may be appropriate for institutions that build a student body during an admission process, experience relatively little attrition for the entering class (cohort), and have an overwhelmingly large percent of students graduate with a bachelor's degree in 4 years.

Like all calculations, there are limitations to this metric. Whenever examining a derived value, one's interest should first turn to determining the limitations of the numerator and the denominator to determine if the metric is appropriate for the intended use. For the numerator, cost needs to be clearly defined, as explained in greater detail in Chapters 3 and 4. In this type of calculation, costs usually relates to institutional expenditures. In some cases, expenditures may be reflective of either education and related activities or traditional education and general (E&G) expenditures. Related activities could include auxiliary enterprises or the operation of a hospital.

For the denominator, "completion" may be defined in different ways, although typically completion is thought of as earning a degree. Institutions offer various types of credentials in addition to the bachelor's degree. In cases where the bachelor's degree is the only degree awarded, the calculation may be appropriate. Bachelor's degree attainment is not an appropriate denominator for all institutions, especially those that primarily award credentials other than bachelor's degrees, have a transfer mission, or enroll students who were previously successful in postsecondary education or are taking courses to upskill or retrain. Second, there is the assumption that students finish a bachelor's degree in 4 years; this is not the case in the 21st century, where the norm is to take 7 years to complete the bachelor's.

For research universities, several other measures of productivity are commonly used: the dollar value of outside research funding, outside research funding per full-time equivalent faculty member, number of patents and licenses awarded, and dollar value of patent and licensure income. These measures are inappropriate for other types of institutions such as community colleges, which do not have a research mission.

For community colleges and, to a lesser extent, universities, providing workforce training or retraining for businesses and industries in the region is considered a productivity measure. Colleges count the number of classes provided and the number of enrollees in special retraining programs that may be offered at a business site or on campus. The University System of Georgia included this measure in its productivity assessments of the 2-year colleges in the system.

Another measure of productivity is to examine the production of degrees in a particular discipline and at the associate, bachelor's, master's, specialist, professional, or doctoral level. In this era of constrained resources, many states are forcing the elimination of programs that are not considered "productive." In this case, productivity refers to delivering a specified number of degrees over a specific time period.

Robst (2001) examined productivity in higher education using a definition of cost efficiency as the difference between actual costs and an estimated minimum cost (p. 731) that he determined for institutions using a frontier cost function. He concluded that institutions that receive a smaller share of their revenues from state appropriations were not more efficient than institutions with higher state appropriations shares. His results were based on data from 1991 and 1995, and it is unclear if the results would be applicable in the new reality of higher education funding in the 21st century.

In 2000, 2002, 2004, and 2006, the National Center for Public Policy and Higher Education (NCPPHE) issued report cards to states on higher education that included measures of productivity, one of which was the ratio of bachelor's degrees produced to the undergraduate enrollment. NCPPHE (2006) concluded that the productivity ratios had remained relatively constant. Consistent with that research, NCES data showed that the number of bachelor's degrees awarded per 100 undergraduate students enrolled in 4-year institutions was the same in 2004 as it was in 1992 (NCES, 2006).

In 2005, the National Center for Higher Education Management Systems (NCHEMS) produced a report entitled *A New Look at the Institutional Component of Higher Education Finance: A Guide for Evaluating Performance Relative to Financial Resources* (NCHEMS, 2005). The report gauged the performance of state public postsecondary education sectors (i.e. research, bachelor's and master's, and 2-year institutions) on a variety of measures relative to the resources made available to them through state and local appropriations and tuition and fees. Measures of performance included graduation rates and degree production for each sector of postsecondary education and research expenditures at the public research universities. While the findings were not conclusive enough to determine which state systems (and sectors within them) are over- or underfunded, the results indicated that some states' institutions perform better than others with the resources they have. This analysis also refutes the argument that more funding always leads to better performance. Kelly (2009) built upon the NCHEMS work and concluded similarly that institutions in some states were more productive than other institutions, based on their level of resources and outputs. Note that Kelly did not base his productivity measure on outcomes.

Titus (2009) examined the relationship between state appropriations to higher education and the productivity of the institutions as defined by the number of bachelor's degrees awarded. He concluded that increases in state need-based financial aid have a positive impact on bachelor's degree productivity and that the number of bachelor's degrees produced is positively related to state appropriations; that is, an increase in state appropriations increases bachelor's degree production.

Auguste, Cota, Jayaram, and Laboissiere (2010) assessed the operational drivers of productivity at eight colleges and universities that were determined to be "high performing" in terms of the number of degrees produced. For this study, the authors defined productivity in two ways: completion efficiency and cost efficiency. Completion efficiency was defined by the ratio of students a school enrolls (measured in full-time equivalent students) to the number of degrees it awards. A low FTE/degree ratio means a completion efficient system, that is, one in which enrolled students have a high chance of gaining a degree. Cost efficiency was defined by an institution's total cost divided by the number of FTEs. A low cost/FTE ratio means a more cost efficient system, that is, one in which more students can be served with a given set of resources (Auguste et al., 2010). They found that there were several "unproductive" credits for an institution: excess credits and failed course credits. Further, they found that 14% of the credits earned by degree completers are over the threshold required by their degree. Such "excess crediting" may constitute up to 10% of total credits taken by all students. Failed credits and credits from which students withdraw constitute another 7% of "unproductive" credits. Although excess crediting may give students extra educational benefit, the authors stated that these credits add to the cost of a degree and so diminish degree productivity (Auguste et al., 2010). They concluded that productivity could be increased by several methods used by the "productive" institutions.

Institutional personnel have logged several criticisms of this research, including the fact that not all students are in college to get degrees. A definition of any credit hours that do not lead to a degree as "unproductive" does not consider the goals of some students and the role and mission of certain colleges.

The Texas Higher Education Coordinating Board released the report to the governor, *Higher Education Cost Efficiencies* (2012), which indicates how the Texas public colleges and universities were "productive" and "efficient" by eliminating degree or certificate programs that were not productive. Of the 105 Texas institutions, 67 reported that "non-productive" programs were eliminated to achieve efficiency and increase the institution's productivity.

The focus on productivity has been taken up by governors in states across the nation and has been defined as the production of bachelor's degrees. In coordination with Complete College America, the Lumina Foundation, and the Gates Foundation, states have been working to drive a particular kind of productivity in the 21st century: increasing the number of bachelor degree recipients by at least 40% to meet the needs of the states' economies for educated workers. Indeed, as noted in Chapter 7, performance funding formulas in some states include components that provide funding directly linked to an increase in graduates, especially in what are called the STEM fields: science, technology, engineering, and mathematics.

Other measures or definitions of productivity are included in the economics literature, including educational production functions. The calculation of production functions is complex, especially in the case of research universities, which produce research results as well as a number of degrees at various levels. Even for community colleges, a production function may be complex because of the variation among certificate and associate degree programs and transfer expectations.

Development of Accountability Systems

The development of performance indicators, accountability systems, and performance-based funding systems is ultimately based on the desire for accountability. At the board, state, and system levels, accountability is implemented by setting goals and objectives for institutions and periodically assessing progress towards those goals and objectives, using accepted indicators.

Perceptions of academic quality and accountability measures used to be based on quantity—the amount of resources, the quantity of students enrolled, the quantity and reputation of faculty research (Astin, 1985). The old measures for accountability were based on inputs and, in some cases, the outputs, but not the outcomes of higher education. In the 1980 and early 1990s, this perception shifted somewhat, and accountability came to include assessment of student outcomes, with indicators that evaluated how much students had learned against some set of learning outcomes, such as the CPA exam (Calcagro, Bailey, Jenkins, Krenzl, & Leinbranch, 2008). Regional accrediting agencies included assessment of student learning as one of the criteria for accreditation. However, the old indicators such as library holdings, admission scores, and count of faculty publications were still included in accountability reports. Over 90% of colleges and universities reported some assessment or accountability measures, but less than 20% of faculty participated (El-Khawas, 1995).

The budget crisis of the early 1990s caused a shift in accountability systems that continues today. Critics, including many legislators and governors, decried the poor state of undergraduate education, while business leaders noted that graduates were unprepared for work. Students were taking too long to graduate and were unable to make a meaningful contribution in the knowledge economy. Rising tuition and fees led to charges of inefficiency, lack of productivity, and lack of effectiveness. Accountability became a hot topic in state houses and in the popular press.

The accountability of the 1990s has been characterized as performance reporting, performance budgeting, or performance funding (Burke, 2004a) and went beyond the accountability of the 1980s. All three of these accountability "programs" had the same purposes: responding to state needs, demonstrating institutional accountability, and improving institutional performance (under the rubric of that which is measured, improves). The measures included all the prior measures of financial accountability, and others were added, most notably the demonstration of progress toward institutional (and state) goals and objectives.

In the 1980s and 1990s, Burke and his colleagues at the Rockefeller Institute at the University at Albany, State University of New York produced a significant amount of research on the state of higher education accountability. Most notable among the research was a series of surveys of all the states' efforts to do performance reporting, budgeting, or funding (Burke, Rosen, Minassians, & Lessard, 2000). The reader is encouraged to visit the Rockefeller Institute website to examine these research reports at www.rockinst.org/education/accountability_higher_ed.aspx

Burke (2004a) concluded that the majority of the states had accountability systems in place, but the majority were performance reporting systems. This finding was confirmed by Christal (1998), who provided a list of the most common performance indicators in use, as shown in Table 6.1. Most of these indicators are output or outcome indicators, but the old accountability measures of inputs and process indicators are still included.

Only three states (Oklahoma, South Carolina, and Tennessee) had accountability reports mandated by legislation before the 1990s, but that number had increased to 23 states by 1997 (Christal, 1998). These

Table 6.1. Most Common Accountability/Performance Indicators Used by States 1997-98.

Indicators	*No. of States Using*
Graduation rates	32
Transfer rates	25
Faculty workload/productivity	24
Follow-up satisfaction surveys	23
External/sponsored research funds	23
Remediation activities and their effectiveness	21
Pass rate on licensure exams	21
Degrees awarded	20
Placement data on graduates	19
Total student credit hours	18
Admission standards and measures	18
Number and percent of accredited programs	13

Source: Christal (1998).

accountability reports were designed to make higher education more responsive to legislators, students, parents, and the general public and included from 10 to 30 indicators. These reports were intended to address concerns about productivity but were somewhat limited by available data and were quantitative in nature, rather than qualitative. Some of the reports were hundreds of pages long, without a summary, which limited their effectiveness with legislators and other policy makers. (Note: Section IV will discuss how these reports should have been presented to policy makers.) Most of the reports presented information in a trend format, and some, most notably the reports of South Carolina, presented comparisons to peer institutions. Some reports also presented targets or goals along with the data and institutions' progress toward the goals. Although the reports were issued by almost every state, the use of the reports by policy makers was not clear, and their use was not studied until Burke and his associates provided their research on the topic.

Other countries were ahead of the states in developing accountability and quality assurance programs for their institutions of higher education. Great Britain adopted academic accountability audits of colleges and published reports in the early 1990s. Norway and Denmark, as well as Spain, established well-regarded accountability, productivity, and quality assurance programs and continue to maintain those programs for higher education today.

The budget crisis of the 1990s drove a change in the accountability paradigm and in funding formulas away from equity and adequacy toward goals of accountability and efficiency (McKeown, 1996a). The new accountability of the 1990s demanded that institutions and systems of higher education do more than just the performance reporting and led to adoption of accountability programs that linked funding to results. Funding for performance appeared to fit with the movement to reinvent and re-engineer government, including higher education (Burke, 2004a). By the time that the Rockefeller Institute had issued the results of its seventh annual survey on accountability and performance, 46 states were using performance reporting, but performance funding had become victim of budget cuts. Legislators appeared to perceive that performance reporting was a "no cost" accountability program, while performance funding required resources (Burke & Minassians, 2003). (Performance funding will be discussed in detail in Chapter 7.)

In response to the Spellings Commission report of 2006, the Association of Public and Land Grant Universities (APLGU) and the American Association of State Colleges and Universities (AASCU) developed the Voluntary System of Accountability (VSA) to demonstrate that public institutions were performing adequately. VSA used three measures of student learning to demonstrate that colleges were adding value to their students and providing a worthy product. Many institutions, especially large research universities, opted out of VSA, leading to a revision in 2013 to make the system more useful to users (Lederman, 2013).

Higher education accountability in the 21st century still includes performance reporting and performance budgeting. However, performance funding has been added to performance reporting and budgeting. Institutions and systems still do performance reporting, but in a manner that is much more transparent to legislators, students, parents, and the general public. Accountability has linked funding to a definition of goals and objectives, a budget to achieve those goals and objectives, *and* funding that is based on some measurement of progress toward or achievement of the goals and objectives. More importantly, the goals and objectives are more likely to be connected to meeting the *needs of students, the state, and its economy* instead of, or in addition to, meeting the *needs of higher education.*

While the setting of goals and objectives is an activity that is unique to every institution/state/system, and may be linked to the economy or other statewide goals, Ewell and Jones (1994, 2006) note four approaches commonly used in measuring progress towards these goals and objectives:

- *The input, process, outcome model*—this is a "production process" model aimed at measuring the value added to departing students, perhaps through pre- and post-assessments.

- *The resource efficiency and effectiveness model*—this approach is designed to measure the efficient usage of key resources such as faculty, space, and equipment, using ratio analyses or similar techniques.
- *The state need and return on investment model*—this approach is built on the assumption that higher education is a strategic investment for states; it is designed to measure the fit between higher education and state needs (e.g., work force preparation and training).
- *The "customer need" and return on investment model*—this approach is built on the notion of consumerism and is designed to measure the impact of higher education in meeting the needs of the individual (e.g., retention and graduation rates, employability and earning potential of graduates).

These four approaches are certainly not mutually exclusive, and most institutions/systems/states employing performance indicators choose from two or more of these areas. Further, no one approach is "better" than the others. Rather, the important thing is that the approach(es) chosen be relevant and appropriate for the institution, system, and state. Research into effective establishment of an accountability, quality assurance, or productivity system has established a set of guiding principles for any accountability or performance funding system that should be followed in the initial design of an accountability system. Table 6.2 outlines 11 guiding principles that are presented in no particular order of importance. The process for developing and establishing a system of performance indicators is unique to every enterprise; however, all 11 of these principles need to be considered during this process to ensure a successful and effective outcome (Layzell, 2001).

These 11 guiding principles have a number of corollaries that should be considered as well:

- *The expectations for institutional performance should be clearly understood and stated at the outset.* Organizations can only "improve" if there is an understanding of the priorities for organizational performance. Clearly, the priorities should grow out of organizational mission and goals; however, it is important that these be understood and agreed to by key participants at the beginning of the process.
- *The starting place for institutional performance measurement and benchmarks for success varies among institutions.* Because each institution operates within its own context, the beginning point for institutional performance measurement also will vary depending on the specific performance indicator. Using "graduation rate" as an

Table 6.2. Guiding Principles for Developing and Establishing Institutional Performance Indicators

Guiding Principle	Definition
Credibility	The performance indicators should have internal and external credibility among all institutional stakeholders.
Linkage to Mission, Strategic Plan, and Policy Goals	The performance indicators should incorporate and reinforce institutional missions and strategic plans, as well as broad policy goals.
Stakeholder Involvement and Consensus	The performance indicators should be developed through negotiation and consensus among key stakeholders.
Simplicity	The performance indicators should be simple to convey and broadly understood.
Reliant on Valid, Consistent, and Existing Information	The performance indicators should be based on data that are valid and consistent and that can be verified by third parties when necessary. The indicators should also be based on established data sources *where possible* in order to maximize credibility and minimize additional workload.
Recognizes Range of Error in Measurement	The performance indicators should be established with wide recognition that there are certain unavoidable ranges of error in any performance measurement activity.
Adaptable to Special Situations	The system of performance indicators should accommodate special institutional circumstances where possible.
Minimizes Number of Indicators	The performance indicators chosen should be kept to the smallest number possible in order to minimize conflicting interactions among the indicators and to maximize the importance of each indicator.
Reflects Industry "Standards" and "Best Practices"	The performance indicators chosen should reflect "industry norms and standards" where possible in order to allow for benchmarking and peer comparisons.
Incorporates Input, Process, Output, and Outcomes Measures	The performance indicator system developed should have a balance of measures related to institutional inputs, processes, outputs, and outcomes.
Incorporates Quantitative and Qualitative Measures	The performance indicator system developed should incorporate both quantitative and qualitative measures in order to present the most complete picture of institutional performance possible.

example, one institution may be at 45% for a 6-year graduation rate while another may be at 85%. Because these types of variances can be due to a variety of potentially valid reasons, no value judgment should automatically be attached.

- *"Continuous improvement" is not infinite.* A related issue that must be dealt with in establishing performance measurement mechanisms is the fact that the rate of "improvement" in any given area is non-linear. Institutions may be able to make great strides toward improving certain operational or programmatic areas initially but then come to a standstill. Or, an institution may move forward in another area and then falter for a period of time. In short, it is important to realize that the process of enhancing institutional performance is imprecise at best and that to expect institutions to "continuously improve" is unrealistic.

- *Performance measures should not be developed only with available data systems in mind.* Implementing a system of institutional performance measurement requires data to be available. In fact, most institutions develop performance measures with this in mind. This practice has both positive and negative consequences. The ability to work with existing data systems reduces the start-up time and cost to implement a performance indicator system. It also improves the comfort level of those involved and thus the credibility of the process. On the other hand, limiting an institution's performance measures according to data availability may not result in the most appropriate or meaningful set of measures in the long run. Thus, notwithstanding the benefits of using existing data systems, the development of performance measures should recognize the current availability of data where appropriate but should be primarily driven by the questions "what are we trying to measure?" and "why?"

Perhaps the greatest challenge in designing a performance indicator system is to achieve some level of balance among all of these competing, and sometimes contradictory, principles. Again, no one of these principles is more important than the others. Rather, it is important that all be considered during the design and implementation of the system.

Burke and Modarresi (2000) identified at least five characteristics common to successful and stable performance or accountability programs:

1. involvement and input from state coordinating boards;
2. accent on both institutional improvement and accountability;
3. sufficient time allowed for both planning and implementation;
4. use of a limited number of indicators; and
5. recognition and protection of institutional diversity.

These findings are consistent with the set of guiding principles discussed earlier and therefore reinforce their importance.

Serban (1998) noted three methods by which progress toward performance goals are measured:

- *Institutional improvement over time*—institutional progress on individual indicators is measured against their own past performance.
- *Comparisons with peer institutions*—institutional attainment is measured against peer institution averages and ranges on individual indicators.
- *Comparisons against predetermined target standards*—institutional performance is measured as progress toward meeting preset target standards on individual indicators.

These measurement methods are not mutually exclusive, and all have their strengths and weaknesses, particularly when considered within the guiding principles described earlier. For example, while benchmarking against one's own past performance may seem to be relatively non-threatening, it can soon bump up against the reality that continuous improvement is not infinite. Likewise, comparisons with external peers add a level of "benchmarking" and independent validation to the process. However, such comparisons invariably introduce data comparability issues that can cloud the validity of the comparisons if not properly controlled. Finally, comparisons against preset targets can enable stakeholders to assess progress toward desired policy outcomes and goals in relatively specific fashion (e.g., improved retention and graduation rates). However, these preset targets need to be designed with the recognition that each institution operates within its own unique context and is starting from a different place. In short, a combination of all three methods is perhaps most desirable in setting success criteria.

Establishing a Quality Assurance or Accountability Program

To set up accountability programs for a college or university, financial officers, institutional research staff, and planning officers have used all of the measures and methods mentioned above. In the 21st century, these programs may be called quality assurance, performance reporting, or accountability systems. All attempt to link qualitative and quantitative data to strategic planning, communication with constituents, and institutional quality improvement efforts.

The goals and objectives of the institution's strategic plan, of the system's planning efforts (for those institutions in a system), and of statewide plans are critical components of an accountability program. Measures of progress toward the goals and objectives must be reported both to internal and to external constituents.

The report *Committed to Quality: Guidelines for Assessment and Accountability in Higher Education* (New Leadership Alliance for Student Learning and Accountability, 2012), issued by a consortia of the major Washington DC higher education actors, is intended to be a tool to help higher education institutions answer accountability questions about student learning and take responsibility for assessing and improving student learning. In the Alliance's view, committing to quality means setting clear goals for student achievement, regularly measuring performance against those goals, reporting evidence of success, and continuously working to improve results (New Leadership Alliance, 2012).

To that end, the Alliance set guidelines within each of these rubrics:

1. Set ambitious goals for learning. Guidelines:

   (a) The institution's statements of learning outcomes clearly articulate what students should be able to do, achieve, demonstrate, or know upon the completion of each undergraduate degree.

   (b) The outcomes reflect appropriate higher education goals and are stated in a way that allows levels of achievement to be assessed against an externally informed or benchmarked level of achievement or assessed and compared with those of similar institutions.

   (c) Institutional practices, such as program review, are in place to ensure that curricular and co-curricular goals are aligned with intended learning outcomes.

   (d) The institution and its major academic and co-curricular programs can identify places in the curriculum or co-curriculum where students encounter or are expected or required to achieve the stated outcomes.

   (e) Learning outcome statements are presented in prominent locations and in ways that are easily understood by interested audiences.

2. Gather evidence of student learning. Guidelines:

   (a) Policies and procedures are in place that describe when, how, and how frequently learning outcomes will be assessed.

   (b) Assessment processes are ongoing, sustainable, and integrated into the work of faculty, administrators, and staff.

(c) Evidence includes results that can be assessed against an externally informed or benchmarked level of achievement or compared with those of other institutions and programs.

(d) Evidence also includes assessments of levels of engagement in academically challenging work and active learning practices.

(e) Results can be used to examine differences in performance among significant subgroups of students, such as minority group, first-generation, and non-traditional-age students.

3. Use evidence to improve student learning. Guidelines:

(a) Well-articulated policies and procedures are in place for using evidence to improve student learning at appropriate levels of the institution.

(b) Evidence is used to make recommendations for improvement of academic and co-curricular programs.

(c) There is an established process for discussing and analyzing these recommendations and moving from recommendation to action. Where feasible and appropriate, key recommendations for improvement are implemented.

(d) The impact of evidence-based changes in programs and practices is continuously reviewed and evaluated.

4. Report the evidence and results. Guidelines:

(a) Regular procedures are in place for sharing evidence of student learning with internal and external constituencies.

(b) Internal reporting includes regularly scheduled meetings, publications, and other mechanisms that are accessible to all relevant constituencies (e.g., faculty, staff, administrators, students, the governing body).

(c) Reporting to external constituencies via the institutional website includes evidence of learning as well as additional descriptive information and indicators of institutional performance (e.g., retention rates, time to degree).

(d) Reporting on student learning outcomes is both accessible to and appropriate for the relevant audience.

(e) The results of evidence-based changes in programs and practices are reported to appropriate internal and external constituencies (New Leadership Alliance, 2012).

This list of guidelines is a good one to follow to ensure that the institution is being accountable for student learning, which is only one component of an accountability or quality assurance program.

The best quality assessment programs derive from and are linked to the institution's mission, strategic plan, and vision and are supported by the executive leadership of the institution, including the governing board. To be successful, the best practice quality assessment programs require, first and foremost, the continued and visible support by the president of the institution and the governing board. As a demonstration of the commitment and support of the president and board, the individual responsible for the quality assessment program should be at the executive level of the organization, as a vice president or vice chancellor. Likely, in today's environment, that condition already has been met by either the president, the board, or by a statewide office. Today institutions not only have a strategic plan with goals and objectives but also have the ongoing support of a senior officer and an office that is responsible for providing measures of progress toward the goals of the plan, maintaining a data system that will ensure that those measures are in place, and issuing reports on the measures. All of the regional accrediting bodies such as the North Central Association now require a strategic plan and accountability measures.

The vice president for quality assessment should be given sufficient financial and staff resources to carry out the essential tasks of a quality assessment program. Best practice quality assessment programs are relatively expensive to operate. For example, there are costs associated with institutional and program accreditation as well as costs for assessing student, graduate, and employer satisfaction using surveys. Some traditional institutions have reduced the number of program evaluations that they do each year because each program evaluation by outside reviewers can cost more than $100,000, and their total budgets have been reduced. The number of surveys also has been reduced even though the costs of an Internet-based survey are significantly less than a snail mail survey. Surveys managed by outside agencies are expensive, and their costs must be balanced against the information received through national comparisons.

The programs that are thought to be best practice are perceived to be critical to the continued success of the institution and are part of the fabric of the institution. Good quality assessment or accountability programs are continuous, in other words, are ongoing programs that do not stop when the institution is regionally accredited or when the strategic plan has been updated; good programs are a natural and ongoing operation that become ingrained or instinctive. Quality assessment should not be perceived as an onerous burden, outside of normal operating procedures, but as an absolutely critical component of normal institutional operations that involve all the staff of the institution. Some institutions have found that an atmosphere of continuous assessment and improvement required a change in the institutional environment so that at least a majority of the faculty and staff were supportive of the quality assurance program.

Faculties are typically the most difficult "staff" members to convince of the importance of ongoing assessment of the learning process. Faculty often do not perceive that the aims of quality assurance (to ensure that the operation of the institution is in sync with its mission, to enhance current operations, and to determine whether the institution is achieving its goals and objectives) have much to do with them and their classrooms.

In many institutions, the quality assessment office grew out of the institutional research (IR) and planning office since this was the place where much research on effectiveness was done and its staff members were qualified in and capable of conducting research on what works, tracking measures of quality, and surveying students, graduates, faculty, and staff. Because this office has the capacity to provide data relatively easily, usually the IR office is part of the quality assessment structure. Similarly, the individual(s) responsible for strategic planning and/or operational planning typically are included in the quality assessment function because quality assessment involves assurance that the institution is working toward achievement of the goals and objectives set out in the strategic plan or vision.

The best practice quality assessment program integrates and synthesizes a variety of measures or modalities to generate data pertinent to the "quality" of an institution and informs internal stakeholders and various external publics on a regular basis about the institution, its programs, and its successes. The challenge is in the integration and application of all the various instruments available to assess the success of the institution—its programs, its students, and its graduates—and to integrate the strategic, tactical, and operational components.

There are multiple components of good quality assessment programs that can be designed for internal or external constituencies, including institutional accreditation, program accreditation, faculty/mentor qualifications, curriculum assessment, student progress assessment, retention, student satisfaction, staff satisfaction, graduate satisfaction, employer satisfaction, financial analyses, and other metrics discussed above, both for the peer institutions and from the benchmark literature.

In the establishment of best practice quality assurance programs, it is essential that who is responsible, what is to be measured or assessed, and how it is to be implemented are determined at the beginning and clearly articulated so that everyone knows what they have to do, when, and why. There should be clarity on from where information will come, who will collect and synthesize the information, where the data will be stored, and how the results will be shared. Coordination of all of the facets of the quality assurance program requires cooperation across multiple levels and across different "arms" of the institution. Cooperation is much easier when the president indicates that quality assurance is of high importance for the institution.

Coordination also implies that one office or one person is responsible for a component of the program, such as surveys. Best practice programs have a central repository or authority that ensures that all surveys that go out are approved and do not overlap.

Determining what the metrics to be used should be is an essential component of a best practice accountability program. There are three kinds of metrics to an accountability program: strategic, tactical, and operational. Strategic quality metrics or components relate to the long-term or macro goals that may be in the strategic plan; strategic metrics are those that are reported to external stakeholders while tactical components are those that move the institution toward achievement of those goals not for the long term, but for an intermediate term. Tactics that are used by and reported to stakeholders internal to the institution may relate to the operation of the institution at a whole, and concern the "how" of accomplishing an objective in the relatively short term. Operational components relate to the daily operations for a particular department or unit within the institution, such as accounts payable or human resources. Operational measures are a very important part of any quality assessment program but usually are not reported to external constituents.

An example of a strategic metric is increasing the number of graduates to 600 per year, or improving the graduation rate to 80%. External stakeholders, including potential students, are very interested in the institution's graduation rate as a measure of how likely a student is to succeed by graduating from the institution. An example of a tactical metric is increasing the number of graduates by 20 next year and 30 the year after; this is a measure that institutional staff members need to know so they can plan. An example of an operational metric is the average time to process an invoice or the time to process a new hire. The operational happens almost daily. In higher education, the distinction between the levels may be blurred. These three categories or levels are not mutually exclusive, as a quality metric can be strategic, tactical, and/or operational. For example, the completion rate of undergraduate students in a particular program is an operational metric for that department for this year but also is a strategic indicator for potential students for the long-term and a tactical measure for next year.

There are hundreds of quality assurance or accountability metrics at the strategic and tactical levels used by colleges and universities. There are thousands of quality metrics at the operational level, mainly because there are so many operational units at a college or university. A college may have 100 academic and non-academic departments, each of which may have 10 quality metrics.

The broad categories for critical quality assurance or accountability metrics include indicators of student enrollment, retention rates, student academic performance and outcomes, graduation and completion rates, and employment status and employer satisfaction.

- *Student Enrollment:* Examples include overall enrollment, enrollment by department/area, undergraduate versus graduate enrollment, percentage of enrollment that is returning graduates, percentage of enrollment that is military students (by affiliation), percentage of enrollment that is online students only, and percentage of enrollment that is transfer students.
- *Retention Rates:* Examples include overall retention rate, retention rate by department/area, freshmen retention, transfer student retention, percentage of returning graduates, and retention by degree level (undergraduate vs. graduate).
- *Student Academic Performance and Outcomes:* Examples include overall performance, performance by department/area, performance by degree level (undergraduate vs. graduate), number of course credits taken and completed, transfer student performance, examination performance (overall, by department/area, by degree level, etc.), overall GPA and GPA by department/area, and internship, assistantship, and student teaching performance.
- *Graduation/Completion Rates:* Examples include overall graduation/completion rates, graduation/completion rates by department/area, number of graduates (overall and by area), graduation/completion rates by degree level, percentage of students graduating on time, and the amount of time to completion (undergraduate vs. graduate, by department/area).
- *Employment Status and Employer Satisfaction:* Examples include employment status (full-time, part-time, or temporary), employment placement (employment by field, time to placement after graduation), employment success (promotions, recognition), level of workforce preparedness (employed in field related to degree area, institutional course offerings' validity to market), average salary one and 5 years after graduation, and employer satisfaction.

Critical metrics used by *almost all* institutions include the number and percentage of degrees awarded, student satisfaction, student performance, faculty/staff satisfaction, and faculty/staff and department performance.

- *Degrees Awarded:* Examples include overall number of degrees awarded, number/percentage of degrees awarded by department/area, number/percentage of degrees awarded by degree type (certificate, associate, bachelor's, master's, doctoral), number/percentage of degrees awarded by degree level (undergraduate vs. graduate), number/percentage of degrees awarded by race/ethnicity or other status, and number/percentage of completions.
- *Student Satisfaction:* Examples include satisfaction of enrolled students and alumni, satisfaction by department/area, satisfaction with course offerings, satisfaction with course delivery, satisfaction with customer service (responsiveness and helpfulness of institutional offices, available services, problem or conflict resolution, etc.), and likelihood that students, graduates, and/or alumni will recommend institution to others.
- *Faculty/Staff Satisfaction:* Examples include faculty/staff satisfaction with the work environment and staff relations, satisfaction with leadership, satisfaction with institution and department operations, overall morale, and satisfaction with professional development opportunities.
- *Faculty/Staff and Department Performance:* Examples include overall performance, performance by department/area, teaching quality, level of faculty/staff productivity, personal awards/recognition received, department awards/recognition received, department accreditation, quality of relationships/interactions with students (responsiveness, helpfulness, reliability, outreach, etc.), and degree or course enrollment and demand.

Other critical quality metrics used by institutions that are less common include the amount of financial aid and resources available for students, number of applications received, a variety of financial measures (related to revenue, budget, and expenditures), amount of alumni support and giving, and the average amount of student debt at graduation/program completion. Metrics may also be classified into the following categories:

- Competitive advantage
- Quality
- Student success
- Finances
- Technology
- Student life

It is important to note that what different institutions may be measuring by a particular type of metric, such as completion rates, may be different. For example, all institutions report completion rates or numbers, but each institution may define the cohort somewhat differently. For some institutions the undergraduate completion rate is the 6-year graduation rate for a cohort of full-time, first-time freshmen, while other institutions may define *one* of its undergraduate graduation rates for a cohort of students who started enrollment at the same time, enroll in at least one class in two out of three semesters or complete nine credit hours within 2 years, and graduate within 10 years. Retention or persistence rates also are defined differently by institutions. Some institutions use the traditional retention of freshmen to sophomore status, while others define retention as enrolling in classes in at least one of the three semesters following initial enrollment. What is important to researchers is to know what definitions are being used so that "apples" can be compared to "apples."

Some metrics used by institutions may be more important for external stakeholders, while others are more important to stakeholders internal to the college or university. In either grouping, some metrics may be strategic while others are tactical. However, institutions typically do not label the metrics they found important as "strategic," "tactical," or "operational;" rather, all were noted as important metrics for the institution.

Generally, quality assurance or accountability metrics relate to the goals and objectives of the institution's strategic plan or action plan and the progress the institution is making toward achievement of the goal or objectives of that plan. For public colleges and universities, some of their quality metrics, such as the number of graduates in STEM fields, relate to specific goals and objectives within the state in which the institution is located. These metrics usually are those items for which the state imposes specific reporting requirements, such as the number and percent of total enrollment of residents of the state enrolled at the college.

Information for the metrics is collected from several sources. The primary methods and data sources used by institutions include the following:

- *Institutional Records and Data:* Offices that generate or collect data include admissions, registrar, finance/business, academic/student affairs, alumni affairs/services, and institutional research, evaluation, and/or planning.
- *Surveys:* Population groups surveyed include enrolled students, graduates and alumni (undergraduate and graduate), employers of graduates and alumni, and faculty and staff. Most institutions conduct surveys of these groups annually.

- *Examination Data, Course Evaluations:* Examination and course evaluation data are typically collected at the end of courses or whenever a national examination is conducted and reported annually.
- *Department Data/Reviews, Faculty/Staff Evaluations:* Department and faculty/staff data are typically collected annually.

Many of the critical quality metrics used by institutions do not have national benchmarks or standards against which to judge. However, some sources are available that list components of a quality assurance program and the metrics for a quality assurance program. *Quality on the Line: Benchmarks for Success in Internet Based Distance Education* (NEA, 2000) provides 24 benchmarks or best strategies in the areas of course development, faculty training, student services, learning resources, infrastructure, outcomes assessment, institutional support, and teaching/learning. *Quality on the Line* is but one example of benchmarks.

Other countries that have adopted quality assurance regulations and benchmarks include Japan, India, the United Kingdom, New Zealand, South Africa, Argentina, and Chile. Quality assurance metrics exist for curriculum, student learning, student support, assessment of student performance, and academic planning. In the United Kingdom, the Quality Assurance Agency has issued guidelines for quality assurance and accreditation and sets benchmarks and standards for all programs. In New Zealand, the Academic Audit Unit (AAU) has produced a quality assurance document that is part-way between an accreditation manual and a guide for external reviewers. Finland audits the quality assurance programs of its colleges and universities, using the European principles and best practices for quality assurance programs. Determination of the success of the quality assurance program is based on the production of useful information for improvement of the operations of the institution and if the quality measures engender improvement. Similarly, the European Association for Distance Learning issued a quality guide for quality assurance metrics in higher education in 2003. The guide lists measures of customer (student) satisfaction, staff satisfaction, and employer satisfaction as some of the quality assurance metrics (Middlehurst, 2001).

Within the United States, the Ohio Board of Regents issued educational accountability metrics that set minimum standards for each institution. Metrics include the percent passage on licensure exams, teacher performance, partnerships with K–12, grants and fellowships received, a survey of teacher education candidates, a new teacher survey to assess the preparation for teaching, an employer satisfaction survey, financial ratios, net income, fund balance, enrollments, academic progress, degrees awarded, post-graduation employment, costs, and financial aid. Ohio focused several metrics on teacher preparation because one of the goals of its statewide master plan was to increase the number of adequately prepared teachers who were competent in their field. Similarly, the Tennessee Higher Education Commission in December 2011 conducted a webinar on the use of quality metrics in Tennessee. Metrics align with the institution's master/strategic plan and with Tennessee's outcomes-based funding formula. Metrics relate to the institution's mission and include time to degree, degrees awarded, on-time progression to degree, percent of credit hours attempted that are completed, number of STEM degrees, and successful transfer students.

In a presentation to the National Governor's Association, William Massey (2011) argued that academic audits similar to financial audits should be a component of a quality assurance system, especially for programs that are provided through alternative means, such as distance education. He pointed out that this kind of metric is done in Australia, Hong Kong, the United Kingdom, and Sweden. Such a system would be based on "generally accepted education quality principles" like the generally accepted accounting principles (GAAP) that guide metrics for financial accountability.

There are a number of critical metrics that should be components of any accountability program. These are discussed below.

- *Institutional and Program Accreditation.* For most institutions, the overarching critical quality assurance metric is accreditation, both of the institution by a regional accrediting body such as Middle States or North Central Association of Schools and Colleges, and of particular programs like engineering accreditation by ABET. Potential students as well as funding bodies seek assurance about the reputation and reliability of the institution and guarantees that the degrees or certificates earned in a particular program of study are evidence of quality learning that will be valued and rewarded by potential employers. The assurance that an institution is accredited is perceived to give this guarantee. Institutional accreditation typically occurs every 10 years but is always reported on the institution's website. Program accreditation occurs periodically and is reported whenever the accreditation is announced by the accrediting body.

- *Employee and Institutional Awards.* Awards made to employees or institutional distinctions are noteworthy accomplishments that provide additional information to potential students, donors, or other funding entities that this is an institution of quality. Examples of awards to employees are Nobel prizes or Pulitzer prizes, while awards to the institution may be a prize for architectural excellence or the Ralph E. Gomory Award for Quality Online Education. Awards are noted on the institution's website when the award is received and typically are included in the institution's annual report.

- *Faculty Quality.* Institutions evaluate the qualifications of their teaching staff, as well as their performance in the classroom, on both an annual basis and at the end of courses. Students evaluate their instructors typically at the end of the course, and student satisfaction with mentors or other instructional personnel is evaluated through a student survey. Before an instructor is hired, institutions evaluate their credentials and then track any change or improvement in credentials or training. In addition, institutions use in-class evaluations by other faculty to determine whether an individual is doing a good job. Also, institutions have a systematic methodology for ensuring that faculty, or individuals who developed each course, were up-to-date on developments in their field or were good teachers.

- *Student Satisfaction.* Measures of student satisfaction with their academic experience and the services received from the institution are critical components of a best practice quality assurance program. Multiple measures of student satisfaction typically are sought through surveys sent to all students, students in a particular class, or students in an academic department. Questions are asked about the student's satisfaction with the class, the institution, advising, faculty, enrollment, and other areas of the college experience. Typically, general student satisfaction surveys are done once per year and provide strategic and tactical information both to the institution and to a department on which the survey is focused. This information may be gathered either through a national survey like the National Survey of Student Engagement (NSSE) or through a survey designed and administered by a department or the institutional research office. The advantage of a national survey is that the institution will have comparative data to other similar institutions. If the survey is repeated, over time trend data will be available to judge progress toward or regress away from goals. Institutions vary in the use they make of the student satisfaction surveys. Some are required to report the results of the surveys to the state governing or coordinating board, while other institutions use the results strategically to plan for the long-term or tactically for the next semester/year. Results also may be posted on websites as a measure of the student experience. Student surveys also are taken at the end of a class and evaluate the classroom experience directly. These surveys by their nature are designed and administered by the institution for use in class evaluations as a quality check on the class, the faculty member, and the way in which the class fits into the total curriculum. The information from the surveys typically is shared with the department, the chief academic officer, and may also be shared with the instructor.

- *Graduate Satisfaction*. Similar to measures of student satisfaction, measures of graduate satisfaction are critical components of a quality assurance program. Graduate surveys typically are conducted annually for the whole institution, but specific departments or academic units may conduct a survey of its own graduates, either for strategic or tactical reasons. Not only the results of graduate satisfaction surveys but also direct quotes from graduates about their programs usually are found on an institution's website as a measure of the relevance and quality of the institution and/or a particular degree or certificate program. Measures of graduate satisfaction are strategically used by institutions to spin the story of the quality of the institution. Some state governing/coordinating boards use graduate satisfaction survey results as one of the items in their performance funding mechanisms rather than as a measure of quality and send out surveys 1 year, 2 years, and 5 years after graduation. Results of the surveys are reported both to the institution as a whole and to specific academic departments or colleges for their use in the quality improvement of their curricula and as an evaluation of their teaching and advising staffs. In addition, graduate surveys are used to determine if graduates are employed in a field related to their training or are seeking an advanced degree or training.

- *Employee Satisfaction*. Just as measures of student and graduate satisfaction are critical quality assurance metrics, so are measures of employee satisfaction, or the quality of employee life. Institutions survey their employees at least once a year on a variety of issues, including satisfaction with pay scales, benefits, working conditions, and technology. Generally, measures of employee satisfaction are used tactically to identify any issues and make short-term corrections to conditions. Also, at the end of each semester, teaching staff usually are surveyed about their courses, the curriculum, use of technology, student ability levels, and other academic issues. Surveys or other information gathered related to teaching and learning are especially critical to an institution's quality assurance program. Through these metrics, departments learn what is working especially well and what is not so that corrective action can be taken.

- *Employer Satisfaction*. Employer satisfaction with the graduates of an institution is one of the more difficult to assess of the quality assurance metrics and one of the critical strategic measures. Potential students want to get a degree at an institution whose graduates are valued and hired by business and industry and where their training relates directly to job responsibilities. Governors and legislators are interested in this measure as well. Surveys gather employer information, typically once per year or every other year. Results of the employer survey are shared on the institution's website (if the results are positive) and shared with individual academic departments as a measure of the appropriateness and efficacy of their programs. Employer surveys are hard to administer because of the difficulty of identifying where graduates are employed. Also, response rates are not high, so the value of the information has to be weighed against the cost of gathering the information. The University System of Georgia has done employer surveys for all the 34 institutions within the system, which certainly helps the institutions.

- *Volunteer or Outreach Activities to the Community.* Several institutions report on the volunteer or outreach activities to the local and/or statewide community. This is an important measure of the way in which the institution interacts with the community in which it is located.

- *Economic Impact.* Several institutions report the economic impact of the institution and their alumni. As states ask more from their public institutions of higher education, the economic impact is one measure of what the institution does for the local community and/ or the state. These studies are done once every several years and reported generally to external constituencies. A more complete discussion of economic impact studies may be found in Chapter 8.

- *Applications and Enrollments.* These metrics relate to the ability of the institution to convert inquiries to applications and applications to registrations or enrollments. The perception is that the overall attractiveness of the institution and how easily a student may complete the application process leads to registration or enrollment and revenues. This is a critical measure for private institutions to monitor to ensure that the institution maintains its revenue flow and its enrollments. There is no national benchmark on what the number of applications should be or what is the acceptable rate of conversion from inquiries to applications to enrollments because this is a metric that is institution-specific. Trends in applications and registrations should be closely monitored because of the strategic implications.

- *Total Course Credits.* The total number of course credits is reported by institutions on both a semester and an annual basis. Some institutions report both the number of credits enrolled and the number successfully completed. Course credits are directly related to institutional revenues, and so the number of credits is an important indicator for institutional management. There has been some national attention to the use of credits completed instead of credits attempted as the measure of enrollment used by states in their funding of higher education. Governors, legislators, and other policy makers appear to perceive that students not completing the courses for which they enroll as a failure of the institution to be productive and a failure of the faculty to ensure student success. There are many reasons that a student does not complete a course, but the critical issue is in the revenue received. In any case, the metric has been given additional prominence in the push to increase the number of college completers.

- *Tuition and Fees of Peer Institutions*. Having lower tuition and fee charges than an institution's competitors provides a competitive advantage, and increases in tuition and fees that are less than a competitor's increase also assist in encouraging potential students to enroll. However, public institutions may be limited in what can be charged. Although the perception has been that the more an institution charges, the higher quality education is provided (e.g., Harvard and Princeton), there is no real correlation between tuition and fees and the quality of the education. In the current economy, students are extremely aware of which institutions are the best value. Institutions monitor the tuition and fees of their competitor institutions to ensure that the institution maintains its competitive advantage. The national standard for reporting is whenever tuition and fees are set for the following academic year. These data are used by the College Board and other groups to calculate average increases in tuition.

- *Examination Results*. Institutions report the passage rates on exams such as the GRE, PRAXIS, bar exam, or the National Nursing Exam to indicate that the quality of their programs is such that almost all completers have passed the exam and/or received high scores. Having the highest passage rate in the state, or in the nation for certain exams, indicates that the institution's programs are high quality. Benchmarks on examination results are institution-specific; that is, the institution wants to increase or maintain its passage rate or scores. These are important measures of the quality of the program that prepared the individual to take the exam.

Student success metrics include those items most often used by colleges and universities in their quality assurance programs. Several of these metrics are so essential that the U.S. Department of Education requires that colleges and universities post these metrics prominently on the institution's website. Similarly, some states require institutions in the state to provide on their websites certain information regarding its costs, faculty, and graduation rates.

- *Enrollment.* All higher education institutions report their enrollment, and unless they have enrollment caps, tout increases in enrollment as a mark of the quality of the institution. Enrollment statistics are critical quality assurance indicators because these statistics demonstrate the institution's role in serving the citizens of the state or region or nation. Enrollment goals by gender, ethnicity, and origin often are set by the state (for public institutions), and the statistics are reported each semester. For purposes of reporting to the state, typically enrollment statistics are done only twice a year coincident with the traditional fall and spring semesters. The benchmark for enrollment may be set by the state, but there is no national standard.

- *Retention and Persistence.* These two items traditionally have measured the continued enrollment of a student at the institution from one year to the next. Retention rates are reported annually to the National Center for Education Statistics and have to be posted on the institution's web site. Historically, this statistic is a measure of the full-time freshmen who re-enroll at the institution in the following year. Some institutions report not only freshman-to-sophomore retention but also sophomore-to-junior and junior-to-senior retention. Persistence can refer to the continued enrollment of a student toward the student's desired goals, whether or not the student is an undergraduate, graduate student, full-time, or part-time. The goal of course is to have 100% retention and 100% persistence, but this is not realistic. The traditional definition of retention and persistence does not fit the clientele of community colleges or institutions that enroll a predominately nontraditional population.

- *Completion and Time to Completion.* Completion metrics are critical components of an institution's quality assurance program. The NGA's Completion Agenda has highlighted this metric, as has President Obama's push for more college graduates. Just as with retention and persistence, the traditional completion metric that is reported to NCES does not fit community colleges or institutions that enroll a part-time or adult population.

- *Degrees and Certificates Awarded.* Given the current national push to increase the number of college and university graduates, the number of degrees and certificates awarded has become a metric of public interest. Several states have begun to fund colleges and universities based on increases in the number of degrees and also based on the number of degrees awarded in fields that are in the state's economic interests, such as graduates in STEM fields. The numbers are calculated and reported annually.

- *Future Education Plans.* Most graduate surveys ask the graduates whether they intend to continue their education. Nationally, about 40% of bachelor's degree recipients go on to more education. This metric is considered important because it is a measure of the quality of the undergraduate education that a graduate school would accept this student.

- *Employment.* Both employment in a field related to the degree or certificate earned and a salary increase after completion of education indicate that the graduate received benefits from the education at the institution. Most institutions consider these metrics to be critical and report the data taken generally from graduate surveys annually.

- *Student Learning.* Assessment of what students learn is an important quality metric. Students are concerned that what they learned in their programs of study will enable them to earn higher salaries, while employers are concerned that students have learned content and thinking skills relevant to their employment. Grades in a course are one measure of student learning, as are scores on standardized tests and rising junior examinations. Special studies have been done by some institutions to determine if one method of teaching or one pedagogy results in students learning more or learning faster. One measure of student learning is an improvement in writing skills. As mentioned above, other measures include student performance on national exams such as the SHRM exam or one of the 10 components of the PRAXIS. Other measures of student learning are to assess whether the student has met the outcomes of an integrated learning assessment. Best practice programs have the outcomes for each program posted on their web sites and then evaluate student performance against the outcomes. Some do this evaluation at the end of the student's program of study, while other institutions do such an assessment at the end of each course.

- *Undergraduate Debt.* There has been considerable interest in the press about the staggering amounts of debt many undergraduates took on to complete their education. Although there is national interest in this measure, most institutions do not consider it to be a critical quality assurance metric.

Higher education institutions have been reporting quality metrics related to finance for many years, at the strategic, tactical, and operational levels. Institutions need to know how much revenue they anticipate, how much they actually receive, and what their budgeted and actual expenditures are against those revenues.

- *Budgeted and Actual Revenues; Budgeted and Actual Expenditures; Fund Balance*. These metrics are typically reported as part of monthly, quarterly, or annual financial statements, or as components of the budget process. Revenues and expenditures must balance, or revenues must exceed expenditures so that the institution will not have to dip into the fund balance. The metrics are reported as a measure of the financial stability and planning of the organization. All institutions report these numbers. Revenues and expenditures are strategic measures during the planning for the future and tactical metrics as the institution balances its budget. The fund balance is an important financial statistic that indicates if the institution has a cushion or bank balance to mitigate the effects of peaks and valleys in revenues. All institutions report fund balances (and revenues and expenditures) as components of the annual audited financial statement. The audit is an outside "accreditation" that the institution is conducting its financial transactions in accordance with generally accepted accounting principles (GAAP). The audit and the certification by the public accountant that all is in order is the benchmark against which these quality metrics are measured.
- *Financial Ratios*. Financial ratios, such as the current ratio or the asset ratio, may be calculated as part of the annual financial audit. Ratios also may be calculated by a state agency, such as a higher education coordinating board, or a state auditor, as a metric on the financial health of the institution. Ratios for higher education institutions are judged against the standards set by major public accounting firms such as Deloitte. For a public college, financial ratios can be early warning signs, but they are not as important an indicator as ratios for private institutions are.
- *Revenues or Expenditures per Full-Time Equivalent Student*. Some public policy analysts perceive that revenues or expenditures per full-time equivalent student are measures of the efficiency of an institution. All other things being equal, for similar institutions, the institution that spends less per student is thought to be more efficient. However, such a measure can mean that the quality of the higher spending

institution is better, that students are enrolled in programs that are more expensive to deliver, or that students require additional counseling and other out-of-class assistance to be successful.

- *Private and Foundation Gifts and Grants.* Gifts and grants to the institution, especially gifts from alumni, in one sense, are measures of the connectedness of the graduates to the institution. Donors give to organizations to whose mission and goals the donor is connected or committed. Not all of the peers report on their private gifts and grants. However, private giving is considered the "margin of excellence" for public colleges and universities.

Metrics related to technology are extremely critical for institutions because technology has become essential for the operation of their programs. Information on student and staff satisfaction with the help desk typically are collected from annual student and staff surveys. Student satisfaction and other measures related to the technology environment currently are collected routinely by many institutions and reported as part of the normal operating metrics. Student surveys ask whether the help desk is available when needed and whether hardware and software were available to deliver services to the students. These really are strategic and tactical metrics because they affect the short-term and long-term operations of the institution.

Most of the metrics that fall into the category of issues related to the student experience are those where a state requires that the institution report these numbers. The number and percentage of in-state or resident students enrolled is a number that is important to state legislators as they fund public higher education institutions. The number and percentage of first generation college students is a statistic that is used by some states in their funding or performance formulas. Research has shown that this group of students requires additional resources for a successful college experience. The number of community college transfers is important in states where the statewide goal is to foster the transfer of students so they may succeed in obtaining bachelors' degrees. Several states include these metrics in their performance funding systems; they are components of the National Governors' Association Complete College America (CCA) initiative, and as such, have become more important nationally. General education learning relates to the CCA initiative and is based on a Gates Foundation study that showed that successful completion of general education courses leads to a successful college experience. These statistics are usually components of the basic student information system of the institution. A list of metrics used in 2012 is shown as an appendix to this chapter.

REPORTING FOR A QUALITY ASSURANCE OR
ACCOUNTABILITY PROGRAM

As the report of the New Alliance suggested, there are several important reporting requirements for an accountability program: reporting to internal constituencies, and reporting to external constituencies. Many institutions use dashboards as one method of reporting. Dashboards are a visual mechanism to display performance information in a user-friendly way. A dashboard shows timely and relevant data and critical information at a glance, usually with graphics. A dashboard allows easy monitoring of key metrics, permits identification of exceptions, and also permits use of detailed data to identify the roots of a problem and take correctional or remedial action (Eckerson, 2006). Performance dashboards are perceived to translate an organization's strategies into objectives and metrics that may be related to each unit within the organization. Dashboards can be thought of as a performance management system that communicates the institution's strategic objectives or goals and enables management to measure and manage the key activities needed to achieve the goals.

There can be three layers to a dashboard: the summary graph, a multidimensional graph, and the detailed or operational view. Users can drill down to the third level, if they choose, to inform day-to-day operations.

Dashboards have become commonplace and provide many benefits to an organization. They can be used to translate strategy into measures and targets, fine tune strategies and make corrections when called for, show daily operations, eliminate silos, increase staff motivation to reach goals, consolidate and integrate information using common definitions, eliminate redundant efforts, give access to information and reduce reliance on special reports from MIS, and provide timely data in a user-friendly format.

Institutions may use three types of dashboards:

- an operational dashboard—used to track core operational processes that would trigger alerts when a potential problem arises;
- a tactical dashboard—used to track departmental projects and can be used for analysis and permits analysis from multiple perspectives; and
- a strategic dashboard—used to monitor strategic objectives and permits management to take correctional action to optimize performance.

An institution may have multiple versions of each type; however, all should include consistent definitions of metrics and rules for shared or related metrics. A prime example is the multiple definitions of "enrolled student" that institutions use in various reports. There should be only one definition of enrolled student used across all the dashboards or reports issued by an institution or a clear definition of what enrolled student means.

Successful use of dashboards requires several things: sufficient resources should be made available, and support must come from the highest level; the right metrics must be chosen, and their meaning should be standardized; there should be good interfaces available; and sufficient plans should be made to ensure end-user adoption.

Each of the dashboards used by an institution should be available on the institution's website and would be designed to communicate with external constituents and/or internal stakeholders. Certain dashboards, namely those related to operational or tactical measures, may be available only to certain constituents because the operational data should be limited in distribution to certain staff and could be limited to specific units within the institution.

There are two forms that such a dashboard could take. The first would be a simple dashboard that would show the institution's performance against a specific metric. Each metric would be shown in a box where the status of the metric is noted by the color of the box and by an arrow showing direction. Green boxes mean that the most recent performance on this metric is at or above target, yellow means the most recent is close to the target or making acceptable progress, while red means that performance is below target. Arrows pointing up mean that there has been improvement on this metric compared to the prior period, arrows pointing down mean a decline in performance compared to the prior period, and arrows pointing sideways indicate no change compared to the prior period. Supporting data would be available and could be accessed by the reader. An example of this type of dashboard is shown in Figure 6.1 and the Appendix.

The second format displays a metric, the definition of the metric, the goal or standard for the metric, and a graph showing the baseline, the actual and targets. Targets can be displayed for each year, for example, during the institution's strategic plan. Supporting data at a granular level could be available by clicking on the graph or components of the graph, depending on the information. An example of this type of dashboard is shown also in the Appendix in Figure 6.1. For those goals for which multiple information bits are available, each of the metrics could be shown as sub-metrics, so to speak. For example, there usually are multiple measures of graduates' or students' satisfaction with the institution, and each of these measures could be shown relative to the benchmark goal. It is visualized that this is a short dashboard, either one screen on the website if it is in the format of the simple dashboard, or several screens if in the format of a more complex dashboard. Readers could click on an entry if they wanted more information.

To link measures to the goals and strategies of the institution's strategic plan, the overarching goals would have the strategies categorized and listed below, in abbreviated form, for those external users of the document. For internal use, the dashboard could be much more complex to include each of the strategies. Readers could go to only those areas in which they were interested. Use of dashboards makes it much more likely that faculty and staff will use the metrics and many reports because the data would be timely, accessible, and easy to use.

SUMMARY

This chapter has introduced concepts of accountability, assessment, and productivity in higher education and has provided information on how to establish, maintain, and report on accountability or quality assurance programs. The following chapter will go into greater detail on performance funding.

EXAMPLE OF A SIMPLE EXTERNAL DASHBOARD

Ivy Tech Community College External Strategic Plan Dashboard

Figure 6.1.   Dashboard Examples.

Ivy Tech Community College has undertaken an extensive update of its 2010 Strategic Plan to support both the 2009 re-accreditation visit by the Higher Learning Commission and the 2009 launch of efforts to create a 2013 Strategic Plan. This update is being orchestrated by a Strategic Planning Council with the support of teams of educators and administrators addressing College-wide strategies and the integration of existing functional and regional plans.

This dashboard serves as a tool to monitor the College's status against specific metrics, aligned with the Strategic Plan. Supporting data is available behind each metric and status is indicated by color and arrow direction.

- Green—The most recent performance is at or above target.
- Yellow—The most recent performance is within 3 percentage points of target.
- Red—The most recent performance is more than 3 percentage points below target.
- ▲ —There has been improvement in percentage of target achieved compared to prior period.
- ▼—There has been a decline in percentage of target achieved compared to prior period.
- ▶ —The percentage of target achieved has not changed compared to prior period or multiple year data is unavailable.

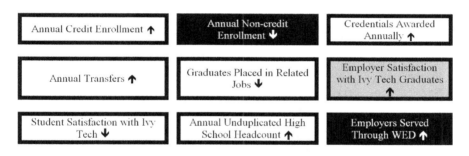

(Dashboard Examples continue on next page)

EXAMPLE OF AN INTERNAL DASHBOARD

Strategic Plan Dashboard—Progress Toward Accelerating Greatness

Strategy 1—Ensure that Students Achieve their Educational Goals

Metric 1.0.2—Number of Students Completing Certificates or Degrees

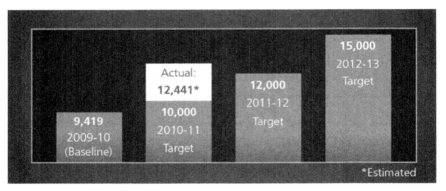

Metric 1.0.2—Statewide Data.

Ivy Tech Community College will increase number of students completing certificates or degrees. The current baseline (2009–2010) for this objective is 9,419. The College has a goal to increase that total to 15,000 by 2013.

(Dashboard Examples continue on next page)

Metric 1.0.3—Rate at Which Students Complete Certificates or Degrees Within 3 Years

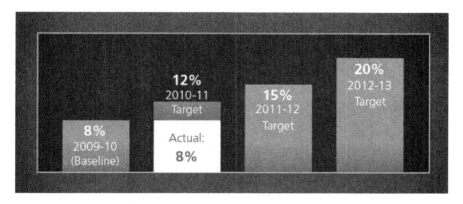

Metric 1.0.3.

Ivy Tech Community College will increase the rate at which students complete certificates or degrees within 150% of the "normal timeframe." The current baseline (2009–2010) rate for the 2006 cohort is 8.0%. The College has a goal to increase that amount to 20.0% by 2013.

Metric 1.0.4—Rate at Which Students Complete Certificates or Degrees Within 6 Years

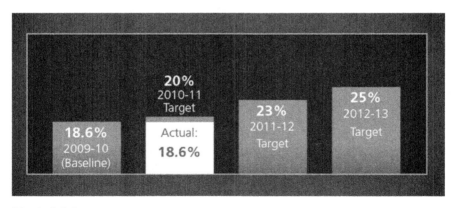

Metric 1.0.4.

(Dashboard Examples continue on next page)

Ivy Tech Community College will track the rate at which students complete certificates or degrees within 6 years. The current baseline (2009-10) rate for the 2003 cohort is 18.6%. The College has a goal to increase that amount to 25% by 2013.

Metric 1.4.1—Number of Students Who Transfer Ivy Tech Credit Hours to 4-Year Institutions

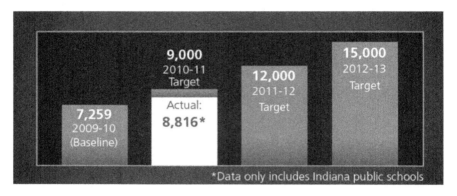

Metric 1.4.1.

Ivy Tech Community College will increase the number of students who transfer Ivy Tech credit hours to 4-year institutions. The current baseline (2009-10) for this objective is 7,259. The College has a goal to increase that number to 15,000 by 2013.

Metric 1.4.3—Rate at Which Students Transfer

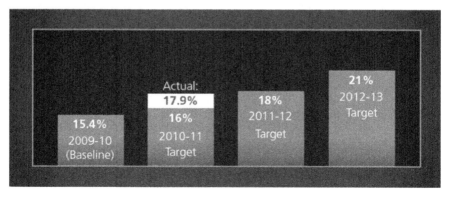

Metric 1.4.3.   *(Dashboard Exmaples continue on next page)*

Ivy Tech Community College will improve rates at which students transfer to a 4-year institution within 3 years. The current baseline (2009–2010) for this objective is 15.4%. The College has a goal to increase that percentage to 21% by 2013.

Metric 1.5.2—Percent of Dual Credit Enrollments Successfully Completed With Grade of A, B, C, Or P

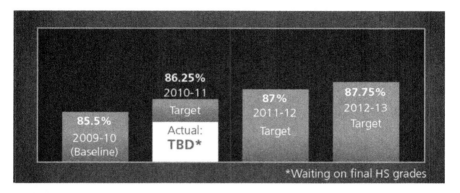

Metric 1.5.2.

Ivy Tech will track annualized dual credit enrollment. The current baseline (2009–2010) for this objective is 85.5%. The College has a goal to increase that percentage to 87.75% by 2013.

Strategy 2—Ensure that Indiana's Citizens, Workforce, and Businesses are Globally Competitive

Metric 2.1.1—Percent of Technical and Professional Development Programs With Current, Validated Statewide Outcome Standards

(Dashboard Examples continue on next page)

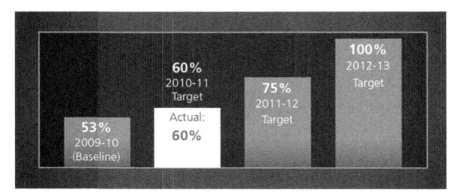

Metric 2.1.1.

Ivy Tech Community College will improve the percentage of its technical and professional development programs with current, validated outcome standards. The current baseline for this objective is 53%. The College has a goal to increase that to 100% by 2013.

Metric 2.2.2—Top 50 Companies Survey Results

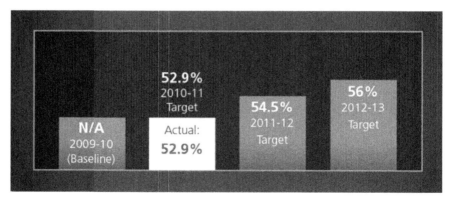

Metric 2.2.3.

Ivy Tech Community College will improve the percentage of positive responses to selected questions in its survey of each region's top 50 employers. The current baseline for this objective is not available. However, the College has a target goal of 56% by 2013.

(Dashboard Examples continue on next page)

Metric 2.2.3—Percent of Graduates Placed in Preparation Related Jobs

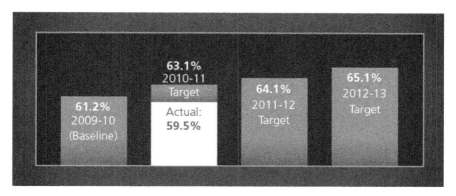

Metric 2.2.3.

Ivy Tech Community College will increase the College's relevance and value to Indiana's employer community. The current baseline for this objective is 61.2%. The College has a goal to increase that percentage to 65.1% by 2013.

Strategy 3—Ensure Optimal Quality and Efficiencies Statewide

Metric 3.1.1—Student Satisfaction With Ivy Tech in General (Very Satisfied or Satisfied)

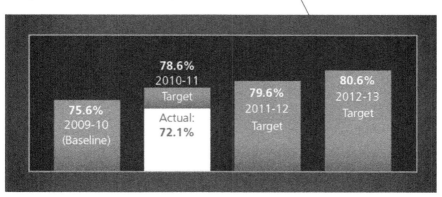

Metric 3.1.1.

(Dashboard Examples continue on next page)

Ivy Tech Community College will improve students' satisfaction and engagement scores. The current baseline (2009–2010) for this objective is 75.6%. The College has a goal to increase that percentage to 80.6% by 2013.

Strategy 4—Ensure an Adequate and Sustainable Resource Base

Metric 4.1.1—Increased Revenues From State

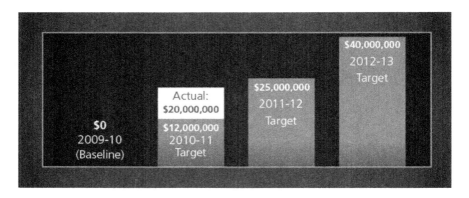

Metric 4.1.1.

Ivy Tech Community College will increase appropriations from the State of Indiana to the College. The current baseline (2009–2010) is $0. The College has a goal to increase that amount to $40,000,000 by 2013.

Appendix:
Performance Metrics Used by Institutions and States in 2012

Metric	Description	Strength	Weakness
Access			
College going rates of high school graduates	% of high school graduates enrolling within a given period of time in the service area/state/region/country	Operationalizes public mission Quantifies market penetration	Less appropriate for private or for-profit institutions
Engagement rates	Percent of the population within a defined service area without a postsecondary credential enrolled	Operationalizes public mission Quantifies market penetration	Less appropriate for private or for-profit institutions
Re-engagement rates	Percent of the population within a defined service area with a postsecondary credential enrolled	Quantifies training aspect of postsecondary education	May not align with institutional mission
Change in enrollment	Percent change in enrollment relative to population change in given service area.	Accounts for change external to institutional efforts Provides context	May not align with institutional mission
Enrollment by level, program, and by minorities	Enrollment numbers for specific populations	Examines trends in enrollments especially when linked to goals	Changes may be beyond control of the institution
Continuing education/extension enrollment	Non-credit enrollment numbers	Measures links to the local community	Not all institutions have continuing education as a mission
SAT/ACT scores of entering students	Average ACT or SAT	Purports to be a measure of the quality of the institution; Useful in projecting completion rates	Not really applicable to open access institutions, or for those serving adult and returning students
Transfer student opportunity	Number of students accepted at 4-year institution after attending a 2 or less than 2 year institution	Highlights systemic efficiency	May not align with institutional mission

(Appendix continues on next page)

Appendix: Continued

Metric	Description	Strength	Weakness
Credentials			
Completions (Degree or Certificate)	The number of degrees or certificates earned (by students) or awarded (by institutions or programs)	Does not rely on defining a cohort	It is possible for a student to earn multiple awards at an institution
Completers	The number of students earning a credential (degree or certificate)	Reflects the number of students attaining an outcome	
Completion rates	The percentage of students in a cohort completing a credential (degree or certificate)	Places counts of students who complete into context	Rates can vary widely, depending on which students are included in the denominator of the cohort calculation
Completion rates of under-represented students	Percentage of completers by race, gender, etc. compared to non-minority completers	Indication of equal opportunity	If populations are small, results can be skewed by one or two students not completing on time
Credentials awarded per 100 full-time equivalent students	Production of credentials (certificates and degrees) in the context of FTEs	Indication of equal opportunity	Does not consider the average time to degree nor type of student
			Credit hours may be earned by students not seeking a credential
Earned a GED	The number, or percentage, of students completing a GED program and passing the tests	Indication of equal opportunity Indication of student body composition	More a secondary school measure unless used as indicative of students that may need help
Transfer			
Transfer-out	The total number of students who transfer out of a program or institution	Indicator of success for institutions with transfer mission	Transfers out happen for many reasons beyond the control of the institution

(Appendix continues on next page)

Appendix: Continued

Metric	*Description*	*Strength*	*Weakness*
Transfer			
Transfer-in	The total number of students who transfer in to a program or institution	Institutional indicator of cooperation with other sectors	Reasons for institution to accept transfer student may not be clear
Transfer-out with a credential	The number of students who transfer out of a program or institution after earning a postsecondary credential	Indicator of success for institutions with transfer mission	Transfers out happen for many reasons beyond the control of the institution
Transfer-in with a credential	The number of students who transfer in to a program or institution after earning a postsecondary credential	Institutional indicator of cooperation with other sectors	Reasons for institution to accept transfer student may not be clear
Transfer-out without a credential	The number of students who transfer out of a program or institution without a credential	Indicator of success for institutions with transfer mission	Transfers out happen for many reasons beyond the control of the institution
Vertical transfer	Number of students who transfer to a 4-year institution from a 2-year institution. May or may not have earned a credential before transferring	Reinforces bachelor's degree as a higher-order outcome	Overlooks economic value of sub-baccalaureate credentials
		Often aligns with student self-expressed intent	Definitions of 2- and 4- year institutions are blurred in data
		Captures student flow and momentum	2- and 4-year institutions offer similar awards
Transfer-out without a credential and at least 15 earned credit hours	The number of students who transfer out of a program or institution without earning a postsecondary credential but at least 15 earned credit hours	Indicator of success for institutions with transfer mission	Transfers out happen for many reasons beyond the control of the institution

(Appendix continues on next page)

Appendix: Continued

Metric	Description	Strength	Weakness
Transfer			
Transfer-in without a credential	The number of students who transfer in to a program or institution without earning a postsecondary credential.	Institutional indicator of cooperation with other sectors	Reasons for institution to accept transfer student may not be clear
Lateral transfer	Number of students who transfer to a 4-year institution from a 4-year institution (or 2-year to 2-year). May or may not have earned a credential before transferring	Captures student flow and momentum	Reason for transfer is not understood
Reverse transfer	Number of students who transfer to a 2-year institution from a 4-year institution. May or may not have earned a credential before transferring	Reinforces upskilling role of 2-year institution Captures student flow and momentum	Reason for transfer is not understood Counters prevailing logic
Transfer-out rates	The percentage of students in a cohort transferring out of an institution and into another institution	Places counts of students who transfer-out into context	Rates can vary widely, depending on which students are included in the cohort
Transfer-in rates	The percentage of students in a cohort transferring into an institution from another institution	Places counts of students who transfer-in into context	Rates can vary widely, depending on which students are included in the cohort
Transfer receptivity	The percent of credits accepted after transfer	Measure of system or institutional cooperation	Reasons for credit acceptance/refusal unclear
Upper division credit hours earned by transfer students compared to hours completed by native students	Average upper division credit hours earned at baccalaureate by transfer students compared to average upper division credit hours earned by native students	Measures equity of treatment and in combination with transfer receptivity, articulation success	Not well understood by faculty

(Appendix continues on next page)

Appendix: **Continued**

Metric	Description	Strength	Weakness
Program or Course Completion			
Complete Adult Basic Education	The number of students completing an ABE program	Reflects the number of students attaining an outcome	n/a
Completed English Speakers of Other Languages (ESL)	The number of students completing an ESL program	Reflects the number of students attaining an outcome	n/a
Completed Developmental Education (DE)	The number of students completing a DE program	Reflects the number of students attaining an outcome	n/a
Completed general education core curriculum	The number of students completing a general education core curriculum	Reflects the number of students attaining an outcome	n/a
Completed apprenticeship program	The number of students completing an apprenticeship program	Reflects the number of students attaining an outcome	n/a
Completed training program	The number of students completing a training program	Reflects the number of students attaining an outcome	n/a
On-time completion	Number of first-time, full-time students who graduate with 2 years for a 2-year program or 4 years for a 4-year program (may also be a rate)	Encourages completion	Assumes enrollment intensity is consistent across all semesters Does not account for students who need to enroll part-time.
Summer enrollment	The percent of students completing a summer term prior to receiving junior status	Captures student momentum	May not be required by institution
Complete 30 credit hours in first academic year	The number of students who finish 30 hours their first year of enrollment	Captures student momentum	Does not account for students who need to enroll part-time
Credit conversion	Ratio of credits earned to credits attempted	Captures student momentum	May result in grade inflation

(Appendix continues on next page)

Appendix: Continued

Metric	Description	Strength	Weakness
Program or Course Completion			
Enrollment at end-of-course or successful course completion	Credit hours earned by students at the end of course	Incentivizes ensuring that students actually learn	May result in grade inflation, depending on definition of "successful" completion
3-year or 6-year graduation rate	Percent of first-time, full-time students who graduate within 3 years from a 2-year program or within 6 years of enrollment in a 4-year program	Provides understanding of success for a particular population	Does not account for students who need to enroll part-time Does not consider any student who is not full-time, first-time
Pass rates on professional licensure exams	Change in pass rates of CPA, Bar, National Nursing, PRAXIS, etc.	Measures graduates' workforce readiness; national or state exams force curriculum alignment with the standards	Can be skewed by small numbers of completers taking the exams
Retention			
Retention rate	1st to 2nd year, fall-to-fall, retention	Captures student momentum	Does not consider reasons for stopping or dropping out, including death of the student
Extended retention rate	1st to 3rd year, fall-to-fall, retention	Captures student momentum	Does not consider reasons for stopping or dropping out, including death of the student
Still enrolled, no credential	The number of students still enrolled at 150 and 200% of normal time that are still enrolled	Captures student momentum	May not be consistent with the student's goals; does not consider part-time students
Developmental or remedial education completion impact	Percent of students completing developmental education and enrolling in a subsequent college level course	Research-based measure that predicts college success	Does not consider reasons for stopping or dropping out, including death of the student

(Appendix continues on next page)

Appendix: Continued

Metric	Description	Strength	Weakness
Persistence			
15 credit hours completed	15 hours completed successfully	Acknowledges student progress, research-based measure	n/a
30 credit hours completed	30 hours completed successfully	Acknowledges student progress, research-based measure	n/a
45 credit hours completed	45 hours completed successfully	Acknowledges student progress, research-based measure	n/a
60 credit hours completed	60 hours completed successfully	Acknowledges student progress, research-based measure	n/a
72 credit hours completed	72 hours completed successfully	Acknowledges student progress, research-based measure	n/a
Learning Outcomes			
Student achievement	Achievement on standardized assessments	Not measured by the institution	May not be consistent with the curriculum
Passing college-level math courses	Passage of gatekeeper math courses	Research-based measure	Not all students take a college-level math course
College grade point average	Percent of students with cumulative grade point average above acceptable threshold	Measure of academic progress and mastery	Students may take lighter course loads to meet GPA requirements
Satisfactory academic progress	Percent of students making progress to completion in accordance with institutional SAP policy	Is required as part of federal Title IV aid participation	Does not consider part-time students; May limit future postsecondary opportunities if slow start observed
Rising junior tests	Competency tests in English and math administered to sophomores	Measures value-added	May eliminate some from continuing their education

(Appendix continues on next page)

Appendix: Continued

Metric	Description	Strength	Weakness
Learning Outcomes			
Passage rates on licensure exams	Pass rates on CPA, HVAC certification, etc.	Measures workforce readiness	May not align with employer demand
% of completers working in related fields or pursuing additional education	Surveys of completers to determine post-completion employment	Proxy measure for workforce/graduate education readiness	Difficult to get a valid survey response
Average first year salaries of graduates/completers	Surveys of graduates/completers or state tax records	Gaining traction in some states	Validity of data; difficult to obtain
Equity Outcomes			
Achievement gap between White and underrepresented minority students	The gap in outcomes (i.e. completion, transfer, persistence, or retention)	Reaffirms commitment to serve all populations equally	Some institutions may not have a large number of underrepresented minority students
Achievement gap between White and underrepresented groups		Reaffirms commitment to serve all populations equally	Depending on definition (i.e. first-time), underrepresented students may be White
Change in achievement rates between White and underrepresented minority students	The change in outcome gaps between White and underrepresented minority students	Reaffirms commitment to serve all populations equally Rewards improvement over time	Large changes in achievement can be made if there are small populations of either group
Programmatic Data			
Program accreditation	Proportion of institutional programs that are accredited	External validation of academic and support programs	Cost of program accreditation in restricted budgets
Participant feedback	Surveys of alumni and current students	Provides a student perspective on program	Obtaining a representative sample
Stakeholder feedback	Surveys of community members and employers	Provides a stakeholder perspective on program	Obtaining a representative sample

(Appendix continues on next page)

Appendix: Continued

Metric	Description	Strength	Weakness
Faculty Data			
Student/faculty ratios	FTE students/FTE faculty	Measure of the quality of the learning environment	Ratios will differ depending on mix of disciplines and levels; Depends on how faculty is defined
% faculty with terminal degrees	Number of faculty with terminal degrees divided by headcount of faculty	Measures credentials of the faculty as a proxy for a quality education	Not all disciplines require a terminal degree to be an effective instructor
Faculty feedback	Opinion survey of faculty	Satisfaction measurement	Low response rate to survey
Full-time faculty share of undergraduate instruction	Undergraduate credit hours taught by full-time faculty divided by total UG credit hours	Measure of faculty involvement in undergraduate education	Not applicable to all institutions
% of courses taught by tenured and tenure-track faculty	Number of courses taught by tenured and t-t faculty divided by the total number of courses	Measure of faculty involvement	Not applicable to all institutions
Women and multi-cultural faculty as a % of total faculty	Number of women and multi-cultural faculty divided by total number of faculty	Reaffirms commitment to equity	n/a
Retention of women and multi-cultural faculty	Retention rates of underrepresented groups compared to retention rates of White male faculty	Reaffirms commitment to equity	n/a
Tenure of women and multi-cultural faculty	Tenure rates of women and multi-cultural faculty compared to tenure rates of White males	Reaffirms commitment to equity	n/a
Average class size		Measure of the quality of the learning environment	May not be applicable to alternate teaching methods such as on-line courses

(Appendix continues on next page)

Appendix: Continued

Metric	Description	Strength	Weakness
Faculty Data			
Average number of credit hours taught by faculty	Total credit hours taught divided by number of faculty	Measure of faculty workload	Misunderstood by policy-makers
Student/faculty ratios by department, compared to peers	Department-specific ratios compared to ratios of a peer group	Measure of workload, relative to peers	Peer selection is difficult at best
Average faculty salaries by rank and by department	Comparison of salaries to national salaries or those of peers	National norms	Misunderstood by legislators
Community and public service activities of faculty	Number and descriptions of public service	Measures community involvement	Not applicable to all types of institutions
Number of publications or creative arts	Number of publications, art shows, etc.; may be limited to peer-reviewed publications	Measure of faculty productivity	Understates creative and professional output of faculty in the arts
Institutional Data			
Expenditure balance	Expenditures for institutional operations relative to a goal	Measure of the quality of the learning environment	May not be appropriate for all institution types
Public/private partnerships	% increase in public/ private partnerships relative to goal	Measure of institutional relevance	n/a
Faculty diversity	Diversity of faculty relative to a goal	Measure of institutional commitment to campus environment	Not all institutions serve a diverse student body
Financial ratios	Current ratio, net assets ratio	Determined by outside agencies	May not be as relevant for public institutions
Tuition and fee rates	Trends over time, and compared to peers	Measures affordability	Seen by the public as increasing too much
Workplace safety record	Report to FLSA and others	Indicator of institutional safety	May not a capture all factors related to safety

(Appendix continues on next page)

Appendix: Continued

Metric	Description	Strength	Weakness
Institutional Data			
Expenditures or revenues by category compared to peers	Per student or % of total by category compared to peers	Identified categories that are out of line	Identification of peer groups
State appropriations per student	Total appropriations divided by number of students	Trend comparison	Definition of student can vary
E&G expenditures per student	Total E&G divided by FTE students	Trend comparison	Definition of student can vary
Cost of attendance	Tuition, mandatory fees, room and board, books, incidental expenses for the average student	Must be reported to IPEDS and maintained on website as part of institutional right-to-know information	Varies significantly by sector
Adoption of a strategic plan	Existence of an institutional strategic plan	Required for accreditation; links budget to goals	n/a
% administrative expenditures	% administrative expenditures compared to academic expenditures	Measure of overhead, trend information important	Varies significantly by type and size of institution; also affected by control
Overhead costs per student	Expenditures for non-academic divided by headcount students	Measure of overhead	Definition of overhead varies by institution or system
% of enrollments in evenings, on weekends, and other off-peak times	Enrollments at off-peak hours divided by total enrollment	Measures use of buildings and somewhat, access	Not all institutions have this mission; on-line classes make measurement difficult
Annual voluntary support	Total gifts to the institution or its related foundations	Indicator of institutional engagement with external communities	Public institutions will have less than private
Annual voluntary support by alumni	Total resources provided by alumni	Measure of loyalty and commitment	Alumni at some institutions in lower-paid fields
Patent or license production	Number of patents or licenses confirmed	Measure of research productivity	Is not applicable to all types of institutions

(Appendix continues on next page)

Appendix: Continued

Metric	Description	Strength	Weakness
Institutional Data			
Sponsored research per faculty member	Outside research expenditures divided by FTE faculty	Measure of research productivity	Is not applicable to all types of institutions
Sponsored research or increase in sponsored research	Amount of sponsored research dollars relative to a goal	Measure of research productivity	Is not applicable to all types of institutions
Program Costs			
Cost by academic program by level of instruction	Academic cost of credit hour	Promotes efficiency	Requires a cost study; Expensive to maintain; Hard to account for fixed and variable costs differences
Cost of non-academic programs	Total program cost per student	Promotes efficiency	Requires a cost study; Expensive to maintain; Hard to account for fixed and variable costs differences
Special Populations			
Low-income	Recipients of a Pell Grant	A proxy for low-income utilizing a national methodology	Some eligible populations do not receive a Pell Grant
High impact completer	Completer in a program determined to have high importance; STEM completers are an example	Targets statewide or local needs	Needs change, and the programs of high impact will have to be changed to continue to serve statewide or local needs
Adults	Students who are 25 or older at time of completion	Targets a special population	Not relevant to all institutions
Dual enrollment	The number of students enrolled in a dual enrollment program	Measures access and reduces the cost of attendance	Not all states permit high school students to get college credit
Economically disadvantaged	Income relative to poverty line, or 150% of poverty line	A proxy for low-income utilizing a national methodology	Not all students know their family income

(Appendix continues on next page)

Appendix: Continued

Metric	*Description*	*Strength*	*Weakness*
Special Populations			
Disabled	Trend in number of disabled students enrolled	Measure of commitment to diversity	
Dislocated worker	Enrollees who have lost jobs	Serving community or state needs for retraining	Not all enrollees self-identify; not applicable to all institutions
First generation	Number of first generation students	Access for underserved populations	Not all students self-report

Note: The metrics provided in this table were informed by the sources listed below. The strengths and weaknesses were developed by the authors of this book.
Sources: Leinbach & Jenkins (2008), Mullin (2012a), Wyner (2012), Layzell (2001), and McKeown-Moak (2012).

CHAPTER 7

PERFORMANCE-BASED APPROACHES IN POSTSECONDARY FINANCE

As we begin examining performance-based approaches to postsecondary finance, it is worth noting that "performance" is subjective, and almost any measure, element, count, or derived value can be considered an indicator of performance. A list of items that have been used as performance measures, as comprehensive as possible, may be found in the Appendix to Chapter 6 because the performance measures used in accountability are similar to, and in many cases the same as, the measures used for performance funding. Additionally, as our understanding of performance and effectiveness is informed by further research within an evolving postsecondary education environment, more indicators of performance will be identified.

PERFORMANCE-BASED APPROACHES

In theory, and rhetoric, performance-based approaches in postsecondary finance are undertaken to incentivize behavior. Governors and legislators appear to believe that what is measured, improves, and as a result they have sought to associate resources with outcomes or performance. Burke

Higher Education Finance Research: Policy, Politics, and Practice, pp. 221–245

(1998) noted that legislators and coordinating or governing boards sought to ensure that institutions' use of scarce resources provided improved results and also contained or restrained costs. States began to approach the issue by publishing reports on critical indicators of effectiveness and efficiency in instruction, research, and service. The total quality movement and the Baldridge Awards accelerated this movement by focusing attention on improvement and by viewing planning, budgeting, and performance as an integrated process (Burke & Modarresi, 2000).

State budgets for higher education traditionally were based on input measures (i.e., enrollments) rather than outcomes or, alternately, on resources rather than results. Although the traditional methods of funding used workload measures, such as the credit hours offered or the number of staff, the focus on inputs encouraged institutions to enroll students in courses and not be concerned with satisfactory completion of the courses or other outcomes. The performance funding movement sought to change this focus.

In addition to this resource dependence perspective, Dougherty and Reddy (2011) suggest three other theories for performance-based funding, including increasing recipient awareness of stated goals, improving recipient performance on stated goals, and stimulating status competition between recipients.

In its most basic form, a performance-based approach to funding is a mechanism used to allocate funds based upon quantifiable indicators. The unit of analysis may be institutions, programs, or students. Each of these units of analysis will be given more attention based on their unique concepts and considerations.

INSTITUTIONAL PERFORMANCE

The idea of aligning institutional funding with student outcomes is not a 21st century idea. The federal government experimented with this kind of budgeting in the 1960s, and the state of Tennessee has had an ongoing performance-based funding program for higher education in place since 1979 (Banta, Rudolph, VanDyke, & Fisher, 1996). In 2000, at the height of what may be called the "old form" of performance funding in higher education, more than three-fifths (35) of all states engaged in at least one form of performance-based funding (McKeown-Moak, 2010b).

Performance as a factor in the allocation of funds to institutions occurs in three ways (Burke, 1998; McLendon, Hearn, & Deaton, 2006). First, the most direct connection between institutional performance and funding is *performance funding*. In this case, funding is tied directly to the institutional outcomes measured. For example, in Tennessee between 1985 and 2005, institutions could receive up to 5% of their appropriation based on achievement on five performance measures (McKeown-Moak, 2013a).

The second, less direct, connection between funding and performance is known as *performance budgeting*, where the allocation process is informed, but not directly tied to, measures of institutional effectiveness, as discussed in Chapter 6. For example, in the 1980s Maryland public institutions reported a series of performance indicators in their budgets, and the measures influenced the State Board's funding recommendations, but allocations were not made based on goals or specific outcomes.

The least direct connection between institutional effectiveness and funding occurs with *performance reporting*, which was the method of accountability most often used prior to 1995. Reported outcomes inform general perceptions of institutional effectiveness and, loosely, allocations (Shin, 2010). For example, in the early 1990s, public colleges and universities in Arizona reported performance measures for each program in the state budget request, but those measures were not used by the legislature in its budget deliberations.

However, the current wave of performance-based funding is quite different from that of a decade ago. State higher education leaders have begun to link calls for additional funding to increased accountability and increased efficiency of operations. *One of the main differences between performance-based funding then and now is the change in the focus from meeting the needs of higher education to meeting the needs of students, the state, and its economy* (McKeown-Moak, 2013a).

Performance funding prior to 2000 generally was linked to, and a component of, the funding formula for higher education institutions. In the first part of the 21st century, however, funding formulas for public higher education underwent a radical change. State after state shifted their funding formulas from the old methods to a new wave of formulas that examine the need for public resources for colleges and universities in a fundamentally different way.

As the national economy went into a period of recession in the last half of the first decade of the 21st century, state appropriations for higher education declined and, in some cases, declined more than 20%. Because higher education enrollments are counter-cyclical, enrollments increased while state appropriations decreased, putting significant pressures on institutional budgets.

At the same time, there was a national focus on performance and in increasing the numbers of college "completers" as a means of improving the economy (HCM Strategists, 2012a). From the White House to state houses to foundations such as the Bill and Melinda Gates Foundation and Lumina Foundation, the demand was made for increased graduation rates, at lower costs for students, and at a lower cost to taxpayers. The economic crisis of the states led to demands for graduation of more students, with higher quality educations, more efficiently, and more quickly (Albright, 2010).

 This shift in focus away from the needs of the college or university to allocation methods that are student-centered, or based on measures of "success," is a sea change in college and university funding (McKeown-Moak, 2012). Measures of success in this case relate to student success and institutional success in meeting the needs of the state or local community. There appears to be a much greater recognition of the fact that higher education is a major driver of the economy and that the state and local community need higher education to provide educated citizens with their greater earning power and ability to pay more in taxes, as well as the other benefits of higher education, including the transfer of knowledge. Policymakers appear to believe that higher education budgets are not aligned with state or local priorities and want institutions to produce graduates in high-demand fields like nursing or teaching (Harnisch, 2011).

The new performance funding models reflect the needs of the state and its citizens, not merely the needs of the institution. Instead of additional funding to educate more students and maintain quality, the economic crisis in states led to reduced funding to educate more students and still maintain quality (McKeown-Moak, 2013a). This has been called the "upending of conventional ways" that are "out-of-touch with economic and demographic realities" (Albright, 2010, p. 1). Instead of funding based on the level of resources needed to maintain the "market basket" of courses, programs, and degrees, given the make-up of the student body, the new funding mechanisms shift to funding based on results as measured by course completions (not enrollments), degrees or other completions, and other measures of institutional success in meeting the state's and the students' needs. This is analogous to funding based on average daily attendance rather than average daily membership in PK–12 funding formulas.

Indeed, in 2013, developing and implementing state performance-based higher education funding systems has been identified as one of the top ten policy issues facing higher education (AASCU, 2013). These funding formulas dominate the current higher education policy landscape—35 states have expressed interest or are currently implementing performance-based funding systems, up from fewer than 10 states just 2 years ago (HCM Strategists, 2012b). The thrust behind the shift to performance-based funding is the longstanding absence of additional state investment and new economic realities that signal the need for better performance on measures of institutional productivity and student success. This has led states to turn attention to *how*—rather than *how much*—state funding is distributed to public colleges and universities (AASCU, 2013). After all, performance funding's ultimate goal is to create stronger incentives for institutions to adopt efficiency, effectiveness, and productivity enhancements that allow them to graduate increasing numbers of students with available revenue (HCM Strategists, 2012b).

The sophistication of these new state appropriations allocation systems has evolved markedly, with institutions incentivized to improve key *outcomes*, such as student retention and degree completion, and less attention to boosting *inputs*, such as student enrollments. Just as important, performance-based funding systems are becoming more equitable. An illustration of this is the provision of a funding premium in some states for graduating low-income students, who are often less academically prepared for college. This encourages public colleges not only to maintain admission standards that promote student access but also to utilize intensive retention strategies that increase the likelihood of student success (AASCU, 2013).

Tennessee has continuously employed performance funding since 1979, and Ohio has used performance funding since the 1980s. Both Tennessee and Ohio shifted their performance funding methods to the new wave, which is based in part on research on what incentivizes institutions. In New York, since 1970 private institutions have been eligible to receive Bundy aid, which is direct, unrestricted state appropriation, based upon the number of degrees conferred. Degrees were used as the basis for allocations rather than enrollments because degrees awarded overcame the difficulties associated with enrollment status (full-time versus part-time, for example), placed an emphasis on productivity, and acted as an incentive to improve retention (Office of Higher Education, 2012).

Some of the new measures in the new wave of funding formulas may sound like the old measures: graduation rates, for example, used to mean the number of full-time first-time freshmen who complete within 150% of the traditional time to degree (i.e., 6 years for a 4-year institution, and 3 years for a community college). The new measure of graduation rate includes students who take longer because of their part-time status or adults who have other responsibilities and are neither first-time nor full-time. The new measure may be called "completions" and refers to not only graduations, but certificates, apprenticeships, and completion of the student's plans, which may be 12 hours of a computing programming strand or qualifying for a teaching certificate, or some other credential.

The new methodology in most states does not do away with the underlying funding formula principles of equity, responsiveness, or adequacy, but rather it calculates the amount of funding by including some different variables. The new methods have state goals as an important component but give institutions flexibility in reaching the goals. In most states, a small proportion of the overall budget is allocated based on performance, but measures consider the differences between institutions and their students. These new models are phased in over time to give institutions time to change and realign their priorities.

States adopting new performance funding models have taken their longstanding formulas and adapted those formulas to emphasize results (such as graduation or course completions) and cost-effectiveness (McKeown-Moak, 2013a). In Ohio, for example, the measure of "enrollment" has moved away from the number of credit hours in which students are enrolled at the beginning of the semester to the number of credit hours for which students successfully complete the course. The weighting of the credit hours remains the same as the old formula to recognize differences in the costs of providing courses in different disciplines and at different enrollment levels (undergraduate, graduate). Texas proposed to do the same for the 4-year colleges and universities—calculate credit hours at course completion rather than enrollment (however, the Legislature rejected this proposal and directed the Texas Higher Education Coordinating Board to come back with a new formula based on completions for the 4-year, non-medical campuses). Other calculations in the funding model in Ohio and Texas remain the same, with calculations for student services, academic support, physical plant, and so on.

There is some concern on the part of faculty that counting only successful completion of a course will lead to grade inflation and pressure to graduate unqualified students (Shin & Milton, 2004). These are real concerns, as is the concern that responding to state priorities that change as the legislature and governor changes results in trying to hit a moving target, making it impossible for institutions to be "successful."

Most states using course completion credit hours are funding performance at the margins, that is, only a small proportion of funds are allocated based on performance. South Carolina's performance funding system of the 1990s failed because it was based on 100% of the funds and was too complex (McKeown-Moak, 2012). Other performance funding systems have failed when the political support from the governor or legislature changes and state priorities change (Dougherty & Natow, 2009; Dougherty, Hare & Natow, 2009). Term limits and legislative turnover also were blamed for the failure of the old South Carolina and Missouri performance funding systems (Dougherty, Natow, Hare, Jones, & Vega, 2011).

As of May, 2013, 37 states are using performance funding or are in the process of adopting performance funding for some or all of their public institutions of higher education. The number is constantly changing, as legislatures and governors push for more accountability. In fact, the National Conference of State Legislatures (NCSL, 2013) lists only 31 states using or considering performance funding. Table 7.1 lists the states currently using performance funding, installing performance funding, or considering performance funding.

Table 7.2 lists performance metrics being used in 2012 by a sample of these states.

**Table 7.1.   2013 Status of
Higher Education Performance Funding Among the States**

Performance Funding in Place	*Installing Performance Funding*	*Considering Performance Funding*
Illinois—less than 1%	Arizona—$5 million in 2014	Alabama
Indiana—5%	Arkansas—5% in 2014	California
Louisiana—15%	Colorado—25% in 2016	Florida
Michigan—3%	Hawaii—based on areas of need	Georgia
Minnesota—1%	Missouri—3% in 2014	Idaho
New Mexico—5%	Nevada—based on completions	Kansas
Ohio—5% for cc; based on completions for 4-yr	North Dakota—2%	Kentucky
Oklahoma—1%	Texas—based on completions	Maine
Pennsylvania—2.4%	Utah—based on completions	Maryland
South Dakota—$6 million	Virginia—based on completions	Mississippi
Tennessee—100%	West Virginia—5%	Montana
Washington—$3.5 million		New York
		North Carolina
		Wyoming

Lessons Learned in Institutional Performance-Based Approaches

The driving force behind any institutional performance-based funding model is the desire to establish a formal link between institutional performance and funding received. These are ultimately translated into a system of performance indicators on which the allocation is based.

The last decade of the 20th century included a number of state efforts to expand enrollment-based funding models to include performance components. Posthumously termed Performance Funding 1.0, the wave of performance funding efforts were not sustainable. Burke (1998) suggests a lesson learned from the first broad-scale attempt at performance funding was that the measures should "encourage the notion that external accountability and institutional improvement, and efficiency and quality, are complementary and not conflicting purposes" (p. 89).

The concept of what is a "best practice" in measuring the performance of higher education institutions continues to evolve. However, there are a number of guiding principles, developed from research studies of what worked and what failed, that are generally accepted as "good practice" in

Table 7.2. Performance Measures Used by Selected States in 2012

Performance Measure	CA	CO	FL	IN	LA	OH	NY	SC	TN	TX	WA	WI
Retention rates	X	X										
Enrollment at end of course				X	X	X			X	X		
Achievement of core competencies	X											
Degrees awarded	X	X	X	X	X	X	X	X	X		X	X
Degrees awarded to adult learners				X	X							
Graduation rates	X	X	X		X		X	X			X	
Time to degree		X	X	X		X	X	X				X
Transfer rates	X			X	X	X	X	X	X		X	
SAT/ACT scores or high school GPA							X	X				X
Faculty workload		X					X	X		X		X
Remediation	X			X							X	
Pass rates on professional licensure exams	X	X		X		X						
Student opinion surveys							X					
Faculty opinion survey							X					
Alumni satisfaction survey												X
Employer satisfaction survey								X				X
Graduate job placement				X				X				
Number of licenses or patents							X					
Sponsored research funds		X	X	X	X	X	X	X	X			X
Workforce development				X	X	X	X	X		X		
Meeting state needs						X						
Momentum points:												
for community or technical colleges						X			X	X	X	
for universities						X			X			
Other indicators chosen by the institution		X	X			X				X		

the development of institutional performance measurement mechanisms, as was discussed in Chapter 6. The 11 guiding principles are the same for performance funding. The process for developing and establishing a system of performance indicators is unique to every enterprise; however, all 11 of these principles need to be considered during this process to ensure a successful and effective outcome (Layzell, 2001).

As mentioned in Chapter 6, the development of performance indicators and performance-based funding systems is ultimately based on the desire for accountability. The four approaches commonly used are the following (Ewell & Jones, 1994):

- the input, process, outcome model;
- the resource efficiency and effectiveness model;
- the state need and return on investment model; and
- the "customer need" and return on investment model.

Some of the earlier performance funding initiatives adopted in the states were not continued for various reasons, both political and financial. Research has shown that there are some characteristics that are common to successful and stable performance-based funding programs:

1. involvement and input from state governing or coordinating boards;
2. accent on both institutional improvement and accountability;
3. sufficient time allowed for both planning and implementation;
4. excellent data systems that provide defensible and accurate information;
5. measures related to institutional missions;
6. use of a limited number of indicators; and
7. recognition and protection of institutional diversity (Petrick, 2009).

NCSL (2013) suggests the following best practices for a successful performance funding model:

1. Put enough funding at stake to create an incentive for institutions to improve results and decide whether the funding will come from new money or base funds. Most states are putting aside 5% to 25% of higher education dollars for performance funding.
2. Allow postsecondary institutions with different missions to be measured by different standards. For example, research universities could be rewarded for research and development performance,

while community colleges could be rewarded for workforce training results.

3. ·Engage all stakeholders—policymakers, higher education leaders,
   and faculty members—in the design of the funding system.

4. Phase in the performance funding system to make the transition
   easier.

5. Keep the funding formula simple, with unambiguous metrics, so
   expectations are clear to everyone.

6. Maintain focus on the goal of improving college completion, while
   rewarding both progress and success. States can reward colleges
   not only for increased degree production but also for retaining students year to year and for helping students transfer between institutions.

7. Include a measure to reward colleges that graduate low-income,
   minority, and adult students to ensure that institutions keep serving these populations.

8. Align the funding formula with state economic and workforce
   needs by providing performance funding to those colleges that are
   graduating students in high-priority fields.

Serban (1998) noted that there are at least four aspects to establishing
and implementing performance funding programs that must be
addressed:

- *success criteria*—the standards by which institutional performance is
  measured;
- *indicators and indicator weights*—the percent of funding to be allocated for each indicator;
- *allocation methods*—the relationship between performance funding
  and operating budgets; and
- *funding levels*—the amounts available for rewarding performance.

Each one of these aspects is addressed briefly below.

Success Criteria

As mentioned in Chapter 6, Serban (1998) noted three methods by
which progress toward performance goals are measured:

- *Institutional improvement over time*—institutional progress on individual indicators is measured against their own past performance.

- *Comparisons with peer institutions*—institutional attainment is measured against peer institution averages and ranges on individual indicators.
- *Comparisons against predetermined target standards*—institutional performance is measured as progress toward meeting preset target standards on individual indicators.

For example, the performance funding model developed by the Oregon University System required that the universities set two separate targets for each of their indicators. The first target represents improvement against the institution's own baseline performance, while the second target takes into consideration the current performance of their external peer institutions (McKeown-Moak, 2010b). This approach provides both an internal and external context for assessing performance improvement.

Indicators and Indicator Weights

In performance funding systems that have more than one indicator, an often thorny issue is what weight to assign each individual indicator in coming up with a composite performance score. The philosophical and political undertones of this issue cannot be understated, in that everyone involved will have at least a somewhat different opinion on the relative importance of each indicator, particularly when the degree to which institutions "excel" varies on each indicator as well. Three approaches to developing indicator weights have emerged:

- *Equal weighting*—each indicator is given the same weighting.
- *Preset, differential weighting*—each indicator has a different weighting.
- *Institutional selection within a preset range of acceptable weights*—each institution is allowed to determine the weight assigned to each of its indicators within a preset range.

The first two approaches certainly have strengths and weaknesses within the context of the guiding principles. Equal weighting is simple; however, it does not enable the recognition of institutional diversity nor priority setting. Likewise, differential weighting may enable the recognition of specific priorities in improving performance; however, it works against the concept of simplicity and may unduly focus institutional attention on those indicators with the greatest weight. The third approach, which was the one used by Kentucky in its now-defunct performance funding program, may strike the greatest balance between all of the guiding principles.

Allocation Methods

Of obvious interest (particularly to recipients of performance funds) is the issue of how the performance funds make their way from the state treasury to institutional budgets. There are two issues related to how the funds get allocated. First, there is the issue of whether performance funds should be kept in a separate pool to be allocated each year over and above institutional base budgets, or whether performance funds should be part of institutional base budgets from the start. Second, there is the issue of whether the use of the dollars received is left up to the discretion of each institution or if there are restrictions on institutional use of the performance funds received (McKeown-Moak, 2010b).

The first issue is largely a question of control versus stability. Obviously, from the state and/or system office perspective, being able to identify, control, and target a separate pool of funding enables great policy (and political) leverage. At the same time, history has shown that such categorical programs are often the first to suffer in times of budgetary downturn, largely because of their status as a separate and relatively "undedicated" pool of funding. Indeed, these types of performance funding were the first to be eliminated during the budget crises of the early 2000s (McKeown-Moak, 2010b). While funding that goes directly into institutional base budgets can also be cut, it is less likely that such cuts would occur. However, state and/or system control over the use and purpose of these funds is greatly minimized once they become part of institutional base budgets.

The second issue is also a question of control versus flexibility, the answer to which depends on the ultimate intent of the program. If the state or system views performance funding as simply a means to reward institutional performance, then there seems to be less of a need to restrict the use of the dollars once they are allocated. However, if the state or system views the program as a way to also improve upon and remediate problem areas at the institutional level, then there would appear to be some logic in restricting at least part of the funds available to institutional improvement activities in those areas.

Funding Levels

The final implementation issue relates to the total dollar amount available for the performance funding initiative. Serban (1998) reported that the amounts vary from state to state and year to year, with a range of 0.5% to 5.5% of state operating appropriations for higher education. (Note: South Carolina was an outlier and allocated 100% of funding by performance criteria.) In 2012, Tennessee's performance funding systems allocated all funding through the performance formulas, and some governors are pushing to allocate more than 10% of budgets through performance methods. (See Table 7.1 for information on the amounts and percentage weights in use in 2013.)

Clearly, the challenge is to have an amount that is large enough to generate institutional interest, within the other competing needs in the state budget. It is also important that the amount available retain a level of stability from year to year to maintain the long-term viability of the initiative. From that standpoint, it is probably better to start out with a relatively small amount and increase it gradually over time as conditions allow, as opposed to starting out large and then have to reduce it in subsequent years, as noted in the best practices from NCSL listed above (2013). In fact, Serban (1998) noted that the effectiveness of the performance funding initiative in Kentucky was ultimately undermined due to the latter approach.

While much effort has been put forth to develop and advocate for performance-based approaches for institutional funding, very little research on the success of these approaches has been conducted. In fact, Dougherty and Reddy (2011) state, "the research literature does not provide firm evidence that performance funding significantly increases rates of remedial completion, retention, and graduation" (p. 43). However, Ohio, Tennessee, and Missouri all cite evidence that their performance funding has had the desired results of increasing graduation in particular fields, increasing graduation rates, improving performance on tests such as the CPA or national nursing exam, or increasing retention (Burke, 1998; Banta & Moffett, 1987).

Burke and his associates at the Rockefeller Institute of Governance at the University at Albany, State University of New York have conducted research into performance funding for over 20 years. Burke and colleagues have produced a series of reports on performance funding and its impact on institutions, students, and faculty, which may be accessed at www.rockinst.org/education/accountability_higher_ed.aspx. These reports contain a wealth of information on the history of the movement as well and are an excellent source of research on the subject. Burke's (2000) study attempted to get at the perceptions of performance funding's impact across a wide variety of campus officials (e.g., campus administrators, faculty leaders) in five states with performance funding programs: Florida, Missouri, Ohio, South Carolina, and Tennessee. Responses to his survey were equally split between no impact and little impact.

One of the important findings of Burke's research is that accountability programs have become increasingly invisible on campus below the vice presidential level, and academic departments are often left entirely out of the loop. This creates a disconnect among societal concerns, institutional goals, and departmental aspirations. Burke noted that the adoption of feedback loops with common departmental indicators can enhance accountability without threatening the unique nature of higher education institutions (Burke, 2006).

Traditional Perspectives of Institutional Performance

The traditional perspective of completion in postsecondary education is the attainment of either an associate or bachelor's degree at the undergraduate level. Institutional funding may be awarded based on the number of degrees awarded in a particular year, as was noted in New York.

Institutions are awarded not only for completions, but also for enrollments. As discussed in Chapter 5, old funding formulas historically used to allocate funds to public institutions rely heavily on credit hour enrollments for the allocation of public funds. In the private non-profit sector, enrollments do not result in formulaic allocations from public entities, but they do result in tuition and fee revenue; a substantial part of which is funded by public, private, and institutional coffers (see Chapter 5). At for-profit institutions, institutions may be incentivized to enroll students. Termed "starts," institutional staff may be rewarded for meeting enrollment targets, though scrutiny in 2010 and beyond has resulted in some institutions shifting their business model to focus more on retention than on starts.

Emerging Perspectives on Institutional Performance

The most common, and often used, metric for institutional performance in postsecondary education at this time is the Student-Right-to-Know completion rates. Research has shown the use of graduation or completion (graduation plus transfer) rates to be highly problematic due to the assumptions applied in determining the denominator of the cohort (Bradburn & Hurst, 2001; Cook & Pullaro, 2010; Hom, 2009). For example, cohorts for the Student Right-to-Know rates reported annually to the U.S. Department of Education's (ED) Integrated Postsecondary Data System (IPEDS) by institutions reflect between seven and 22% of the total student body or enrollment (Mullin, 2012). Furthermore, the Department of Education's congressionally mandated Committee on Measures of Student Success (CMSS) found that "Although federal graduation rates provide important and comparable data across institutional sectors, limitations in the data understate the success of students enrolled at 2-year institutions and can be misleading to the public" (2011, p. 4).

STUDENT PERFORMANCE

Student performance is measured in a number of ways, generally by performance at graduation on standardized tests such as the Graduate Record Exam (GRE), the Law School Admissions Test (LSAT), the Certified Public Accountants (CPA) exam, or the National Nursing Exam. Although these are measures of individual student performance, as is graduation in and of itself, the literature reports these measures as institutional performance statistics.

One perspective of institutional success is informed by the understanding that a student's academic preparation upon entering college plays a substantial role in the likelihood that the student will complete a bachelor's degree. For example, consider two students, Bob and Jolie. Bob recently graduated from high school, was in the top 5% of his class academically, and earned high scores on his aptitude tests. Jolie did not finish high school, did not take an aptitude test, but did take a placement test that identified her need for academic remediation. There are at least two ways to factor individual differences, as exemplified by Bob and Jolie, into measurements of success.

One method is to calculate expected values of student success for an institution given the characteristics of the student body. Research has identified risk factors for success, including high school grade point average, aptitude test score, gender, race, ethnicity, socio-economic status, delayed entry to college after high school, current employment, dependents, single parent, part-time enrollment, lack of a high school diploma, or financial independence (Bailey & Xu, 2012). An institution's "success" rate would then be compared to the expected value from the predictive equation to determine the institution's relative success. The University System of Georgia uses this comparison of expected versus actual graduation rates as one indicator of performance for the system's 34 institutions (McKeown-Moak, 2010b).

A second alternative is to determine an input-adjusted metric for students or a cohort of students based upon the aforementioned risk factors. A synthesis of research (HCM Strategists, 2012a) has indicated that the primary factors to consider include high school characteristics (grade point average, test score, class rank, and curriculum quality), demographic characteristics (race, ethnicity, family income, geography), and incoming student data (academic attitudes, behavior, college goals). A concern about these approaches is that controlling for identifying characteristics associated with traditionally underrepresented populations in terms of success may make comparisons between different institutions more equitable, but it may not result in a focus on better serving underrepresented students.

An alternative approach is to recognize the difference in the academic distance a student has to travel to attain a bachelor's degree and to validate the progress an individual can make along the way. There are points of success along the way to the bachelor's degree (Ewell, 2007) that were developed through cutting edge research done by Teachers College, Columbia University and funded by the Bill and Melinda Gates Foundation. These points of success are called "momentum points" and "milestone events." Momentum points are defined as "measurable educational attainments that are empirically correlated with the completion of a milestone" and milestone events as "measurable educational achievements that include both conventional terminal completions ... and intermediate outcomes, such as completing developmental education or adult basic skills requirements" (Leinbach & Jenkins, 2008, p. 2). The nascent practice is then to acknowledge, and reward, incremental steps towards traditional postsecondary credentials. This approach is used in the new performance funding systems for Washington's Community and Technical College System, and for all colleges and universities in Tennessee. The research base for momentum points at the 4-year institution level, however, is not very robust, and there may be questions as to whether momentum points are effective for research universities.

In 2012, *U.S. News and World Report* issued several reports on which colleges are most and least successful at graduating low-income students and high-income students, defined as those who do not receive financial aid (Morse & Tolis, 2012a). Like other *U.S. News* reports on the quality of higher education, these studies use data collected by *U.S. News* and a methodology with which other researchers have raised questions. We note the reports here as an example of individual student data that are viewed as institutional performance indicators.

In addition to state-specific systems of performance or accountability, there are several notable national measures of state higher education performance, which look at the total statewide picture, not individual institutions. One of these is the Measuring Up reports issued in even-numbered years by Patrick Callan's group, the National Center for Public Policy and Higher Education (NCPPHE). NCPPHE reports are based on a significant amount of research carried out by the staff of the Center. NCPPHE issued these reports in 2000, 2002, 2004, 2006, and 2008, and provided for each state its performance on a number of higher education measures, such as affordability and access. Assessments for 2010 were not available as of 2012. These assessments are valuable in the information that is provided to the public but are not used in state performance funding models.

PROGRAMMATIC PERFORMANCE

Academic programmatic performance has long been of substantial interest. Often, the programs of interest are line-item or grant-funded for workforce development purposes. As these programs have direct funding sources, there is an interest and belief that these programs can be evaluated independently of other factors. In practice, separating out program effects is difficult. One reason is that there are fixed costs associated with a program that are not directly expended on the participants. Examples include equipment, infrastructure, and maintenance of facilities that are necessary to operate a program. This methodological reality makes an evaluation of workforce programs in particular difficult. Inability to document specific outcomes, in addition to inconsistent measures of student success and program participants across states, makes understanding effectiveness of the programs challenging.

Interests in performance of specific educational programs have expanded to include traditional programs at institutions of postsecondary institutions. The focus on programs was heightened with the 2010 program integrity regulations by the U.S. Department of Education.

Program effectiveness may be measured by accrediting groups such as the Accreditation Board for Engineering and Technology (ABET), National League for Nursing Accrediting Commission (NLNAC), and other groups particular to an academic discipline. These groups measure the quality and effectiveness of the programs by evaluating the program on-site. One measure used in the South Carolina performance funding system was the percent of accreditable programs that had received accreditation. Program effectiveness also is measured by the percent of the completers who pass national exams, such as the PRAXIS for teachers, the CPA exam, the bar exam, or the nursing boards.

Increasingly, there is policy attention to the notion that students may be incentivized to complete college. Given that the student is the unit of analysis, proper research requires comparison groups (and rich data to develop proper comparison groups as explained in Chapter 10) and outcomes data. The research on this idea is nascent, yet informative. Some of the measures used for incenting student behavior are displayed in Table 7.3. The new Ohio performance funding system has student incentives as one component. Texas has used a performance incentive of sorts that rewards students graduating on time from Texas A&M and the University of Texas with $1,000 at graduation. Students must sign a contract that says they will graduate within 4 years to be eligible for the award. However, there is no evidence that this program has been successful in increasing the 4-year graduation rates at these two institutions.

Table 7.3.   Student Incentive Criteria

Eligibility Criteria	Characteristics	Maintenance Requirements in College	Outputs
File Free Application for Federal Student Aid	Low-income	Grade point average above a threshold (ex. 3.0)	Enroll in college
Rigorous high school courses completed	Residency	Complete 30 credits a year	.
High school grade point average above a threshold (ex. 3.0)	Merit	Enroll full-time	
Minimum standardized test score		Enroll one summer	
Community service		Engage in academic counseling	
Finish in top ten percent of high school class		Engage in peer advising	
Earn a regular high school diploma		Attend tutoring sessions	
Refrain from drugs and alcohol			
Do not commit crime			

ANALYZING FISCAL ALLOCATIONS

Conducting research on performance funding can be viewed as evaluative, where the research questions examine whether the espoused purposes of the program have been achieved. However, there are important research questions that likely will not align with espoused purposes of a program. For example, the impact of a program on traditionally underrepresented populations may be an important consideration. The work of Mustard (2005) serves as one example of research that showed that the intended impact of Georgia's HOPE scholarship carried with it unintended outcomes.

In a review of state merit-aid program, for example, Morse and Tolis (2012b) found that over half of the students did not quality for the merit aid in the second year of their college experience and that these students would have enrolled at a public institution even without the merit aid. Since one of the goals of the merit aid was to keep the state's brightest students in the state, the merit aid was called unnecessary to prevent "brain-drain."

RESEARCHING INSTITUTIONAL PERFORMANCE FUNDING

Dougherty and Reddy (2011) acknowledged the limited nature of research literature on institutional performance funding in that researchers rarely use multivariate quantitative methodologies and that performance funding variables are usually a dichotomous "yes/no." The ability to link performance mechanisms to outcomes is confounded by factors such as, but not limited to, other accountability practices in the state, accrediting bodies, program initiatives, enrollment size, student composition, tuition dependency, expenditure levels for various institutional functions, faculty composition, institutional mission,
region of country, and amount of institutional aid. Other limitations include the narrow scope of the studies (i.e. institutions and states) and the lack of triangulation in qualitative studies.

In addition to traditional quantitative and qualitative research methodologies, there are other types of analyses that may be appropriate. These calculations are drawn from work in economics and in elementary/secondary finance to examine concepts of fiscal equity.

Fiscal equity has three components: fiscal neutrality, horizontal equity, and vertical equity. Fiscal neutrality refers to the concept that wealth should not be associated with the receipt of funds. Correlations and regressions focused on allocated amounts relative to the wealth of the recipient are methods to examine fiscal neutrality (Berne & Stiefel, 1984).

Horizontal equity refers to the equal treatment of equals. Under horizontal equity, each entity is approximately equal, and the associated allocations should be roughly equal. Calculations associated with the examination of horizontal equity include measures of central tendency and related metrics including the median, range, restricted range, federal range ratio, mean, standard deviation, coefficient of variation, McLoone Index, Gini Index, and the Verstegen Index (see Table 7.4). Regressions also are run to understand how allocations may be related to the variable of interest. It is important to note that, while each of these approaches has its strengths, an analysis that utilizes the greatest number of calculations provides a clearer picture to best understand the phenomena examined. For example, analysts have compared the average of the highest quartile to average of the lowest quartile and made generalizations about the equity of the allocation. This type of approach neglects the rest of the distribution and may be unduly influenced by outliers at either the high or low end, depending upon the number of observations.

Horizontal equity in higher education, however, is the most misused. There are many cases of legislators dividing an institution's state appropriations by the number of headcount students and declaring equity has been achieved if the amounts are equal. Or, an institution will

Table 7.4.   Fiscal Equity Calculations

Calculation	Description	Strengths	Weaknesses
Median	The mid-point of a set of values arranged from least to most.	Not influenced by outliers	Provides no information about the distribution
Range	The arithmetic difference between the largest value and the smallest value of interest; A smaller range indicates a more equitable distribution	Quantifies the magnitude of the distribution	Provides limited information if the maximum and minimum are not understood (A range of 3 to 8 has a different meaning if the maximum value is 50 rather than 10)
Restricted Range	The arithmetic difference between the largest and smallest value after removing the values within the top and bottom 5% of the distribution; A smaller restricted range indicates a more equitable distribution	Removes the influence of outliers	Provides limited information if the maximum and minimum are not understood (A range of 3 to 8 has a different meaning if the maximum value is 50 rather than 10)
Federal Range Ratio	The restricted range divided by value representative of the fifth percentile of the distribution; A smaller value indicates a more equitable distribution	Removes the influence of outliers	Its value is limited in cases with few observations
Mean		Operationalizes normal	Provides no information about the distribution
Standard Deviation		Describes the distribution relative to the mean	May be skewed by outliers
Coefficient of Variation	The square root of a value's variance divided by the mean value; A smaller value indicates a more equitable distribution	Quantifies "equitable"	Not easily understood

(Table continues on next page)

Table 7.4. Continued

Calculation	Description	Strengths	Weaknesses
Gini Index	An indicator depicting the degree to which the distribution of aid matches the distribution of resources; For example, 10% of the students should receive 10% of the resources; Values range from 0.0 to 1.0, with those values closer to 0.0 being more equitable	Long-used economic calculation	Not easily understood
McLoone Index	The ratio of the sum of values below the median to the actual median; It depicts how far the lower half of the distribution is from receiving the median allocation; Values range from 0.0 to 1.0, with those values closer to 1.0 being more equitable	Simple ratio	Uses only 1/2 of the distribution
Verstegen Index	A ratio of the sum of all values above the median to the median value; Values range from 1.0 to 2.0, with those values closer to 1.0 being more equitable	Focuses on "better resourced"	Uses only 1/2 of the distribution

calculate the range, restricted range, or federal range ratio on the same data as the legislator used and mistakenly report that funds are not equitably distributed. For example, the University of Nevada Las Vegas calculates horizontal equity by taking state appropriations plus tuition and fees at each of the Nevada institutions, dividing that number by the number of students, and declaring that the institution is under-funded if the resulting number is not the same as the University of Nevada Reno or that of Truckee Meadows Community College. Reno and TMCC do not offer the same programs as Las Vegas; also Reno is a land-grant institution with a mission to serve all of the state through its agriculture extension programs. No institution offers the same market basket of services and programs to the same students. Therefore, unless the numerator and denominator are equated by using weighted students, this calculation is invalid.

Vertical equity, conceptually, refers to the unequal treatment of unequals and acknowledges differences between populations. Vertical equity is achieved primarily by weighting values, such as the cost of a credit hour, to make the costs roughly equal. Weightings can recognize the higher cost of education for students from disadvantaged backgrounds and relatively lower costs to provide for students from advanced backgrounds. For example, if the cost of education for an advantaged student was $10,000, and the costs associated with educating a disadvantaged student were $25,000, the latter student costs 2.5 times the amount for an advantaged student. These values are then used in equity analyses rather than simple averages. In this discussion, and throughout this book, cost of education refers to the resources required for the institution to provide students the services. The price is what the student pays for tuition and required fees, room and board, books, and other incidental expenses.

Equity analysis in higher education is used most often to determine if resources are being distributed in a fair way to the colleges and universities in a state. Unlike school funding where there have been equity challenges in the courts of almost every state, equity challenges in higher education generally are carried out in the federal courts in what are called the Adams states. The Adams states are those that once ran segregated systems of higher education. Court cases in Alabama, Louisiana, Maryland, Mississippi, and North Carolina relied on funding research that evaluated the equity of the funding system. To complete the analysis, the expert witnesses used the range, restricted range, and federal range ratios on costs per weighted credit hour. Although these measures are imperfect, the federal court accepted the analysis. A better way of doing the study would be to examine the cost of producing a degree in the fields offered by the institutions, adjusted for the abilities of the students, the physical plant of the institution, and certain other factors unique to a particular institution. However, completing such a study would have required a more complete database than was available at the time.

Determining the cost of various programs, and the cost of producing a degree, is a difficult process requiring a significant amount of data. Institutions offer differing market baskets of goods and services, and at best, research can determine only how much the institution is spending, not how much it should be spending, given the types of students and the programs that are offered.

The cost of a degree is not the same as taking the cost per credit hour of instruction and multiplying the credit hour cost by the number of credit hours required for that degree. Cost per credit hour generally is calculated through a cost study, a very expensive and time-consuming process, as discussed in Chapter 5. Cost studies examine the workload of every instructor at the institution and allocate those costs over the courses that each instructor teaches. This information is obtained from surveys of the faculty and administrative staff, so that an instructor who teaches a three-hour course in lower division physics, two four-hour courses in upper division chemistry, two seminars in doctoral level biochemistry, and supervises 10 doctoral students and 16 master's students would have that instructor's "costs" including salary, fringe benefits, travel, and departmental operating expenses allocated across the courses, disciplines, and programs.

Some of the complete cost studies are used to determine the costs of providing credit hours by level and academic discipline. Others are used to document faculty salary inequities or to request additional funding. Amazingly, when these studies of faculty time have been conducted at any time between 1920 and 2010, no matter if the institution is a 2-year college, liberal arts college, major research university, or regional university, faculty members report that they work an average 50–60 hours per week.

As mentioned in Chapter 2, several states complete a cost study every year or every other year and report those findings on their websites. Ohio and Florida also have completed studies of the cost of a degree. Although neither of the methodologies considered the extra costs to provide special services to some groups of students (such as economically disadvantaged students or those needing remediation to succeed), the research is noteworthy.

Florida computed the cost per credit hour by academic discipline and by level of instruction first. Then, each degree program at the associate, bachelor's, master's, specialist, doctoral, and first professional level was costed out by summing the costs per credit hour for a typical student's degree in that discipline and adjusting for the costs of administration and physical plant. Cost of degrees varied widely from less than $5,000 for certain associate's degrees to over $200,000 for certain doctoral degrees. This type of research is not widely disseminated in the research community, although the results of these studies are important in the understanding of what a degree costs and to an understanding of why different institutions spend varying amounts per student.

From the perspective of legislators and other policy makers, Dougherty and Reddy (2011) suggest that the research questions related to performance funding are the following:

- What impacts does performance funding have on student outcomes?
- How are these impacts produced?
- What obstacles and unintended effects are encountered?

Dougherty and Reddy summarize 40 research studies on performance funding and conclude that there is significant additional research needed. As part of their research, they found that there were immediate, intermediate, and long-term changes as a result of performance funding. Among the immediate impacts were changes in funding levels, college awareness of state priorities, and awareness of how one's institution was performing relative to peers. Among the intermediate changes were improvements in instruction and student services and higher numbers of graduates and job placement rates. For example, Banta (1996) reported that after 15 years of performance funding in Tennessee, institutions have improved student learning on campus and increased minority enrollment and retention as well as graduation rates (p. 44).

However, offsetting these gains were weakening of academic standards (a concern of the faculty we talked with about performance funding) and a narrowing of the mission of the institution to those areas that were rewarded (Sanford & Hunter, 2011).

Ultimately, Dougherty and Reddy (2011) concluded that significant additional research needs to be completed to overcome design problems in the studies they examined.

SUMMARY

This chapter has provided information on performance funding, its history of use in higher education, and the current status of performance funding. The new performance funding is quite different from the performance funding of the 1980s and 1990s, in that the goals of the state are primary concerns. It remains to be seen whether performance funding—that is, the linking of higher education funding to specific goals that are in the interests of the state and the student rather than the institution—will be effective in achieving progress or improving the economy. Research on the effectiveness of performance funding in changing the way colleges and universities actually operate and success in increasing the number of college completers is lacking, perhaps because 2013 is too soon to gauge effectiveness of relatively new programs.

To be successful, Lumina Foundation's *Four Steps to Finishing First* (2012) productivity agenda recommend the following minimal conditions in state- and system-level performance funding policies:

- Allocate at least 5% of existing funds allocated through performance funding.
- Build incentives around state goals.

- Take institutional differences into account—providing opportunities for institutions to succeed if they fulfill their missions and contribute to the state's overall higher educational attainment goals.
- Focus on rewarding improvement, particularly for underrepresented students.
- Protect against large shifts in funding by phasing in changes over a few years.
- Measure and publicly report annual progress.
- Continually reevaluate the effectiveness of the funding system once established.
- Maintain a commitment to financial incentives for outstanding performance during good times and bad.

Following these recommendations may help new performance funding policies to result in a good system for higher education.

CHAPTER 8

HUMAN CAPITAL DEVELOPMENT AND RETURNS ON INVESTMENT

Research related to economic impacts of an institution on students or society are often of keen interest to a variety of stakeholders. Students and their families are interested in the short-term and long-term impact of postsecondary education on their quality of life and of the increase in earnings; states are interested in the impact on the workforce, either through meeting the needs for trained workers in all fields or in reducing the costs of poverty. States also are concerned that their investment in providing educational services is resulting in positive financial and societal outcomes. Donors are concerned that their contributions are resulting in a positive impact on the institution or society. Higher education has become so expensive that students, parents, governments, and the general public want to know what they are getting from their investments in higher education.

Recent public press such as *Newsweek* have asked "Is College a Lousy Investment?" (McArdle, 2012). Not only *Newsweek*, but some congressional leaders and talk-show pundits have given frenzied testimony that college is not a good investment and that not all should pursue postsecondary education. The front page of the December 23, 2012 *The New York Times* included an article on the less-than-expected benefits of higher education on individuals from poorer backgrounds, suggesting that postsecondary education was not as good an investment for many as has been thought (DeParle, 2012).

Higher Education Finance Research: Policy, Politics, and Practice, pp. 247–277
Copyright © 2014 by Information Age Publishing

In this chapter we explore the value of a postsecondary education and human capital development, from the perspective of both the individual's and society's return on investment in higher education; we also discuss the economic and societal impact of higher education and provide examples of the methodology for calculating the economic impact of an institution.

HUMAN CAPITAL DEVELOPMENT

Human capital, at its core, is an expression of the value of time at the individual level. Human capital may be thought of as those characteristics of a person that are "productive" in some economic context, such as educational attainment, which then is an investment in the person with returns on that investment, as salaries or social rewards. Human capital also may be thought of as the knowledge, skills, and attributes acquired by investments in education and health. Early investigations of human capital included work by Becker (1964, 1971, 1976), Schultz (1963, 1971), Heckman (1974), and Mincer (1958).

Schultz stressed the significance of the benefits of education on human capital. From the economic perspective, investments in human capital formulation like formal education or on-the-job training can be evaluated on the basis of their ability to generate future returns such as additional lifetime income and greater personal satisfaction (Cohn & Geske, 1986). Thus, the decision to pursue higher education is an investment decision.

Conceptions of human capital as it related to postsecondary education were revisited extensively in 1972 by Bowen and 1988 by Leslie and Brinkman. Building upon the scholars before him, McMahon (2009) examined human capital, offering his conception of modern human capital, which includes "not just narrowly defined economics of job markets and earnings ... [but] the use of human capital at home and in the community during leisure-time hours" (pp. 5, 10). His human capital conception refers to both the social rates of return and the private rates of return. These include both the market returns to investment in education, including jobs, earnings, and economic growth, and the non-market, private benefits such as health, spousal health, child health, child education, fertility rates, longevity, and happiness. In addition, McMahon includes the social benefits such as increased civic participation, reduction of poverty, lower crime rates, and lower public assistance costs. Theoretically, McMahon's human capital model is illustrated in Figure 8.1.

McMahon (2009) states that the "importance of measuring and valuing the earnings, private non-market, and social benefits of higher education and relating their total to the costs of higher education cannot be overstated" (p. 327). Although the econometrics of estimating the return on

Returns to Education
and Costs $

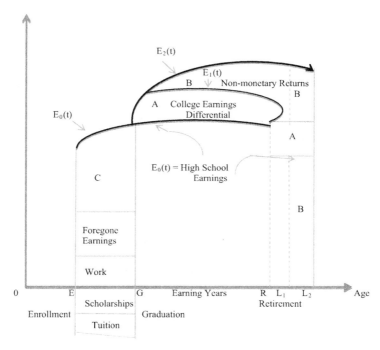

Source: McMahon (2009, p. 95).

Figure 8.1. Investment in education and returns over the lifecycle.

an investment in higher education are beyond the scope of this book, we do present some basic considerations and an equation for calculating the return on investment. In the sections that follow, we also will discuss some of the calculated individual rates of return to higher education.

When expressed as an equation, there is a general formula used to calculate the internal rate of return (IROR):

$$\sum_{t=0}^{[R]} \frac{Et - Ct}{(1+r)^t} = 0, \text{ the net present value}$$

where :

r = the social rate of return,

Et = the net earnings differential before taxes at age t,

Ct = the social cost of the investment (full public and
private institutional costs plus foregone earnings),
and

t = age. For example: t = G at graduation from the
education level in question to retirement at age R.

In this equation, the value of the discount rate that would make Net
Present Value (NPV) = 0 is the solution to the equation. If IROR is
greater than 1, then the "project," in other words, higher education, is a
worthwhile investment (McMahon, 2009).

McMahon and others, including Cohn and Geske (1986), Cohn and
Cooper (1997), Hansen (1963), Becker (1964), and Mincer (1974), have
calculated the return on the investment of various levels of education.
Cohn and Geske (1986) reported that the average return on a bachelor's
degree is about 12%. Others have reported higher and lower returns,
depending on degree, gender, and race/ethnicity. Table 8.1 displays some
of the rates of return.

Table 8.1.   Average Rates of Return to Investment in Higher Education

Author	Sample Year	Private Return	
Return on a Bachelor's in U.S.:			
Cohn	1984	12.0%	
Hansen	1950	11.4%	
Becker	1958	14.8%	
Becker	1956	12.4%	
Mincer	1960	9.6%	
McMahon and Wagner	1976	17.0%	
McMahon	2005	14.0%	16% on associate
Returns on Graduate Education:		Master's	Doctorate
Hanoch	1960	7.0%	
Weiss	1966	12.2%	12.30%
McMahon and Wagner*	1976	0% to 12.7%	0% to 16.4%

Note: * depends on institution and field of study.
Source: Cohn and Geske (1986); McMahon (2009); McMahon & Wagner (1982).

McMahon and Wagner (1981) and others have looked at the return on
the investment also from the perspective of a student's expected and
actual annual earnings 25 years after graduation compared to the earnings without a college education. Ratios calculated by dividing the

expected earnings by earnings before graduation, by dividing salaries after 25 years by beginning salaries, and by dividing actual salaries by expected salaries all give ratios greater than 1.0, meaning that education was a positive investment.

A third method of calculating the return on the investment is to complete a cost/benefit analysis. In this method, the costs of a higher education are compared to the expected benefits. As they say, the devil is in the details. How should cost be defined? How should the benefits be defined? At its least complex, the total tuition and fees plus books are summed over the college experience and then compared to the increase in income from the college experience. In this example, the increase in lifetime earnings is the figure used for the increase in income; no costs of room and board, travel, and other incidental expenses are included in the "cost" of higher education, nor are foregone earnings included in the cost.

LABOR MARKET RETURNS

One component of human capital theory is a focus on workforce outcomes of education. The recent discussions in *Newsweek*, in *The New York Times*, and in legislative conversations have revolved around providing information both for decision making by potential students and their families and also by stakeholders for accountability purposes. Should students and their families invest in programs where there either are no jobs or only low-paying jobs at program completion? Should the states and/or the federal government provide funding for programs that do not lead directly to jobs after program completion? (We in higher education would say yes, because a liberal education is an important driver of the economy.) Programs in this sense can include traditional certificate or degree programs provided by colleges and universities, non-credit workforce programs offered by colleges and universities, adult basic education programs offered by K–12 entities, or other publicly funded workforce training programs.

Workforce data for former students, whether those students are "leavers" or "graduates," may be expressed as changes in median weekly earnings and unemployment rates as the highest level of educational attainment increases; a common source for these data is an annual data release by the Bureau of Labor Statistics of the U.S. Department of Labor titled "Education Pays...." Data show that, on average, as educational attainment increases, earnings also increase while unemployment decreases (see Figure 8.2 and Table 8.2), providing the clearest demonstration of the value of a college education.

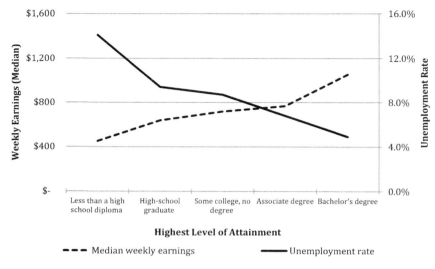

Source: BLS (2012).

Figure 8.2.   Median weekly earnings and unemployment rate by highest level of educational attainment.

Another source of workforce data is the American Community Survey (ACS) of the Census Bureau, available at www.census.gov/acs/www. ACS is an ongoing statistical survey that samples a small percentage of the population each year to give communities and others information for planning. Data from the ACS are available for the nation, for a state, and for a particular community or region within the state. As an example, Table 8.3 displays the 2010 average earnings by educational attainment for the nation, for the state of South Carolina, and for the Charleston regional area. These data can be used to provide support for institutions of higher education in the region.

In general, college graduates, and those with some college, command higher wages and salaries when they enter the labor market. This translates into greater disposable income for spending or saving. Median earnings rise steadily for individuals with increasing educational attainment, no matter what year of data is used. Using 2010 data, assuming inflation equals wage growth and the average worker is employed for 40 years, it is possible to approximate lifetime earnings.

Table 8.2.   **Earnings Metrics**

Metrics	*Description*	*Strength(s)*	*Weakness(es)*
Earnings			
Average earnings (along with earnings) for 1st through 4th fiscal quarter after exit	The total earnings in the quarter as determined from wage records	General understanding of private returns provided Can estimate tax payments of completers	Dependent on the current state of the economy Regional differences exist in earnings Earnings vary by gender and race/ethnicity Earnings change over time
Livable wage	Number of program completers employed with a livable wage, to be determined	General understanding of private returns provided Can estimate tax payments of completers	Dependent on the current state of the economy Regional differences exist in earnings Earnings vary by gender and race/ethnicity Earnings change over time
Earnings at entry	Earnings at a set period after completion, usually six months	General understanding of private returns provided Can estimate tax payments of completers	Dependent on the current state of the economy Regional differences exist in earnings Earnings vary by gender and race/ethnicity Earnings change over time

(Table continues on next page)

Table 8.2. Continued

Metrics	Description	Strength(s)	Weakness(es)
Earnings			
Long-term earnings	Earnings after an extended period of time, such as 5 years	General understanding of private returns provided Can estimate tax payments of completers	Dependent on the current state of the economy Regional differences exist in earnings Earnings vary by gender and race/ethnicity
Full employment earnings	Earnings in a fiscal quarter where the individual was working the entire quarter	General understanding of private returns provided Can estimate tax payments of completers	Dependent on the current state of the economy Regional differences exist in earnings Earnings vary by gender and race/ethnicity Earnings change over time
Change in Earnings			
2nd and 3rd quarters after exit	Earnings in the 2nd and 3rd quarters after exit minus earnings in the 2nd and 3rd quarters before participation among those who were employed in the quarter after exit	Accounts for changes in earnings	Regional differences exist in earnings Earnings vary by gender and race/ethnicity
3rd and 4th quarters after exit	Earnings in the 3rd and 4th quarters after exit minus earnings in the 2nd and 3rd quarters before participation among those who were employed in the quarter after exit	Accounts for changes in earnings	Regional differences exist in earnings Earnings vary by gender and race/ethnicity

(Table continues on next page)

Table 8.2.   **Continued**

Metrics	Description	Strength(s)	Weakness(es)
Change in Earnings			
Average earnings change	The difference in earnings the first full fiscal quarter after leaving the program, for those employed, as compared to earnings the most recent full fiscal quarter prior to entering the program	Accounts for changes in earnings	Regional differences exist in earnings Earnings vary by gender and race/ethnicity Bias favors students who did not work before entry, resulting in larger gains
Pass rates			
Technical skill attainment	Number of career and technical education concentrators who passed technical skill assessments that are aligned with industry-recognized standards, if available and appropriate, during the reporting year	Indicates if student passed barrier to enter the workforce	Skills may not match employer demand
Licensure pass rate	Proportion that complete a state or industry recognized certification or licensure	Proxy for program quality	Content may not match employer demand
Licensure and certification pass rates	The proportion of students who complete or graduate from a program, seek and obtain licensure or certification for the first time within a given year	Proxy for program quality	Content may not match employer demand
Employment			
Entered employment	Employed the first fiscal quarter after exit	Proxy for program quality	Dependent on the state of the economy
Entered employment rate	Percentage of participants who obtained a job by the end of the first quarter after leaving the program	Proxy for program quality	Dependent on the state of the economy Employment changes over time

(Table continues on next page)

Table 8.2.   Continued

Metrics	Description	Strength(s)	Weakness(es)
Employment			
Employment retention rate at 6 months	Of those who had a job in the first quarter after exit, the percent that had a job in the third quarter	Proxy for program quality	Dependent on the state of the economy Employment changes over time
Retained employment	For those employed in quarter after exit, the number of workers employed in the 2nd and 3rd fiscal quarter	Proxy for program quality	Dependent on the state of the economy Employment changes over time
Placement for Tech Prep	The number of tech prep students placed in a related field of employment no later than 12 months after graduation	Proxy for program quality	Dependent on the state of the economy Determining in-field placement requires surveys; not currently included in data systems
Student Placement	Number of CTE concentrators who were placed or retained in employment or placed in military service or apprenticeship programs in the 2nd quarter following the program year in which they left postsecondary education	Proxy for program quality	Dependent on the state of the economy Data only available for certain program participants
Retained employment 3rd quarter after exit	Employed in the 3rd quarter after exit among those who were employed in the quarter after exit	Proxy for program quality	Dependent on the state of the economy Employment changes over time
Retained employment 4th quarter after exit	Employed in the 4th quarter after exit among those who were employed in the quarter after exit	Proxy for program quality	Dependent on the state of the economy Employment changes over time
Employment and credential rate	Employed in the quarter after exit and received credential among adults and dislocated workers who received training	Proxy for program quality	Dependent on the state of the economy Employment changes over time

(Table continues on next page)

Table 8.2. Continued

Metrics	Description	Strength(s)	Weakness(es)
Employment			
Placement rate	The proportion of entering college students who acquire a marketable skill and obtain employment in a field directly related to that skill within one year of last attendance	Proxy for program quality	Dependent on the state of the economy Determining in-field placement requires surveys; not collected
Full-quarter employment	The individual is employed at the beginning and end of the fiscal quarter by the same employer	Proxy for program quality	Dependent on the state of the economy
Cumulative quarters before separation	The number of fiscal quarters a worker is employed before unemployment	Proxy for program quality	Dependent on the state of the economy

Sources: Abowd, Stephens, Vilhuber, Andersson, McKinney, Roemer & Woodcock (2005); Employment and Training Administration (2011); Heckman, Heinrich, Courty, Marschke, & Smith (2011); Carl Perkins Career and Technical Education Act, Public Law 109-270 (2006); Social Policy Research Associates (2011).

Table 8.3. Median Earnings by Educational Attainment

	2010 Median Income			As a % of U.S.		
Educational Attainment	CMSA	S.C.	U.S.	CMSA	S.C.	U.S.
Less than high school graduate	$18,252	$18,116	$19,492	93.6%	92.9%	100.0%
High school graduate (equivalency)	$26,694	$25,600	$27,281	97.8%	93.8%	100.0%
Some college or associate's degree	$32,624	$31,057	$33,593	97.1%	92.5%	100.0%
Bachelor's degree	$41,906	$42,192	$48,485	86.4%	87.0%	100.0%
Graduate or professional degree	$53,430	$52,373	$63,612	84.0%	82.3%	100.0%
Population 25 years + w/earnings	$33,074	$30,860	$34,665	95.4%	89.0%	100.0%

Source: U.S. Census Bureau, American Community Survey (2012).

- Overall, the national median income for all workers is $33,665 with lifetime earnings of approximately $1.4 million.
- Over a career, those who did not earn a high school diploma will earn about $.8 million, or just over $19,492 per year.
- Nationwide, individuals who earn a bachelor's degree have a median annual income of $48,485, or $1.9 million over a lifetime of work.
- Obtaining a bachelor's degree leads to even more education, as nationally, about one-third of all bachelor's recipients earn an advanced degree (Carnevale, Rose, & Cheah, 2010).
- Graduate degree and above holders earn at least twice the amount earned by those with only a high school diploma ($63,612 per year compared to $27,281 per year).

In the calculations of earnings of graduates, Table 8.4 provides an example of lifetime earnings by educational attainment for the nation, for the state of South Carolina, and for the Charleston regional area. These lifetime earnings figures can be calculated from the ACS data for any region or state.

Table 8.4.   Estimated Lifetime Earnings by Educational Attainment (2010)

	Lifetime Earnings		
Educational Attainment	CMSA	S.C.	U.S.
Less than high school	$730,080	$724,640	$779,680
High school graduate	$1,067,760	$1,024,000	$1,091,240
Some college or associate's degree	$1,304,960	$1,242,280	$1,343,720
Bachelor's degree	$1,676,240	$1,687,680	$1,939,400
Graduate or professional degree	$2,137,200	$2,094,920	$2,544,480
Population 25 years+	$1,322,960	$1,234,400	$1,386,600

Source: U.S. Census Bureau, American Community Survey (2012).

Earnings Data

Median earnings data are helpful in initial discussion of the private returns of postsecondary education. Data on median earnings have been advanced by examining earnings associated with a particular major, type of occupation, and level of education. Carnevale (2011) demonstrated that there is in essence a five part aspect to earnings data.

First, in general, the higher the level of educational attainment, the greater the earnings, a point that is supported by the BLS data shown in Table 8.2 (also depicted in Figure 8.2) and by the ACS data in Table 8.3. Second, Carnevale, Strohl, and Melton (2011) examined factors associated with 171 majors including the number of earned credentials, the gender composition, earnings by gender, median earnings, employment status, work status, and earnings boost for a graduate degree. The overall finding of this study was that earnings vary by major.

Third, there is an overlap in earnings depending on occupational choice. Carnevale, Rose and Cheah (2010) estimated the overlap in lifetime earnings for workers with various levels of educational attainment and found that 28.2% of associate degree holders and 23.1% of workers with some college (which would include sub-baccalaureate certificate holders) earn more than bachelor's degree holders. The variation is dependent in part upon occupation as well as credential-type. For example, an engineer with a certificate earns more than a teacher with a bachelor's degree.

Fourth, while there is an earnings overlap across fields of study and occupations, higher levels of education still result in increased earnings. For example, a certificate holder in engineering will make less than a bachelor's degree holder in engineering. Finally, gender and race/ethnicity are factors that trump all else.

For researchers who study earnings then, it is important to control for credential level, occupational field, gender, and race/ethnicity. There also is evidence that pre-college factors such as academic preparedness as measured by high school grade point average and socio-economic status are important to control whenever possible.

There are additional considerations in terms of earnings. As a report from the U.S. Census Bureau (Longitudinal Employer—Household Dynamics Program, 2003) notes, there are three components of wages: human capital, firm effect, and a residual. Their research finds that 30% of earnings variation was due to demographic characteristics including but not limited to education, occupation, age, sex, marital status, and even employer characteristics such as size and industry. However, longitudinal data on workers and firms explain closer to 90% of earnings variation. This is to say that people with the exact same degree from the same college at the same time, with the same level of skills, can have different earnings due to the financial position of the employer. In addition, some people choose to work for companies for non-monetary reasons. For example, take two graduates—who happen to be twins and had all the same grades in courses from an information technology program. Both have been offered the same jobs. By choice, one works in the public sector at a library, and the other chooses to take a private sector job in a leading law firm. There will be differences in earnings as a result of the earnings provided by the employer but also as a result of the choice of the student in terms of where they want to work.

As much as people want to attribute earnings to one factor—an institution—because of these differences, driven by employer and individual choices, such an attribution cannot, and should not, be done. Furthermore, attributing the value of a major to its earnings potential may steer students away from jobs that may pay less but have better fringe benefits (which are not included in earnings), have impact on the community, or be more fulfilling.

Types and Sources of Earnings Data

Earnings data are a valuable part of higher education research. The ability to match individuals, programs, and colleges to earnings provides for a greater understanding of the costs and benefits of postsecondary education and the relative costs associated with attendance. Arkansas, Colorado, Florida, Nevada, Tennessee, and Washington now are providing earnings data for graduates of higher education by institution and by program within the institution. Such data must be viewed with caution because the data may be self-reported or may not include graduates of the institution who left the state or who are self-employed. These are significant limitations. Despite the limitations, at present a bill is pending in Congress to require all colleges and universities to provide the earnings data of their graduates. The American Institutes for Research and conservative pundits are pushing for this type of information to be made available to the general public.

Employment Outcome "Buckets"

There are four primary types of data utilized in the examination of employment outcomes, and thus earnings, for current or former students. Each of these data types can be measured in different ways, as illustrated in Table 8.5, and each has strengths and weaknesses.

The first type of data is earnings data, which may be taken at various points in time. At a minimum, these data are measured six months after completion of a program to allow for the time to transition to a new job and have earnings for a full fiscal quarter.

The second type of data is change in earnings. Change in earnings calculations are important for students/graduates who may be working prior to enrollment to allow for an understanding of the economic impact of a program. Use of the change in earnings also may allow for a better understanding of the impact of specific courses, as some students return to

Table 8.5. Federal Sources of Earnings Data

Database	*Where*	*What*
Unemployment Insurance	State Departments of Labor	Employment records for approximately 90% of the workforce, including private business, state and local governments, some non-profit organizations and Indian tribes
Wage Record Interchange System	U.S. Department of Labor	Facilitates the exchange of wage data among participating states for the purpose of assessing and reporting on state and local employment and training program performance, evaluating training provider performance, and for other purposes allowed under the WRIS Data Sharing Agreement.*
Wage Record Interchange System 2	U.S. Department of Labor	WRIS2 extends the WRIS data sharing model to One-Stop Career Center partner programs such as education programs and other programs not under the jurisdiction of the Department of Labor, as well as other programs.*
Defense Manpower Data Center	Department of Defense	Employment records for maintains data for active duty military in the Army, Navy, Marine Corps, Air Force, Coast Guard, and the National Guard and Reserve
Personnel Compensation and Payroll Records	United States Postal Service	Employment records for current and former USPS employees and postmaster relief/replacement employees.*
Central Personnel Data File	Office of Personnel Management	Employment data for federal civilian employees, most of the executive branch, and the legislative branch. Those employees in the judicial branch are excluded in entirety, and there are exceptions to coverage for the Federal Bureau of Investigation, numerous branches of the executive branch, and some commissioned officers
National Directory of New Hires	U.S. Department of Health and Human Services	Provides employment and unemployment insurance information that enables state child support (IV-D) agencies to be more effective in locating noncustodial parents, establishing child support orders and enforcing child support orders. State Directories of New Hires (SDNHs), State Workforce Agencies (SWAs), and federal agencies provide information to the NDNH.*
American Community Survey	Census Bureau	Provides employment, wage, unemployment, health insurance, and other data on a sample of individuals in communities across the nation.

Notes: (*) reflects a direct quote.

Sources: U.S. Department of Health and Human Services (2012); U.S Department of Labor (2012a; 2012b; 2012c); U.S. Postal Service (2012), Census Bureau (2013).

postsecondary education to upskill and not necessarily to complete a credential. A consideration when conducting earnings change values is the counterfactual, that is to say, the value that is used at re-entry. In some cases a student is returning to college to upskill. In such an instance, a direct change in earnings coupled with an employment rate may be appropriate because upskilling does not always result in increased earnings, though it may help individuals keep their jobs as workplace requirements change. For students without prior earnings, a change in earnings is not appropriate, as there would not be previous earnings. In some cases, students who enter college at age 18 may have had a job in high school; the question then is whether or not to use that data point. Considerations include whether the student completed high school or not and for how long they enrolled in college. These are decisions for the researcher to consider, describe in the limitations section of the research, and note at the bottom of a table showing the findings. The most complicated aspect of change in earnings may be for dislocated workers. Consider an autoworker who loses a job paying $100,000, goes to a college, graduates, and gets a job paying $60,000. The change in earnings in this case would be negative. The question, then, is what is the appropriate comparison point to show the impact of the program for the dislocated worker. Options include the worker did not go to college and remained unemployed ($0 earnings), or got a job at minimum wage for annual earnings of $15,080 in 2012, or the median wage for someone with the dislocated workers educational attainment level. Again, the best answer will depend on contextual factors within the research. The third type of data is a pass rate on licensure and entry examinations. These data are important because in some occupations, students who may have successfully completed a college curriculum cannot begin practice until they demonstrate the skill and abilities required by the exams, such as the CPA or nursing exams. Therefore, it is plausible for some to graduate from a nursing program and not become a nurse because they could not pass the National Council Licensure Exam (NCLEX). These types of measures also were discussed in Chapters 6 and 7 as accountability or performance measures.

The fourth type of data is a measure of employment. Obviously one cannot have earnings without employment. There is, however, a line of inquiry that examines employer tenure and job stability. In addition, the number of graduates who are employed from a particular program is of interest in some policy circles. Some states use the percent of the graduating class that are employed in a field related to their undergraduate major as an accountability or performance measure.

Before we discuss these data, it is important to recognize that there are several sources of earnings data (see Table 8.5). In general, earnings data usually are quarterly wage data and annual earnings data.

Quarterly earnings data for over 90% of the workforce are housed in unemployment insurance (UI) databases held by each state. UI data are the result of a state and federal partnership, which means that each state's data may be different in terms of what is collected and whether or not it is shared with other state agencies and researchers. States do share data with each other for the purpose of evaluating government-funded programs through the Wage Record Interchange System (WRIS) administered by the U.S. Department of Labor; currently all 50 states participate. The tight restrictions on WRIS data led to the development of WRIS2, whose binding agreements allow for a use of the data for broader purposes; at the time of writing just fewer than half of all states participated in WRIS2.

In addition to the UI systems, earnings data for military personnel are housed in the Defense Manpower Data Center; earnings data for workers employed by the United States Postal Service are housed in the Personnel Compensation and Payroll Records database; and earnings data for federal employees are maintained by the Office of Personnel Management. These data are shared with states for the purpose of evaluating government programs through the Federal Employment Data Exchange System (FEDES). In addition to these sources, earnings data are contained in the National Directory of New Hires (NDNH) and other non-public data sources. For example, employees of the Central Intelligence Agency and the Federal Bureau of Investigations, some members of the federal judiciary, and the self-employed are not housed in any of the aforementioned databases.

The self-employed account for 7% of the workforce nationally, with higher percentages in occupations like real estate and construction. A way to include earnings for most U.S. citizens may be accessing data maintained by the Social Security Administration (SSA). In fact, the U.S. Department of Education utilized the SSA data in its gainful employment regulations of 2011. (Currently the program has been struck down by the courts but may be revisited during the second term of President Barack Obama). Because of the lack of self-employment earnings in other databases, researchers may choose to use the data in the American Community Survey. These data, however, are estimates, not actual figures.

While these earnings data are enticing to use for any number of purposes, from research to accountability, there are still substantial shortcomings that researchers and analysts should acknowledge. The first concern is the source of the data. If using SSA data, it is important to note that the researcher does not know if the data reflect earnings from one job or from multiple jobs, whether the person is working full- or part-time, or how

**Table 8.6.   Earnings Outcomes for
Fictitious Program Completers With Located Data: [Year]**

Program Name	Total Number	Percent With Located Earnings Data	Mean	Median	Low	High
		Completers in [Year]		*Earnings*		
A		–%	$–	$–	$–	$–
B		–%	$–	$–	$–	$–
C		–%	$–	$–	$–	$–
D		–%	$–	$–	$–	$–

Note: "Located earnings data" reflect those students for whom data was available. Earnings data reflect __ months after completing. Earnings amounts include those with "$0." There are several factors associated with earnings that may not be accounted for in this analysis.

many hours a week the person is working. With UI data, one can determine how many jobs the person is working but cannot determine whether these are full- or part-time earnings, nor how many hours a week are worked. From an analytical perspective, these issues cause substantial concern and severely limit the comparability of earnings. In addition, there are regional differences in earnings due to variances in the cost of living and due to the factors delineated by Carnevale and shared at the beginning of this section. This is to say, earnings data may not be "clean" enough to use and need to be used in conjunction with other relevant data.

For now, in an era of accountability, the best use of earnings data may be to provide a median earnings amount along with a range and mean to highlight the distribution of outcomes. In addition, the percent of graduates for whom data are available must also be displayed (see Table 8.6).

Earnings Data in Context

Earnings data may be most useful when put into context. If earnings data are not linked with education, corrections, military, and vital statistics data, we cannot be sure if the student/graduate has lower earnings due to participation in further education, is serving time in a correctional facility, has enlisted in the military, or has passed away. When data are finally shared, data privacy concerns limit the usefulness. For example, many educational programs did not receive data back from the U.S. Department of Education gainful employment program because the data match had fewer than 31 students. A benefit of the gainful employment regulations was the availability of data; earnings data were used to estimate whether the debt accumulated by students was an "acceptable" percentage of disposable income on the individual level. However, since many programs did not receive matched data, it was not possible to evaluate debt ratios.

Other Labor Market Returns

In addition to individual wage benefits, higher education also provides spillover effects in the local community. The sharing of knowledge and skills through formal and informal interaction often generates positive benefits, which result in higher wages even for non-college educated workers. In his study on the spillover benefits, Moretti (2004) estimated that a 1.0 percentage point increase in the supply of college graduates in a community raises the wages of high school graduates by 1.6%, those of high school dropouts by 1.9%, and those of other college graduates by 0.4% (see Table 8.7).

Table 8.7.   Impact of a 1.0% Increase in the Number of College Graduates in a Community on Overall Wages

Education Level	*Wage Increase*
High School Dropout	1.9%
High School Graduate	1.6%
College Graduate	0.4%

These estimates of the increase in education can be used to calculate the additional income effects in a community where there is a greater proportion of college graduates. Consider a community that has 2.0% points more college graduates than the U.S. average, which implies that the wages of high school graduates in the community on average are 3.2% higher than they would be without the concentration of college graduates, and the wages of high school dropouts are 3.8% greater. Applying these figures to labor force participation rates by educational attainment and wage levels would result in $179.5 million less income in the community's area if educational attainment levels were similar to the nation. Using the $179.5 million in income as the input to an economic impact model, there would be marginal contributions to the local economy, which are discussed in the section on economic impact of postsecondary institutions.

Citizens with higher education are much more likely to be employed, even during the economic downturn. As shown in Table 8.8, four out of five individuals with some college, a bachelor's degree, or more education participated in the labor force in 2005 and 2010, compared to less than 60.0% of those without a high school diploma.

**Table 8.8.   Labor Force Participation by
Educational Attainment for Adult Population**

	2005	2010
Educational Attainment	*U.S.*	*U.S.*
Less than high school graduate	62.8%	61.3%
High School Graduate	75.3%	74.8%
Some College, or Associates	80.1%	80.7%
Bachelor's Degree (or more)	84.5%	85.8%

Source: U.S. Census Bureau, American Community Survey.

NON-LABOR MARKET RETURNS

Not all of the economic effects of human capital investment in higher
education can be quantified in terms of increased e..nings and productivity. National studies and empirical evidence indicate that higher education helps to reduce poverty, which in turn l(vers state and local
government costs. These amounts can be estimated for any state. For
example, in 2010, approximately 28.8% of South Carolina's population
without a high school degree lived in poverty, compared to only 3.6% of
those with a college degree. In the Charleston region, only about 4.2% of
those with a college degree lived in poverty, compared to about 28.3%
without a high school degree. Of the 43,000 adults who live in poverty,
66.7%, or 29,002 residents, had not attended college (see Table 8.9).

**Table 8.9. Poverty Rate by
Educational Attainment for Adult Population**

	2005			2010		
Educational Attainment	*CMSA*	*S.C.*	*U.S.*	*CMSA*	*S.C.*	*U.S.*
Less than high school graduate	25.0%	25.9%	23.6%	28.3%	28.8%	24.7%
High School Graduate	13.1%	12.9%	11.2%	12.7%	14.2%	12.0%
Some College, or Associates	7.3%	7.7%	7.7%	7.5%	9.0%	8.4%
Bachelor's Degree (or more)	3.0%	3.4%	3.5%	4.2%	3.6%	3.8%

Source: U.S. Census Bureau, American Community Survey (2012).

Higher education is associated with a greater likelihood of starting a small business, a higher rate of business survival, and greater small business success (Dobbs & Hamilton, 2007; Storey, 1994). For example, a Penn State University study (Tripp Umbach Associates, 2004) found that there were 15,000 alumni-owned businesses that employed over 400,000 Pennsylvania residents. Some of the business start-up activity is related to university research and spinoffs of that research. Licensure revenues from patented higher education technologies is one measure of economic value. The Association of University Technology Managers (AUTM) estimated that spinoffs were responsible for $42 billion in economic activity and more than 367,000 jobs in 2002 (Lynch & Aydin, 2004). The University of Florida reported that it had generated 61 spinoff companies that created 91 direct jobs and a total employment impact of 1,925 jobs (Harrington, 2006).

McMahon (2009) showed that the total value of fringe benefits such as medical insurance, pension plans, paid vacations, sick leave, and stock options increase with years of schooling. Additionally, individuals with more education generally are healthier than their less-educated counterparts. Educated consumers are more likely to go to the doctor, to adhere to their medical treatments, and to take advantage of newer medical technologies. In addition, more education is associated with healthier behaviors such as smoking less, maintaining a healthy weight, and using seat belts. McMahon estimated that each additional year of schooling reduces the probability of dying in the following 10 years by at least 3.6 percentage points. Cutler and Lleras-Muney (2006) suggest that the non-pecuniary health benefits represent about half of the private monetary benefit.

U.S. Census Bureau data confirm that private health insurance coverage (employer-based or individually purchased) increases with educational attainment. In the example for South Carolina, health insurance coverage increased from 52.7% for high school graduates to 85.3% for bachelor's degree or higher. Only 36.7% of adult South Carolina residents without a high school degree have private health insurance. Because these people do not have employer-based coverage and are unable to afford an individual plan, a higher percentage of these residents receive Medicaid assistance (see Figure 8.3).

Data also are available to examine health insurance by type by educational attainment. Again, using the Charleston region as an example, 19.6% of working-aged residents (aged 25 to 64 years) do not have any health coverage. For working-aged residents without a high school degree, 42.0% had no form of health insurance, compared to 8.0% of people with at least a bachelor's degree (see Table 8.10).

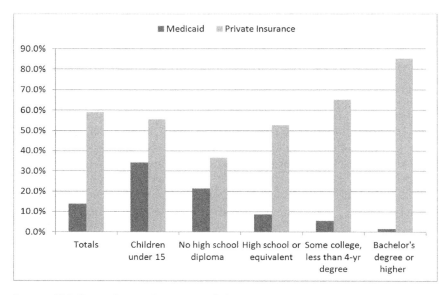

Source: U.S. Census Bureau Current Population Survey, Annual Social and Economic
Supplement (2011).

Figure 8.3.   South Carolina health insurance by educational attainment.

Duncan (1976) showed that the total value of fringe benefits such as
pension plans, paid vacations, sick leave, stock options, and free/subsi-
dized meals also increase with years of education. Some economists
(McMahon, 2009) have estimated that these benefits are equal to or
greater than the value of the monetary benefits. Individuals with higher
educational achievement levels also save money on consumer goods and
achieve higher yields on savings because they generally are more savvy
investors (Solomon, 1975). In addition to greater earning and increased
community wages, public higher education results in better workplace
conditions, more job satisfaction, higher spouse earnings, increased tax
revenue, and lower public assistance costs. Workers with higher educational levels experience lower work turnover rates, which reduce the
costs of worker job searches, and have more options on where to live.

PUBLIC RETURN ON INVESTMENT

Higher percentages of college-educated workers in a region also are
correlated with improved community health, increased education aspi-

Table 8.10. Charleston Region Health Insurance by Educational Attainment

Educational Attainment	Private Insurance	Public Coverage	No Health Insurance Coverage	Total
Less than high school graduate	35.0%	23.0%	42.0%	100.0%
High School Graduate	57.2%	15.3%	27.5%	100.0%
Some College, or Associates	70.7%	12.1%	17.1%	100.0%
Bachelor's Degree (or more)	86.7%	5.3%	8.0%	100.0%
Total Population	68.5%	11.9%	19.6%	100.0%

Source: U.S. Census Bureau, American Community Survey (2012).

rations, lower crime, better child education, lower poverty, better civic institutions, greater political stability, and more community engagement for both college and non-college educated workers in that region. It generally is more difficult to convert these benefits to a dollar value.

Public expenditure savings on social programs and new tax revenues are part of the public or social benefits obtained from higher education. Rephann, Knapp, and Shobe (2009) estimated that an associate or a bachelor's degree resulted in about $7,400 in welfare savings such as food stamps; about $7,300 on Medicaid; and smaller savings on workers' compensation, corrections, and other social programs for a total of $16,000 for an associate degree and $22,500 for a bachelor's degree. Multiplying this by the number of degree holders in a state results in substantial savings of public expenditures. Rephann et al. also estimated that lifetime taxes paid increased from $195,000 for a high school graduate to $250,000 for an associate degree holder, to $323,000 for a bachelor's, to $390,000 for a master's, and to $380,000 for a professional or doctorate degree.

Similarly, Niskanen (1996) found that for each percentage point increase in the population with a bachelor's degree, welfare needs decreased 4%. Baum and Ma (2007) found that food stamps are used in only 1% of households with a college graduate, compared with 6% of households with less education, and that decreasing the food stamp usage rate from 6% to 1% could save governments about $5 billion annually. Medicaid rates also would drop by more than half, and government-assisted school food programs would decrease by 75%.

Economic Impact Studies

Measures of the public return on investment generally are part of a study of the economic impact of higher education, either for one institution, for institutions in a region, or for the institutions in a state. As the public, governors, and legislators have begun to question the value of investments in higher education, public higher education institutions have increasingly produced studies of their economic impact on the region or state to demonstrate that the institution is a driver of the local economy. Typically, institutions hire outside groups to conduct these studies to provide an arms-length view that policy makers are more likely to accept as fact, but occasionally institutions will use their own economics department faculty or other research faculty to complete the study. Recent economic impact studies are available for institutions as diverse as the University of West Florida (UWF, 2009), George Mason University (Fowler & Fuller, 2005), University of Texas at El Paso (Schauer, Gibson, Corral, & Caire, 2010), University of South Carolina (Moore School of Business, 2011), Thomas Edison State College, and Trident Technical College, as well as statewide studies of the economic impact of public higher education in Florida (Board of Governors of the State University System of Florida, 2012), Kentucky (Berger & Black, 1993), Virginia (Knapp & Shobe, 2007), North Carolina (Luger, Koo, Peery, & Billings, 2001), and South Carolina (Moore School of Business, 2009). Readers are encouraged to visit their institutions' websites for each institution's own economic impact study.

The historical approach for conducting higher education economic impact studies was developed by Caffrey and Isaacs (1971) for the American Council on Education. The Caffrey and Isaacs model uses financial data from the institution and information from surveys of faculty, staff, alumni, and students to calculate the economic impact of an institution.

Researchers and economists have found that study to be a starting point for their research, but the methodology has limitations, especially when the included institutions in a region or state are diverse (AASULGC, 1997). Some studies take a narrow approach that focuses on the operational impact of the institutions, while other analyses include a variety of impacts ranging from alumni income to estimating the media value of collegiate sports teams (Blackwell, Cobb & Weinberg, 2002).

To conduct an economic impact study without using the laborious Caffrey and Isaacs model, economists may use any of several econometric models. Three are used most often:

- the MIG, Inc. Impact Analysis for Planning (IMPLAN) System,
- the Regional Industrial Multiplier System (RIMS) developed by the federal government's Bureau of Economic Analysis, and
- the Regional Economic Models, Inc. Policy Insight Plus (REMI PI+) model.

Each of these models has advantages and disadvantages but all produce basically the same types of outputs, which may include delineation of the jobs generated by industry category.

In whichever economic impact model is used, economists use a number of statistics to describe regional economic activity. Four common measures are "output," which describes total economic activity and is generally equivalent to a firm's gross sales; "value added," which equals gross output of an industry or a sector less its intermediate inputs; "employee earnings," which corresponds to wages and benefits; and "employment," which refers to jobs that have been created in the local economy.

In an input-output analysis of new economic activity, it is useful to distinguish three types of expenditure effects: direct, indirect, and induced. Direct effects are production changes associated with the immediate effects or final demand changes. The payment made by an out-of-town visitor to a hotel operator or the taxi fare paid for transportation while in town are examples of direct effects.

Indirect effects are production changes in backward-linked industries caused by the changing input needs of directly affected industries—typically, additional purchases to produce additional output. Satisfying the demand for an overnight stay will require the hotel operator to purchase additional cleaning supplies and services. The taxi driver will have to replace the gasoline consumed during the trip from the airport. These downstream purchases affect the economic output of other local merchants.

Induced effects are the changes in regional household spending patterns caused by changes in household income generated from the direct and indirect effects. Both the hotel operator and taxi driver experience increased income from the visitor's stay, as do the cleaning supplies outlet and the gas station proprietor. Induced effects capture the way in which increased income is spent in the local economy.

A multiplier reflects the interaction between different sectors of the economy. An output multiplier of 1.4, for example, means that for every $1,000 injected into the economy, all other sectors produce an additional $400 in output. The larger the multiplier, the greater the impact will be in the regional economy. For example, Leslie and Brinkman (1988) found that every dollar spent by a community college and its students generated $1.60 in regional income (a multiplier of 1.6); for 4-year institutions, $1 generated $2.20 (a multiplier of 2.2); and 59 local jobs were generated for every $1,000,000 in a community college's operating budget, or 67 jobs generated by a 4-year institution. Various economic impact studies have found multipliers of 0.5 to over 4.0, depending on what inputs and outputs are used. Figure 8.4 depicts the flow of economic impacts.

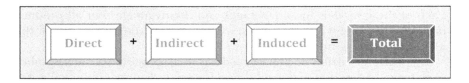

Source: James & McKeown-Moak (2013).

Figure 8.4.   The flow of economic impacts

There are four main categories of inputs to an economic impact study:

1.   Normal Operational Expenditures—this represents the largest input to an economic impact model. The econometric model used generally is adjusted for each institution based on the following inputs. Each institution, for instance, has a different spending pattern for faculty and a different average wage level.

 • Operations: expenditures related to general operations and plant operations and maintenance;
 • Payroll: salaries, wages, and fringe benefits; and
 • Employment: faculty and staff, including graduate teaching or research assistants.

2.   Construction Spending—spending on buildings and construction excluding equipment. This input has the greatest variation.

3.   Student Spending—enrolled students have a positive impact on the local economy by supporting businesses such as restaurants, nightclubs, rental housing, and other retail establishments.

4.   Tourism—parents visiting students, attendees at conferences, and fans at sporting events have a major impact on the local economy. Detailed statistics on these activities, however, often are difficult to obtain because institutions do not typically collect these data.

Sources of data for each of these inputs to an impact model are displayed in Table 8.11.

Table 8.11.   Economic Impact Model Data Sources

Category	*Data Sources*
Employees	IPEDS staff surveys by position; institutional data
Employee compensation	IPEDS finance surveys; institutional consolidated annual financial reports (CAFR)
Expenditures on goods and services	IPEDS finance surveys; institutional consolidated annual financial reports (CAFR)
Capital/construction expenditures	IPEDS finance surveys; institutional consolidated annual financial reports (CAFR)
Student expenditures	IPEDS institutional characteristics; institutional data; student surveys
Visitor expenditures	Institutional data; local tourism and convention bureaus; student and staff surveys
Student enrollment	IPEDS enrollment; institutional data; state higher education coordinating or governing board data
Graduate earnings	IPEDS completions; U.S. Census Bureau; National Crosswalk Service Center
Productivity (employment, etc.)	U.S. Census Bureau; state and U.S. departments of labor

The output for an economic impact study generally consists of a section on the characteristics and history of the institution or institutions being studied, including location, enrollment patterns, and financial characteristics; a section on the model being used and any methodological issues, including those economic impacts that are not included such as any technology commercialization; a section on the financial input and output of the model, including jobs created and the tax benefits derived; a section on other private and social benefits of higher education, including benefits described in the sections above; and a section on some of the institution-specific job creation resulting from higher education.

Table 8.12 provides an example of input and output of the economic section of an economic impact study. Note that this output provides information on jobs created by industry sector. Readers are encouraged to examine several economic impact studies in their entirety to observe the variations in output.

An important component of an economic impact study for a public institution is a demonstration that the institution or institutions generate more tax revenues than are allocated to the institution through appropriations. This is the most complex part of any economic impact study, evaluating the tax revenue implications in terms of return on investment (ROI) and net fiscal impact. For a single business or industry sector, the tax revenue calculations are straightforward. The public sector costs such as those for

Table 8.12.   Sample Output for an Economic Impact Study

Study Inputs

Fiscal Year	Operations	Payroll	Employment	Construction	Student Spending
2006–2007	$74,980,031	$43,425,608	631	$44,174,309 $4,744,678	$4,744,678
2007–2008	$78,358,696	$46,322,053	642	$14,524,051 $4,710,051	$4,710,051
2008–2009	$79,360,812	$48,238,536	665	$26,075,477	$5,224,670
2009–2010	$79,107,284	$48,490,882	639	$7,790,683	$5,388,512
2010–2011	$79,102,672	$49,738,638	632	$4,498,644	$6,386,490

Source: IPEDS Finance Surveys

Estimated Economic Impact FY 2010-11

Region	Output	Value Added	Labor Income	Employment
MSA	$143,439,898	$111,849,775	$83,221,861	1,579
Rest of State	$22,786,527	$13,835,213	$9,021,902	193
Total	$166,226,425	$125,684,988	$92,243,763	1,772

Source: James and McKeown-Moak (2012).

Detailed Economic Impact by NAICS Sector

NAICS Sector	Output	Value Added	Labor Income	Employment
Ag, Forestry, Fish & Hunting	$267,399	$128,541	$85,846	4
Mining	$106,079	$57,080	$18,810	1
Utilities	$1,831,695	$1,521,036	$306,599	4
Construction	$6,870,250	$3,081,653	$2,419,671	58
Manufacturing	$3,470,295	$814,233	$482,365	8
Wholesale Trade	$3,841,552	$2,880,022	$1,537,858	27
Retail Trade	$7,948,392	$5,205,977	$3,697,960	127
Transportation & Warehousing	$3,935,126	$2,472,937	$1,773,554	57
Information	$6,800,031	$3,564,910	$1,214,925	25
Finance & Insurance	$11,274,634	$4,603,241	$2,788,655	65

(Table continues on next page)

Table 8.12. Continued

Detailed Economic Impact by NAICS Sector

NAICS Sector	Output	Value Added	Labor Income	Employment
Real Estate & Rental	$17,316,848	$13,944,075	$1,262,146	72
Professional, Scientific & Tech Svcs	$9,399,171	$6,465,846	$5,489,142	87
Management of Companies	$453,870	$258,988	$226,474	3
Administrative & Waste Services	$6,509,379	$3,943,403	$3,138,847	102
Educational Services	$1,193,818	$624,959	$666,132	18
Health & Social Services	$10,798,392	$6,448,347	$5,932,876	114
Arts, Entertainment & Recreation	$2,209,265	$1,230,270	$738,702	47
Accommodation & Food Services	$7,566,159	$4,095,181	$2,588,754	123
Other Services	$5,012,290	$2,706,107	$2,520,962	120
Government & Non-NAICs	$59,421,781	$61,638,183	$55,353,484	709
Total	$166,226,425	$125,684,988	$92,243,763	1,772

Source: James & McKeown-Moak (2012).

higher education or public safety, however, are more subjective based on location, existing infrastructure, workers drawn to the region because of the project, and wage levels. Too often, the tax revenue estimates are overly aggressive to show a positive return.

With higher education, numerous quantitative and qualitative benefits that economic models do not capture accrue over decades. How should an economic impact study address the long-term value of higher wages associated with a better-educated labor force? Should the calculation factor in social service cost savings? While most higher education institutions' property is tax exempt, surrounding properties typically command higher prices because of the proximity to the institution. Should federal grants and research contracts simply be added to the revenue side of the equation? Ultimately, tax revenue generation is not the primary criteria local and state governments consider when funding education. However, in this age of accountability and performance, it may be important to calculate as part of an economic impact study.

To provide an "order of magnitude" estimate for state tax revenue attributable to publicly supported higher education institutions, one approach focuses on the ratio of state government tax collections to state GDP. Two datasets may be used to derive the ratio: 1) U.S. Department of Commerce Bureau of Economic Analysis GDP estimates by metropolitan area; and 2) the U.S. Census Bureau State Government Tax Collections (STC) report. A brief description of the STC data collection methodology follows:

> Taxes are defined as all compulsory contributions exacted by a government for public purposes, except employer and employee assessments for retirement and social insurance purposes, which are classified as insurance trust revenue. Outside the scope of this collection are data on the unemployment compensation "taxes" imposed by each of the state governments. However, all receipts from licenses and compulsory fees, including those that are imposed for regulatory purposes, as well as those designated to provide revenue are included. (U.S. Census Bureau, 2012)

To calculate the tax impact of an institution, one would apply the percentage of tax revenues in the Census Bureau report to total value added (or GDP) attributable to the publicly supported higher education institutions to determine the increase in tax revenue, calculated as:

> total dollar value added x percent tax revenues = increase in state tax revenue

Then, compare that amount of tax revenue to the total state appropriations for the institution to demonstrate the tax impact. This calculation does not include the tremendous local tax impact of higher lifetime earnings of graduates, federal grants, economic development advantages, and lower social service costs. For example, an institution may generate over $200 million in federal contracts and grants in a fiscal year. Directly and indirectly, these funds help support the overall mission and operations of the university. Without these contracts and grants, state support and student tuition might need to increase to offset this source of revenue. In some fiscal impact studies, a portion of these funds are treated as "savings" or additional state tax revenue generated by the institutions. If a share of federal contracts and grants are included, the state or region would receive an even greater return on investment.

Value added consists of compensation of employees, taxes on production, and imports less subsidies. Value added represents an industry sector's contribution to gross domestic product (GDP). For example, the 2011 GDP for the Charleston (South Carolina) region was $28.0 billion. Direct value added attributable to publicly supported higher education institutions is 5.2% of regional GDP. If one includes the multiplier effects, these entities support 9.9% of Charleston's overall GDP.

SUMMARY

This chapter has presented information on the private and social value of a postsecondary education, including human capital development. The economic and societal impact of higher education was discussed along with information on sources of data and methods for calculating the economic impact of an institution.

CHAPTER 9

STUDENT PERSPECTIVES ON COLLEGE COSTS AND "PRICE"

One of the important components of any calculation of the return on investment (ROI) to a higher education, of course, is how much a student paid or invested to get that education. Included in the "price" are both the out-of-pocket expenses as well as foregone income, as was discussed in Chapter 3. Figure 3.1 depicted both the students' and the institution's revenues and expenditures, showing that what is an expenditure for the student can be a revenue to the institution (e.g., tuition and fees) and that revenues to the student can be an expenditure to the institution (e.g., financial aid).

We also noted that in higher education financial aid parlance, what students pay is referred to as "price" not the "cost" of higher education, even though the amount a student pays to attend a postsecondary institution may rightfully be thought of as a "cost." However, for purposes of determining return on investment, in this chapter we will refer to all the "expenditures" a student makes, including the "expenditure" of foregone income, as a student "price," but we will not refer to student expenditures as the "cost of education."

To better understand the various prices students pay in the pursuit of higher education, this chapter provides an understanding of "price" in all of the variations that price occurs in higher education. The chapter also examines the role "price" plays in postsecondary participation and the ways "price" is communicated to consumers.

Higher Education Finance Research: Policy, Politics, and Practice, pp. 279–295

THE VARIOUS DEFINITIONS OF "PRICE"

To understand price, one must first understand that there are various definitions of "price." There are various ways to quantify price; the following paragraphs provide an overview of many of the variations (see also Figure 9.1).

Tuition and Fees (Sticker Price)

The most basic price of college is the amount published by the institution for tuition and required fees for an academic year for full-time, undergraduate students. These data represent the average for a "typical" student and may vary by program. In addition, the value provided for fees generally represents required fees for all students. In some programs, there may be additional required fees (i.e., the cost of scrubs for a nursing student), and there may also be fees that students may opt out of and are therefore not required to pay. (See Chapter 3 for a discussion of differential tuition and fee policies.) Tuition and fee data also may be presented per course or per credit.

Tuition and Fees and Room and Board (Published Price)

In addition to average tuition and required fees, students need to consider the additional costs of room and board. Together, the total price of tuition and fees and room and board (TFRB) are referred to as the "published price." The published price, or TFRB, is commonly reported and utilized in publications such as the *Digest of Education Statistics* of the National Center for Education Statistics (Snyder & Dillow, 2012) and the annual reports published by the College Board titled *Trends in Student Aid* and *Trends in College Pricing* (trends.collegeboard.org).

Price of Attendance

In addition to the published price, there is the "price of attendance." The price of attendance includes the published price and the price of student expenses. The price of attendance is also referred to as the "cost of attendance" and generally is published on an institution's website.

Student expense budgets, or cost of attendance estimates, are determined each year by each institution both to help the student plan and to inform the development of student financial aid policies. Federal, state, or institutional policy may dictate what expenses can be included in a cost of attendance calculation. The state of California, for example, calculates 9-month student expense budgets for students living on campus, living off

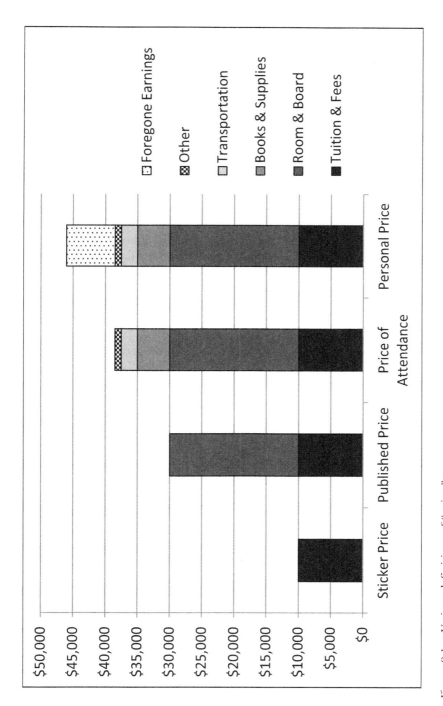

Figure 9.1.   Various definitions of "price."

campus, or with parents inclusive of tuition and fees, books and supplies, food, housing, transportation, personal/miscellaneous, child/dependent care, and loan fees (California Student Aid Commission, 2012). When including these costs, it becomes evident that the "cost of attendance" to the student is much higher than is generally depicted by applying tuition and fee and room and board values.

Personal Price (Foregone Earnings)

There are personal financial costs associated with postsecondary education that extend beyond those mentioned above. Primary among these costs is foregone earnings.

Foregone earnings reflect the amount of money that could have been made during a period of time as compared to the same amount of time the student spent engaged in education-related activities. That is to say, a job paying a $10 an hour would pay $105 a week if a student worked rather than participated in a three credit hour course if class time (3 hours a week), time out of class (6 hours a week), and time commuting (15 minutes each way, 3 times a week) were considered in the calculation.

The ability for students with a high school diploma or less to hold a job and earn money can serve as a disincentive to enroll in college. This is especially true for low-income students who lack stable financial environments or whose local labor market is dominated by jobs requiring less postsecondary education than other areas of the state or nation. For example, many individuals interviewed in Nevada indicated that they did not attend college because they could get a job (parking cars in Las Vegas) that paid over $100,000 per year with tips (McKeown-Moak, 2012). The idea of the counterfactual to college (i.e., no college) for students is real, yet one could imagine a low-income student trying to make a decision seeing one of three options: do not enroll in college, enroll part-time and work part-time, enroll full-time and do not work. In fact, by starting to work earlier, non-college goers may be able to have more financial stability than their college going peers. (This is a fact that is short-lived but may be enticing nonetheless).

For students without financial need, one could assume this value is $0. This is, of course, theoretical, as students without financial need still have the option to spend their time working rather than attending classes or being otherwise engaged in the learning community. In fact, it is an incorrect assumption. While 79% of students worked while enrolled in 2007–2008, only 31% of the wealthiest independent students did not work (see Table 9.1).

Table 9.1.   Hours Worked Per Week by Total Income and Dependency Type, 2007–2008

Total Income by Dependency Type	Hours Worked Per Week (%)				
	$0 <= X <= 0$	$1 <= X <= 20$	$21 <= X <= 40$	$X >= 41$	Total
Dependent: Less than $10,000	21.6	33.3	37	8	100%
Dependent: $10,000–$19,999	21	34.6	38.1	6.3	100%
Dependent: $20,000–$29,999	22.1	34.9	35.7	7.2	100%
Dependent: $30,000–$39,999	18.1	36.1	39	6.8	100%
Dependent: $40,000–$49,999	19.4	36.2	37.5	6.9	100%
Dependent: $50,000–$59,999	20	37.1	37	5.9	100%
Dependent: $60,000–$69,999	21	37.1	35.8	6.1	100%
Dependent: $70,000–$79,999	20	38.5	36.2	5.3	100%
Dependent: $80,000–$99,999	23.7	40.1	31	5.2	100%
Dependent: $100,000 or more	31.2	39	25.7	4.1	100%
Independent: Less than $5,000	36.3	25.2	32.2	6.3	100%
Independent: $5,000–$9,999	24.9	26.5	38.2	10.4	100%
Independent: $10,000–$19,999	15.6	17.6	53.3	13.5	100%
Independent: $20,000–$29,999	12	11.8	56.8	19.4	100%
Independent: $30,000–$49,999	13	10.9	53.2	22.9	100%
Independent: $50,000 or more	14.4	9	47.2	29.3	100%
Total	21	27	40.2	11.9	100%

Source: U.S. Department of Education, National Center for Education Statistics, 2007–2008 National Postsecondary Student Aid Study (NPSAS:08). Note: Dependency status reflects whether the student is fiscally dependent upon someone else (dependent) or is financially independent (independent), though they may or may not have others financially depending on them such as children or other family members.

Research has repeatedly shown that working more than 20 hours a week has negative impacts on college completion, but a fair percentage of all students work more than 20 hours. The decision to work is a factor related to both affordability and human capital development for all students. The need to work may extend to the financial disposition of family members and constitutes a rarely examined personal cost of college.

STUDENT PRICE RESPONSE

The college choice process is complex, as it is influenced by any number of factors, including, but not limited to, parental education and occupation, neighborhood, a student's perception of his or her own ability, proximity to the institution, and, of most importance, price (Feldman, 1972; Immerwahr, Johnson, Ott & Rochkind, 2010; Kinzie, Palmer, Hayek, Hossler, Jacob, & Cummings, 2004). It is this last point that is of most interest.

The influence of price on college enrollment has been repeatedly studied. In fact, meta analyses of the literature by Jackson and Weathersby (1975), Leslie and Brinkman (1987), and Heller (1997) have all concluded that as price increases, enrollment is estimated to decrease. While this finding is consistent across studies, the methods and evolution of the research is not.

Jackson and Weathersby's research made a contribution to the literature by suggesting that a comparison of price responsiveness could be obtained (see Equation 9.1) for studies using various methods by inserting price elasticity estimates (α) into an equation where the other parts (enrollment [E], the eligible population [P], and the cost to the student [C]) were consistent.

$$\text{EQ. 9.1 } \Delta(E/P) = \alpha\,(\Delta C/C)(E/P)$$

In doing so they reached two conclusions. First, in all studies, the cost to the student was significant and negative. Second, student price responsiveness decreases as student income increases; put another way, lower-income students are more price responsive.

Building on the work of Jackson and Weathersby, Leslie and Brinkman (1987) standardized additional research studies through a revised student price response coefficient (SPRC) that transformed the results to a common measure of student price response, corrected all values to reflect consistent price levels, and converted data from various age group populations. After explaining each adjustment, Leslie and Brinkman noted "It is worth noting before leaving this discussion that Jackson and Weathersby's errors often cancel out" (Leslie & Brinkman, 1987, p. 186).

Heller (1997) extended the student price response research by focusing on the effects of student financial aid and the interaction of student financial aid and tuition and fees on students of varying incomes, races, and college sectors. Upon reviewing the research, he found that while increases in student financial aid were associated with increases in enrollment, student financial aid in the form of grants increased enrollments more than loans or work study; that low-income students are more sensitive to price increases than students from comparatively more affluent backgrounds; that while Black students were more sensitive to price than White students, Hispanic students' effects were mixed; and that community college students were more sensitive to price than peers at 4-year institutions.

Hahn and Price (2008) sought to understand the reasons college-qualified students did not enroll in college. Among several findings was the influence of price. Specifically they found that 80% of non-college-goers noted that the availability of aid to bring down the price was an important consideration, and 63% said the price of college was a factor in their decision not to enroll.

The intricacies associated with student perspectives on financing postsecondary education in terms of student factors (student proximity to education, parental level of education, socio-economic considerations), policy considerations (shifting policies from year-to-year, numerous need analysis models, the timing of aid package notice), and analytic capacity, let alone the data to capture it all, suggest that additional student price response research is warranted. Colleges and universities sometimes do their own research to determine the price elasticity of demand. Private institutions, in particular, often will construct a tuition-discounting model that relies on the research on elasticity of demand for their type of institution, as mentioned in Chapter 3. Unfortunately, these studies are not published, and actually results are guarded from competitor institutional staff.

PRICE AND AFFORDABILITY

The relationship between price and affordability is not as direct as often perceived. The price of college provides just one aspect of the dynamic; another is the relative influence of student aid on the price of attendance as illustrated by the development of net price in the higher education finance lexicon. Yet another way to examine the relationship between price and affordability is through an examination of the ability of the family to pay for college. Lastly, price may be compared to earnings to understand its impact on affordability.

Net Price

Both the published price and the price of attendance may not reflect how much students actually have to pay to go to college. These two prices do not account for student financial aid that a student may receive from governmental sources, institutions, and private sources, or through loans. (Note: students may also receive aid from scholarships, employers, and family members. This type of aid is not usually applied to postsecondary education finance research because it is difficult to capture.) Any cost to the student not met by financial aid is termed the net price, at least conceptually.

The Higher Education Act of 1965 (Pub. L. 110-315, 2008) defines net price as "the average yearly price actually charged to first-time, full-time undergraduate students receiving student aid at an institution of higher education after deducting such aid." However, in the College Board annual publications, net price is defined as "what the student and/or family must cover after grant aid and savings from tax credits and deductions are subtracted" (Baum & Ma, 2012, p. 39). So, while the concept of net price (the amount a student pays after deducting aid) is straightforward, just how to calculate it is not. When undefined, consumers of net price data should be sure to understand the source and calculations of the data. The information in Chapter 3 did not differentiate between varying definitions of net price, for example.

While aid is an important part of understanding price, there are times when researchers and analysts inappropriately apply one type of aid to a particular price. For example, the College Board (2012a) published Figure 9 depicting tuition and fees for a sector of higher education that were reduced by total grant aid and tax benefits to arrive at a "Net Tuition and Fees" amount. This may be misleading, as the amount of grant aid may be set to account for the price of attendance, not just the tuition and fee price. The College Board does provide a "Net Tuition, Fees, Room, and Board" value for sectors of higher education, but again there are more costs associated with attending college than just the purchase price of tuition and fees and room and board.

As such, it is most appropriate to use the price of attendance when discussing the price of college relative to an amount of aid. For example Mortenson (1988) provided a depiction of the purchasing power of the Pell Grant in California by placing the maximum Pell Grant amount in the numerator and the price of attendance in the denominator. The analysis was replicated and extended by Baime and Mullin in 2011 for students attending community colleges. Figure 9.2 illustrates these two applications of purchasing power for students attending community colleges. When just TFRB are applied as the cost, as has been done by the

Congressional Research Service (Mahan, 2012), the purchase power of the Pell Grant is nearly twice the amount observed when the cost/price of attendance value is the cost value.

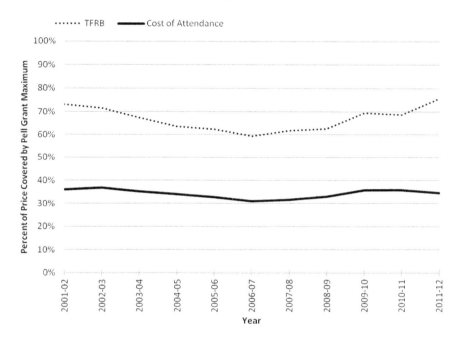

Figure 9.2.   Pell Grants as a percentage of tuition, fees, room and board, and the price of attendance for full-time community college students living off-campus, 2001–2002 to 2011–2012. Source: Authors' analysis of NCES (2012—IPEDS) and Office of Postsecondary Education (2012—Pell EOY).

Price and Family Income

In practice, the amount of aid a student receives is dependent upon the student's or family's ability to pay. Determination of financial need is the result of need analysis formulas implemented by the federal government, state governments, and institutions—which often differ—and is beyond the scope of this volume, but it is important to understand, as determinations of financial need take the family's ability to pay into consideration.

Quantifying price and family income first requires a determination of "price." Cost of attendance values for institutions are available from

IPEDS at the institution level, in addition to tuition and fee, TFRB, and net price. As has been discussed thus far, the type of price selected can have an influence on the analysis and its interpretation. Family income is typically quantified as the median family income.

The relationship between price and family income may be compared several ways. For one, a ratio may be developed with price in the numerator. Another way is to compare trends in cost to trends in family income over a period of time. If the difference between the two values decreases, it is plausible to say college is becoming more affordable; or if the values diverge, it is plausible to suggest that college is becoming less affordable. A third way is to conduct analyses that use the two variables to understand the relationship between the price and family income. Both the College Board and the State Higher Education Executive Officers publications provide tables that examine "affordability" by comparing price to family income. Some of the states' performance indicators cited in Chapter 6 use changes in the affordability index as a measure of performance of higher education.

Price and Earnings

As discussed in Chapter 8, the U.S. Department of Education developed ratios of accumulated debt-to-earnings ratios for completers of gainful employment programs. This situated the price a student paid in terms of loan indebtedness along with earnings immediately after graduation. The idea of price related to discretionary income is not new; Hartle and Wabnick, for example, examined the issue in 1982 where they defined discretionary income as total earnings minus taxes and basic living expenses. The U.S. Department of Education's gainful employment debt measures regulation focused on debt, earnings, and debt repayment rates of former students in certain types of programs offered by institutions of higher education (76 Fed. Reg. 34,386, 2011). This regulation was struck down by the federal court because ED failed to provide a reasoned explanation for the debt repayment measure, a core element of its regulation (*Association of Private Colleges and Universities v. Duncan*, 2012). ED's motion to continue the reporting with more limited metrics was struck down in early 2013 on the grounds that the new data elements expanded a database—the National Student Loan Data System—beyond its original intent (*Association of Private Colleges and Universities v. Duncan*, 2013). At the time of writing this book, the future of gainful employment regulations are being debated in another round of negotiated rule making.

DEVELOPING INFORMED CONSUMERS

Not all students are reared in environments inclusive of members with college knowledge (Vargas, 2004). For those that are, the data and knowledge they may be using may be incomplete or inaccurate, as evidenced by numerous colleges admitting to falsifying data submitted to *U.S. News and World Report* for their influential publications focused on college rankings in 2012 and 2013.

Consumer Information

Consumer information for students about postsecondary institutions has evolved over time from "blue book" directories to college catalogs to commercially produced guides of various types. Yet information provided in these sources has not always been viewed in a positive light. In 1958, one observer noted that "college catalogs, viewbooks, recruiting flyers, and applications materials remain among the most deplorable of all printed literature in America" (Bowles, p. 477).

The federal government has a long history of collecting information about colleges. From 1870 to 1917, the Office of Education of the federal government collected statistics in volumes titled the "Annual Report of the Commissioner of Education." In 1918 and for the next 40 years, statistics were collected and published as the "Biennial Survey of Education in the United States" (Snyder, 1993). Data on institutions did start to improve around 1970, when data from federal and state agencies began to collect common information across institutions (Stark, 1976a). The production of consistent data may be attributed, in part, to the development of state master plans for higher education in the 1960s. In addition, the Higher Education General Information Survey (HEGIS) of the U.S. Department of Education began in 1968 and provided standardized information for all colleges in the country. HEGIS was redeveloped in the mid-1980s and renamed the Integrated Postsecondary Education Data System (IPEDS). At present, IPEDS conducts nine data collection surveys a year, as described in Chapter 2. Data from IPEDS and other federal data collection efforts have been compiled and published annually since 1966 in a volume titled the *Digest of Education Statistics*.

Aside from IPEDS, college submit data to any number of federal and state agencies as outlined in part in Chapter 2. Despite the wealth of information available, there continues to be a focus on collecting more information from institutions and for the data to be made useful to laypersons.

Three Approaches to Consumer Information

The research on consumer protection information appears rather scarce, more frequently showing up as a recommendation to improve the college choice process than anything else. There was, however, a strong interest in the topic in the early 1970s (Stark, 1976a). More recently, research by Morgan and Dechter (2012) echoed a finding by Stark (1976b), suggesting that simply providing students with numerous data points does not mean that students know what the data mean or are interested in it. Furthermore, El-Khawas (1976) and Stark (1976b) independently delineated consumer protection activity into three approaches.

One approach is to provide students information to highlight where abusive practices are taking place, along with the issuance of guidance to help students protect themselves. Developing awareness of program or institutional risks includes institutional disclosure requirements, "shame lists," and public accountability efforts as described in Chapter 6.

A way this information has been pushed to students is in the form of disclosure requirements. A review of disclosure requirements by the National Postsecondary Education Cooperative in 2009 noted that 40 different types of information must be provided to prospective or current students, parents, employees, or the public. Examples include success rates for student athletes, job placement rates, textbook information, transfer of credit policies and articulation agreements, and student financial aid information. The review of these disclosure requirements as obtained from a set of institutions indicated that the information may be difficult to compare and use due to decentralized information management within and between institutions, as evidenced by differences in location of the information and the office responsible for preparing the information. The federal government has also created a set of "shame lists" that highlight changes in both sticker price and net price in an effort to limit college costs while also informing consumers.

Another approach to protect student consumers is to provide comparable information to facilitate individual evaluation of educational opportunities in order to find the best institutional fit for the student. The federal government has required institutions to make a net price calculator available to prospective students.

As discussed previously, net price may be arrived at in any number of ways. The Higher Education Opportunity Act of 2008 (HEOA) requires each institution participating in Title IV federal student aid programs to have a net price calculator on their website that is based upon institutional information and a student's individual characteristics. A template, consisting of a minimum set of data points (see Table 9.2), allows for a consistent treatment of net price (defined as the price of attendance minus grant and scholarship aid). However, institutions are permitted to ask for, but do not require, additional data elements.

Table 9.2.   Net Price Calculator Required Elements

Required Elements	
Input Elements	*Output Elements*
Data to approximate a student's expected family contribution, including but not limited to:	Estimated total cost of attendance
Income	Estimated tuition and fees
Number in family	Estimated room and board
Dependency status	Estimated books and supplies
	Estimated other allowable expenses
	Estimated total grant aid
	Estimated net price
	Percent of full-time, first-time students receiving grant aid

Note: Institutions must also provide the caveats and disclaimers indicated in the Higher Education Opportunity Act of 2008.
Source: NCES (n.d.)

One study found net price calculators that asked for students to answer up to 70 questions (Cheng, 2012). Furthermore, some net price calculators provided estimates of work study or loans, although it was not always clear that the resulting "price" was different than the required net price determination. Five recommendations to make the net price calculator comparable across institutions espoused by Cheng (2012) highlight the reality that though conceptualized initially as a way to better compare the price of institutions after taking various types of aid into account, the varying components of net price calculators have led to more confusion than consistency in helping students understand the "price" of college.

For researchers, this point on net price calculators is important because these data are inconsistent and not appropriate for research purposes, although net price calculators contribute a new avenue to enhance our understanding of student price response.

The federal government took several actions to make federal data more accessible to laypersons. For example, the National Center for Education Statistics of the U.S. Department of Education was authorized to develop the College Opportunities Online Locator (COOL) in 1998 to understand the differences between colleges and the cost to attend college. In 2007 the COOL was enhanced to serve as the primary source for comparing institutions that participate in federal student aid programs, and it was renamed the College Navigator. A study to better understand the usefulness of the College Navigator to students and parents (MacAllum &

Glover, 2012) found that three of the five most valuable pieces of information for students were related to student finance: tuition and fees, estimated expenses before and after aid, and financial aid.

The third approach to consumer information seeks to determine and monitor institutional or program quality through judgments emanating from the collection, comparison, and reporting of data. Quality in post-secondary education has traditionally been the purview of accrediting agencies. To students, the determination of academic fit—that is to say, the relative merit of the person sitting in the chair next to you as determined by performance on standardized test scores—is the traditional indicator of quality. Yet, when academic information from a school was presented during one study of College Navigator, students reacted to low enrollment compared to admitted counts as being a sign of lesser quality of an institution (MacAllum & Glover, 2012). This observation counters what is perceived to be the common perception of quality.

While these three approaches to consumer information each make sense independently, they are on occasion applied in unison. Take, for example, the information tools that constitute the federal government's four-part proposal conceptually designed to work together to better inform student choice designed, in part, because of the switch from lender to government-based students loans. ED felt as though they needed to be sure they were doing all they could to ensure the integrity of the programs through the collection and use of data (i.e., the promulgation of the gainful employment regulations within the program integrity negotiated public rulemaking of 2010). ED began to develop a four-part strategy to better inform consumers (students), consisting of a college scorecard, College Navigator, a shopping sheet, and an aid offer comparison tool (see Figure 9.3). While each of the parts was met with some pushback from advocacy groups in Washington, DC, Morgan and Dechter (2012) solicited the opinions of students. Their research found that the college scorecard had not been subjected to systematic testing with parents and students and that the language utilized was unclear and the purpose of the document to students was unclear. At the time of writing, the future of the four-part strategy is unknown.

Tensions

In addition to the challenges associated with serving multiple purposes, the act of communicating information to students necessitates the use of data for which it may not have been originally intended. There has always been a tension related to the purpose of the data and its ultimate use. For example, there are those who believe that any data collected for consumer

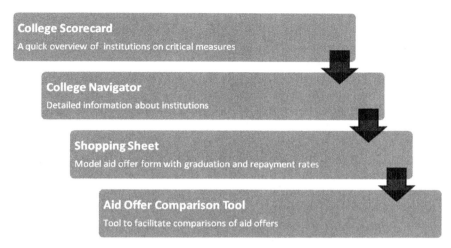

Figure 9.3.   Proposed consumer information tools.

information purposes may ultimately be used for accountability or program eligibility purposes. Misuse of data, therefore, stands as a sustained concern of many and may be reasonable. Just as understanding the effectiveness of a professor requires more than just one metric related to the number of advisees, institutions are more than just graduation or repayment rates. Recognizing this, there is a trend towards multiple measure formats.

There also exists a tension with respect to the level of analysis for accountability. Should it be the institution or the program? On one hand, institutions are responsible for the programs they offer. They therefore should be accountable for the outcomes of those programs and the institutional operations writ large. On the other hand, it may be argued that just because a few programs are not doing well, it does not mean that the institution should be shut down. From a common business perspective, just because Crystal Pepsi failed in the early 1990s did not mean that Pepsi-Co shut down.

There is the question of when enough data will be enough. There seems to be a never ending request for more information without identifying who the end user is and further without understanding if that information is useful to the intended recipient. It may be the case that much of the demand for more "consumer information" comes from researchers seeking ever greater clarity about institutional operations and program evaluation.

Student financial aid, conceptually, perceives higher education as a market whereby students can apply the student aid they have been awarded to an institution of their choosing. Institutions, as actors in a market-based system, then have the burden of communicating the benefits of attending their institution. Further, this market-based perspective suggests that potential consumers would demand the data they felt important. This market-driven approach would then benefit those institutions that provided the information and disadvantage those that did not. Some feel that this is the most appropriate role of data in the consumer information process.

A final tension, for the purposes of this discussion, relates to the development of common metrics. In order to provide comparable information for the selection of an appropriate institution, the metrics being used have to be substantially similar. This is exceptionally difficult when institutional missions and outcomes vary. Institutional retention rates provide one example. At 4-year institutions whose mission is to produce bachelor's degree recipients, monitoring the fall-to-fall semester retention of students is appropriate. However, for institutions that have a transfer function, having students move onto another institution after 1 year is a success—though current retention rates as utilized in IPEDS omit this outcome and therefore treat it as a failure. Yet these data are posted prominently in consumer information vehicles such as College Navigator.

THE FREE APPLICATION FOR FEDERAL STUDENT AID

The Free Application for Federal Student Aid (FAFSA) was discussed in connection with student aid application in Chapter 3. In 2007–2008, 58% of undergraduate students applied for federal aid via the FAFSA, up from 45% nearly a decade earlier (1995–1996). These data suggest a healthy increase in FAFSA filing, but also a large number of students who do not fill out the FAFSA. There is a line of inquiry within postsecondary finance research that examines why students do not receive the financial aid they may be eligible to receive and the impact on students attaining certain levels of attainment.

Reasons for not Completing the FAFSA

College qualified students who do not apply for financial aid provide some insight into the issue. Reasons identified in the research (Advisory Committee on Student Financial Assistance, 2008; Kantrowitz, 2009; King, 2004, 2006) include students not believing they were eligible for aid, students believing they had sufficient funds to pay for college, students finding the financial aid form too complex, and students financing their education from other, non-federal sources.

Research has been conducted to identify ways to reduce these barriers. For example, Bettinger, Long, Oreopoulos and Sanbonmatsu (2009) examined what form simplifying access to financial aid should take, and the Government Accountability Office (2009) examined ideas centered on eliminating questions from the FAFSA and allowing students to access the IRS to populate the FAFSA form with relevant data (a process available to students in 2013).

Influence of not Filing

By not filing the FAFSA, students not only miss out on available aid, they may reduce the likelihood they will be successful in their educational pursuits. Filing a FAFSA is associated with higher within-year persistence rates among low-income students (Novak & McKinney, 2011) and students enrolled part-time at community colleges (McKinney & Novak, 2013).

Not filing a FAFSA extends to the timing of completing the form. King (2004) found that many states and institutions use the FAFSA to allocate aid and that more than half missed the April 1st deadline for state and institutional aid. LaManque (2009) notes that in California the late filing of the FAFSA may result in a student receiving less aid, as fewer fiscal resources are available later in the process.

CONCLUSION

In conclusion, the student perspective on price is not uniform in its definition, interpretation, or presentation. More research is needed to understand student price response and, further, the response of students to consumer information provided as it relates to price and, as an extension, perceived value as indicated by other metrics. Both price and value will continue to be important aspects of the student perspective of higher education as some suggest the paradigm shift has begun from "what is the most expensive is the best" to "the institution providing the greatest value is the best option."

SECTION IV

Presenting Research

In the first three sections of this book we have provided information on the revenues and expenditures for higher education, how these revenues and expenditures are reported, research related to college and university finance, where to locate data to complete research, and what research has been completed relative to accountability, performance, rates of return, and other finance issues.

Now that you have the data and the research, the fourth part of the volume introduces concepts and methods for presenting analysis of postsecondary finance, especially to a policy audience. Chapter 10 examines factors associated with conducting analyses over a period of time, including calculations such as constant dollar conversions, percent change, annualized growth and indexing, and provides examples of these calculations as well as concepts related to internal rates of return, net present value, and discount rates. Chapter 11 addresses comparative methods for the presentation of data including thresholds, indexing, and benchmarking. Chapter 12, perhaps the most important chapter we can leave you with, discusses how to present these concepts to a policy audience. This chapter is especially important and could be called out as a complete section of the book. Little has been written about the nuances of presenting research findings to a policymaking audience, although there is some research on how to influence the policymaking process

Higher Education Finance Research: Policy, Politics, and Practice, pp. 297–297
Copyright © 2014 by Information Age Publishing

CHAPTER 10

THE INFLUENCE OF TIME

Time changes the value of money. Assets such as buildings depreciate or appreciate in value, stock prices go up and down, and the value of money changes. This chapter provides calculations and resources to account for variation in the value of money over time, as well as methodological approaches to evaluate change over time.

TIME-BASED CALCULATIONS

Before conducting more advanced analyses or publishing tables for presentations to a general audience, when trends over time are being presented, it is important to first account for the changing value of money. This can be achieved by determining constant dollar values, indexing values, and calculating percentage changes.

Current and Constant Dollars

Consider a legislator who is 60 years old in 2013 and who attended college beginning at age 18 in 1971. From this legislator's perspective, the current price of college is extremely high. When this legislator was 18, the year was 1971, and the average tuition and fees for a student for an academic year at a private, non-profit institution were $1,820.

Higher Education Finance Research: Policy, Politics, and Practice, pp. 299–314
Copyright © 2014 by Information Age Publishing
All rights of reproduction in any form reserved.

What the legislator needs to understand is that the equivalent price in 2012 was $10,399.

Current dollars, also referred to as nominal dollars, are the value of money at the point in time at which the observation or valuation was made. For example, the nominal value of $1,000 in 2011 is $1,000, and the nominal value of $1,000 in 2012 is $1,000; however, those two $1,000s have a different "value" or purchasing power in 2013. When you are comparing two or more values of money at two different points in time, the values need to be standardized. One way of doing this is to convert current dollars to constant dollars (otherwise termed "inflation-adjusted dollars"). There are three adjustments or methods in higher education finance that will result in constant dollars: the Consumer Price Index (CPI), the Higher Education Price Index (HEPI), and the Higher Education Cost Adjustment (HECA).

The Consumer Price Index (CPI)

The CPI is most commonly used, as it reflects the cost that a consumer would pay for a market basket of goods. There are several types of consumer price indices; the Consumer Price Index for All Urban Consumers (CPI-U) is most commonly used.

There are two places to access CPI adjustments. The first is the online consumer price index calculator of the U.S. Department of Labor (DoL), which may be accessed at http://www.bls.gov/data/inflation_calculator.htm. This calculator allows the user to specify the year for the "constant" and also the year of interest and then calculates the new value for the year of interest with the touch of a button. For example, if you wanted to know what the average tuition and fees at a private, non-profit institution in 1971 were equal to in 2012 constant dollars, you would enter the value in 1971 ($1,820) and then press the button to find it would be equal to $10,399 in 2012.

However, if you are working with numerous years of data, you may want to automate the process, or at least understand how the index is developed. Every month the Bureau of Labor Statistics (BLS) of the DoL releases a consumer price index. Comparing these indices, you can arrive at a factor for yearly or even monthly changes in the value of the dollar.

Calculating a constant dollar conversion involves three steps. To illustrate these steps, we will use the data for published tuition and fee prices at private non-profit institutions for the academic years 2000–2001 to 2010–2011, which are provided in Table 10.1. First, obtain the index for the years of interest. In our example, we use the August Consumer Price Index for the years of interest. The second step is to determine an inflation factor. This is accomplished by dividing the CPI for the current year by the CPI for the base year. For example, in Table 10.1, the base year is 2011, and the August CPI was 218.3. This is the base value into which the other CPI values are divided to arrive at an inflation factor.

Table 10.1. Constant Dollar Conversions for Tuition and Fees at Private 4-Year Institutions: Academic Years 2000–2001 to 2010–2011

			Constant Dollar Conversion			
	Private Four-Year		*Inflation Factor*		*Constant Dollar Amount*	
Academic Year	*Tuition and Fees (current dollars)*	*Consumer Price Index (CPI; August)*	*Base value/ Current value*	*Factor*	*Current Value *Factor*	*Private Four-Year Tuition and Fees (2010)*
2000–01	$16,072	172.8	218.3/172.8	1.263	$16,072 *1.263	$20,305
2001–02	$17,377	177.5	218.3/177.5	1.230	$17,377 *1.230	$21,372
2002–03	$18,060	180.7	218.3/180.7	1.208	$18,060 *1.208	$21,819
2003–04	$18,950	184.6	218.3/184.6	1.183	$18,950* 1.183	$22,411
2004–05	$20,045	189.5	218.3/189.5	1.152	$20,045 *1.152	$23,093
2005–06	$20,980	196.4	218.3/196.4	1.112	$20,980 *1.112	$23,321
2006–07	$22,218	203.9	218.3/203.9	1.071	$22,218 *1.071	$23,788
2007–08	$23,745	207.9	218.3/207.9	1.050	$23,745 *1.050	$24,934
2008–09	$25,177	219.1	218.3/219.1	0.996	$25,177 *0.996	$25,086
2009–10	$26,273	215.8	218.3/215.8	1.012	$26,273 *1.012	$26,579
2010–11	$27,293	218.3	218.3/218.3	1.000	$27,293 *1.000	$27,293

Note: Consumer Price Index (CPI) values reflect the CPI-U, for all urban consumers, for the August of the fall semester. For example, the CPI value for the 2010–2011 academic year is for August 2010.

Source: College Board (2012a), U.S. Census Bureau (2012).

The third step is to multiply the inflation factor by the original, current dollar value for tuition and fees to arrive at an inflation-adjusted constant dollar value. The steps necessary to convert the data for 2002 to a constant value dollar value for 2010 would be the following. First identify the CPI, then divide the 2010 index by the 2002 index (218.312 / 180.7) to arrive at an inflation factor of 1.2081. In this case, the CPI-U inflates each $1 in 2002 by 1.2081, resulting in a change from a current dollar value of $18,060 to a 2010 constant dollar value of $21,819.

In addition to the consumer price index (CPI), two other indices have been developed to account for the changing value of money specifically as it relates to colleges and universities: the Higher Education Price Index (HEPI) and the Higher Education Cost Adjustment (HECA).

The Higher Education Price Index (HEPI)

The HEPI attempts to account for a basket of goods and services colleges and universities purchase, rather than those goods and services that relate to urban consumers and drive the CPI-U calculations; postsecondary institutions purchase a different set of goods than urban consumers. HEPI is determined annually using a methodology that has relied upon a regression formula since 2002 (Halstead, 2001); previously the HEPI was based on over 100 items reflecting 25 budget components. Primary item categories included salaries and benefits, contracted services, library acquisitions, and utilities. HEPI is issued annually by Commonfund Institute and is distributed free of charge at www.commonfundinstitute/HEPI/Pages/default.aspx.

HEPI should be applied to education and general fund expenditure categories and not applied to sponsored research or auxiliary enterprises. The HEPI reflects averages, so it may not be appropriate for individual institutions should they deviate too far from the mean or average purchases. Also, the market basket has remained fixed, so changes in how much an institution spends on one item or another may influence adjusted values.

The Higher Education Cost Adjustment (HECA)

The HECA (State Higher Education Executive Officers, 2012) also attempts to account for the costs associated with higher education while addressing the shortcomings of the HEPI. Rather than relying on a complex calculation, the HEPI is based upon two federally developed price indices: the Employment Cost Index and the Gross Domestic Product Implicit Price Deflator. Advantages of the HECA include that it is constructed using measures of inflation in the broader U.S. economy as compared to items used by institutions. The HECA is a simple and straightforward calculation, and the indices are routinely updated by external sources.

Gillen and Robe (2011) suggest that the HEPI and HECA are inappropriately used in some instances and are subject to some statistical bias as well. Specifically, they note that too often the HEPI and HECA are inappropriately used to adjust tuition, when they were developed for internal budget planning. Gillen and Robe believe that the indices suffer from four types of bias. First, they suggest there exists quality bias in that both indices are input-based rather that an actual measure of the costs; the quality of objects changes from year-to-year, so there are never direct comparisons in most indices, although the CPI has attempted to control for changes in quality. Second, Gillen and Robe assert that the indices assume constant proportionality between inputs and outputs (productivity bias). Third, the indices do not account for substitution opportunities for institutions, such as a shift towards more adjunct faculty. It is also the case that institutions use funds differently to meet similar objectives, thereby suffering from substitution bias. Finally, the HEPI is self-referential—it is a measure of institutional activities influenced by institutional policy decisions.

Despite these criticisms, all three of the price indices are used in higher education studies on trends over time. The College Board, for example, publishes tables of average tuition and fees over time in both nominal and constant dollars using the CPI (College Board, 2012a). SHEEO publishes annual studies that display state support to higher education per student, over time, in nominal and constant dollars using the HECA (SHEEO, 2012).

When conducting analysis where dollar values are being applied, it is advisable to first convert the value to a constant dollar value. If the value is part of a derived value, such as a debt-to-income ratio, than converting to constant dollars is not necessary, as the value is contextualized at that point.

INDEXING

Indexing is the process of equalizing all data points to a certain point in time, normally one that has substantial relevance to the issue being studied, and then examining how the units of interest change relative to that point in time. The indexed value is usually set to 100, although it can be set to 1 or 0. While an index does not need to be, indexes are often used for more than one data series for comparative purposes.

As an example, there is an interest how changes made to federal student aid eligibility during reauthorizations of the Higher Education Act impact Pell Grant recipients enrolled in various sectors of higher education. Table 10.2 shows the number of Pell Grant recipients at public 2-year and 4-year institutions for 10 years after the Higher Education Act reauthorization of 1998. Since the number of recipients varies by sector, an independent index value of 100 was created by dividing the values in 1999–2000 by the base year (1999–2000) and then multiplying by 100.

**Table 10.2.   Federal Pell Grants Recipients at Public Institutions:
1999–2000 to 2008–2009**

Program Year	Pell Grant Recipients		Indexed Value (100 = 1999–2000)	
	Public 2-Year	Public 4-Year	Public 2-Year	Public 4-Year
1999–2000	1,367,889	1,224,269	100	100
2000–2001	1,422,942	1,245,363	104.02	101.72
2001–2002	1,641,186	1,329,257	119.98	108.58
2002–2003	1,799,341	1,464,261	131.54	119.60
2003–2004	1,833,580	1,625,128	134.04	132.74
2004–2005	1,869,531	1,656,289	136.67	135.29
2005–2006	1,800,424	1,600,706	131.62	130.75
2006–2007	1,749,556	1,600,293	127.90	130.71
2007–2008	1,848,472	1,680,160	135.13	137.24
2008–2009	2,084,047	1,751,609	152.35	143.07

Source: Office of Postsecondary Education (2010)

To determine the other values for the years 2000–2001 through 2008–2009, each year value was divided by the base year. The equation is simple:

$$\text{Eq 10.1}\quad V_a = (X_a / X_b) * 100$$

Where V_a represents the indexed value for a given year "a" (i.e. 2000–2001... 2010–2011),

X_a represents the observed data for a given year "a" (i.e. 2000–2001... 2010–2011), and

X_b represents the observed data for the base year "b" (i.e., 2000–2001).

A weakness with indexing data is the assumption that the data have equal trajectories at the time the index is set. That is to say, comparing two data points, where the trend prior to indexing was headed in two different directions, does not tell you much. It is therefore ideal to both ensure that data prior to the base year show similar, though not necessarily exact, trends and to show data in any figures or tables for several years prior to the indexed year.

PERCENT CHANGES

Monthly

In cases where a monetary value has been converted to constant dollars, or for values that are not sensitive to time (such as student counts), there is an interest in how much change occurs from one point in time to another. The process to calculate change is fairly straightforward.

In Table 10.3, we can calculate monthly percent changes in enrollment of first-time students at a college (College A; A definition of the time period is arbitrary and could, for instance, represent a fiscal quarter, a year, or a decade). To calculate a one-month percent change, first-time enrollment in the previous month is subtracted from first-time enrollment in the month of interest; the total is then divided by the previous month amount. This result is then multiplied by 100 to arrive at a percent, as expressed in Equation 10.2.

$$\text{Eq. 10.2} \quad V = ((X_m - X_{m-1}) / X_{m-1}) * 100$$

Where V represents the monthly percent change,

X_m reflects the value in the month of interest, and

$X_m - 1$ reflects the value for the month prior to the month of interest.

Applying this calculation, the percent change from July to August would be calculated as $((1{,}577 - 1{,}601) / 1{,}601) * 100 = -1.5\%$, a 1½% decrease.

Before continuing, it is worth noting that the data presented in Table 10.3 may appear a little absurd given that enrollment patterns typically are not even, rather they tend to be seasonal with larger enrollments in the fall than at other times of the year. Yet, for some institutions such as online or for-profit institutions that have new enrollments continuously throughout the year, or each month, also termed "starts," this type of analysis may be appropriate. For institutions that exhibit a traditional enrollment pattern, the unit of analysis for enrollment comparisons should be a year, whether with fall enrollments, 12-month unduplicated headcounts, or full-time equivalent student counts.

Table 10.3.   First-Time Student Enrollment at College a by Monthly, Annualized, and Annualized Year-to-Date Percent Changes, 2012

Month in 2012	First-Time Student Enrollment (Headcount) at College A	Percent Change (Growth Rate)		
		Monthly	Annualized	Annualized Year-to-date
January	1,421			
February	1,560	9.8%	206.45	75.06
March	1,575	1.0%	12.17	50.92
April	1,643	4.3%	66.07	54.57
May	1,490	(9.3%)	(69.06)	12.05
June	1,564	5.0%	78.90	21.14
July	1,601	2.4%	32.39	22.69
August	1,577	(1.5%)	(16.58)	16.91
September	1,704	8.1%	153.31	27.40
October	1,622	(4.8%)	(44.67)	17.21
November	1,499	(7.6%)	(61.18)	(4.67)
December	1,408	(7.6%)	(52.84)	(12.58)

Annualized Percent Change

Annualizing data results in a growth rate that reflects the amount a value would have changed over a year, had the monthly growth rate held constant for an entire year. Annualizing data allows for a quick comparison of percentage changes for periods less than a year. The first step is to determine the length of the various observations and how they relate to an entire year. In this example, illustrated in Table 10.3, we are examining monthly changes. The second step is to apply Equation 10.3.

$$\text{Eq. 10.3} \quad V = [((X_m / (X_m - 1))^{12} - 1] * 100$$

Where V represents the annualized percent change,

X_m reflects the value in the month of interest, and

$X_m - 1$ reflects the value for the month prior to the month of interest.

For example, if the percent change in enrollments of −1.5% observed from July to August continued for 1 year, the annualized growth rate would be −16.58%.

Annualized Year-to-Date Percent Change

In some cases, you may want to know the direction a data point may be taking partway through the year to better understand future performance. Annualizing year-to-date is a method that contributes to this understanding.

The first step in this calculation is to determine the length of the various observations and how they relate to an entire year. In this example, illustrated in Table 10.3, we are examining changes occurring from the beginning of the year (January) until a point within the year (April). The second step is to conduct the calculations in Equation 10.4.

$$\text{Eq. 10.4} \quad V = [((X_m / (X_m - 1))^{12/m} - 1] * 100$$

Where V represents the annualized year-to-date percent change,

X_m reflects the value in the month of interest,

$X_m - 1$ reflects the value for the month prior to the month of interest, and

m denotes the number of months that have passed.

Using our example for enrollments at College A, we can see that new starts from January to April would portend a growth rate of 54.57%.

MOVING AVERAGES

Interruptions in data may be repetitive, as in the case of cycles like the hiring of temporary workers during the holiday season, or due to a disruption, like Hurricane Katrina's impact on enrollments in Louisiana in 2005. There are methods to address these interruptions in data. One way is to provide a moving average, which will smooth volatile data by consolidation.

A moving average may be calculated by adding up the values for a determined number of years and then dividing by the determined number of years. Generally data are smoothed for 3 years, but they may be smoothed over longer periods of time. A simple moving average is calculated as shown in Equation 10.5.

$$\text{Eq. 10.5} \quad A = (A_t + A_{t-1} + \dots) / n$$

Where A represents the simple average,

t represents the time period, and

n represents the number of cases used to smooth the data.

For example, consider College B. Enrollment in each of the last 10 years was as follows:

Academic year	Enrollment	3-Year Rolling Average
2003–2004	17,500	–
2004–2005	19,800	–
2005–2006	18,400	18,567
2006–2007	20,300	19,500
2007–2008	21,900	20,200
2008–2009	24,100	22,100
2009–2010	22,600	22,866
2010–2011	24,700	23,800
2011–2012	27,500	24,933
2012–2013	31,600	27,933

The data do not indicate a consistent pattern of increases, decreases, or steady enrollment.

Applying moving averages allows researchers to see the underlying trends in the data by minimizing the influence of cycles or anomalies in data. When displayed visually, a moving average also allows for a clearer picture of trends, especially if there are a substantial number of observations of data. Moving averages are limited, in that the timeliness of recent data is removed if a substantial number of values are used, as each year is treated equally. In practice, rolling averages are used to stabilize enrollments in funding formulas and establish institutional enrollment projections.

Some feel as though weighting the data, so that the most recent data have more or less importance to data points than others when developing an average, is a better way to smooth the data. Examine College B's enrollment for the last 3 years again. This time we are going to weight the enrollment data for the most recent years to give them either greater or less influence over the result. We use two approaches: one where the most recent of the three observations has the least weight (50-30-20) and one where the most recent of three observations has the greatest weight (20-30-50). Naturally, it would follow that if the most recent observations were given the greatest weight, they would most closely reflect the value for the most recent observation. This is illustrated in Table 10.4. When enrollments increased and the most recent observation (2012–2013 academic year) were most heavily weighted, the highest value results (28,990 for 2012–2013). When the 50-30-20 weighting approach is used while enrollment increases, the lowest value results (26,920) for 2012–2013.

Table 10.4. Comparison of Weighting Approaches at College B Over Three Years, Assuming Increasing and Decreasing Enrollments

Weighting Approach	Academic Year			Weighted Total
	2010–2011	*2011–2012*	*2012–2013*	
Enrollment	24,700	27,500	31,600	
20/30/50	24,700*.20 = 4,940	27,500*.30 = 8,250	31,600*.50 = 15,800	28,990
50/30/20	24,700*.50 = 12,350	27,500*.30 = 8,250	31,600*.20 = 6,320	26,920
33/33/33	24,700*.33 = 8,233	27,500*.33 = 9,167	31,600*.33 = 10,533	27,933
Enrollment	31,600	27,500	24,700	
20/30/50	31,600*.20 = 6,320	27,500*.30 = 8,250	24,700*.50 = 12,350	26,920
50/30/20	31,600*.50 = 15,800	27,500*.30 = 8,250	24,700*.20 = 4,940	28,990
33/33/33	31,600*.33 = 10,533	27,500*.33 = 9,167	24,700*.33 = 8,233	27,933

Weighted enrollments are used most often in funding formulas to smooth out changes in funding that would be greater than those to which institutional managers can effectively respond. Legislators seem to prefer the use of a weighting factor that gives actual enrollments a higher weight than projected enrollments. For example, budget requests typically include at least 3 years of enrollment data: the last actual, the current year, and the projected or request year. Because of concerns that institutions might inflate possible or budgeted enrollments, enrollments may be weighted 50-30-20, with the highest weight given to the last actual count of enrollments. This works well for institutions when enrollments are declining but is perceived to work less well when enrollments are increasing. In the case of declining enrollments, legislators may perceive that they are funding "phantom" enrollments. In the case of increasing enrollments, institutions perceive that they are not receiving adequate funding to serve the current students.

There are more advanced research methods that apply averages and apply more aptly to time series models. Examples, whose examination extends beyond the scope of this volume, include but are by no means limited to autoregressive moving average (ARMA) and auto regressive integrated moving average (ARIMA) models. Additional models are discussed in the following chapter.

ESTIMATING CHANGE

There are various measures of time as they relate to money. This section contributes to an understanding of the terminology needed to engage in planning discussions related to the use of current and future funds. The various concepts are introduced as extensions of an answer to one question.

> *How much do I have to save annually if I want to provide my daughter $32,000 for 4 years of college, which she will start in 12 years?*

The simple answer is that I save $2,666.67 a year for 12 years. Problem solved, right? Wrong, it ignores the interaction of time and money. My intent is for her to have an amount of money that equals the amount of purchasing power of $32,000 today. I need to account for the time value of money.

Compounding Interest (Future Value)

We start with the definition of compound interest as provided by Bannock, Baxter, and Davis (1992), "the calculation of total interest due by applying the rate of the sum of the capital invested plus the interest previously earned and reinvested" (p. 81). The amount of compounded interest earned at the end of the time period plus the initial capital is referred to as the future value. This is what I am interested in, the future value of my initial amount (principal) given some compounding interest rate over a set period of time.

Written out as a research question, it may be expressed as the *value of an amount of money (principal)* left on deposit/invested for a *set number of years* at *a set interest rate*. This definition is actually a script (this script and the others in this section were derived from Droms, 1979). Scripts are invaluable to you. They help add clarity to an issue as you try to think it through. If we take the information put forth in our problem statement, combined with the thought I could deposit $3,000 and receive an interest rate of 6%, the definition of compound interest for my situation can be written to say:

What is the future value of a *$3,000 certificate of deposit* invested for *12* years at a set interest rate of *6% annually?* Written as an equation, this would say:

$$\text{Eq. 10.6} \quad V_n = P\,(1+i)^n$$

Where V equals Future Value (FV),

P equals the principal amount ($3,000),

i represents the interest rate (6%), and

n equals the number of years (12).

At the end of 12 years, my initial investment of $3,000 would be worth $6,036.

$$V_n = P\,(1+i)^n = (\$3,000)(1+.06)^{12} = (\$3,000)\,(2.012) = \$6,036$$

A shortcut to understanding how long it takes to double the initial investment is the Rule of 72. If you divide 72 by the interest rate, one can find how many years it will take to double the initial investment. This was illustrated in the previous example; 72/6 equals 12.

Additionally, the interest rate may be applied monthly rather than annually. In such a case, the equation would be:

$$\text{Eq. 10.7} \quad V_n = P\,[(1+i/m)^{nm}]$$

Where V represents the Future Value,

P equals the principal amount ($3,000),

i represents the interest rate (6%),

n reflects the number of years (12), and

m reflects the number of times per year that interest is compounded (12).

$$V_{nm} = \$3,000\,[(1+.06/12)^{12(12)}] = \$3,000\,[(1+.005)^{144}] = \$3,000\,[2.050751] = \$6,152.25$$

In 12 years, my initial investment of $3,000 at a rate of 6% will be worth $6,036 if compounded annually or $6,152.25 if compounded monthly. Neither approach gets me to my goal of $32,000, and clearly I need to find out how much principal I need to invest now to reach my goal. I can either recalculate future value rates until I arrive at the value I seek or work backwards from the goal—the present value.

Present Value

Present value seeks to determine the amount of money needed currently, and invested at a certain rate, to end in a set amount. Essentially it is compound interest in reverse.

In seeking to determine the present value of $32,000, I am trying to answer the following question. What is the present value of *an amount (V)* to be received *number of years (n)* from now if invested at a *set annual rate of interest (r)*?

$$\text{Eq. 10.8} \quad PV = V_n \left[1/(1 + r)^n \right]$$

Where PV denotes Present Value,

V denotes future value,

n represents years, and

r reflects the discount rate (conceptually the inverse of interest rate).

Applying this process to the $32,000 goal, I find that I will need to deposit $15,903.01 now.

$PV = \$32,000 \left[1/(1 + .06)^{12} \right] = \$32,000 \left[1/(2.012196) \right] = \$32,000 [0.496969] = \$15,903.01$

I am not in the position, financially, to deposit $15,903.01 to meet my goal. Also, I have come to realize that if the value of money changes over time, I may not need to have exactly $32,000 in 12 years. What is more likely is that I will make an initial investment and then contribute monthly—which is an annuity.

Annuities

An annuity is a guaranteed series of payments (or receipts) for a set period of time in the future purchased immediately for a lump sum (Bannock, Baxter, & Davis, 1992). My $32,000 goal was developed when I was not aware of the time value of money. I was thinking I would have $8,000 a year to help her for 4 years. Knowing what I know now about the changing value of money, I need to first rethink how much money I need to provide $8,000 a year for 4 years. I need to determine the present value of the annuity.

Present Value of the Annuity

The question then becomes, how much money do I need (the present value of an annuity) in 12 years if I want to receive annual payments of *$8,000 a year* for *4 years* with a *discount rate of 6%*?

$$\text{Eq. 10.9} \quad A_n = R[(1 - (1/(1+r)^n))/r]$$

Where A equals the present value of an annuity,

R reflects the amount of future receipts,

r reflects the discount rate, and

n equals the number of years.

$$A_4 = \$8,000\ [(1 - (1/(1+.06)^4))/.06] = \$8,000\ [(1 - (1/(1.06)^4))/.06]$$

$$= \$8,000\ [(1 - (1/1.262477))/.06] = \$8,000\ [(1 - (.792094))/.06]$$

$$= \$8,000\ [.207906/.06] = \$8,000\ [3.4651]$$

My goal has been reset. In 12 years, I need to invest $27,720.80 at 6% so that $8,000 can be disbursed every year for 4 years to support my daughter's college education. Again, I cannot afford to invest half of this amount at 6% now, nor can I just divide it by 12 to understand how I can most wisely—and affordably—meet my goal. I need to make payments.

Compound Value of an Annuity

A series of payments made for a set period of time that earns a certain rate of interest per period describes the compound value of an annuity. It is very similar to the concept of compound value previously discussed, though expanded to include a payment set at regular intervals, as depicted in Equation 10.10.

$$\text{Eq. 10.10} \quad S_n = P\ [(1+i)^{n-1}/i]$$

Where S denotes the compound sum,

P equals the principal amount deposited each year,

i reflects the interest rate, and

n represents the number of years.

In terms of the calculation I am undertaking, the following would be true:

$$S_{12} = P\,[(1+.06)^{12\text{-}1}/.06]$$

$$\$27{,}720 = P\,[(1.06)^{11}/.06]\ \$27{,}720 = P\,[1.898299/.06]$$

$$\$27{,}720 = P\,[31.638317] = \$876.15$$

I need to deposit $876.15 a year for 12 years at 6% interest to accumulate $27,720.

In this chapter, we examined ways to account for the changing value of money. As researchers, these practical applications and calculations are of utmost importance to understand and apply where appropriate.

CHAPTER 11

ON GROUPS AND EVENTS

Research is undertaken to further our understanding of topics of perpetual interest or issues of the day. Research requires information about specific groups, such as students with disabilities; the influence of some event, such as participation in a training program funded with public dollars; or a combination of both.

The way groups are determined matters as much as the finding resulting from the analysis. For institutions, the appropriate selection of peers and the benchmarks used for comparison contribute to our understanding of the postsecondary enterprise. In addition to institutional perspectives, cohorts of students are also of interest to understand the postsecondary enterprise, especially as they experience certain events.

In this chapter, we examine both the development of peers and benchmarks along with the development of cohorts and the analysis of them pertaining to the occurrence of an event.

DETERMINING PEER INSTITUTIONS

One of the more difficult concepts to convey to stakeholders is a comparison of an institution or system to another institution or system. Colleges and universities develop sets of "peer" institutions, or peer departments, or peer systems with which to compare themselves on a group of variables.

Higher Education Finance Research: Policy, Politics, and Practice, pp. 315–328
Copyright © 2014 by Information Age Publishing
315

A "peer" is a college or university that is "most like" another college or university based on similarities on a group of variables like mission, size, organization, control, location, mix of programs, and student body characteristics. Colleges and universities use groups of peers to compare their performance on characteristics and/or to request additional funding to support initiatives. Peers may be determined for one institution based on sets of characteristics that indicate "alikeness" or "similarity," or peers may be determined for a set of institutions.

A set of peers typically includes at least ten colleges or universities because not all will elect to participate in data collection efforts. A peer group smaller than ten may not provide sufficient data to yield valid or reliable information. The peer group may include all actual peers, or it may include "aspirational" peers. Aspirational peers are those that the institution aspires to be like on some criterion, such as faculty salary or compensation levels, or academic reputation.

Colleges, state systems, and legislative analysts have used peers to set tuition, recommend faculty salaries, compare expenditures per full-time equivalent student, compare legislative appropriations, and adjust student/faculty ratios. In 1996, a majority of states were using peers in their funding models; 26 states used peer data for salary purposes, 17 for tuition and fee setting, 10 for determining overall funding levels, and six for determining funding for libraries (McKeown, 1996b). That number declined in the early 2000s but is on the rise again as performance funding and performance assessment becomes more prevalent.

An individual institution may use peers for internal comparison purposes. For example, peers can be established for each academic department or for each business office in the university. Generally, peers are determined for "general" purposes, and the same set of peers is used for all comparisons that a college or university may make. However, some colleges have one set of peers for determining tuition, another set of peers for comparisons of faculty and staff salaries and compensation, and a third set for funding comparisons.

To determine a set of peers, colleges or coordinating/governing boards may use several methods: geographic location, membership in an organization or externally determined group, or statistical analysis.

Geographic Proximity

All of the colleges in the contiguous states or other colleges in the same state that have been assigned the same Carnegie Classification may be used as peers. Geographic proximity is used because it is thought that the nearby colleges are those with which the college or university competes for students and staff. The Southern Regional Education Board (SREB) and the Western Interstate Commission on Higher Education (WICHE) maintain detailed databases on the colleges and universities in their respective regions and form the basis for some geographic peer comparisons. Geographic peer selection is used most often for comparisons of tuition and fees.

Membership in Athletic Conferences, Organizations, or the Same Carnegie Classification

While most are familiar with the National Collegiate Athletic Association (NCAA), there are a few other governing bodies in collegiate athletics. Member institutions administer student financial aid programs as well as acquire revenue and have expenditures.

The NCAA is comprised of three memberships classifications: Division 1, Division II and Division III. While the NCAA develops the overall governing principles, each division sets its own rules applicable to a broad set of actions related to the provision of athletic opportunities for student athletes. In addition to the NCAA, the National Association of Intercollegiate Athletics (NAIA) serves as a governing body for about 350 athletic programs at small colleges. Community colleges are members of one of three governing bodies: The National Junior College Athletic Association, the Northwest Athletic Association of Community Colleges, or the California Community College Athletic Association.

Data for athletic programs are collected and made available by the Office of Postsecondary Education via the Equity in Athletics Disclosure Act (EADA) data analysis cutting tool (http://ope.ed.gov/athletics/). Data elements include participants by gender, head and assistant coaches by gender, coaches' salaries, athletically-related student aid by gender, recruiting expenses by gender, operating expenses, and revenues. Data may be grouped by state, sanctioning body, conference, enrollment size, and institutional sector. Each membership association also may provide data on student athletes, such as graduation rates of student athletes.

Carnegie Classifications are categorizations of colleges and universities using a method designed by the Carnegie Commission for the Advancement of Teaching. (See Chapter 1 for a discussion of Carnegie Classification.) At the time of writing this book, there were six main Carnegie Classifications, most of which had subsets for further delineation of institutions. The five main categories are Doctoral Granting, Master's, Baccalaureate, Associates, or Specialized Campus. The sixth category is Tribal Colleges. These classifications include some differentiation by size and location.

Some colleges and universities use membership in Carnegie Classification or in an athletic conference as the only criterion for determining peers. For example, members of the Big Ten Athletic Conference compare data on physical plant, libraries, planning, enrollment trends, and other data items. The universities that are members of the Association of American Universities (AAU) have detailed data that are shared among member institutions. Data include items such as rank of faculty and class size by discipline and level. Membership is used most often for peer selection for plant, library, and faculty comparisons.

Statistical Analysis

To determine peers, some colleges or governing/coordinating boards use statistical analysis techniques. The analysis may be simple or quite complex. A simple analysis may use only one variable to select peers, such as all colleges of a certain size, no matter what the location, organization, or control.

More complex statistical methodologies involve upwards of 100 variables in determining the set of peer institutions. Variables include size, location, organization, control, mix of academic programs, types of students served, graduation rates, or any of a number of other variables.

Typically the peer selection will start with one variable that is used as the major criterion to eliminate most of the 4,900 colleges and universities in the United States. For example, only public colleges may be included in the selection group. Then, the group may be further winnowed by elimination of all colleges above or below a certain enrollment.

The most complex method for selecting peers involves completing factor analyses or cluster analyses to determine which colleges have the most alike factor scores, or which cluster together based on the variables used. A set of "difference" scores may be computed, which are used to determine how alike two institutions are on a variable or factor. The difference scores are summed across all variables or factors, and those colleges with the smallest total difference score become the set of peers. Factor analysis also may be used after a criterion variable is used, such as enrollment within a certain range.

Criteria for Peer Selection

The process of identifying peers for an institution begins with development of a set of criteria or variables that will be used to determine "similarity." In identifying peer institutions, usually the primary selection criterion reflects the mission of the institution as identified by their control type and Carnegie Classification. Public institutions typically include only public institutions in their selection pool, because of the difficulties in comparing revenues and expenditures because of the differences in reporting under GASB and FASB. Variables chosen for comparison purposes will vary related to the mission and goals of the institution. Table 11.1 displays a generalized set of variables from which specific variables related to each institution's mission usually is chosen.

Table 11.1. General Variables/Criteria for Use in Determining Peers

1. Control (Public or Private non-profit or Private for-profit)

2. Carnegie Classification

3. Number of headcount students by level and part-time or full-time status

4. Percent part-time and percent full-time students

5. Location in urban/rural/suburban area

6. Number of full-time equivalent students

7. Number of degrees awarded

8. Degrees awarded by field and percent degrees awarded by field

9. Total sponsored research expenditures

10. Land grant status

11. Medical school

12. Highest level degree awarded

13. Program mix: Technical; 2-year; undergraduate only; undergraduate and master's; undergraduate, master's, and doctoral

14. Number of staff by category

For each category, a sample of institutions will be drawn from the list of all colleges and universities in the U.S. that are public, or private. For example, for doctoral-granting institutions, all public institutions classified as doctoral may be included. For the master's sector, all public master's campuses may be included in the list; for baccalaureate institutions, all public baccalaureate institutions may be included; and, for associate campuses, all public associate colleges may comprise the list. Or the list of possible peers may include only those institutions that are in one of the sub-categories of each Carnegie Classification. Data should be taken from the most recent and available IPEDS institutional characteristics, fall enrollment, staffing, degrees awarded, and finance surveys, and combined into one file for each classification.

It is important in conducting this type of research to provide a copy of the data file to the institutions being studied if the research is being done by a person or a group outside the institution.

Under the most complex methodology, to develop an initial listing of "peers," a factor analysis is completed on the combined data file for each group. Factor analysis identifies underlying variables called "factors" that explain the pattern of correlation within a set of observed variables. Because there usually are over 100 variables in the data set, factor analysis permits the reduction in the number of variables to a more manageable set of factors that enables comparison among colleges or universities. To ensure that there is a valid comparison, factors identified by the statistical technique should explain at least 80% of the variance or differences among campuses.

This type of factor analysis will result in "factor scores" for each institution for each factor identified in the analysis. A factor analysis that identified 22 factors would result in each institution having 22 factor scores, one for each of the 22 factors.

Then, the factor scores for each institution in the sample would be compared to the factor scores for each other institution in its "sector" to get "distance scores." A distance score is defined as the difference between one campus and another on each factor score. Distance scores usually are squared to eliminate the negatives, or the absolute value of the score is used. All institutions in the group then are rank-ordered based on their total distance score, that is, the sum of all the individual distance scores, and arrayed in a list from low to high total distance score. The institution with the smallest distance score from the target institution is the institution most like the target institution. We have used SPSS statistical package to complete a general factor analysis with no constraints placed on the number of factors, and with weighted or unweighted variables. The biggest critique of this methodology is that it may be difficult to explain to stakeholders.

BENCHMARKING

Another way to conduct a comparison is to identify benchmarks, or standards by which the unit of analysis can be measured. Two types of benchmarks include operational and strategic.

Operational benchmarks are focused on within-institution operations including the various revenue and expenditure categories associated with GASB or FASB accounting standards (see Chapter 2). There are any number of metrics, outside of standard institutional reporting, that are beneficial for institutions to examine and benchmark themselves against. Examples of institutional surveys include the National Survey of Student Engagement (NSSE), Community College Survey of Student Engagement

(CCSSE), the Survey of Entering Student Engagement (SENSE), the Noel-Levitz Satisfaction Inventory, the Noel-Levitz Institutional Priorities Survey, and the ACT student opinion and Alumna Surveys.

Strategic benchmarks are focused on the future and aspirations. Generally, they include comparative rankings and performance on leading indicators within a sector.

In addition to the data sources identified in Chapter 2, there are numerous data sharing groups. Examples include the Higher Education Data Sharing consortium (HEDS), the National Community College Benchmarking Project (NCCBP), the Association of American Universities Data Exchange (AAUDE), Achieving the Dream (AtD), and the Southern Universities Group (SUG).

Benchmarks allow institutions to compare themselves to their prior performance on a set of metrics and to other, peer institutions, on metrics. While institutionally developed surveys and data collection instruments have a place, surveys created by national entities are usually tested to be reliable and valid, a factor that goes a long way with external stakeholders (Bers, 2012).

COHORTS

As discussed in Chapter 2 and elsewhere in this book, postsecondary finance includes examinations of both raw and derived values, such as the total cost of a program or the cost of a program per participant, respectively. In both cases, researchers and analysts need to be sure there is consistency in measurement. That is to say, the number of programs or institutions being funded or the number of students being served will change. Furthermore, in cases where there is interest in a particular group—or cohort—some members may not be present in each observation. This is true whether the data are cross-sectional (a point in time) or longitudinal (following a unit of analysis over time).

While each type of data will be discussed, it is first proper to acknowledge that there are threats to the validity of data when examined over a period of time. Time related threats to validity include the following:

Type of Threat	Description	Postsecondary Finance Example
History	A coincidental event influences the outcome	Super-storm Sandy in fall 2012
Reactivity	Previous experience influences the outcome	Previous appropriation amounts

(Threat Table continues on next page)

(Threat Table continued)

Type of Threat	Description	Postsecondary Finance Example
Maturation	A subject's development influences the outcome	A change in governing perception of postsecondary education value
Instrumentation	A shift in how measures are collected or reported influences the outcome	Changes to accounting practices
Mortality	The loss of participants influences the outcome	Institutional classification changes

While there may be ways to address these threats in controlled experiments (Dooley, 2001), it is difficult in the field of postsecondary finance when the unit of analysis is beyond the control of the analyst: researchers don't control the weather, legislator knowledge, elections, procedural changes, or classification qualifications.

GROUPS AND CROSS-SECTIONAL DATA

Cross-sectional data depict values for a point in time and usually cover a specific time period. Examples include revenues for the 2012–2013 academic year or a state appropriation for higher education institutions. As mentioned in Chapter 2, these data may be contextualized by deriving institutional revenues per student or appropriations per student. Doing so is one way to make cross-sectional data comparable over time. For example, the State Higher Education Finance Survey (SHEF; State Higher Education Executive Officers, 2012) frequently depicts appropriations per FTE over a 25 year period of time, after adjusting for inflation. Cross-sectional data can be used for time-based calculations in other ways as well. These methods include turning cross-sectional cohorts into estimates of cohorts into the future.

Developing a cohort for a particular study purpose and following that cohort over an extended period of time requires substantial resources and may not be possible for all. There are some ways to turn cross-sectional data into quasi-longitudinal data, a common method used in cohort survival rates.

Cohort survival rates reflect an estimate of the proportion of an entering cohort at some point in the future. Calculations can vary as researchers try to control for changes in both the numerator and denominator of the calculation. For example, the UNESCO Institute of Statistics calculates a primary completion rate that is the number of students successfully completing the last year of primary school in a particular year divided by the number of children who would be of that age in the entire population (The World Bank, 2003).

All survival rate calculations have limitations. Common challenges for the determination of a numerator relate to determining who is a non-completer, as compared to who was held back to repeat a grade, who may have skipped a grade, who may have dropped out for a year only to return later, or who may have moved out of or into the group from outside the unit of analysis (i.e. moved into or out of one school district, college, or country from another). The denominator suffers many of the same challenges as the numerator, including the use of population estimates and timing of age determination for the population. In cases where parents are holding back their children, also termed "redshirting," to put them in the best position to be successful in curricular and co-curricular activities, tying completion to age is further complicated.

Groups and Longitudinal Data

Longitudinal data follow a cohort for a determined period of time. A cohort may be defined in any number of ways. A relatively simple or less complex way is to group units of analysis by a general characteristic such as gender for students or sector for institutions. The primary strength of longitudinal data is that individuals or institutions may be assigned to groups that may then be followed over a period of time with the intent to understand how and why aspects of the group change.

Exactly how groups are created has analytical ramifications. Ideally, members of the cohort would be randomly assigned to a group as a means to ensure that each subject has an equal chance to be in a group. There are also threats associated with groups, including selection, selection-by-interaction, and regression towards the mean (Dooley, 2001).

In education, random assignment is difficult to achieve given the concern for human subjects and ingrained perceptions of programmatic gatekeepers and the mechanisms or processes needed to enact such a research methodology. Matching is one alternative to random assignment. Matching is the process of aligning two or more subjects on similar criteria. It may be accomplished in a variety of ways.

One method is to create a matched set of units over time to account for mortality. This practice is employed most prominently by the Delta Cost Project (Desrochers & Wellman, 2011), where their trend analyses account only for those institutions who have data available for each year during the time period studied. This method limits the influence in the outcomes attributable to institutions leaving the group or being added to a grouping of interest. It does, however, leave some institutions out.

Another method, a propensity score, suggests that routine demographic variables are not sufficient to match subjects (Shadish & Steiner, 2010). Rather, characteristics associated with the selection process must be considered. A propensity score is developed when covariates are combined to arrive at a single number, as it is suggested that individuals with similar scores are similarly likely to be in either the treatment or in the control group. A propensity score ranges from 0 to 1, the closer to 1 the stronger the prediction a participant would be in the treatment, the closer to 0 the stronger prediction the participant would be in the comparison group, with 0.50 reflecting equal probability.

EVENT-BASED ANALYSES

While many analyses are conducted on data observed at a particular point in time (cross-sectional), data may be plotted at points in time. When data for one variable are plotted as points that result in a continuously changing line over some period of time, a trend is observed. In some cases, data are cyclical. Employment provides an example, where seasonal employment results in increases in employment each winter. In cases where data have cycles, observing data over time is especially important because a pattern repeats itself. It is possible to have both a trend (a general trajectory) and cycle (patterns in the data) occur at the same time.

Events cause shifts in data trends. Baker and Richards (2004) outlined three types of events in data. The first is a level shift, epitomizing sustained change, where an event shifts a mean value from one level to another, and the new mean continues for a period of time without returning to prior levels. The second is a temporary change, where gradually the effects of the event erode, and the new mean reverts back to the previous "old" mean. Closely related is a one-time response, the third type of change. In such an instance an event causes a disruption in a sequence, only to be short lived, with the value quickly returning to the original mean value (see Figure 11.1). The change can either be negative or positive in direction.

Events may be lengthy processes from beginning to end. The evaluation of events, or treatments, are complicated by the fact that often initiatives are not given time to gestate before a response occurs.

From a research perspective, treatments, or events, are of primary interest. Analytically, there are several ways to conduct time analyses. We

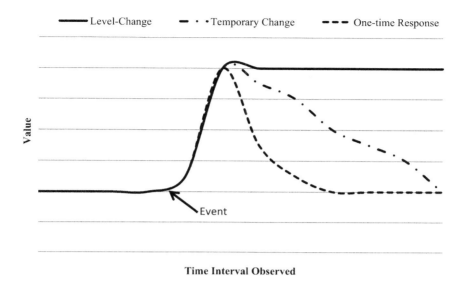

──── Level-Change ▬ · · Temporary Change ▬ ▬ ▬ One-time Response

Value

Event

Time Interval Observed

Figure 11.1.   Three types of changes in temporal data.

briefly outline a few major categories of methods, providing further sum-marization in Table 11.2, to provide a general overview. Each overview is just the beginning to countless revisions and evolutions that attempt to account for weaknesses in the models. Readers are encouraged to learn more about each method as appropriate to their research needs.

Synthetic Cohorts

Synthetic cohorts are one evolution of cross-sectional analysis including follow-back designs that attempt to look at data retrospectively. Synthetic cohorts differ in that the cohort is developed around an event of interest, such as college graduation, relying on data both before and after the event of interest (Campbell & Hudson, 1985). These pre- and post-event data are then utilized for analytical purposes to answer questions of interest.

In higher education finance, synthetic cohorts have been applied to calculate lifetime earnings estimates for various levels of educational attainment (e.g., "The College Payoff").

Table 11.2. Overview of Time-Based Groupings and Analysis

Concept	Description	Strength	Weakness
Similar Groups			
Cohorts	Representative of population defined by some characteristic(s)	Allows for trend analysis	Groupings may be purposeful or not; Groupings may be a result of self-selection that is unaccounted for in the use and interpretation
Cohort Survival Rates	Uses cross-sectional data from one stage/ category to project into the future	Can be applied to existing data to provide estimates; Simplicity makes it comparatively easier to understand than other options	Cohort mobility and mortality
Matched set	The aim is to remove the influence of change in measurements over time due to the addition or attrition of units under analysis by studying only units available during all observations	Changes over time are not influenced by units entering or leaving the dataset during the observed time period	Leaves out some data
Propensity Score (Matching)	The aim is to imitate a balance between two groups on a set of pre-treatment variables that would be observed in a randomized experiment; Propensity scores may be used for matching, weighting, or as a regression covariate	Pre-treatment variables are condensed to one number; The balancing process assists in determining if assembled data can be used for causal purposes	Process usually fails when relying on routine demographic variables; Requires substantial knowledge about the selection process; Much still needs to be known about the statistical qualities of a propensity score, such as balancing, various uses, and appropriate estimates of standard errors

(Table continues on next page)

Table 11.2. Continued

Concept	Description	Strength	Weakness
Time-Based Analysis			
Synthetic Cohorts	The aim is to develop a cohort based upon the occurrence of an event of interest, such as college graduation	Can be applied to existing data to provide estimates; Similar amounts of pre and post event data are available; Each subject acts as the control	Not a true cohort; Assumptions may not hold true
Event History Analysis	The aim is to understand the causes of an event for those who experience it	Follows individual for a period of time	Unknown, or censored data, can bias the analysis; Explanatory variables may vary in time
Regression Discontinuity Design	Accounts for measurement error around a point of demarcation	Closely resembles a natural experiment given natural error in measurement	Findings are most relevant for data close to the point of demarcation (cut score)

Event History Analysis

At its core, event history analysis models attempt to understand what may cause an event—such as taking out college loans—to happen. Allison (1984) noted that "there is no single method of event history analysis but rather a collection of related methods that sometimes compete but more often complement each other" (p. 10).

Regression Discontinuity Design

Regression discontinuity design is a method that has been compared to random assignment (Cook, 2008). The rationale for using regression discontinuity design is that the selection process is completely known because there is an assignment score, or a cut-score. This is like an experiment because there is error in any measurement, so a chance exists that the subject may be above or below the cut-score.

SUMMARY

In this chapter, we examined ways in which the construction and application of groups and events influence fiscal analysis. The purpose of this chapter was to introduce the topics and issues for consideration, with the realization that, in some cases, the topics and methodologies introduced will require further extensive study.

CHAPTER 12

PRESENTING RESEARCH TO AN AUDIENCE OF POLICYMAKERS

It is a challenge to present data in a manner so that an audience of policy-makers will be interested. An effective presentation requires presenters to first know how knowledgeable their audience is about the topic and then to understand that other interested parties, such as press and members of the higher education community who are very knowledgeable about the topic and are interested in the details, will likely be present. The need then is to inform policymakers without overwhelming them with details: to balance the general and the specific.

INFORMING AND EDUCATING

While the purpose of presenting information to a policy audience is primarily to advise, a framework for interacting with policy audiences may be centered around two objectives: to inform and to educate. Researchers complain that their work is not connected to policy, and policy analysts complain that research is out of touch with what really matters. Part of this debate or discussion has to do with the unit of analysis being examined and the timeliness of the topic. There also is a part of the disconnect that has to do with the way data are presented.

Before presenting data, it is helpful to understand the difference between policy-related work and academic research. Majchrzak (1984) described the nature of policy research in terms of its focus and action-orientation. Research has either a technical focus or one based on a fundamental social problem. Technically focused research can have either a low action orientation (policy analysis) or a high action orientation (technical research). Fundamentally based research can have a low action orientation (traditional academic research) or a high action orientation (policy research). The question for academic researchers then becomes, how do I make my research more action-oriented? Majchrzak asserts that policy research scrutinizes all possible options to solving a fundamental problem, rather than just documenting the problem.

It is possible to conduct research that serves both academic and policy audiences. The difficulty comes in determining how to take the same bits of data and present those in different ways: to inform and to educate. The practice of informing and educating are not mutually exclusive. There are, however, defining characteristics of each.

Informing

Information in and of itself is descriptive in nature. The goal of informing is to share data with little to no interpretation of what the data might mean.

A Single Data Point

The most basic type of information to share is a data point. The right data point has the ability to stand on its own. When constructing single data points, assume the audience does not have background knowledge on the topic.

The single data point may also serve to elicit the interest of the reader for more information. For example, one data point is "84% of community college students work."

For researchers, a thorough study that attempted to resolve a research question will result in a single data point. For policy analysts, this may be a single value. In both cases, the resulting data point connects to either a more elaborate study or other data points.

There are limitations to the use of a single data point, however. In many cases a stand-alone, single data point is neither sufficient nor appropriate. Consider the cost-per-completer metric we discussed in Chapter 9. Applying this metric to an institution that has multiple missions is misleading. A conversation about a population, in this case the implied relationship of success of all students to cost, should include data points that describe outcomes for all members of the population.

Multiple Data Points on a Topic

A single point of data can stand by on its own, but without context, it tells the reader very little. When combined with other data points, greater detail starts to emerge. Expanding our previous example, 84% of community college students work, and 60% work more than 20 hours each week. Without saying it, these two data points lead the reader to think more critically about the first data point without the author having to provide commentary.

In other cases, multiple data points can provide a comprehensive picture of a topic. Consider, for example, enrollments. There are several ways to count enrollments, such as fall headcounts of all students; first-time, full time students; 12-month unduplicated students; and full-time equivalent students. Providing all these data in one place can be informative to the reader, as the reader will begin to see there are multiple ways to determine how many students an institution serves as depicted in Chapter 2, Table 2.2.

Multiple Data Points on Multiple Topics

There are also times when, through experience, researchers understand that certain questions are continually asked. In such cases, it is helpful to develop a fact sheet, also referred to as a one-sheet. Whether it applies to institutions, a state system, or a sector of postsecondary education, a one-sheet that presents all of the relevant data is an important tool for communicating with policy audiences. A one-sheet has the added benefit that legislators and other policymakers are more likely to read a one-page document than a multiple-page treatise.

A tool for researchers (and often a requirement for institutional researchers) is the compilation of a fact or data book. Fact/data books present multiple data points on multiple topics about an institution, state system, or sector in one volume. In the state of Illinois since 1966, for example, the Illinois Community College Board has released a compilation of statistics about each college in the system. The U.S. Department of Education has released the *Digest of Education Statistics* annually, save two instances, since 1962. In both cases, a short narrative may introduce a section of the volume and highlight trends; however, the publications provide multiple data points on multiple topics.

The criticism to data/fact books and sheets is that these types of publications, consisting of primarily figures and data tables, are dumps of administrative data. It is, however, one way to describe the state of institutional finances and serves as a resource for further analysis and commentary. To mitigate this criticism, many institutions and systems have gone to the use of dashboards as discussed in Chapter 6. Dashboards present a significant amount of data in a very brief form with some analysis.

The saying "A picture is worth a thousand words" could be rewritten to say, "A picture is worth approximately three written pages." Advancements in technology allow information to be communicated visually more readily than ever before. One only needs to look at the various templates provided by software programs to see the demand for and appreciation of presenting a polished visual.

One form of building a narrative is to use an infographic—*or string of related data points presented visually*—to tell a story. The data points can be sequential (i.e., point 1 is a precursor to point 2) or relational in their orientation. To researchers, infographics may be seen as a parallel to conceptual models, where the connections between data, resulting from previous research, are tied together to describe a theorized network of activities.

Educating

George Orwell once wrote "The great enemy of clear language is insincerity" (1946, p. 116). By this he suggests that one should be direct and purposeful in what he or she writes, rather than indirect through expansions of literary eloquence and profuse posturing as a way to come to describe the point one wishes to convey.

Writing for a Policy Audience

Writing for a policy audience is fundamentally about building a narrative. It attempts to pull together the relevant data on an issue of importance. It may be presented as an executive summary or a policy/issue brief.

For academic researchers, writing policy briefs requires a mental shift in the way information is presented. Rather than applying the general structure of a research paper—where one introduces the problem, builds upon the literature to inform the reader, states the purpose of the paper, describes the methodology, and then delineates and answers the research question(s)—the focus is on the problem and supporting data from the start. The structure is not set.

Some feel briefs should loosely represent a research paper: a problem statement, a purpose followed by an outline of topics addressed in the brief, and a discussion of each topic. Another perspective is that a brief should be structured as either a persuasive or argumentative essay. The former aligns more closely with a data-informed examination of the issue, whereas the latter may be more reflective of an advocacy position. In cases where policy requires changes to current law, the audience you may be trying to influence with your work may be more familiar with argumentative essays than research reports. Ultimately, the work environment and purpose for the brief will dictate which structure is appropriate. Baker and Richards (2004) and Majschrak (1984), among numerous others, put forth model structures for research and analytic reports.

If you want the policymaker to read your document, make it brief—a general rule is that board members, legislators, governors, or congresspersons will read one page; a chief staff person will read two to three pages; and interns will read complete documents. Include an executive summary as well as a summary and conclusion section, even in a "brief."

Concise analyses of data have become increasingly common. For example, the National Student Clearinghouse has established a research center that fairly frequently releases data "snapshots" consisting of a few graphs with text that speaks directly to the data as presented without providing interpretation or analysis. Others groups, such as the Economic Policy Institute, incorporate a data visual with a brief description and commentary as part of a blog. These data are often extracts from a larger report. The essential elements include a title, subtitle, a chart (rarely, if ever, a table), three to five sentences of commentary, and a link to a document from which the chart was extracted. By embedding a link to a longer document, these one-page documents serve as gateways to additional research.

Presenting to a Policy Audience

No matter what one writes, it is likely the case that it will eventually have to be presented to an audience. One way to present information is through a speech or lecture, methods that have their place and rely on a strong narrative to capture the listeners' attention. Another method is through a formal presentation in person or through synchronous or asynchronous technologies—at this point often utilizing presentation software such as Microsoft PowerPoint.

The focus in presentations should be on the visuals. People learn better from visuals and narrative rather than from words alone. Reading the same text displayed on the screen actually confuses the audience, as reading and listening to the same thing at once is difficult, and people can only hold a limited amount of information in their brain at once (Harrington, Bers, Carr, Daly, Kalb, & Ronco, 2012).

Additionally, the automatic levels built into software programs like PowerPoint can minimize equally important data through the size of the text displayed. PowerPoint and similar systems also require complex information to be truncated into a few words, when they are used rather than a visual that is then explained verbally.

When presenting to policy audiences, it is helpful to present the problem, then the data to support the findings in a visual format (table, figure, etc.), and at the end of each research question or topic, a summary of the main points. Think of it as telling a story, ending with a clear message. Do not talk for a time period beyond that designated for your presentation; practice your presentation beforehand, and time it to ensure you can complete it within the allotted time.

Finally, when creating the presentation, think through the elements of designing a presentation including, but not limited to, using a plain background, using a font such as Calibri that does not have a serif, keeping all fonts at 18 point or larger, using phrases rather than sentences, decluttering the presentation by removing graphics unless absolutely necessary, and using bullets sparingly.

Communicating to a Policy Audience

Thus far this chapter has addressed the presentation of information in written formats. What is also important to discuss is the most effective way to present the data you have gathered and the knowledge you have obtained. While each person develops their own communication style and professional presence, this section provides advice from the experience of the authors. We first outline a few rules of thumb to consider when presenting to an audience of policymakers and then share input for how to interact with the press or media.

There are certain lessons one learns from experience. While not exhaustive, there are a few we have learned along the way.

1. You are trying to help the policymakers communicate an idea to their constituencies. If you approach the presentation from the perspective of what would the policymakers' constituents want to hear rather than what you think is most important, it is more likely that the presentation will be received well.

2. Credibility is your most important characteristic. Be explicit with your data and its limitations and sources. Only answer the questions you can at the time, but be sure to follow-up on the ones you cannot answer. Do not make up answers. Admit that you cannot answer the question right now and get back as quickly as possible with the answer.

3. Provide both quantitative and qualitative data to support your points. If you are discussing the impact of an intervention on affordability, have a story or two about what you have researched. If you are talking about student experiences with the student finan-

cial aid process, provide some type of data relating to how many people are served by student financial aid to quantify its prevalence. Legislators are moved by anecdotal stories from their constituents, so having an anecdote from one of the legislator's constituents will help make your point.

4. You will not be the only expert relied upon to make a policy decision. Savvy leaders will, in fact, ask the same question of multiple researchers and compare the information.

5. Clarify if you are using actual, estimated, or revised values. This is especially important if you are talking about appropriated funds that can change during an academic year.

6. Accept alternative interpretations where plausible. Data can be seen through multiple lenses, not only the one you apply. Be gracious when an alternative is suggested, but stand by your particular interpretation when needed.

7. You know you have done a good job if you are asked back to present again, assuming you were asked to give the presentation in the first place.

8. Remember that the three "Cs" of policy analysis impact are primacy, frequency, and recency. In presenting to policymakers, be there first, be there often, and be there last.

Interacting With the Press and Media

Members of the press will call you, an identified expert or knowledgeable source, for one of three reasons. First, they are exploring a topic and trying to obtain general information to develop or frame their story. If they are early in the research process and fishing around, it may be an indication that they think of you as an expert and are testing different ideas with you to better understand how best to approach the topic. Second, the press may already have the story framed and are looking for more information, and perhaps your perspective, on the issue. Finally, the press person already has what they want you to say in mind and is trying to get you to say it.

When interacting with the press, it is appropriate to suggest that you will provide any background information—that is, information that is not to be quoted—and that, upon more fully understanding what is being asked, you are happy to provide an appropriate quote and/or provide a specific piece of information. It has been our experience that the press will attempt to get you talking about the topic in general, to develop a rapport with you. Upon doing so, they may then try to catch you off guard and ask the question they really wanted answered with the aspiration you will respond without fully realizing it or thinking it through.

When contacted by the press about work you have completed, several practical suggestions come from our experiences. First, be available. Reporters are often on a tight deadline. If you happen to be away from the office, get back to the media as quickly as possible. Second, be sure to have a set of talking points coming from the research, and stick to those talking points. These can, and often do, form the foundation of a press release. Do not make up data on the fly. Third, have a list of others familiar with your research or analysis and the topic to which you can refer the reporter.

DATA VISUALIZATION

After the data are collected, checked for quality, coded, recoded, and analyzed, the resulting information needs to be communicated in a manner that is accessible. By accessible, we refer specifically to both an academic audience as well as a general audience. While accompanying written material speaks to your understanding of the topic and is necessary for answering questions, how you present data will lend to building the utility of your data. Together, accessibility and utility speak to your credibility.

A focus on visual presentation of information is critical as most people learn better from narrative accompanied by visuals rather than from words alone. A proper visual presentation of data reinforces the points you are making.

Presenting Quantitative Data

The old adage "lies, damn lies, and statistics" endures for a reason. If your intent is to develop work for the purpose of causing action, or at least careful contemplation or consideration, then a transparent presentation is a must. Data may be presented as a table or a figure.

Elements of a Table

This discussion of an effective table will be informed by comparing Table 12.1a to Table 12.1b. Table 12.1a reflects a slide common to any presentation of a university budget or research session. While minimally sufficient, there are ways this table may be enhanced without detracting from the message, as exemplified in Table 12.1b.

Table 12.1a. Enrollment at Hudson University

	Undergraduate Enrollment				
Year	*Estimated Fall Headcount*	*Total Fall Headcount*	*First Time, Full Time[a] Fall Headcount*	*12-Month Unduplicated Headcount*	*FTE[b]*
2000–2001					
2001–2002					
2002–2003					
2003–2004					
2004–2005					
2005–2006					
2006–2007					
2007–2008					
2008–2009					
2009–2010					
2010–2011					

Table 12.1b. Undergraduate Enrollment at Hudson University: 2000–2001 to 2010–2011

	Undergraduate Enrollment				
	Fall Headcount			*12-Month Unduplicated Headcount*	*FTE[b]*
Academic Year	*Estimated*	*Total*	*First Time, Full Time[a]*		
2000–2001					
2001–2002					
2002–2003					
2003–2004					
2004–2005					
2005–2006					
2006–2007					
2007–2008					
2008–2009					
2009–2010					
2010–2011					

Note: Undergraduate data are presented because this presentation focuses on funding at the undergraduate level. Funding for graduate and professional students are treated differently by the state and institution and therefore beyond the scope of this presentation.

    a. First-time, full time students are a proxy for traditional, freshman students.

    b. Full-time equivalent (FTE) students are determined by dividing the total number of credit hours by 30.

Source: National Center for Education Statistics (2012a).

Title of the Figure or Table

Specificity of the title is very important; stay away from vague words such as "some," "many," or "few." There is a substantial difference between enrollments that include undergraduate, graduate, and first professional students, and only undergraduate enrollments. Descriptive information that clarifies any potential confusion needs to be provided.

When discussing financial data that reflect a point, or points, in time, it is important to include the year to which the data refer. In Table 12.1a, this information is missing.

Table Elements

Specificity matters within the table as well, where it serves to clarify ambiguous terms. The term "year" as constructed in postsecondary education primarily refers to either an academic year or a fiscal year, though it may also be interpreted as a calendar year. Further, similar constructions of the word "year" may apply to different periods in time. A fiscal year may cover the same period of time as a calendar year, for example. In the two tables (12.1a and 12.1b), utilizing the term "year" is vague and may mislead the reader.

Specificity can extend beyond the words used to include the presentation of information with similar characteristics. For example, fall headcount enrollment can represent the total, an estimated total, or first-time, full-time students. Rather than creating separate columns Total Fall Headcount, Estimated Total Fall Headcount Enrollment, and First-time, Full-time Fall Headcount Enrollment (Table 12.1a), spanner heads may be created.

A narrow column should exist between columns to separate the data. This is especially important when more than one spanner head is used.

Source

Providing data without a source at the bottom of a figure or table is not an acceptable practice. Publishing formats vary in the amount of information required; however, at a minimum, a source should include the author(s) and year. A more detailed citation can be included in either accompanying materials, if presenting information from an available paper, or, if giving a presentation on slides, in an appendix.

Notes

A general note can be included to clarify the table. Specific notes, identified by notes in the table, provide exacting information such as a definition or outline a calculation. For example, note "b" clarifies to the reader what an FTE is in relation to enrollment; FTE are determined by dividing the total number of credit hours by 30.

Elements of a Figure

A figure can present tabular data in a visual format or may be a linked set of related ideas. For the purposes of this chapter, we will focus on the display of tabular data.

Like tables, figures need to be properly labeled. Accompanying detail should also be included in notes. In one of the most popular books on statistics, titled "How to Lie with Statistics," Huff (1954) suggested that figures may be misleading if they had the following characteristics: 1) graphs presented out of proportion; 2), graphs starting at a value other than zero (see Figure 12.1); or 3), in the case of pictograms, the size of the image changes in more than one dimension. For example, if a pictogram was intended to show a 100% increase, yet it was expanded both vertically and horizontally, the resulting image would actually represent a 300% increase. Wong (2010) suggests the y-axis does not have to start at 0 when depicting nondiscreet values.

PRESENTING QUALITATIVE DATA

When thinking of a way to present data, the use of words may not immediately come to mind. However, there are a couple of ways that words are being used to communicate findings.

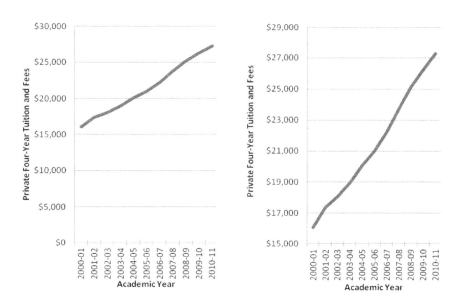

Figure 12.1.   Two ways to depict the same data

One way is to identify terms that are important to the topic you are studying. In the case of postsecondary finance, terms such as "affordability," "cost," and "working" are barriers that research (Heller, 1997; Cook & King, 2007) has found to influence college going and completion. Interviews with college students that afterwards quantify the use of these terms may be one informative way to display qualitative data. *The New York Times* (Corum, 2011) applied the method of capturing word frequency, then displaying the frequency using circles of various sizes to represent the magnitude of frequency, to commencement speeches for college class of 2011.

Another, fairly popular method is a word cloud. A word cloud is a visual depiction of word usage. The more frequently a word was used, the larger the word was presented in the cloud. The cloud, then, is an arrangement of frequently used words. A critic (Harris, 2011) of word clouds suggests that clouds present data only without providing a common theme or narrative; for example, a word cloud about a war that has the word "car" as the largest and biggest word in the cloud does not tell the reader much about the role of "car" in the war. Harris' strongest complaint is that word clouds merely describe events and may be inappropriate to explain events. This is a point to which researchers should give careful consideration.

There is a difference between using words as captured by interviews, focus groups, and other qualitative approaches and presenting the words together with financial data as context and applying a mixed-method approach where one form of inquiry informs the other. From a research perspective, the latter signifies greater rigor. In policy research, employing more than one approach is often necessary to best address the issue of interest, as it allows for the use of "hard" data and includes the voice of stakeholders.

Morse (2003) provides an overview of mixed methods approaches where four multi-method designs are categorized as qualitatively driven and four are categorized as quantitatively driven. The interaction of qualitative and quantitative approaches can be either simultaneous or sequential. In simultaneous designs both approaches drive the study at the same time, with one approach taking precedence. For example, a quantitative approach and a qualitative approach are employed at the same time. In sequential designs, one approach informs the second approach. For example, a qualitatively driven project is supplemented by a quantitative project.

ELEMENTS OF DESIGN

Publishing in peer-reviewed or edited outlets often requires adherence to a certain format set forth either in a style guide or in a publication manual such as American Psychological Association, Modern Language Association, or Chicago style manuals. There are instances, however, where the traditional formats limit the ability to present research results and findings in a more considered manner.

Outside of required publication formats, researchers have the liberty to decide how their information is to be shared in presentations, blogs, infographics, or when working with a graphic designer. In such instances, it helps to have a basic understanding of two design elements: color and typeface.

Color

Color combinations can elicit certain emotions or feelings. The book *My Many Colored Days* by Dr. Seuss (1996) clearly demonstrates the connection between color and emotions.

Because each color has a quality (Whelan, 1994), it can contribute to, or distract from, the presentation of research results and findings. For example, the color red evokes strength and aggression and is not a color one would want to use when presenting sensitive data. Blue, which conveys calmness and dominance, may be a better choice.

Color	Related Feeling
Red	strength and aggression
Orange	optimism and positive social interaction
Yellow	cheerfulness and competence, trust
Green	balance, growth, self-reliance
Blue	calmness and dominance
Purple	creativity
Turquoise	clarity of thought
Magenta	harmony, balance
Pink	immaturity, silliness
Brown	security, protection
Grey	compromise
Gold	success, achievement

The meaning of a color may vary by culture. If a color scheme is selected for a purpose, it is worthwhile to reference a source, such as the infographics colors in culture by McCandless (2009), to ensure you are utilizing a culturally appropriate hue. It may also be the case, when presenting to an institution, that a set of school colors carries a different meaning and may be appropriate or appreciated by the audience.

While colors alone can connote certain emotions, they may also be combined into one of ten color schemes that are used by many word processing programs (see Table 12.2). Each color scheme depicts how colors from the color wheel are grouped or how tints and shades (adding white or black) provide a spectrum of the same hue.

Table 12.2.   Color Schemes

Color Scheme	Description
Complementary	A color and its direct opposite on the color wheel
Clash	A color and a color either to the right or left of its complement on the color wheel
Split Complementary	A color and the two colors on either side of its complementary color
Primary	The application of red, blue, and yellow
Secondary	The application of green, violet, and orange
Tertiary	The application of red-orange, yellow-green, and blue-violet or blue-green, yellow-orange, and red-violet
Achromatic	The application of black, grey, and white
Analogous	The application of three consecutive colors on the color wheel
Monochromatic	The application of one color in combination with its shades and tints
Neutral	The application of a color that has been neutralized by the addition of black or its complementary color

When harmonized, color schemes project meaning, such as royalty, dependability, professionalism, elegance, or richness (Sutton & Whelan, 2004; Whelan, 1994). For example the deep hues of blue, burgundy, tan, and green express traditional themes.

In a practical example, when discussing revenue sources you may want to use a monochromatic scheme for the various revenue sources to indicate they are all similar.

Naturally, expenditures are the opposite of revenues; therefore, it would be appropriate to express expenditures in a complementary color. If presenting two types of expenditures (i.e., restricted and unrestricted) and one revenue source, it may be appropriate to use a split complementary color scheme to reinforce the contrast; orange for revenues and light blue for restricted expenditures and dark blue for unrestricted expenditures.

In another example, statistically significant data displayed in a figure can be identified with a complementary color to make it stand out. The same could be true for the presentation of data for control and treatment groups.

To display data for a specific university, often the institution's colors are used. For example, a figure for major research universities' expenditures per student might use red for Indiana, green for Michigan State, navy blue for the University of Michigan, burnt orange for University of Texas Austin, maroon for Arizona State University, and so on.

While the colors you choose to use will not change the findings or results of your analysis, when considered appropriately, colors can support your narrative while adding to the professional appearance of your presentation. Such actions suggest that you are making a decision with a purpose and therefore moving beyond standard color scheme templates available in software packages.

Typeface

While used interchangeably, typeface and font are not synonymous. Typeface refers to the design of the letter form, whereas font refers to the standard delivery of the letter form in its size for example (Lupton, 2010).

Typeface has its own affiliated mood that can be emphasized if italicized, bolded, or by adjusting spacing (Götz, 1998). Italic forms were created to give an impression of handwritten letters. They are therefore of value in presenting qualitative work. However, *too many italic words next to each other may diminish the impact of font.* Lupton (2010) portrays the use of various fonts as a mixing bowl, where each word has its own identity.

Fonts can be used as a means of expression. ALL CAPITALS GIVE THE APPEARANCE YOU ARE SHOUTING, fonts with serifs connote traditional values and honesty, whereas san serif fonts seem modern and less traditional (Garfield, 2010).

When selecting font for a word cloud or other presentation of information, it is important to think about what the font conveys rather than selecting your favorites. Does the font communicate the findings appropriately?

CONCLUSION

How you present your research can be as important as the quality and content of that research. Presenting research results to a policy audience can be stressful, no matter how many times you have presented the same data, and even to the same audience. It is wise to remember, especially when presenting to elected officials, that they were elected, and you were not. Politics does enter into the effectiveness of your presentation and to the believability of your results. Although it should not matter what political party you personally align with, remember to keep any political opinions to yourself and present material in a totally non-biased manner. Answer questions honestly, and if you don't know the answer, say so, but get back with the answer as soon as possible.

In the long run, if your research is done well and presented in a professional manner, you likely will be asked back to lend your expertise to policymakers. Good luck.

REFERENCES

Abowd, J. M., Stephens, B. E., Vilhuber, L., Andersson, F., McKinney, K. L., Roemer, M., & Woodcock, S. (2005). *The LEHD infrastructure files and the creation of quarterly workforce indicators* (Technical Paper No. TP-2006-01). Washington, DC: U.S. Census Bureau, Longitudinal Employer—Household Dynamics.

Advisory Committee on Student Financial Assistance. (2008). *Apply to succeed: Ensuring community college students benefit from need-based financial aid.* Washington, DC: Author. Retrieved from http://www2.ed.gov/about/bdscomm/list/acsfa/applytosucceed.pdf

Albright, B. (2010). *Reinventing higher education funding policies: Performance funding 2.0—funding degrees.* Paper for the Making Opportunity Affordable Initiative of the Lumina Foundation.

Allison, P. D. (1984). *Event history analysis: Regression for longitudinal event data* (Sage University Paper series on Quantitative Applications in the Social Sciences, No. 07-046). Thousand Oaks, CA: SAGE.

American Association of Community Colleges. (n.d.). Community college growth by decade. Washington, DC: Author. Retrieved August 1, 2007 from http://www.aacc.nche.edu/Content/NavigationMenu/AboutCommunityColleges/HistoricalInformation/CCGrowth/CCGrowth.htm

American Association of State Colleges and Universities. (2007). *Tuition discounting at AASCU institutions.* Washington, DC: Author.

American Association of State Colleges and Universities. (2013). *Top ten higher education state policy issues for 2013.* Washington, DC: AASCU.

Anderson, G. L. (1976). *Land-grant universities and their continuing challenge.* East Lansing, MI: Michigan State University Press.

Ashworth, K. H. (1994). *Formula recommendations for funding Texas institutions of higher education.* Austin, TX: Texas Higher Education Coordinating Board.

Association of Governing Boards. (2012). *Tuition discounting.* Washington, DC: AGB.

Association of Private Sector Colleges. & Universities. v. Duncan, 870 F. Supp. 2d., (D.D.C. 2012). *Association of Private Colleges and Universities v. Duncan* (D.D.C. 2013).

Astin, A. W. (1985). *Achieving academic excellence.* San Francisco, CA: Jossey-Bass.

Auguste, B. G., Cota, A., Jayaram, K., & Laboissiere, M. C. A. (2010). *Winning by degrees: The strategies of highly-productive higher education institutions.* Boston, MA: McKinsey & Company.

Bailey, T. & Xu, D. (2012). *Input-adjusted graduation rates and college accountability: What is known from twenty years of research?* New York, NY: Teachers College Columbia University.

Baime, D. S. & Mullin, C. M. (2011, July). *Promoting educational opportunity: The Pell Grant program at community colleges* (Policy Brief 2011-03PBL). Washington, DC: American Association of Community Colleges.

Baker, B. D., & Richards, C. E. (2004). *The ecology of educational systems: Data, models, and tools for improvisational leading and learning.* Upper Saddle River, NJ: Pearson Education.

Bannock, G., Baxter, R. E., & Davis, E. (1992). *The Penguin dictionary of economics* (5th ed.). New York, NY: Penguin Books.

Banta, T. W. (Ed.) (1986). *Performance funding in higher education: A critical analysis of Tennessee's experience.* Boulder, CO: National Center for Higher Education Management Systems.

Banta, T. W.. & Moffett, M. S. (1987). Performance funding in Tennessee: Stimulus for program improvement. *New Directions in Higher Education, 59,* 35–43.

Banta, T. W., Rudolph, L. B., VanDyke, J., & Fisher, H. S. (1996). Performance funding comes of age in Tennessee. *Journal of Higher Education, 67*(1), 23–45.

Baskin, P. (2012). Public no longer? NSF sounds alarm over cuts at state research universities. *Chronicle of Higher Education.* P. 1. October 5.

Baum, S., & Lapovsky, L. (2006). *Tuition discounting: Not just a private college practice.* New York, NY: College Board.

Baum, S., & Ma, J. (2007). *Education pays: The benefits of higher education for individuals and society.* Washington, DC: College Board.

Baum, S., & Ma, J. (2012). *Trends in college pricing 2012.* Washington, DC: College Board.

Baum, S., Lapovsky, L. & Ma, J. (2010). *Tuition discounting: Institutional aid patterns at public and private colleges and universities.* New York, NY: College Board.

Becker, G. (1964). *Human capital.* Chicago, IL: University of Chicago Press.

Becker, G. (1971). *The economics of discrimination.* Chicago, IL: University of Chicago Press.

Becker, G. (1976). *Economic approach to human behavior.* Chicago, IL: University of Chicago Press.

Berger, M. C., & Black, D. A. (1993). *The long-run economic impact of Kentucky public institutions of higher education.* Lexington, KY: Center for Business and Economic Research, University of Kentucky.

Berne, R., & Stiefel, L. (1984). *The measurement of equity in school finance: Conceptual, methodological, and empirical dimensions.* Baltimore, MD: The Johns Hopkins University Press.

Bers, T. (2012). Surveys and benchmarks. *New Directions for Institutional Research, 153,* 33–48.

Bettinger, E. P, Long, B. T., Oreopoulos, P., & Sanbonmatsu, L. (2009, September). *The role of simplification and information in college decisions: Results from the*

H&R Block FAFSA experiment (NBER Working Paper No. 15361). Retrieved from www.nber.org/papers/w15361

Betts, J. R., & McFarland, L. L. (1995). Safe port in a storm: The impact of labor market conditions on community college enrollments. *Journal of Human Resources, 30*(4), 741–765.

Biemiller, L. (2012, April 5). Tuition discounts rise again, but their effectiveness lags. *Chronicle of Higher Education*, p. 1.

Blackwell, M., Cobb, S., & Weinberg, D. (2002). The economic impact of educational institutions: Issues and methodology. *Economic Development Quarterly, 16*(1), 88–95.

Board of Governors of the State University System of Florida. (2012). *Economic contributions of the State University System of Florida in fiscal year 2009–10*. Tallahassee, FL: State University System of Florida.

Bogue, E., & Brown, W. (1982). Performance incentives for state colleges. *Harvard Business Review, 60*, 123–128.

Boling, E. J. (1961). *Methods of objectifying the allocation of tax funds to Tennessee state colleges*. Nashville, TN: George Peabody College of Vanderbilt University.

Bowen, H. (1972). *Who benefits from higher education—and who should pay?* Washington, DC: American Association for Higher Education.

Bowen, H. R. (1980). *The costs of higher education*. San Francisco, CA: Jossey-Bass.

Bradburn, E. M., & Hurst, D. G. (2001, May). *Community college transfer rates to 4-year institutions using alternative definitions of transfer* [NCES 2001–197]. Washington, DC: U.S. Department of Education, National Center for Education Statistics.

Brademas, J. (1983). Foreword. In R. H. Fenske & R. P. Huff (Eds.), *Handbook of student financial aid* (pp. ix - xii). San Francisco, CA: Jossey-Bass.

Brainard, J., & Hermes, J. J. (2008, March 28). Colleges earmarks grow amid criticism. *Chronicle of Higher Education*, p. 5.

Brinkman, P. T. (1989). Instructional costs per student credit hour: Differences by level of instruction. *Journal of Education Finance, 15*(1), 34–52.

Brinkman, P. T. (1990). Higher education cost functions. In S. A. Hoenack & E. Collins, *The economics of American universities* (p. 139). Albany, NY: State University of New York Press.

Brinkman, P., & Leslie, L. (1986). Economies of scale in higher education: Sixty years of research. *Review of Higher Education, 10*(1), 1–28.

Broomall, L. W., McMahon, B. T., McLaughlin, G. W., & Patton, S. S. (1978). *Economies of scale in higher education*. Blacksburg, VA: Virginia Polytechnic Institute Office of Institutional Research.

Brubacher, J. S., & Rudy, W. (1997). *Higher education in transition: A history of American colleges and universities* (4th ed.). New Brunswick, NJ: Transaction.

Bureau of Labor Statistics. (2012). *Education pays...* Washington, DC: U.S. Department of Labor.

Burke, J. C. (1997). *Performance-funding indicators: Concerns, values, and models for two-and four-year colleges and universities*. Albany, NY: The Nelson A. Rockefeller Institute of Government.

Burke, J. C. (1998). Performance funding: Arguments and answers. *New Directions for Institutional Research, 97*, 85–90.

Burke, J. C. (2000, February). *The new accountability performance reporting and funding*. Presentation to the House Commission on Postsecondary Education, Subcommittee on Institutional Efficiency.

Burke, J. C. (2003). The new accountability for public higher education: From regulation to results. *Journal of University Evaluation of National Institute for Academic Degrees.*

Burke, J. C. (2004a). *Achieving accountability in higher education: Balancing public, academic, and market demands.* San Francisco, CA: Jossey-Bass.

Burke, J. C. (2004b). Balancing all sides of the accountability triangle. *Association of Governing Boards of Universities and Colleges, Trusteeship, 12*(6).

Burke, J. C. (2006, September/November). Closing the accountability gap for public universities: Putting academic departments in the performance loop. *Planning for Higher Education*, 19–27. Retrieved from http://www.rockinst.org/pdf/education/2005-11-closing_the_accountability_gap_for_public_universities_putting_academic_departments_in_the_performance_loop.pdf

Burke, J. S., & Minassians, H. (2003). Performance Reporting: "Real" Accountability or Accountability "Lite" Seventh Annual Survey 2003. State University of New York, NY: The Nelson A. Rockefeller Institute of Government.

Burke, J. C. & Modarresi, S. (2000). To keep or not keep performance funding: Signals from stakeholders. *The Journal of Higher Education, 71*(4), 432–454.

Burke, J. C., Rosen, J., Minassians, H., & Lessard, T. (2000). *Performance funding and budgeting: An emerging merger? The fourth annual survey.* Albany, NY: The Nelson A. Rockefeller Institute of Government.

Burke, J. C., & Serban, A. M. (1998a). Performance funding for higher education: Fad or trend? *New Directions for Institutional Research, 97.*

Burke, J. C., & Serban, A. (1998b). State synopses of performance funding programs. *New Directions for Institutional Research, 97*, 25–48.

Caffrey, J. & Isaacs, H. H. (1971). *Estimating the impact of a college or university on the local economy.* Washington, DC: American Council on Education.

Calcagro, J. C., Bailey, T., Jenkins, D., Krenzl, G., & Leinbranch, T. (2008). Community college success: What institutional characteristics make a difference? *Economics of Education Review, 27*(6), 632–645.

California Student Aid Commission. (2012, November 7). *2013–2014 student expense budgets.* Retrieved from http://www.csac.ca.gov/pubs/forms/grnt_frm/studentexpensebudget.pdf

Campbell, R. T., & Hudson, C. M. (1985). Synthetic cohorts from panel surveys: An approach to studying rare events. *Research on Aging, 7*(1), 81–93.

Carl D. Perkins Career and Technical Education Improvement Act of 2006. (2006). Pub. L. No. 109-270, 120 STAT. 683.

Carnegie Commission on Higher Education. (1970a). *A chance to learn: An action agenda for equal opportunity in higher education.* New York, NY: McGraw-Hill.

Carnegie Commission on Higher Education. (1970b). *The open-door colleges.* New York, NY: McGraw-Hill.

Carnegie Commission on Higher Education. (1971). *New students and new places.* New York, NY: McGraw-Hill.

Carnegie Commission on Higher Education. (1972). *The more effective use of resources.* New York, NY: McGraw-Hill.

Carnegie Commission on Higher Education. (1973). *Higher education: Who pays? Who benefits? Who should pay?* New York, NY: McGraw-Hill.

Carnegie Foundation for the Advancement of Teaching. (2012). *The Carnegie classifications of institutions of higher education.* Retrieved from http://classifications.carnegiefoundation.org

Carnevale, A. P. (2011, August). *Postsecondary education and jobs.* Paper presented at the Congressional Program of The Aspen Institute, Washington, DC.

Carnevale, A. P., Rose, S. R., & Cheah, B. (2010). *The college payoff: Education, occupations, lifetime earnings.* Washington, DC: Georgetown University, The Center of Education and the Workforce.

Carnevale, A. P., Strohl, J., & Melton, M. (2011). *What's it worth? The economic value of college majors.* Washington, DC: Georgetown University, The Center of Education and the Workforce.

Caruthers, J. K. (1989, May). *The impact of formula budgeting on state colleges and universities.* Paper presented at the meeting of the American Association of State Colleges and Universities. San Francisco, CA.

Caruthers, J. K., & Marks, J. (1994). *Funding public higher education in the 1990s: What's happened and where are we going?* Atlanta, GA: Southern Regional Education Board.

Chambers, M. M. (1968). *Higher education: Who pays? Who gains? Financing education beyond the high school.* Danville, IN: Interstate Printers and Publishers.

Cheng, D. (2012). *Adding it all up 2012: Are college net price calculators easy to find, use, and compare?* Oakland, CA: The Institute for College Access & Success. Retrieved from from http://ticas.org/files/pub/Adding_It_All_Up_2012.pdf

Christal, M. E. (1998). *State survey on performance measures: 1996-97.* Denver, CO: State Higher Education Executive Officers (SHEEO).

Chronicle of Higher Education. (2008). Database on congressional earmarks for higher education, 1990–2003. Retrieved from http://chronicle.com/premium/stats/pork/legacyindex.php

Clotfelter, C. (1976). Public spending for higher education: An empirical test of two hypotheses. *Public Finance, 31*(2), 177–195.

Cohen, A. M. (1998). *The shaping of American higher education: Emergence and growth of the contemporary system.* San Francisco, CA: Jossey-Bass.

Cohn, E., & Cooper, S. T. (1997). Internal rates of return to college education in the United States by sex and race. *Journal of Education Finance, 23*, 101–133.

Cohn, E., & Geske, T. G. (1986). Benefit-cost analysis of investment in higher education. In M. P. McKeown & S. K. Alexander (Eds.), *Values in conflict: Funding priorities for higher education* (pp. 183-216). Cambridge, MA: Ballinger.

Cohn, E., & Geske, T. G. (1998). Why Is a high school diploma no longer enough? The economic and social benefits of higher education. In T. Fossey & M. Bateman (Eds.), *Condemning students to debt: College loans and public policy* (pp. 19–35). New York, NY: Teachers College Press.

Cohn, E., & Hughes, W. W. (1994). A benefit-cost analysis of investment in college education in the United States, 1969–1985. *Economics of Education Review, 13*(2), 109–133.

Cohn, E., & Leslie, L.L. (1980). The development and finance of higher education in perspective. In Subsidies to Higher Education: The Issue New York, NY: Praeger.

Cohn, E., Rhine, S., & Santos, M. (1989). Institutions of higher education as multi-product firms: Economies of scale and scope. *Review of Economics and Statistics, 71*(2) 284–290.

College Board. (2006). *Trends in college pricing, 2006.* Washington, DC: Author.

College Board. (2012a). *Trends in College Pricing 2012.* Miami, FL: Author.

College Board. (2012b). *Trends in Student Aid 2012.* Miami, FL: Author.

Committee on Measures of Student Success (CMSS). (2011). *Committee on measures of student success: A report to Secretary of Education Arne Duncan.* Washington, DC: U.S. Department of Education. Retrieved from http://www2.ed.gov/about/bdscomm/list/cmss-committee-report-final.pdf

Cook, T. D. (2008). Waiting for life to arrive: A history of the regression-discontinuity design in psychology, statistics and economics. *Journal of Econometrics, 142,* 636–654.

Cook, B. J., & King, J. E. (2007, June). *2007 Status report on the Pell Grant program.* Washington, DC: American Council on Education, Center for Policy Analysis.

Cook, B., & Pullaro, N. (2010). *College graduation rates: Behind the numbers.* Washington, DC: American Council on Education.

Cope, R. G. (1968). Budget formulas and model building. In Association for Institutional Research, *Institutional Research and Academic Outcomes.* Athens, GA: Association for Institutional Research.

Cornwall, C., Mustard, D. B., & Sridhar, D. J. (2006). The enrollment effects of merit-based financial aid: Evidence from Georgia's HOPE program. *Journal of Labor Economics, 24*(4), 761–786.

Corum, J. (2011, June 11). The class of 2011: Word usage in 40 speeches given at graduation this year. *The New York Times.* Retrieved from http://www.nytimes.com/interactive/2011/06/10/education/commencement-speeches-graphic.html

Cunningham, A. F., & Merisotis J. P. (2002). National models for college costs and prices. *Planning for Higher Education, 30*(3), 15–26.

Cutler, D. M., & Lleras-Muney, A. (2006). *Education and health: Evaluating theories and evidence.* Working Paper 12352. Cambridge, MA: National Bureau of Economic Research. Retrieved from http://www.nber.org/papers/w12352

Davis, J. S. (2003). *Unintended consequences of tuition discounting.* Indianapolis, IN: Lumina Foundation for Education.

Delaney, J. A. (2011). Earmarks and state appropriations for higher education. *Journal of Education Finance, 37*(1), 3–23.

Delaney, J. A., & Doyle, W. R. (2011). State spending on higher education: Testing the balance wheel over time. *Journal of Education Finance, 36*(4), 343–368.

Delta Cost Project. (2009). *Metrics for improving cost accountability.* Washington, DC: Author.

DeParle, J. (2012, December 23). For poor, leap to college often ends in a hard fall. *The New York Times,* p. A1.

Desrochers, D. M., & Wellman, J. V. (2011). *Trends in college spending, 1999–2009.*Washington, DC: Delta Cost Project. Retrieved from http://www.deltacostproject.org/resources/pdf/Trends2011_Final_090711.pdf

Division of Performance Audit. (2006). *Recent Kentucky tuition increases may prevent the achievement of the commonwealth's 2020 postsecondary education goals, briefing report.* Frankfurt, KY: Auditor of Public Accounts.

Dobbs, M., & Hamilton, R. T. (2007). Small business growth: Recent evidence and new directions. *International Journal of Entrepreneurial Behavior and Research, 13*(5), 296–322.

Dooley, D. (2001). *Social research methods* (4th ed.). Upper Saddle River, NJ: Prentice-Hall.

Dougherty, K. J., Hare, R. J., & Natow, R. S. (2009). *Performance accountability systems in community colleges: Lessons from the voluntary framework of accountability for community colleges.* New York, NY: Teachers College, Columbia University, Community College Research Center.

Dougherty, K. J., & Natow, R. S. (2009). *The demise of higher education performance funding in three states.* Working Paper Number 17. New York, NY: Teachers College, Columbia University, Community College Research Center.

Dougherty, K. J., Natow, R. S., Hare, R. J., Jones, S. M. & Vega, B. E. (2011). *The politics of performance funding in eight states: Origins, demise, and change.* New York, NY: Teachers College, Columbia University, Community College Research Center.

Dougherty, K. J., & Reddy, V. (2011). *The impacts of state performance funding systems on higher education institutions: Research literature review and policy recommendations.* (CCRC Working Paper No. 37). New York, NY: Teachers College, Columbia University, Community College Research Center.

Dr. Seuss. (1996). *My many colored days.* New York, NY: Alfred A. Knopf.

Dressel, P. L., & Faricy, W. H. (1972). *Return to responsibility.* San Francisco, CA: Jossey-Bass.

Droms, W. G. (1979). *Finance accounting non-financial managers.* New York, NY: Addison Wesley.

Duncan, G. J. (1976). Earnings functions and non-pecuniary benefits. *Journal of Human Resources, 11*(4), 462–483.

Dundar, H., & Lewis, D. R. (1995). Departmental productivity in American universities: Economies of scale and scope. *Economics of Education Review, 14*, 119–144.

Dynarski, S., & Scott-Clayton, J. (2013). *Financial aid policy: Lessons from research.* (Working Paper # 18710). Washington, DC: National Bureau of Economic Research.

Eckerson, W. W. (2006). *Performance dashboards: Measuring, monitoring, and managing your business.* Hoboken, NJ: John Wiley & Sons.

Eddy, E. D. (1957). *Colleges for our land and time.* New York, NY: Harper & Brothers.

El-Khawas, E. H. (1976). Clarifying roles and purposes. *New Directions for Higher Education, 13*, 35–48.

El-Khawas, E. (1995). *Campus trends.* Washington, DC: American Council on Education.

Employment and Training Administration. (2011). *Coverage*. Washington, DC: U.S. Department of Labor.

Ewell, P. (2007). *Community college bridges to opportunity initiative: Joint state data toolkit*. Austin, TX: Bridges to Opportunity Initiative and Community College Leadership Program, University of Texas at Austin.

Ewell, P. T., & Jones, D. (1994). Pointing the way: Indicators as policy tools in higher education. In S. Ruppert (Ed.), *Charting higher education accountability: A sourcebook on state level performance indicators* (pp. 18-25). Denver, CO: Education Commission of the States.

Ewell, P. T., & Jones, D. P. (2006). *State level accountability for higher education: On the edge of a transformation*. Denver, CO: Education Commission of the States.

Feldman, K. A. (1972, Winter). Some theoretical approaches to the study of change and stability of college students. *Review of Educational Research, 42*(1), 1-26.

Fenske, R. H. (1983). Student aid: Past and present. In R.H. Fenske & R. P. Huff (Eds.), *Handbook of student financial aid* (pp. 5-26). San Francisco, CA: Jossey-Bass.

Fowler, L., & Fuller, S. S. (2005). *Economic impact of George Mason University on the Northern Virginia economy*. Fairfax, VA: Center for Regional Analysis, School of Public Policy, George Mason University.

Garfield, S. (2010). *Just my type: A book about fonts*. New York, NY: Gotham Books.

General Accounting Office. (2010). *College and university endowments have shown long-term growth, while size, restrictions, and distributions vary*. Washington, DC: Author.

Glaser, E. (2013, January 26). College planning: A crash course on paying the bill. *The Wall Street Journal*. Retrieved from http://online.wsj.com/article/SB10001424127887323468604578248013503238302.html

Glenny, L. A. (1959). *Autonomy of public colleges: The challenge of coordination*. New York, NY: McGraw-Hill.

Gillen, A. (2009). *Financial aid in theory and practice: Why it is ineffective and what can be done about it*. Washington, DC: Center for College Affordability and Productivity.

Gillen, A., & Robe, J. (2011). *Stop misusing higher education-specific price indices*. Washington, DC: Center for College Affordability and Productivity. Retrieved from http://centerforcollegeaffordability.org/uploads/Stop_Misusing_Price_Indices.pdf

Goetzmann, W. N. & Oster, S. (2012). *Competition among university endowments*. Working Paper No. 18173. Cambridge, MA: The National Bureau of Economic Research.

Goldin, C., & Katz, L.F. (1999). Education and Income in the Early 20th Century: Evidence from the Prairies (National Bureau of Economic Research Working Paper No. 7217).

Goldstein, L. (2002, August). To measure or not to measure—That's still the question. In *Business Officer Magazine*. Washington, DC: National Association of College and University Business Officers.

Goldstein, L. (2005). *College & university budgeting: An introduction for faculty and academic administrators.* Washington, DC: National Association of College and University Business Officers.

Goldstein, L. & Meditto, S. (2005, January). GASB and FASB. In *Business Officer Magazine.* Washington, DC: National Association of College and University Business Officers.

Götz, V. (1998). *Color & type for the screen.* East Sussex, UK: RotoVision SA.

Government Accountability Office (GAO). (2005). *A glossary of terms used in the federal budget process* (GAO-05-734SP). Washington, DC: Author. Retrieved from http://www.gao.gov/new.items/d05734sp.pdf

Government Accountability Office (GAO). (2009). *Federal student aid: Highlights of a study group on simplifying the Free Application for Federal Student Aid* (GAO-10-29). Washington, DC: Author.

Grapevine (various years). Accessed at HYPERLINK http://www.grapevine .illinoisstate.edu" www.grapevine.illinoisstate.edu

Gross, F. M. (1973). *A comparative analysis of the existing budget formulas used for justifying budget requests or allocating funds for the operating expenses of state-supported colleges or universities.* Unpublished dissertation, University of Tennessee, Knoxville, TN.

Gross, F. M. (1979). Formula budgeting and the financing of public higher education: Panacea or nemesis for the 1980s? *The AIR Professional File, 6,* 1–6.

HCM Strategists. (2012a). *Rules of the game: Data for input adjusted metrics* (Context for Success). Washington, DC: Author.

HCM Strategists. (2012b). *Tracking momentum: Edition 10.* Washington, DC: Author.

Hahn, R. D., & Price, D. (2008). *Promise lost: College-qualified students who don't enroll in college.* Washington, DC: Institute for Higher Education Policy.

Hale, J. A., & Rawson, T. M. (1976). Developing statewide higher education formulas for use in a limited growth environment. *Journal of Education Finance, 2,* 16–32.

Halstead, K. (2001). *College and university higher education price index: 2003 update.* Washington, DC: Research Associates.

Harclerod, F. F. (1980). *Accreditation: History, process, and problems.* Washington, DC: American Association for Higher Education.

Harnisch, T. (2011). *Performance-based funding: A re-emerging strategy in public higher education financing.* Washington, DC: AASCU.

Hansen, L. W. (1963). Total and private rates of return to investment in schooling, *Journal of Political Economy, 71*(2), 128-140.

Harrington, J. (2006). *Office of IP Development and Commercialization: Final report.* Tallahassee, FL: Florida State University, Office of Economic Forecasting and Analysis.

Harrington, M., Bers, T., Carr, R., Daly, R., Kalb, J., & Ronco, S. (2012). *Bulletproof presentations: An important note from the AIR bet visual presentation committee.* Tallahasse, FL: Association for Institutional Research.

Harris, J. (2011, October 13). Word clouds considered harmful. *Nieman Journalism Lab.* Retrieved from www.niemanlab.org/2011/word-clouds-considered-harmful/

Hartle, T. W., & Wabnick, R. (1982). *Discretionary costs and college costs*. Washington, DC: National Commission on Student Financial Assistance. (ERIC Document Reproduction Service No. ED 228944).

Hawley, M., Boland, M., & Boland, H. (1965) Population size and administration in institutions of higher education. *American Sociological Review, 30*, 252–255.

Heckman, J. J. (1974). Shadow prices, market wages and labor supply. *Econometrica, 42*(4), 679-694.

Heckman, J. J., Heinrich, C. J., Courty, P., Marschke, G., & Smith, J. (2011). *The performance of performance standards*. Kalamazoo, MI: W.E. Upjohn Institute for Employment Research.

Heller, D. E. (1997). Student price response in higher education: An update to Leslie & Brinkman. *Journal of Higher Education, 68*(6), 624–659.

Hillman, N. W. (2010a). Who benefits from tuition discounts at public universities? *Journal of Student Financial Aid, 40*(1), 17.

Hillman, N. W. (2010b, November). *Tuition discounting for revenue management*. Paper presented at the Association for the Study of Higher Education Annual Meeting, Indianapolis, IN.

Hoenack, S. A., & Collins, E. (1990). *The economics of American universities*. Albany, NY: State University of New York Press.

Hom, W. C. (2009). The denominator as the "target." *Community College Review, 37*, 136–152.

Hovey, H. A. (1999). *State spending for higher education in the next decade: The battle to sustain current support*. San Jose, CA: National Center for Public Policy and Higher Education.

Huff, D. (1954). *How to lie with statistics*. New York, NY: W.W. Norton & Company.

Hungate E., Meeth, J., & O'Connell, T. (1964). The quality and cost of liberal arts college programs. In J. E. McGrath (Ed.), *Cooperative long range planning in liberal arts colleges* (pp. 8-36). New York, NY: Columbia University.

Immerwahr, J., Johnson, J., Ott, A., & Rochkind, J. (2010). *Squeeze play 2010: Continued public anxiety on cost, harsher judgments on how colleges are run*. New York, NY: Public Agenda and The National Center for Public Policy and Higher Education. Retrieved from http://www.publicagenda.org/pages/squeeze-play-2010

Jackson, G. A., & Weathersby, G. B. (1975). Individual demand for higher education. *Journal of Higher Education, 46*(6), 623–652.

James, T., & McKeown-Moak, M. (2012). *The impact of publicly supported higher education on the Charleston, South Carolina region*. Austin, TX: TXP.

Kantrowitz, M. (2009). *FAFSA completion rates by level and control of institution*. Washington, DC: Student Aid Policy Analysis

Kelly, P. (2009). *The dreaded "P" word: An examination of productivity in public postsecondary education*. Washington, DC: Delta Cost Project.

Kiley, K. (2013, May 7). Price of a bad economy. *Inside Higher Education*. Retrieved from http://www.insidehighered.com/news/2013/05/07/nacubo-survey-reports-sixth-consecutive-year-discount-rate-increases

King, J. (2004). *Missed opportunities: Students who do not apply for financial aid* (Issue Brief). Washington, DC: American Council on Education, Center for Policy Analysis. Retrieved from http://www.acenet.edu/news-room/Documents/

IssueBrief-2004-Missed-Opportunities-Students-Who-Do-Not-Apply-for-Financial-Aid.pdf

King, J. (2006). *Missed opportunities revisited: New information on students who do not apply for financial aid* (Issue Brief). Washington, DC: American Council on Education, Center for Policy Analysis.

Kinzie, J., Palmer, M., Hayek, J., Hossler, D., Jacob, S. A., & Cummings, H. (2004). *Fifty years of college choice: Social, political, and institutional influences on the decision-making process* (New Agenda Series, Vol. 5, No. 3). Indianapolis, IN: Lumina Foundation for Education.

Knapp, L. G., Kelly-Reid, J. E., & Ginder, S. A. (2012). *Enrollment in postsecondary institutions, fall 2011; financial statistics, fiscal year 2011; and graduation rates, selected cohorts, 2003–2008: First look (preliminary data)* (NCES 2012- 174). Washington, DC: U.S. Department of Education, National Center for Education Statistics.

Knapp, J. L., & Shobe, M. H. (2007). *The economic impact of the University of Virginia.* Charlottesville, VA: Weldon Cooper Center for Public Service, University of Virginia.

Koshal, R. K., & Koshal, M. (1999). Economies of scale and scope in higher education: A case of comprehensive universities. *Economics of Education Review, 18,* 269–277.

LaManque, A. (2009). Factors associated with delayed submission of the Free Application for Federal Financial Aid. *Journal of Applied Research in the Community College, 17,* 6–12.

Lasher, W., & Sullivan, C. (2005). Follow the money: The changing world of budgeting in higher education. In J. C. Smart (Ed.), *Higher education: Handbook of theory and research* (Vol. 19, pp. 197–240). Dordrecht, Netherlands: Kluwer.

Lapovsky, L., & Hubbell, L. L. (2003). Enrollment management and tuition discounting. *Educational Considerations, 31*(1), 7–11.

Lapovsky, L. & Hubbell, L. L. (2004). Tuition discounting: 15 years in perspective. *Business Officer.* Retrieved from http://www.nacubo.org/Business_Officer_Magazine/Business_Officer_Plus/Online_Articles/Tuition_Discounting_15_Years_in_Perspective.html

Layzell, D. (2001). *Issues and models of performance indicator usage and performance funding in higher education.* Harrisburg, PA: Pennsylvania State System of Higher Education.

Lederman, D. (2013). Public university accountability 2.0. *Inside Higher Ed.* Retrieved from http://www.insidehighered.com/news/2013/05/06/public-university-accountability-system-expands-ways-report-student-learning

Leinbach, D., & Jenkins, D. (2008). *Using longitudinal data to increase community college student success: A guide to measuring milestone and momentum point attainment* (CCRC Research Tools No. 2). New York, NY: Community College research Center, Teachers College, Columbia University.

Leslie, L. L., & Brinkman, P. T. (1987). Student price response in higher education: The student demand studies. *Journal of Higher Education, 58*(2), 181–204.

Leslie, L. L., & Brinkman, P. T. (1988). *The economic value of higher education.* New York, NY: MacMillan.

Leslie, L. L., & Ramey, G. (1986). State appropriations and enrollments: Does enrollment growth still pay? *Journal of Higher Education, 57*(1), 1–19.

Lingenfelter, P. E. (2004). The state and higher education: An essential partnership. In *New Directions for Higher Education: Special Issue: Restructuring Shared Governance in Higher Education, 127,* 47–59. Retrieved from http://onlinelibrary.wiley.com/doi/10.1002/he.v2004:127/issuetoc

Lochner, L. & Moretti, E. (2004). The effect of education on crime: Evidence from prison inmates, arrests, and self-reports. *The American Economic Review, 94*(1), 155–189.

Longanecker, D. A. (2007). *Thinking outside the box: Policy strategies for readiness, access, and success.* Boulder, CO: Western Interstate Commission for Higher Education.

Longitudinal Employer—Household Dynamics Program. (2003). *A layman's guide to the LEHD human capital measures* (Informational Document No. ID-2003-04). Suitland, MD: U.S. Census Bureau.

Lucas, C. J. (1994). *American higher education: A history.* New York, NY: St. Martin's Griffin.

Luger, M. I., Koo, J., Peery, J., & Billings, S. (2001). *The economic impact of the University Of North Carolina System on the state of North Carolina.* Chapel Hill, NC: Office of Economic Development, University of North Carolina at Chapel Hill.

Lumina Foundation. (2012). *Four Steps to finishing first: An agenda for increasing college productivity to create a better-educated society.* Indianapolis, IN: Author.

Lupton, E. (2010). *Thinking with type: A critical guide for designers, writers, editors, & Students* (2nd ed.). New York, NY: Princeton Architectural Press.

Lynch, T., & Aydin, N. (2004). *Literature review of the economic and social impact of higher education research funding.* Tallahassee, FL: Leadership Board for Applied Research and Public Service, Florida State University.

MacAllum, K., & Glover, D. (2012). *Student and guidance counselor feedback on the College Navigator website.* Washington, DC: U.S. Department of Education, National Postsecondary Education Cooperative.

Mahan, S. M. (2012). *Federal Pell Grant program and the Higher Education Act: How the program works, recent legislative changes, and current issues* (Report No. R42446). Washington, DC: Congressional Research Service.

Majchrzak, A. (1984). *Methods for policy research* (Applied Social Research Methods Series, Volume 3). Thousand Oaks, CA: SAGE.

Massey, W. (2011). *Metrics for efficiency and effectiveness in higher education: completing the completion agenda.* Washington, DC: National Governors' Association.

McArdle, M. (2012, September 17). Is college a lousy investment? *Newsweek.* Retrieved from http://www.thedailybeast.com/newsweek/2012/09/09/megan-mcardle-on-the-coming-burst-of-the-college-bubble.html

McCandless, D. (2009). *The visual micellaneum: A colorful guide to the world's most consequential trivia.* New York, NY: HarperCollins.

McCarthy, J. R., & Hines, E. R. (1986). Public and private funding of U.S. higher education: 1840–1985. In M. P. McKeown & S. K. Alexander (Eds.), *Values in conflict: Funding priorities for higher education.* Cambridge, MA: Ballinger.

McDowell, G. R. (2001). *Land-grant universities and extension into the 21st century: Renegotiating of abandoning a social contract.* Ames, IA: Iowa State University Press.

McKeown, M. P. (1974). *An empirical test of a tuition funding model for higher education.* Unpublished doctoral dissertation, University of Illinois at Urbana-Champaign, Urbana, IL.

McKeown, M. P. (1981). *Use of budget guidelines among the states.* Annapolis, MD: Maryland State Board for Higher Education.

McKeown, M. P. (1982). *Funding formula use in higher education.* Annapolis, MD: Maryland State Board for Higher Education.

McKeown, M. P. (1986). Funding formulas. In M. P. McKeown & S. K. Alexander (Eds.), *Values in conflict: Funding priorities for higher education* (pp. 63-90). Cambridge, MA: Ballinger.

McKeown, M. P. (1994). Federal student financial aid in the 1990s: Crisis and change? *Educational Considerations, 22*(1).

McKeown, M. P. (1995). *Arizona University System budget primer.* Phoenix, AZ: Arizona Board of Regents.

McKeown, M. P. (1996a). *State funding formulas for public four-year institutions.* Denver, CO: State Higher Education Executive Officers.

McKeown, M. P. (1996b). State funding formulas: Promise fulfilled? In D.S. Honeyman, J. L. Wattenbarger, & K. C. Westbrook (Eds.), *A struggle to survive. Funding higher education in the next century* (pp. 49-85). Thousand Oaks, CA: Corwin Press.

McKeown, M. P., & Layzell, D. T. (1994). State funding formulas for higher education: Trends and issues. *Journal of Education Finance, 19*, 319–346.

McKeown-Moak, M. P. (1999a). *Financing higher education: An annual report from the states.* Denver, CO: State Higher Education Executive Officers.

McKeown-Moak, M. P. (1999b). Higher education funding formulas. *New Directions for Higher Education, 107*, 99–107.

McKeown-Moak, M. P. (2000a). A view from the states: A survey of the collection and use of cost data by states. In C. T. O'Brien & J. V. Wellman, *Higher education cost measurement public policy issues, options, and strategies* (pp. 6-12). Washington, DC: Institute for Higher Education Policy.

McKeown-Moak, M. P. (2000b). *Financing higher education in the new century: Second annual report from the states.* Denver, CO: State Higher Education Executive Officers.

McKeown-Moak, M. P. (2001a). *Financing higher education: Third annual report from the states.* Denver, CO: State Higher Education Executive Officers.

McKeown-Moak, M. P. (2001b, March). *Performance indicators/funding in higher education: Case studies from Iowa, Pennsylvania, Virginia and Georgia.* Paper presented at the American Education Finance Association Conference, Cincinnati, OH.

McKeown-Moak, M. P. (2002). *Financing higher education: Fourth annual report from the states.* Denver, CO: State Higher Education Executive Officers.

McKeown-Moak, M. P. (2003). *Financing higher education: Fifth annual report from the states.* Denver, CO: State Higher Education Executive Officers.

McKeown-Moak, M. P. (2004, March). *Financing higher education in 2004: Fiscal crisis is the state of the states.* Paper presented at the American Education Finance Association Annual Meeting.

McKeown-Moak, M. P. (2005, March). *Trends in state support for higher education, 2004–05.* Paper presented at the American Education Finance Association Annual Meeting, Louisville, KY.

McKeown-Moak, M. P. (2006a). *Funding formula use.* Denver, CO: State Higher Education Executive Officers (SHEEO).

McKeown-Moak, M. P. (2006b, March). *Trends in state support for higher education, 2005–06.* Paper presented at the American Education Finance Association Annual Meeting, Denver, CO.

McKeown-Moak, M. P. (2010a). *Evaluation of the Nevada system of higher education funding formula.* Austin, TX: MGT of America.

McKeown-Moak, M. P. (2010b). *Options for funding Arizona higher education: Phase I report.* Phoenix, AZ: Getting AHEAD Arizona.

McKeown-Moak, M. P. (2012, May). *The "new" performance funding in higher education.* Paper presented at the National Education Finance Conference, San Antonio, TX.

McKeown-Moak, M. P. (2013a). The "new" performance funding in higher education. *Educational Considerations, 40*(2), 3–12.

McKeown-Moak, M. P. (2013b, May). *Trends in funding higher education, 2012–13: Continued crisis.* Paper resented at the National Education Finance Conference, Indianapolis, IN.

McKinney, L., & Novak, H. (2013). The relationship between FAFSA filing and persistence among first-year community college students. *Community College Review, 41*(1), 63-85.

McLendon, M. K., Hearn, J. C., & Deaton, R. (2006). Called to account: Analyzing the origins and spread of state performance-accountability policies for higher education. *Educational Evaluation and Policy Analysis, 28(1),* 1–24.

McLendon, M. K., Hearn, J. C., & Mokher, C. G. (2009). Partisans, professionals, and power: The role of political factors in state higher education funding. *Journal of Higher Education, 80*(6), 686–713.

McMahon, W. W. (2009). *Higher learning, greater good: The private and social benefits of higher education.* Baltimore, MD: Johns Hopkins University Press.

McMahon, W. W., & Wagner, A. (1981). Expected returns to investment in higher education. *Journal of Human Resources, XVI*(2), 274-285.

McMahon, W. W., & Wagner, A. P. (1982). The monetary returns to education as a partial social efficiency criteria. In W. W. McMahon & T. Geske (Eds.), *Financing education: Overcoming inefficiency and inequity.* Urbana, IL: University of Illinois Press.

Medsker, L. L., & Tillery, D. (1971). *Breaking the access barriers: A profile of two-year colleges.* New York, NY McGraw-Hill.

Middlehurst, R. (2005). *Quality assurance and accreditation for virtual education: A discussion of models and needs.* Zurich, Switzerland: UNESCO.

Miller, J. L., Jr. (1964). *State budgeting for higher education: The use of formulas and cost analysis.* Ann Arbor, MI: University of Michigan.

Miller, J. L., Jr. (1968). *An introduction to budgetary analysis.* Athens, GA: Southern Regional Education Board.

Miller, C. & Munson, L. (2008). *University endowment reform.* Washington, DC: Center for College Affordability and Productivity.

Millett, J. D. (1974). *The budget formula as the basis for state appropriation in support of higher education.* Indianapolis, IN: Academy for Educational Development.

Mincer, J. (1958). Investment in human capital and personal income distribution. *Journal of Political Economy, 66*(4), 281–302.

Mincer, J. (1974). *Schooling, experience, and earnings.* New York: National Bureau of Economic Research.

Moore School of Business. (2009). *The economic return on investment in South Carolina's higher education.* Columbia, SC: University of South Carolina.

Moore School of Business. (2011). *The economic impact of the University of South Carolina.* Columbia, SC: University of South Carolina.

Moretti, E. (2004). Estimating the social return to higher education: Evidence from longitudinal and repeated cross-sectional data. *Journal of Econometrics, 121,* 175–212.

Morgan, J. M. & Dechter, G. (2012). *Improving the college scorecard: Using student feedback to create an effective disclosure.* Washington, DC: The Center for American Progress.

Morse, J. M. (2003). Principles of mixed methods and multimethodresearch design. In A. Tashakkori & C. Teddie (Eds.), *Handbook of mixed methods in social & behavioral research* (pp. 189–208). Thousand Oaks, CA: SAGE.

Morse, R., & Tolis, D. (2012a, October 4). How successful are colleges at graduating low-income students? *U.S. News and World Report.* Retrieved from http://www.usnews.com/education/blogs/college-rankings-blog/2012/10/04/how-successful-are-colleges-at-graduating-low-income-students

Morse, R., & Tolis, D. (2012b, October 25). Which colleges are successfully graduating high-income students? *U.S. News and World Report.* Retrieved from http://www.usnews.com/education/blogs/college-rankings-blog/2012/10/25/which-colleges-are-successfully-graduating-high-income-students

Mortenson, T. (1988, May). *Pell Grant program changes and their effects on applicant eligibility 1973–74 to 1988–89* (ACT Student Financial Aid Research Report Series 88-1). Iowa City, IA: American College Testing Program.

Moss, C. E. & Gaither, G. H. (1976). Formula budgeting: Requiem or renaissance? *Journal of Higher Education, 47,* 550–576.

Mullin, C. M. (2012a). Understanding the workforce outcomes of education. *New Directions for Institutional Research, 153,* 75–88.

Mullin, C. M. (2012b). *Why access matters: The community college student body* (Policy Brief 2012-01PBL). Washington, DC: American Association of Community Colleges.

Mullin, C.M. (in press). Analysis of the Pell Grant program. *Journal of Education Finance, 38*(4).

Mullin, C., & Honeyman, D. (2007). The funding of community colleges. *Community College Review, 25*(2), 113–127.

Mullin, C. M., & Honeyman, D. S. (2008). Statutory responsibility for fixing tuition and fees: The relationship between community colleges and undergraduate institutions. *Community College Journal of Research and Practice, 32*(4-6), 284–304.

Mustard, D. (2005, March). *Evaluation of the Georgia Hope Scholarship program.* Paper presented at the Annual Meeting of the American Education Finance Association.

National Association of College and University Budget Officers (NACUBO). (2013). *2012 NACUBO/Commonfund Study of Endowments.* New York, NY: Author.

National Association of State Budget Officers (NASBO). (2012). *Fiscal Survey of the States.* Washington, DC: Author.

National Association of State Universities and Land-Grant Colleges. (1997). *Value added: The economic impact of public universities.* Washington, DC: Author.

National Center for Education Statistics. (n.d.). *Net price calculation information center.* Washington, DC: Author. Retrieved from nces.ed.gov/ipeds/resource/net_price_calculator.asp

National Center for Education Statistics. (2006). *Digest of Education Statistics: 2005.* Washington, DC: Author.

National Center for Education Statistics. (2010a). *Glossary.* Washington, DC: Author. Retrieved from http://nces.ed.gov/ipeds/Glossary/index.asp?id=135

National Center for Education Statistics. (2010b). *IPEDS finance survey tips, scholarships, grants, discounts, and allowances.* Washington, DC: Author. Retrieved from http://nces.ed.gov/ipeds/factsheets/fct_ipeds_finance_03072007_3.asp

National Center for Education Statistics (NCES). (2011). *Glossary* [Data base]. Washington, DC: Author. Retrieved from http://nces.ed.gov/ipeds/glossary

National Center for Education Statistics. (2012a). *IPEDS Finance Survey.* Washington, DC: Author. Retrieved from http://surveys.nces.ed.gov/ipeds/downloads/forms/package_5_67.pdf (FASB format) http://surveys.nces.ed.gov/ipeds/downloads/forms/package_5_68.pdf (GASB format) http://surveys.nces.ed.gov/ipeds/downloads/forms/package_5_12.pdf (for-profit format)

National Center for Education Statistics (NCES). (2012b). *NPSAS.* Washington, DC: Author.

National Center for Higher Education Management Systems. (2005). *A new look at the institutional component of higher education finance: A guide for evaluating performance relative to financial resources.* Denver, CO: Author.

National Center for Public Policy and Higher Education. (2006). *Measuring up 2006: The national report card on higher education.* San Jose, CA: Author.

National Conference of State Legislatures (NCSL). (2013). *Performance funding for higher education.* Denver, CO: Author.

National Education Association. (2000). *Quality on the line: Benchmarks for success in internet based distance education.* Washington, DC: Author.

National Postsecondary Education Cooperative. (2009). *Information required to be disclosed under the Higher Education Act of 1965: Suggestions for dissemination* (Updated; NPEC 2010-831v2). Washington, DC: U.S. Department of Education.

New Leadership Alliance for Student Learning and Accountability. (2012). *Committing to quality: Guidelines for assessment and accountability in higher education.* Washington, DC: New Leadership Alliance.

Niskanen, W. A. (1996). Welfare and the culture of poverty. *The CATO Journal, 16*(1), 1–15.

Novak, H. & McKinney, L. (2011). The consequences of leaving money on the table: Examining persistence among students who do not file a FAFSA. *Journal of Student Financial Aid, 41*(3), 5–23.

Ochoa, E. M. (2011, March 18). *Dear colleague letter: Guidance to institutions and accrediting agencies regarding a credit hour as defined in the final regulations published on October 29, 2010* (GEN-11-06). Washington, DC: U.S. Department of Education, Office of Postsecondary Education, Assistant Secretary.

Office of Higher Education. (2012). *Aid to independent colleges and universities (Bundy Aid).* Albany, NY: University of the State of New York, New York State Education Department. Retrieved from http://www.highered.nysed.gov/oris/bundy/

Office of Postsecondary Education. (2010). *Pell end-of-year report, 2008–09.* Washington, DC: U.S. Department of Education.

Orwell, G. (1946). Why I write. In G. Orwell, *Politics and the English language* (pp. 309–335). Boston, MA: Mariner Books.

Paulsen, M. B. (1989). Estimating instructional cost functions at small independent colleges. *Journal of Education Finance, 15*(1), 53–66.

Peterson, R. G. (1976). Environmental and political determinants of state higher education appropriations policies. *Journal of Higher Education, 47*(5), 523–542.

Petrick, R. (2009, April). *Aligning state resources to better promote student success.* Presentation Made to the Texas Higher Education Coordinating Board Leadership Conference, Austin, TX.

Rawson, T. M. (1975). *A study to develop alternative statewide higher education funding formula models for possible use in New Mexico.* Unpublished doctoral dissertation, University of New Mexico, Albuquerque, NM.

Rephann, T., Knapp, J. L., & Shobe, W. M. (2009). *Study of the economic impact of Virginia public higher education.* Charlottesville, VA: Weldon Cooper Center for Public Service, University of Virginia.

Robins, G. B. (1973). *Understanding the college budget.* Athens, GA: University of Georgia Press.

Robst, J. (2001). Cost efficiency in public higher education institutions. *Journal of Higher Education, 72*(6), 730–750.

Roche, J. P. (1986). *The colonial colleges in the War for American Independence.* Millwood, NY: Associated Faculty Press.

Rourke, F. E. & Brooks, G. E. (1966). *The management revolution in higher education.* Baltimore, MD: The Johns Hopkins Press.

Rudolph, F. (1990). *The American university: A history.* Atlanta, GA: The University of Georgia Press.

Ruppert, S. S. (Ed.). (1994). *Charting higher education accountability: A sourcebook on state-level performance indicators.* Denver, CO: Education Commission of the States.

Russell, J. D. (1954). *The finance of higher education.* Chicago, IL: University of Chicago Press.

Rutledge, V. B., & Stafford, J. H. (1977). Unit cost funding for university systems. *Journal of Education Finance, 2*(3), 324–334.

Sanford, T. & Hunter, J. M. (2011). Impact of performance-based funding on retention and graduation rates. *Education Policy Analysis Archives, 19*(33), 1–30.

Schauer, D. A., Gibson, E. K., Corral, G., & Caire, M. (2010). *2010 economic impact of the University of Texas at El Paso. IPED Technical Reports. Paper 93.* El Paso, TX: Institute for Policy and Economic Development, University of Texas at El Paso.

Schneider, M.B. (2006). *Endowments can become too much of a good thing. Chronicle of Higher Education.*

Schultz, T. W. (1963). *The economic value of education.* New York, NY: Columbia University Press.

Schultz, T. W. (1971). *Investment in human capital.* New York, NY: Free Press. *Servicemen's Readjustment Act,* Public Law 346-268 (1947).

Serban, A. M. (1998). Performance funding criteria, levels, and methods. *New Directions for Institutional Research, 97,* 61–67.

Shadish, W. R., & Steiner, P. M. (2010). A primer on propensity score analysis. *Newborn & Infant Nursing Reviews, 19*(1), 19–26.

Shin, J. C. (2010). Impacts of performance-based accountability on institutional performance in the United States. *Higher Education, 60*(1), 47–68.

Shin, J. C., & Milton, M. (2004). The effects of performance budgeting and funding programs on graduation rates in public four-year colleges and universities. *Educational Policy Analysis Archives, 12*(22), 1–26.

Snyder, T. (Ed.). (1993). *120 years of American education: A statistical portrait.* Washington, DC: U.S. Department of Education, Office of Educational Research and Improvement, National Center for Education Statistics.

Snyder, T. D., & Dillow, S. A. (2011). *Digest of education statistics: 2010* (NCES 2011-015). Washington, DC: U.S. Department of Education, Institute for Education Sciences, National Center for Education Statistics.

Snyder, T. D., & Dillow, S.A. (2012). *Digest of Education Statistics 2011* (NCES 2012-001). National Center for Education Statistics, Institute of Education Sciences, U.S. Department of Education, Washington, DC.

Social Policy Research Associates. (2010). *PY2009 WIASRD Data Book* (DOL No. DOLF091A20934). Oakland, CA: Social Policy Research Associates.

Solomon, L. C. (1975). The relation between schooling and savings behavior. In F. T. Juster (Ed.), *Education, income, and human behavior* (pp. 253–294). Washington, DC: National Bureau of Economic Research. Retrieved from www.nber.org/chapters/c3700.pdf

Stark, J. S. (Ed.). (1976a). Promoting consumer protection for students. *New Directions for Higher Education, 13.*

Stark, J. S. (1976b). Is more information better? *New Directions for Higher Education, 13,* 59–73.

State Higher Education Executive Officers (SHEEO). (2012, March 24). *State Higher Education Finance: Fiscal year 2011.* Boulder, CO: Author. Retrieved from http://www.sheeo.org/finance/shef/SHEF_FY11.pdf

Storey, D. J. (1994). *Understanding the small business sector.* London: Thomson Learning.

Sutton, T. & Whelan, B. M. (2004). *The complete color harmony: Expert color information for professional color results.* Gloucester, MA: Rockport.

Texas Higher Education Coordinating Board (THECB). (2012). *Higher education cost efficiencies.* Austin, TX: Author.

Titus, M. A. (2009). The production of bachelor's degrees and financial aspects of state higher education policy: A dynamic analysis. *Journal of Higher Education, 80*(4), 439–468.

Tripp Umbach and Associates, Inc. (2004). *The Pennsylvania State University economic impact statement 2003.* Pittsburgh, PA: Author.

Troop, D. (2013). In a volatile economy, colleges' endowment returns fall flat. *Chronicle of Higher Education.*

University of West Florida. (2009). *The economic impact of UWF Emerald Coast on the regional economy.* Pensacola, FL: Haas Center for Business Research and Economic Development, University of West Florida.

U.S. Census Bureau. (2011). Current population survey annual social and economic supplement. washington, DC: Author. Retrieved from http://www.census.gov/cps/data/

U.S. Census Bureau. (2012). *American community survey.* Washington, DC: Department of Labor. Retrieved from http://www.census.gov/acs/www

U.S. Department of Education. (2010). *Issue paper #7: Proposed regulatory language* Washington, DC: Author.

U. S. Department of Education. (2012). *College completion tool kit.* Washington, DC: Author.

U.S. Department of Health and Human Services. (2012). *A guide to the National Directory of New Hires.* Washington, DC: Administration for Children & Families, Office of Child Support Enforcement. Retrieved from http://www.acf.hhs.gov/sites/default/files/programs/css/a_guide_to_the_national_directory_of_new_hires.pdf

U.S. Department of Labor. (2012a). *Unemployment compensation: Federal-state partnership.* Washington, DC: Office of Unemployment Insurance, Division of Legislation. Retrieved from http://workforcesecurity.doleta.gov/unemploy/pdf/partnership.pdf

U.S. Department of Labor. (2012b). *Wage Record Interchange System.* Washington, DC: Employment & Training Administration. Retrieved from http://www.doleta.gov/performance/WRIS.cfm

U.S. Department of Labor. (2012c). *Wage Record Interchange System (WRIS) 2.* Washington, DC: Employment & Training Administration. Retrieved from http://www.doleta.gov/performance/wris2.cfm

Vargas, J. H. (2004). *College knowledge: Addressing information barriers to college.* Boston, MA: The Education Resources Institute.

Van Wijk, A. P., & Levine, J. B. (1969). *The pros and cons of existing formula financing systems and a suggested new approach.* Toronto, Canada: Systems Research Group.

Vidovich, L., & Slee, R. (2001). Bringing universities to account: Exploring some global and local policy tensions. *Journal of Education Policy, 16*(5), 431–453.

Wellman, J. (2011). *Delta study.* Washington, DC: Delta Cost Project.

Wellman, J. V. & Ehrlich, T. (2003). How the student credit hour shapes higher education: The tie that binds. *New Directions in Higher Education, 122*.

Whelan, B. M. (1994). *Color harmony 2: A guide to creative color combinations.* Gloucester, MA: Rockport.

Wilson, L. (1971). Analyzing and evaluating costs in higher education. *The Educational Record, 42*, 102.

Wong, D. (2010). *The Wall Street Journal guide to information graphics.* New York, NY: W.W. Norton & Company.

The World Bank. (2003, April). *03: World development indicators.* Washington, DC: International Bank for Reconstruction and Development.

Wyner, J. (2012, August). *The Aspen Prize for Community College Excellence.* Presentation to the Board of the American Association of Community Colleges, Washington, DC.

ABOUT THE AUTHORS

Mary McKeown-Moak, PhD, has over 40 years of experience as an educational administrator working with colleges and universities, school districts, boards, state legislatures, executive offices, and non-profit agencies. She specializes in financial and capital planning, human resource management, budgeting and resource allocation, organizational reviews, and strategic planning and is considered a national expert on higher education funding formulas and performance funding.

She has served as senior financial officer of the Arizona University System, which includes more than 150,000 students at Arizona State University, Northern Arizona University, and the University of Arizona; director of strategic planning for Arizona State University; business manager of the University of Illinois Foundation; and associate director of finance and facilities for the Maryland Higher Education Commission. She has taught courses in educational finance and management at five universities. After retiring from the Arizona University System, she was a senior partner with MGT of America, Inc., a national public sector research and management consulting firm.

She has assisted 36 states and/or systems of higher education in development of their resource allocation systems, funding formulas, and performance funding and also has developed funding formulas for special education, pupil transportation, categorical aid, and general school aid. In her consulting practice, she has worked with more than 400 colleges and universities on educational management issues. She also has served as an expert witness in education finance court cases.

Dr. McKeown-Moak is a past president of the Association for Education Finance and Policy, of the Fiscal Issues, Policy, and Education Finance Special Interest Group, and the Futures Research and Strategic Planning Special Interest Group of the American Education Research Association. She is also a past chair of the State Higher Education Financial Officers (SHEFO). Working with the State Higher Education Executive Officers (SHEEO), she published an annual series of reports on the state of higher education funding. In addition, she has authored or edited five books on educational finance and management, published over 200 articles and chapters in books, and written more than 200 consulting reports. Currently, she sits on four editorial boards for national journals and is associate chair of the National Education Finance Academy's board of advisors.

Dr. McKeown-Moak earned a BA in mathematics and accounting from Michigan State University, an MA in guidance and personnel from Michigan State, and a PhD in administration, higher, and continuing education from the University of Illinois at Urbana-Champaign.

Christopher M. Mullin, PhD, serves as the assistant vice chancellor for policy and research at the State University System of Florida, Board of Governors where he provides leadership and direction with regard to academic and student affairs policies and programs, strategic planning, research, analysis, and special projects in support of the Board of Governors' constitutional responsibilities. Prior to joining the Board of Governors, Dr. Mullin served as the program director for policy analysis at the American Association of Community Colleges (AACC). In this capacity, his chief responsibility was to provide analysis and supporting data to guide and enhance AACC's advocacy efforts, with an emphasis on federal student financial assistance, the performance of community colleges in serving low-income and minority students, accountability, institutional performance, college costs, and related institutional policies. Additionally, he responds to immediate needs for the analysis of federal legislative, regulatory, and related policies, while also playing a central role in shaping AACC's long-term federal policy agenda. Prior to joining AACC, he worked for the Illinois Education Research Council where he focused on a longitudinal study of high school students into college and career and conducted analyses of the state's funding structures for education. He has also been an educator at the pre-K, elementary, middle, high school and graduate school levels.

His work has been reported in *The Wall Street Journal, The Chronicle of Higher Education, Inside Higher Education, EdWeek* and *NBC Nightly News*. Dr. Mullin interacts regularly with members of national media, including the *CBS Evening News*, the *TODAY* show, *The New York Times, The Wall Street Journal, Bloomberg News*, and *The Huffington Post*.

To date, Dr. Mullin's research interests include the influence of state P-20 education structures on the educational decisions of both institutions and individuals. His completed research has been published in over 30 policy documents, 13 articles in peer-reviewed journals, and 5 book chapters. In addition to co-authoring this volume, he has co-edited two books. He has given over 70 presentations at the national, state, and local level.

Dr. Mullin serves the postsecondary community in many ways, including his service on the editorial advisory boards of the *Journal of Education Finance*, the *Community College Review*, and the *Community College Journal of Research and Practice* and serving as the coordinating editor of the peer-reviewed *AIR Professional Files*. Further, he was selected to serve on the Expert Panel to Support Federal Measures of Workforce Education and Credentialing and serves on several advisory boards.

Dr. Mullin earned a Bachelor of Arts degree from the University of Florida in 1999, a Master of Education degree from Teachers College, Columbia University in 2005, and a Doctorate of Philosophy in higher education administration from the University of Florida in 2008.

INDEX

Performance-based funding, 108–109,
170–173, 239
allocations for, 232
characteristics of stable programs,
229–230
funding levels, 232–234
indicators for, 231
and institutional performance,
222–227
lessons learned from, 227–234
research and analysis of, 238–244
success criteria for, 230–231
Physical plant operation, 56, 134
funding formulas for 155–157
Post-graduate plans, 193
Postsecondary education levels, 10–12
Postsecondary education sectors, 4–5
Present value (PV), 310
Price of education; *see also* Student
costs, Student debt
affordability of, 285–287
definitions of, 280–284
and family income, 287–288
influence on college enrollment,
284–285
Private colleges, religious origins of,
6–7
Private gifts and grants, 52
Private institutions, definition, 5
Private nonprofit institutions, 6–7
Productivity
measurement of, 166–170
state appropriations, 169
Programmatic performance, 237
Proprietary 90/10 revenue percentages,
44–45
Public institutions, 7–8
definition of, 5
Public service, 55
funding formulas for, 151–152

Q
Qualitative data, 339–340
Quality assurance, 177ff
benchmarks for, 186

R
Regression discontinuity design, 327
Remedial education, 17–18
Research, 54
funding formulas for, 151
Retention rates, 192, 225
Return on investment (ROI)
labor market returns, 251–265
methods of calculating, 248–251
non-labor market returns, 266–268
public, 268–276
tax revenue implications, 275–276
Revenue categories (operating vs. non-
operating), 50–53
Revenue deduction, 157–158
Revenue, budgeted vs. actual, 194
Revenues/expenditures per FTE
student, 194–195
Rockefeller Institute, 233

S
Scholarships/fellowships, 56, 70, 134
funding formulas for, 157
IPEDS definition of, 71–72
Service academies (West Point, Naval
Academy, Air Force Academy), 8
Servicemen's Readjustment Act of 1947
(GI Bill), 8
Southern Regional Education Board
(SREB), 105
Southern Universities Group (SUG),
319
Spellings Commission report of 2006,
173
Stafford Guaranteed Student Loan, 83
State and local appropriations to
higher education, 96–106
methods of, 106–110
State Higher Education Executive
Officers (SHEEO), 47, 101, 303
State Higher Education Finance Survey
(SHEF), 47, 101
State-level data 47–48
Student body characteristics, 316
and student success, 235
Student costs, pre-enrollment, 64–65;
See also Price of education

CPSIA information can be obtained
at www.ICGtesting.com
Printed in the USA
LVOW13s1423270217
525552LV00009B/118/P